WITHDRAWN

The Social Psychology of Female–Male Relations

A Critical Analysis of Central Concepts

The
Social Psychology
of
Female–Male Relations

A Critical Analysis of Central Concepts

Edited by

RICHARD D. ASHMORE

Department of Psychology
Rutgers University
The State University of New Jersey
New Brunswick, New Jersey

FRANCES K. DEL BOCA

Department of Psychology
Bard College
Annandale-on-Hudson,
New York

1986

ACADEMIC PRESS, INC.
Harcourt Brace Jovanovich, Publishers
Orlando   San Diego   New York   Austin
London   Montreal   Sydney   Tokyo   Toronto

Acknowledgment is gratefully made for permission to quote from
F. C. Bartlett, *Psychology and Primitive Culture,* 1979, Westport,
CT: Greenwood Press. (Originally published by Cambridge University Press, 1923.)

ACADEMIC PRESS, INC.
Orlando, Florida 32887

United Kingdom Edition published by
ACADEMIC PRESS INC. (LONDON) LTD.
24–28 Oval Road, London NW1 7DX

LIBRARY OF CONGRESS CATALOGING-IN-PUBLICATION DATA

Main entry under title:

The Social psychology of female-male relations.

    Includes index.
    1. Interpersonal relations—Addresses, essays,
lectures.   2. Sex role—Addresses, essays, lectures.
3. Identity (Psychology)—Addresses, essays, lectures.
4. Men—Psychology—Addresses, essays, lectures.
5. Women—Psychology—Addresses, essays, lectures.
I. Ashmore, Richard D.   II. Del Boca, Frances K.
HM132.S569   1985   305.3   85-9138
ISBN 0-12-065280-3 (alk. paper)
ISBN 0-12-065281-1 (paperback)

PRINTED IN THE UNITED STATES OF AMERICA

86 87 88 89   9 8 7 6 5 4 3 2 1

Contents

Chapter Seven
Women and Men in Task Groups
Kathryn M. Bartol and David C. Martin

Chapter Eight
Male–Female Relations:
A Summing Up and Notes toward
a Social-Psychological Theory
Frances K. Del Boca and Richard D. Ashmore

Contributors

Numbers in parentheses indicate the pages on which the authors' contributions begin.

ASHMORE, RICHARD D. (1, 69, 121, 167, 311), Department of Psychology, Rutgers—The State University of New Jersey, New Brunswick, New Jersey 08903

BARTOL, KATHRYN M. (259), College of Business and Management, University of Maryland at College Park, College Park, Maryland 20742

DEL BOCA, FRANCES K. (1, 69, 121, 311), Department of Psychology, Bard College, Annandale-on-Hudson, New York 12504

HUSTON, TED L. (167), Departments of Psychology and Home Economics, The University of Texas at Austin, Austin, Texas 78712

KATZ, PHYLLIS A. (21), Institute for Research on Social Problems, Boulder, Colorado 80302

LIBBY, PAM L. (211), Department of Psychology, Rutgers—The State University of New Jersey, New Brunswick, New Jersey 08903

MCMANUS, MARGARET A. (121), Department of Psychology, Rutgers—The State University of New Jersey, New Brunswick, New Jersey 08903

MARTIN, DAVID C. (259), College of Business Administration, American University, Washington, D.C. 20016

STAINES, GRAHAM L. (211), Department of Psychology, Rutgers—The State University of New Jersey, New Brunswick, New Jersey 08903

WOHLERS, ARTHUR J. (69), Department of Psychology, Rutgers—The State University of New Jersey, New Brunswick, New Jersey 08903

Preface

Over the last decade and a half there has been a significant rise in research on topics related to female–male relations. This research is scattered (there are a number of different literatures that crosscut several disciplines) and largely atheoretical, and the extant empirical work is highly variable in quality. Further, little attention has been paid to the implicit conceptual frameworks that guide research. Our book is intended as a step toward remedying this situation. More specifically, it has two major objectives: (1) to bring together and organize the available research and theory, and (2) to critically evaluate past and current efforts.

Our goal of organizing the accumulated literatures is accomplished by introducing a new field of study, "the social psychology of female–male relations," that is guided by a cognitive social-psychological framework. This conceptual framework focuses on the thoughts, feelings, and behaviors of individuals in social interaction and explicitly considers *women and men in relation to one another*—as individuals, as representatives of social categories, and as significant social groups. Within this framework, three individual-level gender-related constructs (gender identity, sex stereotypes, and gender-related attitudes) are evaluated, and women and men are examined in the context of three related, yet distinguishable, social relationships (close, personal relationships, role relationships, and task groups).

Our second objective, the critical evaluation of extant work, is achieved, first, by appraising past and current paradigms for conceptualizing and investigating aspects of female–male relations and, second, by offering specific prescriptions to guide future work. That is, our authors address the strengths and weaknesses of the present literature and suggest what they regard as the most profitable directions for future theory development and research.

The book comprises eight chapters. The first provides an introduction to the volume. It lays out the parameters of the social psychology of female–male relations and describes the context (time and place) in which the book was written. The six content chapters that follow (Two through Seven) are grouped into two parts. Part One, ''Gender and the Individual,'' includes three chapters, each focusing on a specific individual-level, gender-related construct. Taken up in turn are gender identity, sex stereotypes, and gender-related attitudes.

Chapter Two contains two major insights: first, that gender identity is a complex, multifaceted construct, and, second, that the structure and degree of differentiation of gender identity develop and change over the life course. This occurs in response to major life events (both social and biological) and in interaction with the social environment.

Together, Chapter Three and Four present a relatively general cognitive social-psychological framework for two important constructs, sex stereotypes and gender-related attitudes. Sex stereotypes are the structured sets of beliefs about the social categories *female* and *male,* and gender-related attitudes are evaluations of, and summary feelings toward, the sexes and related objects or issues. Both are conceptualized as elements of the individual's long-term social memory. It is argued that ''thinking about the sexes'' includes a good deal more than a set of beliefs about the characteristics of women and men. Of particular importance is the fact that we have beliefs and feelings about types of men and women. That is, in addition to stereotypic conceptions of the sexes, individuals and society as a whole partition the overarching social categories *female* and *male* into gender subtypes (e.g., ''career woman,'' ''ladies' man'').

Part Two, ''Gender and Interpersonal Relationships,'' also includes three chapters: These consider women and men in three different, but interconnected, types of interpersonal relations—in close, personal relationships, in role relationships, and in task groups.

The fifth chapter of the book offers a critique of analyses that explain the behavior of women and men in close, personal relationships in terms of sex differences in the individual dispositions of the participants. The authors contend that gender-related patterns in personal relationships must be accounted for not only in terms of the dispositions of the individuals involved but also, and often more importantly, in terms of the qualities of the relationships themselves and the immediate and broader societal contexts in which a particular relationship is situated.

Chapter Six presents a strong and straightforward critique of the current usage of the term *sex role* to describe a global set of behavioral prescriptions that apply to all women and to all men. Suggesting that the global approach involves too high a level of aggregation with a resulting loss of information, the authors adopt a "role-specific" approach that analyzes female–male role relationships in terms of the differential experience and performance of women and men in three major pairs of social roles: spouse (wife–husband), parent (mother–father), and worker.

Chapter Seven presents a comprehensive review of research on gender-related patterns of behavior in task groups that cannot be found elsewhere. This review serves as a backdrop for considering several explanations for the real-world problem of differential recruitment to, and advancement in, managerial positions by women and men.

The concluding chapter of the book summarizes points made in earlier chapters and offers a set of notes toward a theory of female–male relations. The social psychology of relations between the sexes is placed in a broader context that explicitly considers biological and societal-level factors and more generally analyzes female–male relations as an instance of intergroup relations.

This book is aimed at social scientists concerned with gender and with relations between the sexes. (In fact, it is our hope that the volume will alter the nature of research and theory on these general topics.) We believe it will be primarily of value to the social scientist (especially, psychologists, sociologists, and anthropologists) doing research on women, on men, or on women and men in relationships or in social interaction. Such individuals may identify themselves as working in the areas of sex (or gender) roles, psychology (or sociology or anthropology) of women, psychology (or sociology or anthropology) of men, close relationships or interpersonal attraction, marriage and the family, and/or sex differences. In addition, scholars in any discipline who have an interest in women's studies or feminist studies should find this book useful.

Although not primarily designed to be a textbook, this volume would be appropriate for graduate or advanced undergraduate courses on Female–Male Relations (or, Sex Roles, Psychology and Gender, Psychology of Women/Men) and Intergroup Relations (or, Psychology of Prejudice, Intergroup Conflict). Together with other books, it could be used for Social Problems and Applied Social Psychology courses. It might also be useful as a supplementary text for sociology, anthropology, or political science courses concerned with gender or intergroup relations.

We are indebted to several people who read and provided thoughtful feedback on early drafts of one or more of our chapters: David S. Titus (Chapters 1, 3, 4, and 8), Margaret A. McManus (Chapters 1, 3, and 8), Wendy Ashmore and Graham L. Staines (Chapter 1), and Michael P.

Johnson (Chapter 3). In referring to these specific individuals, we are certain that we have left many intellectual debts unacknowledged. We are grateful to those unnamed students and colleagues who have triggered an insight or reacted to the germ of an idea that was later developed in one of our chapters.

Other individuals assisted in equally important ways. We thank Margaret A. McManus, Arthur J. Wohlers, and Dieter Papke for the time and effort they devoted to library research, and Pat Freeman and Mary Ann Grandinetti, who diligently typed successive drafts of all four of our chapters. In addition, we owe a great deal to the editors and staff at Academic Press.

Finally, and perhaps most important, we wish to thank the authors of chapters in this volume—Phyllis A. Katz, Ted Huston, Graham L. Staines, Pam Libby, Kathryn M. Bartol, and David C. Martin—for their patience and for their willingness to respond to our questions and suggestions at all stages.

One

Toward a Social Psychology of Female–Male Relations

RICHARD D. ASHMORE

FRANCES K. DEL BOCA

Vive la différence
The battle of the sexes
Women and children first
It's a man's world
The mating game

Introduction

If, as Lakoff and Johnson (1980) argue, metaphors are experientially grounded and reflective of fundamental cultural values, the foregoing phrases suggest the complexity of female–male relations in American society. "Vive la différence" highlights, in an apparently approving fashion, the differences between women and men. The next four statements directly concern relations between the sexes. According to the "Battle of the sexes" metaphor, men and women are combatants engaged in open conflict. "Women and children first" and "It's a man's world" reflect the twin aspects of traditional American sex-role ideology—the code of chivalry which places women before men in certain instances (e.g., emergencies), coupled with "a man's world" in which men have greater personal freedom and women are denied access to formal public power. "The mating game" captures yet another facet of female–male relations, the cooperative (and playful?) venture to establish and maintain interpersonal and physical intimacy. These metaphors not only suggest the complexity of relations between the sexes, but also point to some of the major issues: the differences (both actual and perceived), the conflicts, the differentials in status and prestige in various domains, and the need to coordinate conduct so that the mating game and other games can be played successfully.

This book is concerned with one approach to these and related issues, what we term the "social psychology of female–male relations." It is not claimed that any such field currently exists—it does not. A major goal of the present volume is, in fact, to begin the process of creating such a field, hence the word "toward" in the title of this introductory chapter. The work covered is drawn from a variety of sources, and much of it is not indexed as "social psychology" or as "female–male relations." An important task, then, is to bring together and to organize the available research and theory. Further, the extant literatures constitute an intellectual jungle. The empirical research is highly variable in quality (some is quite good, too much is not good at all), and very little attention has been paid to conceptual analysis. Hence, a second major goal is to critically analyze key concepts.

The concepts to be considered follow from a consideration of what a social psychological analysis of relations between the sexes entails. Because social psychology focuses on the individual in a social context, both the individual and the social context must be included. The body of the present volume comprises six chapters organized into two parts. The first three chapters are devoted to individual-level concepts: gender identity (most broadly, how gender is represented in one's behavior and view of self), gender stereotypes (beliefs about men and women), and gender-related attitudes (evaluative predispositions toward women and men as social categories and toward the many issues relevant to relations between the sexes). The second part of the book directs attention to the social context. Three such contexts are considered: women and men in close personal relationships (e.g., a couple "in love"), in role relationships (e.g., a father and mother), and in groups (e.g., a mixed-sex task group in an organizational setting).

In order to set the stage for the critical analysis of central concepts in the following six chapters, the remainder of this chapter is devoted to two topics. We first place this volume in historical and intellectual context. That is, we describe where it stands in time and space and in relation to other approaches to understanding relations between the sexes. Then, we provide a working conceptual framework for the social psychology of female–male relations by considering what is here meant (and not meant) by social psychology and by female–male relations.

The Context of This Book

THE WHERE AND THE WHEN

The idea for this volume was conceived late in 1980, and most of the writing was done between 1981 and 1984. All but one of the authors is American by birth and all presently reside in the United States. The overwhelming bulk of the work cited is by Americans and based on American samples. Thus, this book is, strictly speaking, about male–female relations in the United States in the early to mid-1980s, as seen by American psychologists.

The where and when of this work is important for many reasons, three of which we highlight. First, the United States has its own distinctive physical and cultural make-up. It is a large, ethnically heterogeneous, economically advanced state. It has a ranked class structure and a system of values that emphasizes freedom and individual self-reliance. Further, present relations between the sexes in the United States are conditioned by a unique set of historical events (see Andreas, 1971, Chapter 6; Bernard, 1981). Thus, it is necessary to exercise care in generalizing to other cultural settings the conclusions reached in this book about female–male relations.

This (rather obvious) caution is needed because not only the observed (i.e., male–female relations) but also the observers (i.e., authors) are American. Although our scientific training helps us to view phenomena in a more objective light than we might without this training, a truly disinterested or value-free social science is not possible (and, some would argue, not advisable [see Tajfel, 1981]). In addition to having what might be called an American cultural perspective, the authors, trained and employed in the United States, share an American approach to psychology. This approach is not independent of the American society and cultural values of which it is a part. Indeed, Sampson (1978) has argued "that the needs of a male-dominant, Protestant-ethic oriented, middle-class, liberal, and capitalistic society initially helped found and nourish and, in social psychology (among other social sciences), continue to help maintain" a research paradigm stressing the goal of establishing universal laws concerning the causes of behavior of autonomous individuals (p. 1335). (For a critique of American social psychology from a European perspective, see Israel and Tajfel, 1972.)

Second, it is our view that the 1980s in the United States is a time of unusual uncertainty and possibly of transition, and that this affects relations between the sexes. In the 1980 election, conservatives made impressive gains, and their standard-bearer, Ronald Reagan, was re-elected by a wide margin in 1984. And, the economy, which in early 1983 was on the brink of a depression, is at this time (February, 1985) seemingly healthy. The confusing and seemingly unpredictable political and economic picture is accompanied by ferment in female–male relations. Some events were part of the confusing overall political picture (Geraldine Ferraro was nominated as the first female Vice-Presidential candidate, while the Equal Rights Amendment failed to be ratified), but other changes are part of trends that have been developing over the past two decades.

These latter changes were occurring in both the work world (traditionally regarded as the masculine domain in American society) and in the family (traditionally the woman's domain). Women are entering the work world in large numbers—an increase of 21 million (or 95%) in the past 20 years (Prial, 1982, p. 1A). Further, married women with children are a major part of this increase. In 1960, only 27.6% of all married women with children under the age of 18 worked outside the home. In less than one generation (i.e., by 1980) this figure had climbed to 54.2% (Hacker, 1983, p. 133). During this same period, the percentage of mothers with children under the age of 6 years who are employed increased from 18.6% to 45.0% (Hacker, 1983, p. 133). Not only are more women (including mothers) working, but many are working in jobs that were historically filled overwhelmingly by men (Prial, 1982, p. 1A). Over the past two decades, women have become a majority in six major traditionally male job categories, including "insurance adjustors, ex-aminers, and investigators" (from 9% in 1961 to 58% in 1981) and "bill col-lectors" (from 22% to 63% during the same period). Pay differentials be-tween the sexes continue (in 1981, a full-time employed woman earned just 59.8% of a comparable male), but today the world of work is clearly not "For Males Only."

The American family, too, has been undergoing significant changes. The figures on working mothers indicate part of the alteration. There have also been changes in family stability and structure. Since the mid-1960s, there has been a dramatic rise in divorce rates and this increase is especially marked for couples with children (Hetherington, 1979, p. 851). As a consequence, ap-proximately 20% of American children live in single-parent families (Conger, 1981).

Third, this book is written after a decade of considerable interest—among academics, the popular press, and the public at large—in the whole range of issues concerning the sexes. In the social science corner of scholarly activity, this interest is easily documented. A large number of review articles have ap-peared (e.g., Mednick & Weissman [1975], Parlee [1975, 1979], and Vaughter [1976] in psychology; Lipman-Blumen & Tickameyer [1975], Huber [1975], Lopata [1976] and Gould [1980], in sociology; Stack et al. [1975], Quinn [1977], Lamphere [1977], Rapp [1979], and Atkinson [1982], in anthropology; Chapman [1975], Jusenius [1976], and Kahne [1978] in economics; Boals [1975], Carroll, B. A. [1979, 1980], and Jacquette [1976] in political science). Several bibliographies have been published (e.g., Astin, Parelman, & Fischer, 1975; Een & Rosenberg-Dishman, 1978; Rosenberg & Bergstrom, 1975). Many journals have published special issues concerned with the sexes (e.g., *American Anthropologist*, 1980, *49*, #1; *Counseling Psychologist*, 1979, *8*, #1; *International Journal of Group Tensions*, 1974, *4*, #1; *Sociology and Social Research*, 1979, *63*, #3). (Although most of these review articles, bibliographies, and special issues have focused on women, there has been some attention paid to men, e.g., special issues of *Family Coordinator*, 1979, *28*, #4, and *Journal of Social Issues*, 1978, *34*, #1, and a review article, Harrison, 1978.) Finally, a number of new journals (e.g., *Sex Roles, Signs, The Psychology of Women Quarterly*) have been founded, and these new outlets are becoming more specialized (e.g., *Women and Politics* with volume one issued in Spring, 1980, and *Women and Therapy* which began in 1982).

We wish to stress two points about the high level of interest in female–male relations in the 1970s. First, there is some evidence that the concern reached a plateau or perhaps even began to subside. Figure 1 presents the number of abstracts per 1000 total abstracts indexed each year in the *Psychological Abstracts* under the following headings: "sex roles," "sex-role attitudes," "human females," "human males," and "human sex differences." As can be seen, there was a relatively steady increase in all categories from

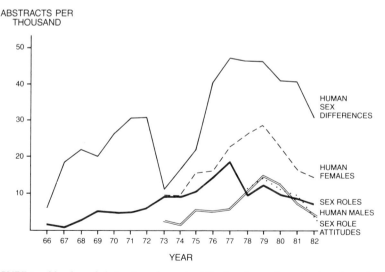

FIGURE 1.   Number of abstracts under each of five headings relevant to female–male relations (per 1000 total abstracts) appearing in *Psychological Abstracts*, 1966–1982.

1966 until 1979[1] and a decline in the years since 1979. The figures for 1983 and 1984 reveal (1) a continuing decline for "human males" and "human sex differences" abstracts and (2) a leveling off for the other three headings (i.e., "sex roles," "human females," "sex-role attitudes"). Although this analysis of gender-related abstracts appearing in *Psychological Abstracts* suggests that there has been in the 1980s an apparent decline in the volume of new work appearing, the literature pertinent to male–female relations is huge and growing.

The second major point about the interest in the sexes is that the concern is not distributed equally. The overwhelming majority of books, articles, bibliographies and so on are concerned with women. This point is also apparent in Figure 1—in every year that "human females" and "human males" appear as index headings, there are many more entries under the former.

One Perspective among Many

There are many approaches to understanding relations between the sexes. (By "understanding," we simply mean representing some insight—in this case, about women or men or their relations—in such a way that others can apprehend this insight.) These approaches take a wide variety of forms—works of literature and art (e.g., Virginia Woolf's *A Room of One's Own*, Michelangelo's *David*, Ibsen's *A Doll's House*), literary and art criticism (e.g., Garrard & Broude, 1982), and analyses of legal and religious systems (e.g., Silk, 1982). There are also scientific approaches that rely on the interplay of theory construction and empirical testing of hypotheses to provide insight into female–male relations. Here we partition the scientific approaches according to level of analysis. At the most micro end are biologically oriented researchers who seek to understand the sexes in terms of genetic or hormonal factors, while the macro end of the continuum is anchored by historians, political scientists, economists, and sociologists who account for male–female relations in terms of societal or, in some cases, global variables. In between are psychological (analyzing the sexes in terms of the abilities, interests, and personalities of individuals) and social psychological levels of analysis. These various approaches to understanding relations between the sexes are neither mutually exclusive nor competing alternatives. Any comprehensive account would require the integration of a wide variety of perspectives, a point we return to in Chapter Eight. Because this volume presents a social psychology of female–male relations, we turn now to consideration of what such a level of analysis entails.

[1] There was, however, a sharp decline in the number of "human sex differences" abstracts in 1973; this was most likely due to the addition of two new headings, "human females" and "human males," that year.

Framework for a Social Psychology of Female–Male Relations

The social psychological analysis of relations between the sexes to be presented in the following chapters is not theory driven or theory derived. That is, the present volume did not begin with a single theory which was then applied to the topic of male–female relations. The reason for not choosing this path is simple—we do not believe that there is, at present, any single theory that can adequately be so applied. This volume, which focuses critical attention on central concepts, is one step toward a social psychological theory of female–male relations.

Although no single theory guides this work, the authors (not all of whom would be labelled by self or others as "social psychologist") do share a general orientation toward social psychology. This shared orientation provides the first part of a framework for the specific chapters to follow and for the social psychology of female–male relations more generally. The second part of the framework involves specifying what is here meant by "female–male relations."

A Cognitive-Social Psychological Orientation

Although there is no single universally accepted definition of *social psychology*, probably the one most often cited was phrased by Gordon Allport, "*an attempt to understand and explain how the thought, feeling and behavior of individuals are influenced by the actual, imagined, or implied presence of others*" (1968, p. 3; italics in original). While accepting the general spirit of this formulation, we offer as a guiding definition for the present volume that social psychology is the scientific study of "*how individuals interact with their social environments during the life span, with mutual and reciprocal consequences*" (Sherif, 1981, p. 1 mimeo; italics in original). The latter definition is preferred for three primary reasons.

1. In contrast with the Allport definition, the latter emphasizes that social psychology is concerned with both individuals and social environments. It is, thus, not as tilted toward what has been termed "psychological social psychology" as distinguished from "sociological social psychology" (House, 1977; Strykker, 1977; Taylor & Johnson, 1984). Although all of the present authors are "psychologists," the analyses to follow do not center solely on the individual.

2. The Sherif definition explicitly recognizes a mutually causative relationship between the individual and the social environment. That is, not only are individuals "influenced by . . . others," but also individual humans can and do influence others as well as the social environment more generally.

3.   The second definition is also preferred because it includes the phrase, "during the life span." Many psychological social psychologists may find the phrase unnecessary and perhaps a distraction. We do not. It emphasizes that humans are born into social groups, that they are "socialized," and that this "socialization" is a lifelong process.[2]

The preceding working definition contains two key terms, "individual" and "social environments." It is important at this point to make explicit the assumptions made here about the individual and the most continuing social environment, human society. Human nature is too complex for a single "(wo)man is . . . " metaphor to be adequate (Harré, 1980, p. 204). Thus, several such metaphors or models must be elaborated and ultimately be brought together (Harré & Secord, 1973). Our working model of (wo)man is built around what we regard to be two central "facts" about *Homo sapiens*—humans are cognitive and social.[3]

By asserting that "(wo)man is a cognitive creature," we mean that humans represent external reality internally (Fodor, 1981), that much of this representation is in language-like format (Fodor, 1975), that this internal representation can be manipulated (transformed, reorganized) in a variety of ways, and that internal representations guide human action. Basically, when we say that "(wo)man is a cognitive creature" we mean that the "mind" has an active, causal role in human conduct. And, we agree with Sperry that "mind can rule matter in the brain and exert causal influence in the guidance and control of behavior, on terms acceptable to neuroscience and without violating monistic principles of scientific explanations" (1977, p. 239).

There has been considerable controversy about the exact nature of internal representations. For example, there is a debate among cognitive psychologists about the format of these representations. Some contend that all knowledge is represented in a propositional form (cf. Pylyshyn, 1973), whereas others argue for a dual code model, which includes both propositional or analytic information and image or analog representation (cf. Glass, Holyoak, & Santa, 1979, pp. 7–24). Our position is catholic. Quite simply, a representation is a discrimination made by the person (Kelly, 1955), and

[2]The notion that social psychology should have a life span perspective is not new. As Murphy, Murphy, and Newcomb stated in their highly influential *Experimental Social Psychology* published in 1937, "Social psychology overlaps both child psychology and psychology of personality. Social psychology is the study of the way in which the individual becomes a member of, and functions in, a social group" (Murphy et al., 1937, p. 16).
[3]One further implication is that we, as all humans, are to a large extent shaped by our culture. Thus, our working model of (wo)man may really be of "Homo Euroamericans" (Jahoda, 1980) and our analysis specific to American culture to an unspecified degree. Shweder and Bourne (1982) have presented evidence suggesting important Western–Nonwestern differences in models of (wo)man and of society.

discriminations can take many forms. That is, we feel that several types of mental contents (also termed "internal codes," see Posner, 1973) must be considered: (1) verbal "knowledge" (e.g., "The Human Life Amendment would prohibit all abortions"); (2) images (e.g., the mental "picture" of my spouse); (3) feelings (e.g., the joys and fears experienced by a newlywed); (4) generally nonconscious "programs" for motor activity (e.g., a male in American society opening a door for a female).

It is essential to briefly note what we do *not* mean by "(wo)man is a cognitive creature." First, it does not mean that (wo)man is a computer (see Estes, 1980). As a corollary, the presumed cognitive nature of (wo)man does not mean that humans are logical–rational beings. Although the present "cognitive creature" metaphor is quite similar to Kelly's (1955) notion of "(wo)man the scientist," we do not regard humans as always behaving as good scientists. There are a number of reasons why the lay scientist deviates from the ideal scientific model, e.g., humans have a limited capacity to process and store information; humans tend to selectively attend to evidence that confirms their "implicit theories" (see Ashmore & Del Boca, 1979, pp. 244–245).[4]

Second, it does not mean that there is nothing out there and that humans create or construct cognitions from impoverished stimulus displays. Thus, although we see humans as active cognizers, we do not assume that all of the action is in the head (see Neisser, 1976, on this general point). That humans internally represent external reality does not deny or significantly diminish the importance of the external reality.

Finally, as should be clear from our catholic position regarding the nature of internal representation, the "(wo)man is a cognitive creature" metaphor does not mean that we take a narrow view of cognition. Thus, it does not mean that the proper subject matter of psychology is conscious experience or that we are urging a phenomenological social psychology (whatever that might be). And, it does not mean that emotion is absent from (wo)man. Cognition and affect, which can be separated for analytic purposes, are complexly intertwined phenomena (Fransella, 1980; Lazarus, 1982). Within the present cognitive-social psychological framework, emotions or feelings are, at least in part, simply one form or type of internal representation, just as are images and propositions.

"(Wo)man is a cognitive creature" is a good metaphor for *Homo sapiens*, but it is not sufficient. Its shortcomings point up the second aspect of human nature we wish to stress—"(Wo)man is a social being." A purely cognitive view of human nature ignores a very important fact: *Homo sapiens* is born

---

[4] Nisbett and Ross (1980) have provided a detailed analysis of deviations from optimal performance by an intelligent being.

into established and continuing social contexts ("families," "kin groups," "societies"), is generally dependent on others (note the especially prolonged and pronounced helplessness of the human infant) and is seldom if ever "completely alone." That (wo)man is a social animal has several implications. First, humans are, in a sense, programmed to respond to others and to "culture." That is, human nature cannot be separated from culture because culture has influenced the evolution of the species (cf. Geertz, 1973, pp. 33–51). Second, there are no purely psychological events.

> The individual who is considered in psychological theory, in fact, is never an individual pure and simple. The statements about him always have reference to a particular set of conditions. The individual with whom we have to deal may be the individual-in-the-laboratory, or the individual-in-his-everyday-working environment, or—and in social psychology this is always the case—the individual-in-a-given-social-group. (Bartlett, 1923, p. 11).

Third, (wo)man has goals or purposes other than cognizing. And, these goals are often social in nature, for example, maintaining a particular image in the eyes of others (cf. Ashmore, 1981).

Our "cognitive-social psychological" framework is quite similar to the "social-cognitive perspective" of Tajfel and the Bristol school (see Turner & Giles, 1981). Like them, we hesitate to affix such a label and for much the same reason. "Social cognition" has come to denote the application of the information processing theory and methods of cognitive psychology to social entities. We do not intend this.[5] Rather, we mean that a social psychological level of analysis requires recognition that (wo)man is both a cognitive creature and a social being. Further, these are not separate aspects of human nature but are inseparably connected (cf. Turner & Giles, 1981, p. 30). (Sherif [1981] presents a similar argument in her paper, "The social and psychological bases of social psychology.")

FEMALE–MALE RELATIONS AS AN INSTANCE
OF INTERGROUP RELATIONS

The early classic statements by Hacker (1951) and Myrdal (1944) notwithstanding, the notion of "female–male relations" would not have made much sense to most social scientists as recently as 1966 (when the National

---

[5] Our objection here is not with cognitive psychology per se. In fact, Bower's definition of the field—"Cognitive psychology is concerned with how organisms cognize or gain knowledge about their world, and how they use that knowledge to guide decisions and perform effective actions" (1975, p. 25)—is perfectly compatible with our assertion that "(wo)man is a cognitive creature." Rather, we reject the often tacit assumption that certain theoretical models and certain methods define the domain of ways of doing cognitive psychology, or, by extension, cognitive social psychology.

Organization of Women was founded). There was recognition that individual women and men did relate to one another. For example, psychologists investigated sexuality and sexual behavior, and sociologists, marriage and the family. However, the idea that the relations between the sexes might be similar to those between ethnic or national groups would have seemed far-fetched. Since about 1970, both social scientists and the lay public—in part because of the efforts of that loose confederation of individuals and groups termed the Women's Liberation Movement—have come to accept the proposition that females and males relate to one another both as individuals and as groups. In addition to considering gender as an individual difference factor or personality variable, there has been increasing recognition by social scientists that male and female are important social categories (cf. Deaux, 1984).[6] Viewing gender in these terms leads to a consideration of male–female as a relation between social categories or groups—that is, as an instance of intergroup relations (see Babad, Birnbaum, & Benne, 1983). A number of concepts have been borrowed from analyses of race and ethnic relations (e.g., stereotype, prejudice, discrimination) and various intergroup relations models have been applied to relations between the sexes. Political scientists have addressed the issue of women as an "interest group" (cf. S. J. Carroll, 1980), and sociologists have debated how best to conceptualize the position of women in society (e.g., Are women a minority group? a class? a caste? Do they differ from men primarily in terms of their relation to modes of production? [cf. Lipman-Blumen & Tickameyer, 1975]). It is our belief, however, that an intergroup relations perspective has not fully informed social psychologists' analyses of the various topics we feel are relevant to female–male relations.

An intergroup relations perspective involves both an external reality (societal level) and the internal (psychological) representation of this reality. Quite simply, the world of humans is partitioned into groups. In today's world, nation states are one important level of grouping and within each state or society there is further partitioning. If we focus on an individual society (for example, that of the United States), we can see that not only are there a variety of different groups (or social categories) but also that this social categorization involves multiple and cross-cutting classifications. For example, a person can be a member of many social categories (e.g., a white male college professor born in Glendale, California) and a given social category can share members with many others (e.g., there are a variety of different types of college professors, though most are white males).

Perhaps the most important aspect of external reality concerning in-

---

[6]In this volume the terms *sex* and *gender* are used interchangeably to denote the socially defined categories male and female. See Unger (1979) for suggested distinctions regarding these terms.

tergroup relations is that any two groups can stand in various relations to one another. If they are interdependent, this interdependence can be either positive (what Deutsch, 1949, terms "promotive interdependence") or negative ("contrient interdependence"). Historically, negative interdependence has taken two primary forms: dominance (where one group clearly establishes itself "on top", e.g., slavery in the U.S.) and competition (where the two groups openly compete for resources, e.g., the U.S. and the U.S.S.R.).

At the psychological level, individuals internally represent the relevant social categories. And, the state of intergroup interdependence comes to shape beliefs about and evaluations of social categories. For example, Americans see Russians (especially Russian leaders) as aggressive and warlike and Russians share the same view of Americans (the mirror-image phenomenon, see Ashmore, Bird, Del Boca, & Vanderet, 1979).

An intergroup relations perspective on female–male relations raises a number of significant questions. At the societal level, what is the nature of the interdependence between the social categories "men" and "women"? We will not devote much attention to this issue. It is essentially a sociological question, requiring societal-level analysis. However, we take as given that males have the dominant position in American society.[7] And if, as we asserted earlier, the state of intergroup interdependence is reflected at the level of the individual, then partial answers should appear in all the following chapters.

While much is to be gained by considering female–male relations as an instance of intergroup relations, it is also necessary to recognize that relations between the sexes have a number of unique features. Probably the most obvious and most important is that they often live together. As Hacker (1951) noted, "accept into my family by marriage" is the indicator of smallest social distance (and hence least amount of prejudice) when ethnic and race relations are considered. Asking such a question with regard to the "other sex," however, makes absolutely no sense because marriage between men and women is the rule. Thus, the fact that individual males and females are drawn to one another, that they form relationships, and that societies legitimize and define such relationships through informal norms and formal laws provides a unique and very important facet to female–male relations.

A consideration of the general intergroup relations perspective in conjunction with an appreciation of the special nature of relations between the sexes leads to a set of questions that serve to define and delimit the domain of the social psychology of female–male relations. First, how are gender categories

---

[7] Whether male dominance is a cultural universal has stirred a great deal of debate, particularly among anthropologists. For contrasting perspectives on this topic, see Rogers (1978), Rosaldo (1980), and Sanday (1981).

psychologically represented? How do women and men come to think about and evaluate themselves as members of the social categories female and male? What are the beliefs we hold about men and women? How do we evaluate these social categories and issues such as the ERA that are relevant to the relations between the sexes? Second, what are the forms of social relationships between individual women and men and how are these conditioned by overarching societal relations between the sexes? How do women and men enter into, maintain, and dissolve personal relationships such as love? What are the various role relationships that bind (and separate) the sexes? How do the sexes interact in group settings?

A SOCIAL PSYCHOLOGY OF FEMALE–MALE RELATIONS:
WHAT IT IS, WHAT IT IS NOT, AND HOW WE HOPE TO BUILD IT

The preceding questions have been addressed primarily by psychologists and sociologists. There are established literatures concerned with these and closely related topics. And, specialty areas have been established in each discipline, for example, "marriage and the family" in sociology, "sex differences" in psychology, and "sex roles" in both. It is, thus, important to articulate how the present volume (and the social psychology of female–male relations more generally) relates to, and yet is distinguishable from, these established literatures and areas of professional specialization. The social psychology of female–male relations is new. We propose bringing together a set of topics that are united by their relevance to what we regard as the overriding issue—how men and women relate to one another as individuals, as members of groups, and as groups.

To adequately begin to address this issue we must draw from a variety of academic disciplines (though primarily from sociology and psychology) and from several specialty areas within each discipline. Thus, the focus of the present book is related to, but not reducible to or coterminous with, several existing topics. This is not a book on "sex differences." That is, we are not writing in the tradition of Maccoby (1966), Maccoby and Jacklin (1974), and Block (1976, 1979). The reader will find considerable discussion of differences between men and women, but this is not designed to add to, modify, or correct an existing catalogue of such differences. Rather, the aim is to identify female–male differences that have implications for how the sexes relate to one another. The present book is not a "sex-roles" text. Here, "sex role" is regarded as just one concept, albeit an important one, that is necessary for a social psychological analysis of male–female relations. And finally, this is not a book on the "psychology of women" or the "sociology of women." Although these subdisciplines are valuable in their own right, it is our view that it is also necessary to recognize that women and men are interrelated and interconnected at both the individual and the societal level. As a consequence, the following chapters deal with both men and women and with their interrelations. We hope that practitioners in these other areas will find much of interest in this volume. There are likely to be many specific theories and research paradigms that they may find helpful. Perhaps more importantly, the ensuing chapters may provide fresh insights to issues of mutual concern.

To begin building a social psychology of female–male relations we have brought together six topics. The book is divided into two parts, each containing three chapters. Part One focuses on the individual, while Part Two is concerned primarily with social interaction and the social context of individual action. Chapter Two, on gender identity, is concerned with how an individual relates to his/her own gender category. Chapters Three and Four deal with the beliefs about (*stereotypes*) and evaluations of (*attitudes*) the social categories male and female. That is, these chapters detail how the individual thinks and feels about women and men as groups. The next two chapters deal with men and women in relationships, first voluntary personal relationships and then role relationships. The final chapter of Part Two focuses on how women and men think, feel, and behave in group settings. The six chapters cover female–male relations in terms of individual-to-own-category and individual-to-other-category relations (gender identity, stereotypes, and attitudes) as well as the relationships between individuals (personal and role relationships) and the behavior of women and men in small, face-to-face groups.

Each chapter takes a critical approach to the topic at hand. Such an approach involves a careful analysis of both the empirical literature and of existing theoretical frameworks. Where possible, the focus is on specific concepts (e.g., gender stereotype, sex role). This volume is not intended as an encyclopedic review of six literatures. Rather, it is a critical analysis of a set of topics which, when taken together, constitute the social psychology of female–male relations. Because our goal is to provide a beginning in building a new field, the authors have been encouraged to not only describe with a critical eye "what is," but also to be prescriptive, to indicate "what is not but should be." It is hoped that such an approach will be a successful first step toward a social psychology of female–male relations.

References

Allport, G. W. (1968). The historical background of modern social psychology. In G. Lindzey and E. Aronson (Eds.), *The handbook of social psychology* (2nd ed., Vol. 1). Reading, Ma: Addison-Wesley Publishing Co.

Andreas, C. (1971). *Sex and caste in America*. Englewood Cliffs, NJ: Prentice-Hall.

Ashmore, R. D. (1981). Sex stereotypes and implicit personality theory. In D. L. Hamilton (Ed.), *Cognitive processes in stereotyping and intergroup behavior*. Hillsdale, NJ: Erlbaum.

Ashmore, R. D., Bird, D., Del Boca, F. K. & Vanderet, R. C. (1979). An experimental investigation of the double standard in the perception of international affairs. *Political Behavior, 1*, 123–135.

Ashmore, R. D., & Del Boca, F. K. (1979). Sex stereotypes and implicit personality theory: Toward a cognitive-social psychological conceptualization. *Sex Roles, 5*, 219–248.

Astin, H.S., Parelman, A., & Fisher, A. (1975). *Sex roles: A research bibliography*. Washington, DC: U.S. Government Printing Office.

Atkinson, J. M. (1982). Review essay: Anthropology. *Signs, 8*, 236–258.

Badad, E. Y., Birnbaum, M., & Benne, K. D. (1983). *The social self: Group influences on personal identity*. Beverly Hills, CA: Sage Publications.

Bartlett, F. C. (1923). *Psychology and primitive culture*. Westport, CN: Greenwood Press.

Bernard, J. (1981). The good-provider role: Its rise and fall. *American Psychologist, 36*, 1–12.

Block, J. H. (1976). Issues, problems, and pitfalls in assessing sex differences: A critical review of *The psychology of sex differences*. *Merrill-Palmer Quarterly, 22*, 283–308.

Block, J. H. (1979, September). Personality development in males and females: The influence of differential socialization. Paper presented at the Annual Convention of the American Psychological Association, New York.

Boals, K. (1975). Review essay: Political science. *Signs, 1*, 161–174.

Bower, G. H. (1975). Cognitive psychology: An introduction. In W. K. Estes (Ed.), *Handbook of learning and cognitive processes* (Vol. 1): *Introduction to concepts and issues*. Hillsdale, NJ: Erlbaum.

Carroll, B. A. (1979). Review essay: Political Science, Part I: American politics and political behavior. *Signs, 5*, 289–306.

Carroll, B. A. (1980). Review essay: Political Science, Part II: International politics, and feminist radicals. *Signs, 5*, 449–458.

Carroll, S. J. (1980). Women as candidates: Campaigns and elections in American politics. Unpublished doctoral dissertation, Indiana University.

Chapman, J. R. (1975). Review essay: Economics. *Signs, 1*, 139–146.

Conger, J. J. (1981). Freedom and commitment: Families, youth, and social change. *American Psychologist, 36*, 1475–1484.

Deaux, K. (1984). From individual differences to social categories: Analysis of a decade's research on gender. *American Psychologist, 39*, 105–116.

Deutsch, M. (1949). A theory of co-operation and competition. *Human Relations, 2*, 129–152.

Een, J. D. & Rosenberg-Dishman, M. B. (Eds.) (1978). *Women and society—Citations 3601 to 6000: An annotated bibliography*. Beverly Hills, CA: Sage Publications.

Estes, W. K. (1980). Is human memory obsolete? *American Scientist, 68*, 62–69.

Fodor, J. A. (1975). *The language of thought*. New York: Thomas Y. Crowell.

Fodor, J. A. (1981). *Representations: Philosophical essays on the foundations of cognitive science*. Cambridge, MA: MIT Press.

Fransella, F. (1980). Man-as-scientist. In A. J. Chapman & D. M. Jones (Eds.), *Models of man*. Leicester: British Psychological Society.

Garrard, M. D., & Broude, N. (Eds.) (1982). *Feminism and art history: Questioning the litany*. New York: Harper & Row.

Geertz, C. (1973). *The interpretation of cultures*. New York: Basic Books.

Glass, A. L., Holyoak, K. J., & Santa, J. (1979). *Cognition*. Reading, MA: Addison-Wesley Publishing Co.

Gould, M. (1980). The new sociology. *Signs, 5,* 459–467.

Hacker, A. (Ed.) (1983). *U/S: A statistical portrait of the American people.* New York: The Viking Press.

Hacker, H. M. (1951). Women as a minority group. *Social Forces, 30,* 60–69.

Harré, R., & Secord, P. F. (1973). *The explanation of social behavior.* Totowa, NJ: Littlefield, Adams & Co.

Harré, R. (1980). Man as rhetorician. In A. J. Chapman & D. M. Jones (Eds.), *Models of man.* Leicester: British Psychological Society.

Harrison, J. B. (1978). Review essay: Men's roles and men's lives. *Signs, 4,* 324–336.

Hetherington, E. M. (1979). Divorce: A child's perspective. *American Psychologist, 34,* 851–858.

House, J. S. (1977). The three faces of social psychology. *Sociometry, 40,* 161–177.

Huber, J. (1975). Review essay: Sociology. *Signs, 1,* 685–698.

Israel, J., & Tajfel, H. (Eds.) (1972). *The context of social psychology: A critical assessment.* New York: Academic Press.

Jacquette, J. S. (1976). Review essay: Political science. *Signs, 2,* 147–164.

Jahoda, M. (1980). One model of man or many? In A. J. Chapman & D. M. Jones (Eds.), *Models of man.* Leicester: The British Psychological Society.

Jusenius, C. L. (1976). Review essay: Economics. *Signs, 2,* 177–189.

Kahne, H. (1978). Review essay: Economic research on women and families. *Signs, 3,* 652–665.

Kelly, G. A. (1955). *The psychology of personal constructs.* New York: Norton.

Lakoff, G., & Johnson, M. (1980). *Metaphors we live by.* Chicago: The University of Chicago Press.

Lamphere, L. (1977). Review essay: Anthropology. *Signs, 2,* 612–627.

Lazarus, R. S. (1982). Thoughts on the relations between emotion and cognition. *American Psychologist, 37,* 1019–1024.

Lipman-Blumen, J., & Tickameyer, A. (1975). Sex roles in transition: A ten year perspective. *Annual Review of Sociology, 1,* 297–337.

Lopata, H. Z. (1976). Review essay: Sociology. *Signs, 2,* 165–176.

Maccoby, E. E. (Ed.) (1966). *The development of sex differences.* Stanford, CA: Stanford University Press.

Maccoby, E. E., & Jacklin, C. (1974). *The psychology of sex differences.* Stanford, CA: Stanford University Press.

Mednick, M. T., & Weissman, H. J. (1975). The psychology of women: Selected topics. *Annual Review of Psychology, 26,* 1–18.

Murphy, G., Murphy, L. B., & Newcomb, T. M. (1937). *Experimental social psychology.* New York: Harper & Row.

Myrdal, G. (1944). *An American dilemma* (Appendix 5). New York: Harper & Row.

Neisser, U. (1976). *Cognition and reality.* San Francisco, CA: W. H. Freeman.

Nisbett, R., & Ross, L. (1980). *Human inference: Strategies and shortcomings of social judgment.* Englewood Cliffs, NJ: Prentice-Hall.

Parlee, M. B. (1975). Review essay: Psychology. *Signs, 1,* 119–138.

Parlee, M. B. (1979). Review essay: Psychology and women. *Signs, 5,* 121–133.

Prial, F. J. (1982, November 15). More women work at traditional male jobs. *New York Times,* p. 1A and C20.

Posner, M. I. (1973). Coordination of internal codes. In W. G. Chase (Ed.) *Visual information processing.* New York: Academic Press.

Pylyshyn, Z. W. (1973). What the mind's eye tells the mind's brain: A critique of mental imagery. *Psychological Bulletin, 80,* 1–24.

Quinn, N. (1977). Anthropological studies on women's status. *Annual Review of Anthropology*, 6, 181–226.

Rapp, R. (1979). Review essay: Anthropology. *Signs, 4*, 497–513.

Rogers, S. (1978). Women's place: A critical review of anthropological theory. *Comparative studies in society and history, 20*, 123–162.

Rosaldo, M. Z. (1980). The use and abuse of anthropology. *Signs, 5*, 389–417.

Rosenberg, M. B., & Bergstrom, L. V. (Eds.) (1975). *Women and society: A critical review of the literature with a selected annotated bibliography*. Beverly Hills, CA: Sage Publications.

Sampson, E. E. (1978). Scientific paradigms and social values: Wanted—A scientific revolution. *Journal of Personality and Social Psychology, 36*, 1332–1343.

Sanday, P. R. (1981). *Female power and male dominance: On the origins of sexual inequality*. Cambridge: Cambridge University Press.

Sherif, C. W. (1981, August). Social and psychological bases of social psychology. G. Stanley Hall Lecture on Social Psychology. Paper presented at the Annual Convention of the American Psychological Association, Los Angeles, CA.

Shweder, R. A., & Bourne, E. J. (1982). Does the concept of the person vary cross-culturally? In A. J. Marsella & G. White (Eds.), *Cultural conceptions of mental health and therapy*. Boston: Reidel.

Silk, M. (1982, April 11). Is god a feminist? *New York Times Book Review*, pp. 11, 20–21.

Sperry, R. W. (1977). Bridging science and values—A unifying view of mind and brain. *American Psychologist, 32*, 237–245.

Stack, C. B., Caulfield, M. D., Estes, V., Landes, S., Larson, K., Johnson, P., Rake, J., & Shirck, J. (1975). Review essay: Anthropology. *Signs, 1*, 147–160.

Strykker, S. (1977). Developments in "two social psychologies": Toward an appreciation of mutual relevance. *Sociometry, 40*, 145–160.

Tajfel, H. (1981). *Human groups and social categories: Studies in social psychology*. Cambridge, England: Cambridge University Press.

Taylor, M. C., & Johnson, M. P. (1984). *Strategies for linking individual psychology and social structure: Interdisciplinary and crossdisciplinary social psychology*. Unpublished manuscript.

Turner, J. C., & Giles, H. (Eds.) (1981). *Intergroup behavior*. Chicago: University of Chicago Press.

Unger, R. K. (1979). Toward a redefinition of sex and gender. *American Psychologist, 34*, 1085–1094.

Vaughter, R. M. (1976). Review essay: Psychology. *Signs, 2*, 120–146.

Part One

GENDER AND THE INDIVIDUAL

Two

Gender Identity: Development and Consequences*

PHYLLIS A. KATZ

Introduction: Definitions and Concepts

If one had to predict a person's life course on the basis of a single attribute, the best choice would probably be gender. After 9 months of gestation suspense, gender is the first piece of information given to parents and relatives. "What did you have?" (i.e., what gender is your baby) is usually the first question asked of new parents, and "It's a boy" or "It's a girl" are probably the first three words heard by most newborns in an English-speaking environment. The answers are associated with very different life scripts.

The meaning and implications of those three little words will take the child quite a few years to absorb, and this chapter will review some of the major milestones in this process. Despite the lengthy and gradual course of gender socialization, however, the early age at which gender learning begins is one of the most remarkable phenomena in child development. The average 2-year old, for example, has a vocabulary of about 29 words, talks in two-

gross error- 15 months 200 words .

*Preparation of this chapter was made possible by Grant No. R01 HD 16218–01 from the National Institute of Child Health and Human Development, Phyllis Katz, Principal Investigator. The author is particularly grateful to Diane Coulter, Tamara Russell, and Susie Gulbrandsen for their extensive assistance in library research, editing, and typing of this chapter.

word sentences, has been walking for about 10 months, and is probably in the process of being toilet-trained. In contrast to this relatively primitive functioning, however, such a child is already quite advanced with regard to gender knowledge. It is likely that he or she can use the words "girl" and/or "boy" correctly as a self-referent and can select gender-associated toys and future occupations at greater than chance levels.

Gender is an extremely prominent cue for both self-definition and societal reaction and becomes so very early in life. The developmental period without gender awareness is remarkably short, and one's core gender identity, once formed, may be quite difficult to change even if a mistake has been made in the original definition (Money, Hampson, & Hampson, 1957). The content, quality, and salience of an individual's gender identity does, however, develop and change in meaningful ways across the life cycle.

This chapter examines the concept of gender identity and traces these developmental changes from infancy through adulthood. A final section examines the implications of cross-cultural research, androgyny research, and social change for conceptualizations of gender identity.

THE MEANINGS OF GENDER IDENTITY

The concept of gender identity has been used widely in a variety of ways, both in the popular and in the scientific literature. Many different terms with both overlapping and distinctive meaning have been used interchangeably. This has been reflective of (and is perhaps contributive to) considerable theoretical confusion in this area. It is undoubtedly because gender is of such broad concern (i.e., has the reader ever encountered anyone with no thoughts on the subject?) that the implicit but perhaps unwarranted assumption of shared meaning is made.

The terms in this area that have often been used interchangeably include gender identity, gender role, gender-typing, gender-role preferences, gender concepts, gender schemas, gender attitudes, and gender-role behavior. It has been generally assumed that strong relationships exist among these concepts even when they are differentiated as to meaning (e.g., Kagan, 1964). This presupposition, however, has not been unequivocally supported on an empirical level (e.g., Spence & Helmreich, 1978; Spence, Helmreich, & Stapp, 1975). Additionally, "sex" has been used synonymously with "gender" in all of these terms (i.e., sex roles, sex-role preferences, etc.), thereby doubling the number of overlapping terms. Although good arguments have been proposed for distinguishing "sex" from "gender" (e.g., Kessler & McKenna, 1978; Unger, 1979), most investigators (including those in this book) continue to use them synonymously.

This chapter is concerned primarily with gender identity, which in many ways is the most vague of the previously mentioned constructs. At its most basic, gender identity is a psychological construct, referring to an individual's phenomenological experience of being masculine and/or feminine. Most definitions offered have included at least this aspect. Kagan (1964), for example, suggests that gender identity represents "the degree to which an individual regards himself as masculine or feminine" (p. 144) as these are defined by cultural standards. Yorburg (1974) notes that gender identity refers to one's "image of self as a male or female and convictions about what membership in that group implies" (p. 1).

Storms (1979) has attempted to operationalize gender identity by measuring degree of experienced masculinity and femininity. The present writer believes that such a quantitative approach may be too oversimplified. A more complete operationalization should take into account not only quantity, but also structure and degree of differentiation of gender identity and its relation to other components of self-identity. Current theory suggests (e.g., Bem, 1981a; Katz, 1979) that both individual and developmental differences exist along each of these dimensions.

Several related and perplexing issues have been discussed with regard to the gender identity construct. The first is whether all aspects of such identity are consciously experienced or whether there are some components that typically lie outside of an individual's awareness. This issue has important implications for both measurement and conceptualization. Although most theories have treated gender identity as a predominantly conscious entity, it should be noted that psychoanalytically oriented theorists have not. Stoller (Green, 1974), for example, suggests that sex-role identity recognition is largely "motivated by awareness, conscious and unconscious, of our past" (p. xi). The present writer does not subscribe to the premise that gender identity is primarily unconscious. Nevertheless, insofar as its formation begins very early in life, the possibility clearly exists that such rudimentary processes may not be typically remembered.

A second issue that has been raised concerns the relationship of gender identity to other aspects of an individual's self-concept. Work by Bem (1981a), Markus, Crane, Bernstein, & Sikadi (1982), and Sherif (1980) has explored, with somewhat different hypotheses, how gender-relevant knowledge is organized into self-conceptualization. This work has demonstrated that: (1) individuals differ with regard to the salience of masculinity and/or femininity to general self-concept, and (2) those with sex-typed identities process information differently from those who do not. A more detailed discussion about individuals who do not fit with traditional conceptions of masculinity or femininity is presented later in the chapter.

Sherif (1980) has pointed out the critical importance of reference groups in determining the degree of personal integration of one's gender identity (whether sex-typed or not) with the self-system.

Gender identity has been a central construct in many theories of socialization, although it has been less prominently employed in research than other gender-related concepts, in part, because of difficulties in operationalizing it. There appear to be several explanations for why this concept seems difficult to define with precision. The major one, shared with many other psychological constructs, is the difficulty in assessing another person's internal experience, a state that can be inferred only on the basis of observable behavior. The behaviors from which we infer gender identity often include the other overlapping terms referred to earlier, such as preferences and role behavior. In adults we typically assume that a variety of gender-related behaviors are indicative of an individual's sense of gender identity—that is, if a person feels himself to be strongly male, he will have preferences for and engage in multiple pursuits that are culturally designated as masculine. Thus, in this context, gender identity is conceptualized as an independent variable. In contrast, when children are being observed, these same behaviors are often regarded as contributing to one's sense of gender identity. Thus, with younger groups, identity is often regarded as a dependent variable. It is the present author's view that an interactive process between gender self-conceptualization and behavior occurs at all developmental levels once initial gender labeling occurs. Certain aspects of one's gender identity (such as basic self-identification) may be quite primitive and constant, whereas other aspects may be ever changing (such as the complexity and degree of differentiation of one's inner experience).

A conceptualization of how gender identity should be defined, together with its anticipated theoretical relationships to the aforementioned constructs, are contained in Figure 1. It should be noted that gender identity, insofar as it is an internal construct, is viewed here as subsuming at least a portion of other internal constructs, such as the gender schemata, gender concepts, gender stereotypes, and gender attitudes subscribed to by the individual. Each of these terms may well affect one's gender identity, although they are not identical to this construct. Gender schemata, concepts, stereotypes, and attributes can be applicable in different degrees to others as well as to the self. Only that portion that is relevant to self would be subsumed under gender identity. For example, one can believe that males are generally stronger than females (i.e., a stereotype). If one is female, this might translate in various ways, such as (1) I am weaker than men, or (2) I am not like most women, and therefore, this comparison is not relevant to me. In the first instance, the stereotype affects one's sense of identity; in the second case it does not. Although the present conceptualization is heavily

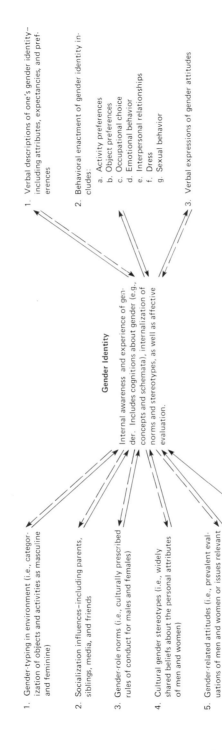

Developmental Antecedents

1. Gender-typing in environment (i.e., categorization of objects and activities as masculine and feminine)

2. Socialization influences—including parents, siblings, media, and friends

3. Gender-role norms (i.e., culturally prescribed rules of conduct for males and females)

4. Cultural gender stereotypes (i.e., widely shared beliefs about the personal attributes of men and women)

5. Gender-related attitudes (i.e., prevalent evaluations of men and women or issues relevant to male–female relations)

6. Biological factors (i.e., puberty, pregnancy, menopause, hormonal balances, etc.)

Experiential Phenomena

Gender Identity

Internal awareness and experience of gender. Includes cognitions about gender (e.g., concepts and schemata), internalization of norms and stereotypes, as well as affective evaluation.

Behavioral Consequents

1. Verbal descriptions of one's gender identity—including attributes, expectancies, and preferences

2. Behavioral enactment of gender identity includes:
   a. Activity preferences
   b. Object preferences
   c. Occupational choice
   d. Emotional behavior
   e. Interpersonal relationships
   f. Dress
   g. Sexual behavior

3. Verbal expressions of gender attitudes

FIGURE 1. Relation of gender identity construct to other gender-related constructs.

cognitive, it also includes nonverbal, emotional, and perhaps biologically based components (see Hines, 1982) of one's gender identity.

The solid arrows in Figure 1 depict the more typical developmental stages. In the case of constructs listed under the column labeled "Developmental antecedents," the dotted arrows are more pronounced after the individual becomes a parent—that is, their own gender identity as developed at that point will affect how they socialize their offspring. The biological factor is conceptualized as unidirectional. With regard to the constructs listed in the "Behavioral consequents" column, the dotted arrows can be viewed as providing interactive feedback. For example, if a male is experiencing some anxiety or uncertainty with regard to the degree of his masculinity, then engaging in many masculine activities may serve to lessen such anxiety.

Operationalization and Interdisciplinary Aspects of Gender Identity

There are several other points that need mentioning with regard to the developmental antecedents, the operationalization, and the interdisciplinary relevance of gender identity. First, it should be noted that the construct of gender identity is based on the concept of gender, which developmentally precedes it. In the first year of life, one has a gender prior to an awareness of gender identity. Gender categorization of individuals takes place at birth and is based on inspection of the infant's genitalia. There are only two dichotomous categories used. For most individuals there is a concurrence of biological sex, gender categorization, and gender identity, but not for all. There are multiple biological cues for gender, and they are not always perfectly correlated. A variety of anomalies exist in which external genitalia and genetic makeup are not in the same category. Additionally, some individuals (transsexuals) experience a gender identity that is different than their assigned gender—that is, they feel as if they have been placed in the wrong body. For these reasons, investigators such as Kessler and McKenna (1978) have argued that gender attribution is at least as much a social construction as a biological one. The latter portions of this chapter include some discussion about individuals who do not readily fit the two-category gender assignment system.

The manner in which constructs are defined is determined partially by theoretical usage and partially by the measures designed to assess the constructs. There are few existing measures that purport to directly measure gender identity. The two that appear to overlap most with the preceding definitions include Storms' (1979) Sex-Role Identity Scale for adults and a similar self-rating for children used in our laboratory (Katz & Boswell,

_e asked to rate the degree of self-perceived
_egard to their personality and social image.
_nts are asked to rate the degree of similarity
_rsonalities and those of other boys and girls.
_o measure a construct often reveal a good deal
_.. It is instructive in this regard, then, to look at
_i of tests and measures purporting to assess various
_, stereotypes, and attitudes. This book describes 235
_vhich 59 purport to measure gender roles, a rubric that
_.ole adoption, preference, orientation, and identity. Of
_z for use with children and 29 with adults.
_.ity of the children's measures assess preferences for toys and
_one measures knowledge of sex-role stereotypes, and four utilize
_parent or teacher ratings of masculinity in boys. Six claim to measure degree
of masculinity or femininity, using either preferences or self-descriptive adjectives (e.g., Feldman, Nash, & Cutrona, 1977), or projective drawing completion (Franck & Rosen, 1949). Only three measures specifically label
themselves as scales of gender orientation or identity. These do not report
established reliability or validity and have little in common with the
previously described theoretical definitions of this construct.

How about the available adult measures? Of the 29 adult sex-role
measures described by Beere, 25 assess either masculinity, femininity, or
both (either individually or together as a bipolar scale); 1 claims to measure
sex-role preference; 1 sexual identification (based on psychoanalytic theory);
and 2 gender identity. Those labeled sex-role preference and gender identity
do not differ essentially from those labeled masculinity and/or femininity, in
that they utilize either adjectives, activities, or occupational preferences and
yield masculinity or femininity scores. Just as toy preferences are the most
popular assessment of sex roles in children, adjective checklists are most frequently employed for adults. Other measures of masculinity and femininity
include interests, values, preferences, semantic differentials, activities, word
associations, and generally almost anything that has been found to
distinguish males from females. This brief perusal of measuring instruments
suggests that most measures have been empirically rather than theoretically
defined and, therefore, do little to advance theoretical conceptualization.

Since the mid-1970s, the most widely employed scales of masculinity and
femininity have been those employing adjectives (e.g., Bem, 1974; Spence,
Helmreich, & Stapp, 1974). There also have been a number of disclaimers,
often by test constructors (e.g., Spence, 1982; Storms, 1979), stating that
such attribute measures have nothing to do with gender identity. It has been
argued that the Bem Sex-Role Inventory and the Personal Attributes Questionnaire, the two most popularly used assessments of masculinity and

femininity, do not actually measure these global constructs, but rather measure degree of instrumentality and expressiveness. It appears, however, that even if such relabeling were to occur, these attributes would continue to be construed in gender-related terms by the general public and by many psychologists. These disclaimers are based on the fact that adult measures of gender identity components (including personality attributes) do not correlate well with one another. The inference that Spence draws—that is, that attributes have nothing to do with gender identity—seems overly broad, however. Another equally tenable interpretation of such low intercorrelations is that any one measure may only tap a small portion of the identity construct as delineated in Figure 1. The structure of gender identity appears to be quite complex, and multiple measures may be needed to accurately assess the concept.

Another aspect of gender identity that merits some discussion is the relevance of this concept to a wide variety of scientific disciplines. At one end of the continuum, there is the possibility that a host of biological factors (e.g., hormonal balances) might affect an individual's sense of identity. At more-macro levels, complex sociological factors such as institutional sexism might have substantial impact on an individual's phenomenological experience of gender. Weitz (1977) has argued that the persistence of differential gender behavior and beliefs over the centuries has been maintained by a tripartite system involving biological, psychological, and societal factors. Thus, the analysis of gender identity (as the experiential portion of this behavior) is inherently interdisciplinary in nature, requiring the perspectives of biology, psychology, and sociology–anthropology. (In Chapter Eight, this volume, Del Boca and Ashmore propose that three levels of analysis—biological, social psychological, and societal—are also necessary for understanding female–male relations more broadly.)

Numerous biological factors have been explored that are assumed to underlie gender differentiation, including genetic makeup, prenatal hormone levels, gonadal hormones, and anatomical differences themselves. Although animal evidence suggests that each of these variables affects gender behavior, it is not clear from research on humans how much such biological variables affect a person's gender identity. Results have indicated, for example, that prenatal hormone levels are pertinent to the behavior of some groups with medical anomalies (e.g., Ehrhardt, 1979), but comparable relationships have not been found in more broadly defined populations (Green, 1974; Hines, 1982). While it does not seem too far-fetched to expect that particular bodily experiences associated with being male or female might well have important impact on gender identity, the pertinent evidence to date is far from convincing.

The psychological correlates of gender identity that have been most widely researched include phenomena such as direct sex-typing (e.g., this is for girls and that is for boys), differential reinforcement for conventional and nonconventional gender-related behavior, direct instruction (e.g., "You're a girl and girls are supposed to . . . "), modeling by significant others and identification. All may serve as developmental antecedents of gender identity as noted in Figure 1.

At the societal level, there are a number of variables that, like the biological substrates, may affect an individual's gender identity either directly or indirectly. The existence of consensually validated norms and beliefs about what constitutes the ideal female and male can have very direct effects on gender identity, particularly on the developing child. In contrast, factors such as the nature of the economy (i.e., who does what kind of work) may have more remote effects.

Numerous other societal variables that have been prominently investigated for their relationship to gender socialization include language usage, religion, myths, household patterns, educational systems, and political institutions. Exposure to particular cultural beliefs about masculinity and femininity is redundant and unavoidable. The degree to which such beliefs affect a particular individual's feelings of gender identity is determined by a number of factors, including how much they are enforced within their immediate social environment and their level of cognitive maturity. How these relate to each other constitutes the theme of most of the rest of this chapter.

The Developmental Course of Gender Identity

As far as we know, an individual is not born with gender identity. A young child's rudimentary sense of identity is based on a simple label, boy or girl. As previously noted, this label does not exist in a vacuum. It acquires its meaning for the child in many ways, including the fact that the social environment differentiates a wide variety of objects, activities, television programs, books, personality attributes, et cetera as more appropriate for one gender than for another. This process both precedes and occurs concomitantly with the cognitive process of gender-labeling and continues long after it. As can be seen in Figure 1, environmental gender-typing impacts gender identity, which in turn reveals itself in behavioral consequences, although these concepts (identity and gender-typing) are conceptually distinct and are not necessarily congruent for any given individual at any given point in time. Huston (1983) has also suggested the need to demarcate more clearly the various components and constructs of gender-related phenomena.

Various aspects of gender identity do change developmentally for a variety of reasons. At the societal level, normative expectations with regard to gender are age-graded. Fifteen-year old girls are expected to behave very differently from 5-year old girls. At the psychological level changes in biological and cognitive capacities have profound implications for gender identity. As children get older, for example, they are more capable of taking other people's roles or projecting themselves into a hypothetical future. Thus, although one's gender classification does not generally change (barring surgery), the structure of one's gender identity changes across the life cycle. The criteria for masculinity and femininity are quite different at 5, 25, and 55 years of age.

The remainder of this chapter charts the developmental course of the gender-identity construct. It first considers the social context of early gender identity and then explores the cognitive aspects of gender-identity formation during infancy and early childhood. Other major developmental stages discussed include the school age child, adolescence, and adulthood. A final section considers the possibilities of alternate gender identities and societal change.

Infancy

THE SOCIAL CONTEXT

The social environment of the infant is geared up for the gender dichotomy long before he or she enters it. Parents themselves, of course, have undergone a long period of gender socialization. They, therefore, have long-standing notions about maleness or femaleness and mold the child's behavior to the appropriate category, apparently as soon as possible.

Parental propensity to respond to very young infants on the basis of gender cues has been demonstrated in a number of studies. Rubin, Provenzano, and Luria (1974) found that parents perceived their day-old sons as bigger, firmer, more alert, and stronger than did those with day-old daughters, although in actuality the infants did not differ in height or weight. A number of other laboratory studies have demonstrated that differential responses to infants are made rather generally by adults. A study conducted by the present author and colleagues several years ago (Seavy, Katz, & Zalk, 1975) demonstrated that when the same infant was introduced to adults with either a male or female name, footballs and dolls were selected accordingly as play objects. Moreover, when a gender label was not given (our Baby "X" condition), adults evidenced confusion and discomfort in playing with the child. Differences in adult behavior based on gender labels have also been found by Condry and Condry, 1976; Sidorowicz and Lunney, 1980; Smith and Lloyd, 1978; and Will, Self, and Datan, 1976.

There are three major areas in which the gender socialization of infants occurs. These include (1) differential structuring of physical environments, (2) choice of different play objects, and (3) use of different interactional styles with boys and girls. It should be noted that while these differences have been documented, their effects on gender identity have not.

To illustrate the first area, physical environments of male and female infants have been found to differ consistently (Rheingold & Cook, 1975) in both obvious and subtle ways. The obvious cues include pink and blue color-coding. Additionally, girls' rooms are more likely to contain muted, pastel colors, smaller prints, more finely detailed and ruffled fabrics, while boys' rooms are more likely to have bright colors, bold stripes, prints with large predatory animals, and many fewer frills. The effects of these early environmental differences have not been ascertained, although they should be. It does not seem too far-fetched to predict that a bright, lively environment might well have energizing effects on both the infant and the caretakers, whereas a muted, softer one will be more calming and serene. This may affect both present levels and volume of interactions, as well as later preferred noise thresholds. Overall environmental softness may elicit protectiveness, whereas liveliness may elicit stimulation.

The second area, differential object choice, has been demonstrated both in experimentally controlled studies and in most home environments. Potent effects of gender labels can be demonstrated in a laboratory with adults and unfamiliar infants, but the magnitude of gender-typing in the real world is even greater. Because the child's gender is known, parents, grandparents, and friends typically supply the young infant with a wide variety of toys and other objects that vary reliably by gender. Dolls for girls and trucks for boys are merely the most obvious. Even ostensibly gender-neutral toys have gender-added cues. Rattles and teething rings, for example, while used by both sexes come in color-coded models. Stuffed animals, a popular choice for a young child's gift, are also ostensibly gender-neutral, but docile animals such as kittens and rabbits are recommended for girls, whereas wilder ones such as lions and tigers are seen as more appropriate for boys. Almost all toy stores categorize objects by gender and direct potential purchasers to so-called "appropriate" items (Kutner & Levinson, 1978) of toys and clothing, as do most mail-order toy catalogues (Schwartz & Markham, 1985).

The final area of differential early interaction patterns is more subtle and is not completely consistent across the infancy period. During the first 3 months of life, for example, male infants are touched by their mothers more frequently than are female infants (Lewis, 1972). Until the 1980s, very little research had been conducted on father–infant interaction, but this is being remedied (see Lamb, 1981). With regard to mothers, boys are rocked and handled more, but in a less-gentle manner (Moss, 1967; Parke & O'Leary, 1976; Yarrow, Rubinstein, Pederson, & Jankowski, 1972). Girls are touched less frequently during the first few months, but they are talked to and looked at more (Lewis & Cherry, 1977; Lewis & Goldberg, 1969; Moss, 1967). For as-yet-unexplained reasons (greater early male infantile vulnerability and irritability have been suggested) the pattern of sex differences observed during the first 3 months reverses itself by 6 months of age. By the middle of the first year, girls are touched more frequently than are boys (Lewis, 1972), a pattern that approximates and perhaps encourages future behavior where touching and physical expression of affection are considered more female-appropriate. With regard to general social interaction, female infants typically receive more social stimulation of all kinds, including more verbal interaction (Lewis & Weinraub, 1979; Thoman, Leiderman, & Olson, 1972).

The effects of these differential interactional patterns may well have consequences for gender identity, although this remains to be documented. More-frequent exposure of female infants to verbal stimulation, for example, may account for greater emphasis on and proficiency in verbal skills. Less emphasis on social stimulation for boys may lead to greater interest in the exploration of inanimate objects. Such sex differences in cognitive style may well be forerunners of later gender identity. Many investigators have spoken, for example, of stronger affiliative behavior in women (e.g., Crandall, 1969; Gilligan, 1977), and strong ties to one's familial and social environment are often integrally related to women's feelings of femininity. Thus, such differential socialization practices may well have lasting impact on gender identity.

We might consider for a moment why the social context of the infant is so pervasively gender-typed. Unlike other periods of life, the activities of boys and girls themselves do not differ. Moreover, in the absence of genital or clothing cues, unfamiliar adults cannot distinguish infant gender very well. In the aforementioned Seavy, Katz, and Zalk study, 70% of the adults incorrectly believed that the unnamed Baby "X" was a boy and found substantiating cues (e.g., no hair, strong grip, etc.).

Although admittedly speculative, several possible reasons can be suggested for early gender socialization. First, manufacturers of infant products may offer gender-coded items in the belief that this constitutes their best marketing strategy, irrespective of parental beliefs. Such products do give the purchaser an additional choice and an opportunity to personalize a gift more. Studies of pre-industrial societies might permit the evaluation of this factor. A second possibility is that many parents simply believe that it is necessary for boys and girls to get used to the appropriate gender-identified things right from the outset. A third possibility is that parents do not like others to mistake their child's gender and, therefore, guarantee against such errors by announcing their gender to the world. It is not clear why this should be the case, but adults clearly exhibit discomfort with an infant of unknown gender, and in our study, mothers who watched their own infant behind a one-way vision screen were upset that other adults could so easily accept an incorrect gender label for their child.

The announcement of an infant's gender may well set up an inexorable chain of events. Both previous research and anecdotal evidence suggests that adults respond to infant gender cues with differential social responses and expectations. Ruffles may elicit one set of responses (such as higher voice tone, smiling, comments about attractiveness, etc.), whereas "little slugger" t-shirts may elicit a different set (e.g., lower voices, more teasing, comments about strength, etc.). More theory and research is needed with regard to the analysis of this process itself, as well as to its consequences, which are often self-fulfilling ones. Of particular interest and almost totally absent from the research literature are the long-term effects of these very different kinds of social environments on children. We have evidence of differential treatment on one hand and later behavioral sex differences on the other, but we have very few notions of how (or whether) these things are, in fact, linked. Even if they are, our theoretical frameworks have not yet delineated which particular variables may be most relevant.

COGNITIVE ASPECTS OF EARLY GENDER IDENTITY

It is generally agreed that one's core or basic gender identity is formed during the first 2 or 3 years of life. What appears to be meant by the term core gender identity is Yorburg's (1974) definition of sex-role identity, namely one's fundamental perception of maleness or femaleness of the self. This is the foundation on which other aspects of identity rest and which some investigators regard as relatively impervious to change.

The issue of how an infant constructs a gender identity, while critically important, is not very well understood. A major difficulty in delineating this process developmentally has to do with the relative absence of measures to assess this construct in the preverbal child. It is clear that one milestone is the child's ability to self-label gender correctly. Prior to such verbalizations, however, infants do make differential responses to gender in others, suggesting that gender concepts may precede self-labeling. Some investigators (e.g., Fagot, 1983) have argued that gender socialization will not affect children until after they have acquired some sense of gender identity. It would appear, then, that cognitive understanding of and phenomenological experience of gender, while related, may be conceptually distinct even during infancy.

The two most widely cited positions concerning childhood gender identity acquisition are social learning theories (e.g., Mischel, 1966, 1969), which emphasize the primary role played by environmental determinants, and cognitive-developmental theories (e.g., Kohlberg, 1966), which stress the fundamental importance of cognitive level. The primary cognitive milestone in this process is the self-labeling of gender. There are no currently available theories, however, that operationalize what the earliest forerunners of gender identity development might be. It appears that there are both cognitive and perceptual components to this process. The cognitive component (which has been discussed more extensively in the literature) involves the learning of gender labels, the application of such labels to oneself, and the consequent elaboration of its meaning.

While correct self-labeling and gender conceptualization require cognitive skills that are not yet present in the first 2 years, some environmental precursors include the very frequent use of gender labels by others. From the child's point of view, the repeated use of statements such as "Aren't you a strong little boy" may be an important way of organizing early social experience. With the exception of one's first name (which itself is ordinarily gender-linked), few words are used toward the infant with such consistency as "boy" or "girl." Probably because of this, most children can correctly label themselves with regard to their gender with a fair degree of accuracy by 2 years of age (Kuhn, Nash, & Brucken, 1978; Slaby & Frey, 1975).

The perceptual component that antedates self-classification (contrary to Kohlberg's belief) involves the child's increasing ability to differentiate aspects of gender in others. The process by which this occurs is not well understood. A number of preverbal cues are probably used, including voice pitch as well as other differences based on olfactory, tactile, and visual cues. In the olfactory area, women's cosmetics are more likely to be perfumed and to contain different scents. Infants are usually handled differently by male and female adults. Differential visual cues are apparent in multiple areas, including height differences and systematic variations in dress and/or hair styles. At a proximal level, skin contact with a male or female is also a differential experience. One does not usually feel stubble on mommy's face. Thus, in all sense modalities, gender cues are potentially discriminative. Perhaps the most significant gender cue, however, has to do with differential availability: Mommy (or a female substitute) is there; Daddy is usually not.

Parents are delighted to discover that their child's first words usually include "mommy" and/or "daddy." The child's correct use of these nouns, together with their incorrect generalization to other adults demonstrates that children have rudimentary gender concepts by the time they can speak. While the use of the word "daddy" to a strange male adult might be embarrassing to a parent, the fact that it is almost never used in conjunction with a

Discussion

strange female adult suggests the child's concepts about adult gender may be surprisingly accurate.

The child's increasing ability to discriminate gender cues during the first few years has also been demonstrated with regard to peers, as well, in the same-sex preferences of 10-month old infants (Lewis & Brooks, 1975) and the social behavior of 2½-year-olds (Jacklin & Maccoby, 1978).

The underpinnings of these social preferences are not well understood. Despite these lacunae in our conceptualization about early gender identity formation, the documentation of sex-typed behavior in the postinfancy period suggests that the first 2 years of life may be of particular importance. Preferences for sex-appropriate toys have been found in children as young as 2 years of age (Blakemore, LaRue, & Olejnik, 1979; Fagot, 1974, 1977). Knowledge of sex-typing[1] has also been obtained with regard to adult possessions (Weinraub, Brown, Sockloff, Ethridge, Gracely, & Myers, 1981) and jobs (Kuhn et al., 1978) between 2 and 3 years of age. Finally, correct verbal identification of one's own and other people's gender is present before the age of 3 years (Thompson, 1975). Thus, considerable learning about gender occurs in the first years of life.

IS THERE A CRITICAL PERIOD FOR GENDER IDENTITY?

An intriguing finding by Money, Hampson, and Hampson (1957) is often quoted in psychology textbooks. The findings of these investigators with anatomically atypical children (i.e., those in which chromosomal, gonadal, hormonal, and anatomical indices of gender are not in accord) has been widely cited as suggesting that psychological problems result if a child's gender is surgically changed after the age of 2 years (see Money & Ehrhardt, 1972). The implication of this finding is that there may be a critical period during infancy in gender identity development.

In a series of papers, Money and his associates (Money, Hampson, & Hampson, 1955, 1957) have discussed findings with over 100 hermaphroditic patients for whom either initial sex assignment was difficult to make because of ambiguous genitals or later evidence contradicted earlier gender assignments. Based on a variety of evidence, sex of assignment and

---

[1]The terms "sex-typing," "sex roles," and "sex-role learning" have been used frequently and interchangeably in the children's literature and are used in this chapter for convenient reference to this literature. Staines and Libby argue in Chapter Six that the usage of the general term "sex roles" is not as useful as more-differentiated role terms (e.g., father, worker, etc.) in adults. I believe that although this critique is germane to adults, it may not be completely applicable to children whose concepts about gender roles may be more global.

rearing appears to be a more potent influence of gender identity than any of the other biological variables.

Although these findings attest to the significance of the early social context in the development of gender identity, their conclusion that identity is relatively irrevocable after the first 2 years of life remains problematical, and contradictory evidence does exist. One problem has to do with extrapolating general principles from a group of anatomically deviant children to those who are not. Indeed, Diamond (1965) has argued that the child's hormonal ambiguity itself may account for the apparent flexibility in accepting the assigned gender. The case history material presented suggests that these children, not surprisingly, have major preoccupations about their genitalia and have strong needs for psychological resolution with regard to gender.

Moreover, other findings have not supported the notion that gender identity is invariably and irrevocably formed in infancy. Transsexuals, for example, do not always exhibit acceptance of their early gender assignment even when it is in accord with observable anatomical cues (e.g., Stoller, 1968) but are often desirous and capable of changing their gender identity. Imperato-McGinley, Guerrero, Gautier, and Peterson (1974) discuss the "gueva-doces", (i.e., literally, penis at twelve) a small group of children in Central America who appear (and are raised as) female but who develop a penis and masculine secondary sex characteristics at puberty. At that point they are raised as and regarded as boys, both by themselves and by others. If early gender identity were indeed irrevocable, one would predict all kinds of disturbances for these children which apparently do not occur. Finally, findings from the anthropological literature suggest that in societies where male children are reared almost exclusively by women, they may form an initial feminine identity that is reversed by the culture through the use of stringent adolescent initiation rites in which boys must demonstrate physical prowess and toughness (Burton & Whiting, 1961). This also contradicts the notion that gender identity is fixed.

It would appear then that there are conflicting data regarding both the role of biological factors and the critical-period hypothesis. While basic gender identity is formed for most but not all individuals by the end of infancy, the status of the critical period hypothesis remains in doubt.

To summarize this age period, it would appear that while gender conceptualization is far from complete and some gender confusion is evident, the young child's development of gender identity is well on its way. By 3 years of age, a child's gender identity has developed to include (1) the ability to differentiate both children and adults on the basis of gender and (2) the correct classification of themselves and others on the basis of gender cues. This early gender identity seems relatively resistant to change and includes information about what things constitute gender-appropriate behavior. Possible factors that underlie these developmental processes include (1) the salience of gender for adults, (2) the redundancy of sex-typed cues, and (3) the differential social and physical environments of male and female infants.

Early and Middle Childhood

THE PRESCHOOL PERIOD

The period between 3 and 6 years of age is generally referred to as the preschool period, which may be a misnomer for the large percentage of children who attend nursery school or day care facilities. It is meant, however, to differentiate these years from mandatory, formal schooling, which starts with the first grade. The preschool period is characterized by very active sex-role learning, which builds on earlier acquired skills. The child can be seen as continuing to develop the sense of identity begun during the first 3 years. In contrast to the first 3 years of life, where the largely nonverbal child is the recipient of gender-role information and differential socialization practices, the preschooler is a most active participant in the whole process. For this reason, the age period between 3 and 6 years has been considered by investigators of varying theoretical persuasions as being a most significant one for sex-role socialization and gender identity. Researchers have focused on two factors that seem particularly salient during this phase: (1) the readily observed sex differences in boys' and girls' behavior and concomitant differential treatment by adults, and (2) the child's cognitive elaboration of the gender concept.

With regard to the first factor, the frequency of observed behavioral sex differences increases markedly after infancy, and these have riveted psychologists' attention for decades. Over 75% of the more than 1600 studies reviewed by Maccoby and Jacklin (1974) deal with sex differences in preschoolers. Multiple reports of boys and girls in group settings report great divergence in social behavior. Boys are described as more physically active and aggressive and as interacting more frequently with same-sex peers. Girls are generally described as quieter, more emotionally mature, having longer attention spans, interacting more with teachers, and seeking help more frequently.

The preschool period appears to be marked by rapid learning of the culturally designated gender-appropriate categories in many areas, including toys, activities, future occupations, and domestic roles. A broad literature shows this to be true for a wide variety of responses, including verbal preferences, knowledge of stereotypes, nonverbal preferences, play behavior, choice of playmates, books, favorite television characters, and some personality attributes (e.g., Barry, 1980; Birns, 1976; Blakemore, et al., 1979; Connor & Serbin, 1977; Eisenberg-Berg, Boothby, & Matson, 1979; Gold & Berger, 1978; Haugh, Hoffman, & Cowan, 1980; Peterson & McDonald, 1980). There is probably no other area in the child's life (with the possible exception of language) that is as overlearned as gender. There may well be 5-year-olds who do not know the alphabet or color names, but there probably is not one who does not recognize the separate play worlds of boys and girls and which objects belong to each.

Although the documentation of sex differences remains a relatively popular area of research, it is no longer as all pervasive. Changes in adult sex-role norms and the impact of the women's movement has caused rethinking of many of our old assumptions about child-rearing and has caused some changes in research trends as well. There has been less concern with the documentation of sex differences, per se since the mid-1970s. Preferences for sex-stereotyped toys and activities, while still conceptually regarded as evidence of gender learning, are not necessarily treated as the sine qua non of the socialization process. In accordance with newer conceptions of adult sex roles (e.g., Bem, 1975, 1977), investigators have begun to look at non-sex-typed or androgynous patterns in children (Hemmer & Kleiber, 1981; Lott, 1978). Interest has been expressed in individual differences in sex-typing, and departures from traditional patterns in children are no longer regarded to be as invariably deviant as they once were (e.g., Sutton-Smith & Rosenberg, 1960). A number of attempts to modify highly sex-typed behavior have also been reported (e.g., Flerx, Fidler, & Rogers, 1976; Nilsen, 1977), and more interest has been expressed in the school-age child as well as in adolescence (see Worell, 1981).

In contrast to sex-difference research, which has been largely atheoretical, the issue of how the child develops the gender concept has generated considerable theoretical interest. The mechanisms suggested as underlying the preschool child's seeming absorption with gender and gender-related activities have derived from four particularly prominent classical theoretical views (Katz, 1979), which include (1) shaping or reinforcement paradigms, (2) modeling theories that stress observational learning, (3) parental bonding and identification (psychoanalytic theory), and (4) cognitive-developmental theory. These have all been somewhat revised in recent years.

The first two do not specify any given developmental period as more significant than others. The latter two positions, initially exemplified by the writings of Freud (1927) and Kohlberg (1966), respectively, postulate the occurrence of specific critical events during the preschool period, which are presumed to have lasting effects on the development of gender identity. According to psychoanalytic theory, at age 3 or 4 years, the child forms a strong positive attachment to the opposite-sex parent and develops concomitant negative feelings toward the same-sex parent. This engenders considerable conflict, which is presumed to be resolved (by the age of 6 years) when the child relinquishes desires for the opposite-sex parent and identifies with the same-sex one. Revisions in the classical position have been offered by Chodorow (1974) and Dinnerstein (1976). Both of these have stressed that antifeminine feelings are an outgrowth of being raised by a primary female caretaker.

In contrast to the affective factors postulated by psychoanalytic theory, the cognitive-developmental position postulates two entirely different events as critically important. The first is the occurrence of correct self-labeling as to gender (present in most children by 3 years of age). The label "boy" or "girl" generalizes to objects and activities classified by the society as masculine or feminine, and gender-related objects take on enhanced value and the child actively seeks them out. This process, then, is regarded as an active and self-reinforcing one. The second event occurs, according to Kohlberg, at approximately 5 or 6 years of age and consists of the achievement of *gender constancy*, the recognition that one's gender is an unmodifiable trait, despite changes in age and outward appearance. Updates of the cognitive-developmental view have suggested the importance of adolescence (Ullian, 1976) and the importance of sex differences in orientation (Gilligan, 1977), but most research has still focused on Kohlberg's concept of gender constancy.

Although this phenomenon has been of considerable interest, the age at which it occurs has been found to vary from 3 years (Kuhn et al., 1978) to 8 (Emmerich, Goldman, Kirsh, & Sharabany, 1977). Moreover, a literature review by Huston (1983) suggests that gender constancy may not be the most significant aspect of gender learning, because it does not relate to other measures of such learning. This could be interpreted as a critique of Kohlberg's emphasis. It also points to the fact that gender identity is a multifaceted construct even in young children, which is consistent with our earlier conceptualization.

The classical positions alluded to have all stressed the importance of parents as the major socializers of gender, often to the exclusion of others. The present author has previously questioned (Katz, 1979) the narrowness of this socialization focus as well as the overemphasis on the preschool period. Considerable evidence has been amassed since these older views were espoused, suggesting that an individual's sex role and other aspects of gender identity continues to develop and change throughout childhood, adolescence, and adulthood (e.g., Feldman, Biringen, & Nash, 1981; Fischer & Narus, 1981; Katz, 1979; Rebecca, Hefner, & Oleshansky, 1976; Urberg & LaBouvie-Vief, 1976). Moreover, the general assumption made by earlier theorists that children will imitate, identify, and generally be more similar to their same-sex parent than anyone else has not received much empirical substantiation (e.g., see Fling & Manosevitz, 1972; Hetherington, 1965; Lazowick, 1955; Lott, 1978). Although parents are important socializers during the preschool period (Downs & Langlois, 1979; Fagot, 1978a; Greif, 1979), it is clear that many additional sources of social influence play a role, including books (e.g., Mortimer, 1979; St. Peter, 1979), nursery school teachers (Fagot, 1978b, 1979), television (McArthur & Eisen, 1976; Sprafkin & Liebert, 1978), siblings (Brown & Weinraub, 1981; Katz & Rank, 1981), and peers (Fagot, 1979; Lamb & Roopnarine, 1979; Serbin & Connor, 1979).

Increased theoretical attention needs to be devoted to the cognitive mechanisms that underlie gender identity aside from gender constancy and how these relate to particular socialization practices. Common agreement exists that children in the preschool period are extremely involved with the understanding of gender categories and their implications (Kuhn et al., 1978; Masters & Wilkerson, 1976), but a young child's cognitions about gender cannot be adequately understood without a concomitant understanding of the social and developmental context in which they occur (Katz, 1976).

There are a number of characteristics of preschool thinking that may profoundly affect gender identity development. The preschool child is generally thought to be at a preoperational level of cognition (Inhelder & Piaget, 1958). What this means is that he or she is not yet capable of conserving certain formal aspects of objects (such as number and quantity) and is very much affected by an object's changing perceptual qualities. Thus, gender itself may be thought of as potentially changeable. A peculiarly illogical type of reasoning called transductive reasoning is also evident at this age. This type of reasoning involves making conclusions by going from one particular to another particular. Thus, if boys are similar in one respect, they may also be assumed to be alike in others as well. Finally, the child is particularly prone to understanding concepts in terms of their opposites, which forms a ready cognitive basis for the simplistic kinds of "us" versus "them" beliefs held in both the sex-role and the racial-attitude areas. Positive evaluations are associated with the child's own sex, whereas negative evaluations are elicited by the other, a trend that becomes less pronounced with age but is still evident in middle childhood (Zalk & Katz, 1978). This rather inflexible and evaluative mode of thinking about group differences may have the effect of making gender identity particularly salient and chauvinistic.

THE SCHOOL-AGE CHILD

The present author has previously outlined a model depicting the major developmental steps involved in the formation of gender identity (Katz, 1979). In that paper, it was suggested that there are three distinctive but overlapping stages, including (1) the learning of child gender roles (i.e., what is appropriate for boys and girls), (2) the preparing for adult gender roles (i.e., occupational, sexual, and domestic future roles); and (3) developing and enacting adult gender roles, which themselves change across the life cycle. It is important to keep these conceptually distinct because the connotations of what constitutes masculine and feminine behavior and their relation to each other differ widely as a function of developmental level and societal expectations. Somewhat different substages within each period are delineated for males and females with differing crises and milestones. Finally, differing patterns of socialization influences are assumed to be operative at varying points in the cycle.

As was seen in the previous sections, the preschool period is a stage of proliferating learning about what boys and girls do, play with, and are like. When children enter their formal education period, they bring these suppositions with them. They then influence and are influenced by other children in a more consistent way. The school-age period marks the flowering of boy and girl roles, as well as the beginnings of preparation for adult gender roles.

It is interesting to note that official sex-role expectations for boys and girls within the formal school environment are remarkably similar. Both sexes are expected to sit quietly, to pay attention to the teacher, and to master the rudimentary mysteries of reading and mathematics. Generally speaking, grade-school classrooms are not as physically sex-typed as most nursery school classrooms—that is, there are no separate play areas. Thus, if adults were the major gender-role socialization agents at this stage, there should be diminished behavioral differences between grade school boys and girls than at earlier levels of development. This is not the case, however. More sex-related differences have been found in grade school than in preschool children (Block, 1978). Boys and girls exhibit differential ability in mastering the early school environment (boys seem to have more difficulty), differential interests and activities (both in and after school), and strong preferences for same-sex friends. At 7 or 8 years of age, the peer group takes on an increasingly prominent role in determining what constitutes appropriate standards of behavior for boys and girls (Hartup, 1976). Such standards are set with little input from the other group because sex segregation reaches its zenith in middle grade school. Best friends are almost always same-sexed (Katz & Boswell, 1984), and voluntary activities are with same-sexed groups.

The implications of growing up in different worlds may be quite profound for future gender identity. For one thing, it has the effect of accentuating perceived sex differences. For another, evaluative patterns are present that may have future effects. Each gender group typically favors its own, although boys are often evaluated negatively within the school environment both by students (Zalk & Katz, 1978) and by teachers (Silvern, 1978).

In addition to peer-group socialization, a number of other sources maintain the view that boys and girls are expected to be different and have different future aspirations. Analyses of children's books, for example, have repeatedly documented systematic differences in the portrayals of males and females (e.g., Key, 1977). Boys are overrepresented in action and adventure stories, whereas girls are typically portrayed as smiling onlookers. Most toys designed as appropriate for boys have a heavy action component, whereas toys for girls are more passive. Television transmits similar impressions about occupations. Doctors, lawyers, and detectives tend to be depicted as males, whereas the few female characters who aspire to careers are shown as conflicted. Sex differences are even more pronounced in television advertisements than in program content. Authoritative voiceovers are almost invariably male, whereas females are all too frequently shown as becoming ecstatic over laundry detergents. Media affects the way children think about gender (Frueh & McGhee, 1975)[2] and more flexible role models are not readily available. Within the school environment itself, factors such as textbooks, course content, career counseling, and teachers themselves maintain differential and stereotyped gender-role behavior (Levitin & Chananie, 1972; Minuchin & Shapiro, 1983).

The issue of how all this impinges on gender identity is not entirely clear. Evidence suggests that school-age children are as aware of and knowledgeable about gender-role stereotypes in a variety of areas as are adults (Best, Williams, Cloud, Davis, Robertson, Edwards, Giles, & Fowles, 1977; Masters & Wilkerson, 1976), and behavioral preferences and social interactions of boys and girls are quite discrepant (Katz & Boswell, 1985). Some evidence, however, suggests that children's concepts about gender might become more flexible and less dichotomous by the end of grade school (Urberg, 1979). Moreover, although children are aware of adult definitions of what constitutes masculine and feminine behavior, their own assessments of each other in these areas may differ considerably (Silvern, 1977; Vreogh, 1971). Another interesting trend relevant to gender identity is the absence of self-esteem differences in childhood, a trend that begins to change during prepubescence, when girls start viewing themselves more negatively (Loeb & Horst, 1978; Silvern, 1978). Interestingly, there are not consistent sex differences in self-esteem in adults, or at least not in the college-age young adult samples most often studied. Thus, at least during childhood (and the college years), each gender seems equally happy with their own identity as they elaborate on it in largely separate social spheres.

---

[2]The precise nature of the effects and how these are mediated, however, are not completely clear. See Ashmore et al., Chapter Three, this volume.

Adolescence

The period prior to puberty is a time in which the gender identities of boy and girl are at their zenith. The onset of physiological sexual maturity, however, may dramatically alter the stability of all aspects of this identity. The sweeping biological changes of puberty must be adjusted to, and these adaptations may ultimately comprise a significant portion of adult gender identity. New patterns of interpersonal skills must be acquired in preparing for appropriate adult sex roles. Both the physiological and psychological aspects of sexual maturity, therefore, may render much of the previously acquired child gender identity obsolete. It seems useful to conceptualize this transition from child to adult sex roles as occurring in two stages: early adolescence, where the focus is on adjustment to biological changes, and later adolescence, where significant heterosexual patterns are established, and occupational paths are chosen.

EARLY ADOLESCENCE

During early adolescence (from approximately 12 to 15 years of age), the same-sex peer group remains a primary source of influence. Same-sex friends provide social continuity from childhood and serve as a comparison group with which to evaluate one's own physical changes. Physical maturity occurs about 2 years earlier in girls than in boys and has many psychological implications. This developmental asynchrony between males and females makes within-sex bonding more likely during this time because same-sex developmental experiences are more similar.

Many investigators (e.g., Money & Ehrhardt, 1972) have noted that the influence of pubertal hormones make sexual dimorphism the foremost feature of adolescent growth and development. Physically, males and females become more divergent at puberty, not only in terms of reproductive physiology but with regard to body build and strength differentials. It should be noted, however, that underlying hormonal differences between males and females are not dichotomous. Both males and females have androgen, estrogen, and progestin. The difference is in the balance, and considerable individual variability exists.

Although the task of adjusting to the physical changes of adolescence is difficult for both sexes, some investigators (e.g., Bardwick, 1971) have suggested that girls may have a harder time because of both menstruation and the greater visibility of their secondary sex characteristics. Menarche, which signals a female's reproductive capacity, is often fraught with ambivalence. On the one hand, it is a positive symbol of growing up and potential maternity; it also, however, has negative associations to blood, physical discomfort, and derogatory labels (Ernster, 1975). Sanday (1981) has summarized the considerable cross-cultural evidence with regard to menstrual taboos, which suggests a sharp demarcation in the way females are treated after their first menses in many societies. Although such taboos are not institutional-ized within our own culture, some remnants may still be present. Breast development may be associated with similar ambivalence—being feminine and grown-up, on the one hand, but also being more visibly sexual and hav-ing to deal with differential societal responsiveness. Boys undoubtedly also have problems dealing with voice changes, beard growth, and ejaculation, but less has been written about their responses to these phenomena.

Discrepancies between an adolescent's actual rate of physical development and his or her self-concept may be quite common at this time. If a female views herself psychologically as a child, for example, but has early breast development, she may experience a very negative body image; analogously, if her fantasy is to be a sexy movie star and she is a later developer, she may curse her flat-chestedness. Boys have analogous problems and anxieties associated with pubertal changes. In some cases, the visibility of these changes (e.g., size of their penis) is confined to the gym locker room. In other cases (e.g., body build and size), would-be football stars who are short and develop late may be quite unhappy.

For many individuals, early adolescent experiences often remain central to both physical and psychological aspects of gender identity (see Pleck, 1981). Adult body images are often based on early adolescent perceptions (Stunkard & Mendleson, 1967). Individuals who were extremely thin or obese at this time, for example, still think of themselves the same way even when their body configuration has changed. Such body images may also af-fect future expectations. Although there are no data on this, the possibility exists that early-maturing, well-developed girls might receive more social reinforcement for following a traditional feminine script and consequently be less interested in pursuing a career. Late-maturing boys might elicit fewer expectations to fulfill an adult male role, and this, in turn, may affect their interest patterns and interpersonal reactions.

While rate of pubertal change is important in its own right, adult reactions to such changes may be equally important, and insufficient research atten-tion has been devoted to this area. Parents may be considerably less per-missive, for example, toward daughters who are capable of maternity and may attempt to curtail their activities more at adolescence than they did before. Thus, for girls, psychological freedom may be restricted in both overt and subtle ways at the same time that psychological maturity is being experienced. Boys do not generally have to contend with increased parental protectiveness, but early maturers may have to contend with increased parental expectations to "act like a man" and to fulfill new chores as the result of their increased body strength.

On a cognitive level, adolescents are capable of much more complex thought processes, entering what Inhelder and Piaget (1958) term the period of formal operations. They are more capable of inferential thought and hypothesis testing. The ramifications of this are that they are no longer bound to the present and the observable but are more capable of projecting themselves into future roles (Hill & Monks, 1977). Thus, their gender identity is no longer as concrete as it previously was but can now incorporate some hypothetical elements as well. Urberg (1979) has found that adolescents are more capable of thinking about gender in nonsimplistic ways and can begin to recognize some of the arbitrary qualities of earlier gender-role norms. This increased cognitive capability, however, may not manifest itself until later in adolescence, however, because of countervailing pressures such as increased anxiety about physiological changes and greater consequent need to conform to peer-group expectations.

This increased anxiety about sexuality and identity may reveal itself in a number of pathological ways during early adolescence, and the increased frequency of some of these conditions suggest that the current cultural climate may be exacerbating such conflicts. There has been, for example, a dramatic increase in the incidence of young teenage pregnancy. There has also been a corresponding rise in weight disorders such as obesity, bulimia, and anorexia nervosa among this age group, particularly in girls. Another indication of general psychological malaise in this age group is the higher incidence of suicide, a leading cause of death in adolescents. These grim statistics suggest that early adolescent identity changes are quite profound and that a number of adolescents are finding them more difficult to deal with.

Cross-cultural evidence shows that some less-complex societies may formalize these changes by initiation ceremonies that may make the task of adaptation somewhat simpler. Although such rites are often arduous and in some instances physically painful (involving such things as circumcision, skin cutting, and other genital mutilation), they do serve the purpose of having the new status of the adolescent acknowledged by the society and confirming the sexual gender identity of the individual. After the initiation rites are completed, the person is considered as having adult status, is free to behave sexually, to marry, and to enact adult occupational roles. In more-technological societies, of course, there is often a very long delay between the onset of sexual maturity and the time that adult status is achieved, a delay often fraught with ambivalence about one's identity.

LATER ADOLESCENCE

The second stage of adolescence extends from approximately 15 to 19 years of age. The major sex-role tasks of later adolescence include (1) more serious development of heterosexual interactions, and (2) more concentrated development of vocational interests and life goals. Sex differences are evident in both of these areas. Dating, for example, becomes a very prominent concern and activity in late adolescence. Success in this area, however, involves different factors for boys and girls. Although cultural mores are changing, adolescent girls are still typically the recipients of male attention rather than the initiators of social interactions. As recipients, the dimension of physical attractiveness takes on more importance for females (Lerner, Orlos, & Knapp, 1976), and their success with males (at least initially) is based more on factors beyond their control. Thus, female gender identity may take on more aspects of a social object quality. Concern with how others (particularly male others) respond may lead to preoccupation with social skills and pleasing others rather than pursuing one's own goals. Excessive concern with appearance may relate to the increased frequency of eating disorders previously alluded to, which are quite prominent in late adolescent females as well. For many adolescent females, the acknowledgment of gender identity is seen as coming from others. Although males of this age are also concerned with whether or not girls will find them attractive, the dimensions are not as far-reaching, because this factor is not necessarily the major determinant of their gender identity. There are many other factors that may serve to validate and diffuse their masculine identity, including reinforcement for athletic pursuits, for working hard in school, and for pursuing an occupation that will lead to financial success.

Female and male perceptions of life goals are also likely to differ at this time. Marriage remains a more significant option for many adolescent girls than does occupational success, and they often see academic interests as less relevant for them. This is particularly clear in mathematics and science. Boys perceive these subjects, quite accurately, as opening up future career options, whereas girls' interest (Boswell, 1979; Parsons, Kaczala, & Meece, 1982) and performance (Mullis, 1975) begins to decline in junior and senior high school.

While career interests are certainly becoming more common in adolescent females, the importance of marriage does not seem to be declining very much, and even girls who are strongly committed to feminist ideals apparently become more aware of realistic options for themselves during late adolescence and lower their previous expectations with regard to total domestic equality (Komarovsky, 1973).

The sources of socialization influence during late adolescence are multiple and differ for the two tasks discussed. Although same-sex friends continue to be important, opposite-sex peers and the media take on renewed importance with regard to what constitutes appropriate heterosexual and dating behavior. Television, movie, and rock star models can also be very influential—in part because parents do not usually serve as models in this area, unless they are divorced and are themselves involved in dating. (Parents do, however, serve as models for marriage and child-rearing behavior, which has ramifications for sex-role behavior in later points in the life cycle.) Career decisions, on the other hand, are very much influenced by parents (Kandel, 1981; Katz & Boswell, 1985), as well as by teachers and peers.

In summary, the major components in the development of gender identity during adolescence include (1) adjusting to physical sexual maturity, (2) developing social skills and relationships with the opposite sex, and (3) considering future options with regard to vocation and marriage. There appears to be wide divergence between boys and girls during this period, in that physical maturity may be more stressful for girls, and interpersonal goals often take precedence over intellectual ones. Same-sex peers are strong sources of influence during early adolescence; in later adolescence, opposite-sex peers (both as a group and as individual dating partners) become more significant. Television, movies, magazines, and books also contribute heavily to transmitting information about appropriate heterosexual behavior and courtship patterns. The direct influence of parents in some areas may decline during adolescence, although their cumulative influence as role models and socializers remains.

Adulthood

Young Adulthood

The three most important tasks that typically impact on the gender identity of young adults are (1) finding a marriage partner,[3] (2) becoming a parent, and (3) establishing one's vocational competence. The relative importance of these areas differs considerably for men and women. As noted earlier, although a higher proportion of women now hold career aspirations than formerly, the majority still perceive marriage and raising a family as their primary goals, whereas career success is more significant to most men's gender identity.

In many ways, the period of young adulthood represents the epitome of prior gender-role socialization, at least for the traditional script. The roles of wife and mother are central for female identity; the role of breadwinner is central to the male (Bernard, 1981). The problem is, however, that existing sex-role socialization practices have not kept pace with a social environment that is becoming considerably more complex. Dramatic changes, brought

[3]The development and maintenance of close, personal relationships between individual men and women is an important part of the social psychology of female–male relations, which is analyzed by Huston, Chapter Five, this volume.

about in part by the women's movement, advances in contraceptive technology, and changing economic conditions, have altered traditional adult gender-role behavior for many. We still prepare children for traditional roles, but the two-child, father-sole-breadwinner household now represents only about 7% of all American families (Hoffman, 1977). People are marrying later, having children later, and divorcing with greater frequency. The 1960s, 1970s, and 1980s have witnessed the massive entry of women of all ages into the work force. The two-breadwinner and the single-parent variations of the family are now more common than the traditional one.

The question can be raised as to what effect these changes are having on gender identity. For some, there is more overlap in gender roles (see Chapter Six of this volume). Fathers are taking an increasingly active role in parenting, whereas mothers are taking on a more significant role in family economics. Many economists believe that the work world will also soon be modified to reflect these trends. At the level of the individual, however, these types of behaviors may not be something they anticipated in their earlier years, and the consequences may be quite profound for identity issues.

It has been noted (Rossi, 1968) that the formal educational process teaches us surprisingly little about being either a marital partner or a parent. Thus, few women are psychologically prepared for the biological aspects of pregnancy and childbirth, and few new parents have any real concept of what caring for a child entails. Playing with dolls as a child probably has as much applicability to caring for a noisy, intrusive infant as playing with cars has to becoming president of General Motors. Because of this, I have previously argued that the skills involved in marriage and parenting are learned largely through delayed modeling of one's own parents. If the guidelines have changed in the interim, however, how are young adults now handling these issues? What happens to gender identity when an enormous discrepancy exists between present behavior and norms, on the one hand, and older expectations on the other?

Research has been relatively sparse on these issues, but their importance clearly suggests the need for further investigations that go beyond the documentation and frequency of sociological change. Anecdotal observations suggest, however, that considerable conflict is being experienced by those who are now in their 20s and 30s. Women who have invested heavily in a career and have delayed child-bearing are becoming increasingly anxious about the decision to have a child; men who have subscribed to egalitarian marriages, feel cheated at some levels, particularly if they do not have children. New kinds of pressures are being placed on relationships, with few successful role models to emulate. It is as if people are caught up in the earlier affective components of gender-role preparation (e.g., Can one really have a feminine identity unless one is a mother?), while enacting more contemporary kinds of roles.

From the point of view of this chapter, one of the most significant aspects of parenthood is that it begins a new cycle of gender-role socialization and identity. As noted earlier, parents are, at least initially, formative influences on the gender identity of their offspring, and all cultures apparently transmit a sex-role template to their children. Is this template changing? Are parents of young children now trying to transmit different messages?

Research conducted in our laboratory (Katz & Boswell, 1985) suggests that a substantial number of highly educated parents do wish to change the template, but they are not uniformly successful with young children for a variety of reasons. One has to do with the multiple socialization influences that children are exposed to. No matter how liberal the parents, peers and television programs are very potent forces, which often override parental values. Another reason may reside in the previously discussed cognitive capacities of children. Their sensitivity to dichotomous categories may lead them to accentuate sex differences even where parents attempt to minimize them.

The final, and perhaps most far-reaching problem, however, has to do with parental anxiety over tampering with something that seems so basic. They fear upheaval of a social order that they believe has been in effect for centuries. Even where the pernicious effects of the system are acknowledged, the alternatives seem bewildering, and there is discomfort in the thought that their children might become misfits. Intertwined with this is the often unverbalized fear that if traditional gender identities are discarded, homosexuality will result. Even the most ardent feminists often do not have the complete courage of their convictions when it comes to their own children. Current child-rearing practices in this area deserve considerably more research attention than they are receiving, for in many ways they reveal much about current gender-identity conflict.

LATER ADULTHOOD

The question can also be raised with regard to what happens to gender identity after the establishment of occupational and family stability. Because research and theoretical emphasis has been heavily oriented toward childhood, this question has only recently received attention.

There are three phenomena that have been discussed with regard to gender identity in middle and later adulthood. Two of these primarily concern women and the other affects both sexes.

With regard to women, there has been a substantial increase in the number of middle-aged women who are going back to school and starting new careers after their child-rearing responsibilities have diminished. This suggests that female gender identity is far from completed during the early adult years and that even where women have followed a traditional script, they are becoming more desirous of incorporating components of occupational success into their lives (Barnett & Baruch, 1977). This transition of women in their middle years may mean either that gender identity development in women takes a longer time to develop or that it changes more over the life span than does male gender identity. As was noted in the section on adolescence, female gender identity may develop in ways that are more intrinsically tied to other people's expectations and responses. It is, perhaps, not until after the child-bearing and child-rearing years are over that some women feel free to consider their own needs, independently of others. This appears to be a relatively new phenomenon, and its occurrence may offer an alternative model for other cohorts as to how to combine several facets of gender identity over time.

The occurrence of menopause can also be a crucial biological event for women, which may or may not alter their gender identity. The psychological implications of loss of reproductive capacity vary greatly, but it is clearly both a period and an event that all women must come to terms with. It is interesting to note that in many cultures, postmenopausal women occupy higher status than younger ones and are accorded greater respect than they previously received. This does not appear to be the case in our youth-oriented culture, and in fact, this particular milestone is accorded neither formal status nor very much research interest. Rather, women are left to deal with it by themselves or with their (generally) male gynecologists as a medical problem. As was the case with puberty, if we wish to understand the impact of menopause, we need to take into account the nature of the biological event itself, the psychological meaning of that change to the individual, and the societal reaction and interpretation of it.

Although males do not experience anything directly comparable to menopause, the general aging process may elicit somewhat similar psychological reactions, such as concern about sexuality and whether one's life will be diminished in meaningful ways. Additionally, retirement has traditionally been a critical event of greater concern to men. It is of interest to note that people's conceptions about aging and sexuality have themselves been in transition since the mid-1970s. The widely publicized work of Masters and Johnson (1966), for example, suggests that a diminishment of sexual activity is not the invariant accompaniment of aging that many previously believed. Thus, current generations may not have this expectation, and their gender identity in later life may consequently be more sexual than was true for earlier cohorts.

There is some suggestion in the literature that both men and women may broaden their gender identities as they grow older to include more traits they previously associated with the opposite sex (Neugarten, 1968). The possibility that males may become more nurturant with age, whereas females become more assertive has been discussed. There is some evidence that suggests that older adults (particularly males) describe themselves less exclusively in terms of masculine and feminine adjectives than do younger ones (e.g., Feldman, 1974; Hyde & Phillis, 1979). Considerably more work needs to be done with older populations in this area. To further substantiate these trends, other behavior needs to be looked at, as well, including such things as grandparenting behavior.

It is interesting to speculate on what mechanisms might be related to this broadening of gender identity development in later life. One possibility may relate to the underlying biological aspects of gender itself. The evolutionary raison d'etre for sexual dimorphism is reproduction. In one sense, then, the cultural overlay of gender socialization may simply provide redundant cues of sex differences to reinforce this dimorphism. Once the reproductive phase is over, however, such sharp distinctions may no longer be necessary. Another possibility is that living does bring wisdom at least to some. After enacting many roles and observing males and females in action for many years, one may finally come to recognize and experience the arbitrariness of differentiated gender roles.

In summary, I believe that one's gender identity, while basic in one sense, is also in continual transition throughout one's life. The template and developmental sequence appear less clear for later life than for earlier stages. This may be because of relative lack of empirical attention, prior theoretical focus on childhood, and earlier, erroneous beliefs that identity is fixed early in life.

Developmental Course of Gender Identity: A Summary

Considerable expenditure of effort throughout life is devoted to acquiring and modifying one's gender identity. The various developmental milestones discussed are summarized in Figure 2.

Figure 2 represents an attempt to present schematically some of the trends previously discussed. The time line goes from the top of the figure to the bottom. Note that it begins prior to the birth of the child. The social context[4]

---

[4]It should be noted that this developmental sequence presented is probably most applicable to white, middle-class, heterosexual Americans. Considerable diversity exists across ethnic groups in gender scripts. Both family environments and the larger social environments in which they are embedded differ significantly for various groups. More research on the implications of this diversity would contribute to our knowledge of how gender identity is formed and maintained.

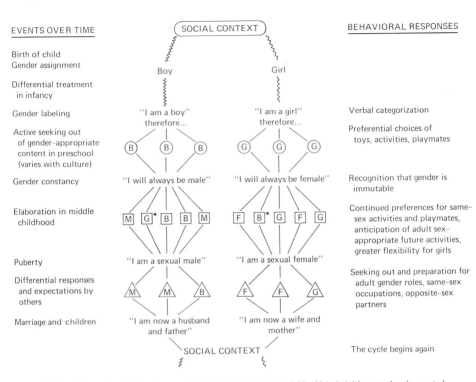

KEY: B = Boy, G = Girl, F = Female (adult) —actual and expected, M = Male (adult) —actual and expected.

FIGURE 2.   Schematic representation of gender identity development. *No one is completely stereotyped; there are always some cross-gender interests.

that the child is born into has two existing channels or templates to assist the child in establishing gender identity.

The four major internal steps in this process over time involve (1) initial self-labeling as to gender, (2) recognition that gender is an immutable category, (3) addition of sexual aspects of gender, and (4) enacting the reproductive fulfillment of gender roles. Gender identity continues to change throughout life. At the point of reproduction, however, the cycle becomes a repetitive one in terms of the next generation.

The relationships among these four major transitions in gender identity (early gender awareness and labeling, recognizing the immutability of the gender category, coordinating the gender concept with sexuality, and integrating this enlarged gender concept with reproduction and child-rearing) merits some discussion. Insofar as we are postulating a stage theory, the question can be asked (as with all developmental stage theory) as to what happens to pre-existing levels when a higher one is reached? One possibility is that these levels are additive. Older ones may remain in place as the concept is enlarged by new cognitions and experiences. Another possible model is transformational in nature, with each addition qualitatively changing the concept so that it is experientially unrecognizable from the pre-existing one.

Although this is admittedly speculative, it appears to me that both types of models may be relevant to the formation of gender identity, one to its cognitive aspects and the other to its affective components. On a cognitive level, the transformational model may be the more appropriate one. Once one has achieved gender constancy, for example, it is hard to imagine being able to conceptualize gender changing as a function of irrelevant cues. Once one has incorporated sexual responses into gender role, it is more difficult to conceptualize gender in a nonsexual way. Yet if this were the whole story, why do so many individuals continue to experience anxiety about their gender identity? Why should there ever be doubt about one's masculinity or femininity once gender constancy is established? That such doubts are fairly widespread suggests that on an affective level, these developmental components of gender socialization may be additive. Earlier emotional phases may not be completely transformed but may instead remain as residual influences on later gender-related behavior and experience. Even though one knows (on an intellectual level) that gender does not usually change, there may still be primitive, perhaps unconscious affective responses suggesting it could. Gender identity is a pervasive construct that clearly has both cognitive and emotional elements that interact and change over time. Recent theoretical emphases have focused on the cognitive aspects, but more attention needs to be devoted to its affective factors as well. Interestingly, current developmental approaches have been practically synonymous with a focus on cognitive change (witness cognitive-developmental). Needed now are some affective-developmental theories that are more amenable to empirical investigation than earlier ones.

Are There Other Gender Identities Possible Besides Masculine and Feminine?

The prior discussion has assumed that most people do view gender as a dichotomous variable and that gender socialization develops more or less in accordance with this supposition. Each sex has typically been reinforced for engaging in behavior designated as appropriate (i.e., masculine for males, feminine for females), and one's psychological experience of gender was presumed to reflect this basic bipolarity. This analysis was not meant to imply that the social world is or has to be dichotomous or that most people are completely masculine or feminine in their behavior. On the level of gender identity, however, it seems that a substantial majority of individuals do define themselves as primarily masculine or feminine. The final question to be raised in this chapter is whether such an analysis is too oversimplified and whether other types of gender identities exist.

Three pieces of evidence have brought this question to the fore. First, cross-cultural research has pointed out that there have always been individuals who have not fit the two-category gender system. Second, the medical literature has also dealt with conditions that seem to expand the gender system. Finally, theoretical and ideological positions have been espoused (e.g., Pleck, 1975; Rebecca, et al., 1976) that suggest that individuals may (and should) transcend bipolar gender identities by integrating male and female characteristics. This latter approach is very much related to the rapidly proliferating research on androgyny. Each of these are discussed in turn.

It should first be noted that individuals may deviate from a bipolar gender system along a number of dimensions. Biologically, they may, for example, be born with both male and female genitals or exhibit sexually ambiguous hormonal patterns during adolescence. On a psychological level, they may prefer activities primarily associated with the other gender. They may prefer opposite-sex attire (e.g., transvestites) or prefer same-sex sexual partners (homosexuals). Finally, they may experience a psychological gender identity opposite to that of their original gender assignment (transsexuals). Within our culture, there are differing degrees of stigma and confusion associated with these departures from a two-category system.

Anthropologists have long noted the existence of such individuals across a variety of cultures. They have been referred to collectively by the French term *berdache*. Because this term covers all of the aforementioned discrepancies, concern has been expressed by some investigators about its specificity (Angelino & Shedd, 1955; Forgey, 1975).

Although the particular condition is usually apparent in the individual study, widely differing treatments have been accorded cross-culturally to individuals classified as berdache. Edgerton (1964) studied the treatment of hermaphrodites among the Pokot tribe in Western Kenya. Such individuals were often put to death at birth (as was always true in ancient Greece). Those that were not the victims of infanticide were subject to continual ridicule because they were regarded as neither male nor female and incapable of sexual behavior. In contrast, the Navaho regarded such intersexed individuals as favored by supernatural powers and thus were treated with respect and reverence (Hill, 1935).

Studies of the berdache phenomenon among American Indians have dealt not with hermaphrodites but with transvestites, homosexuals, and possibly incipient transsexuals. Forgey (1975) summarized this research. Among most of the American Indian tribes, berdache was a socially recognized category, defined as individuals who were physiologically clearly male or female but who assumed the role and status of the opposite sex (including cross-dressing). Such individuals were viewed by the community with attitudes ranging from tolerance to great esteem. Among the Cheyenne, such individuals were sought out for their great power. The Dakota and Omaha tribes believed they were prophets. They were tolerated in a neutral manner among the Sioux. In all instances, the condition was attributed to divine mandate. For Plains Indians, only biological males and not females could be classified as berdache. Forgey explains this as a way for deviant males in a warlike, hypermasculine culture to achieve social prestige. Both male and female berdaches existed in other American Indian tribes, such as the Navajo, Mojave, and Nevada Shoshone. In all of these cultures the berdache was a socially recognized means by which someone could assume the dress, role, and status of the opposite sex without undue conflict. Thus, there appear to be some societies that have expanded the two-category gender system on the basis of an individual's experienced (rather than biological) identity.

The fate of such individuals in our own society appears more problematic in some ways. Generally, their treatment is under the aegis of the medical community, and some of this treatment might well be regarded as quite barbaric if it were discussed in the context of a less familiar culture. A summary of surgical treatment of transsexualism (Roberto, 1983), for example, lists such procedures as augmentation mammaplasty, rhinoplasty, testicular implants, bilateral mastectomy, penectomy, depilation, and bone cartilage insection into tubed penile flaps, and these are not always successful.

Transsexualism is, of course, a particularly interesting case for considerations of gender identity, precisely because there is a lack of relationship between one's psychological experience of gender and one's anatomy and gender label. Although such individuals comprise a very small minority (as do most of the aforementioned deviations), the intriguing question about transsexuals is how nonpsychotic individuals can maintain a strong sense of identity that goes contrary to their anatomy, so strong that they frequently seek surgery to put the two in congruity. Although much has been written about transsexuals (see Gagnon, 1974; Green, 1974; Green & Money, 1969; Money, 1968; Money & Brennan, 1968; Money & Primrose, 1968; Roberto, 1983; Stoller, 1968), the process by which an individual can remain convinced that they should be a member of the opposite sex in the face of redundant and overwhelming sex-role socialization still remains somewhat of a mystery. Speculations about mechanisms have included incipient parental attitudes toward the child's gender (Green, 1974), possible biological determinants (Stoller, 1968), faulty early gender identity (Luria & Rose, 1979), and cultural components (suggested by the lower frequency of females who resort to surgical sex change). Although this phenomenon is not well understood, that it occurs at all represents a challenge to all theories about gender identity, as well as to a strong cultural insistence on dichotomous gender roles.

Since the mid-1970s, psychologists have been concerned with another phenomenon that also is related to the central question posed in this section of whether it is possible to have a gender identity other than masculine or feminine. A rapidly proliferating body of research has been concerned with defining, measuring, and criticizing the concept of androgyny, which in its most basic form suggests that individuals are (or can be) neither masculine nor feminine but rather some combination of both. This body of work differs considerably from the aforementioned deviations because its primary concern has been limited to nonpathological individuals and the traits they use to describe themselves. Another significant difference is that whereas other deviations are reacted to with anxiety and stress, the androgyny alternative has been regarded as a positive one, both in terms of theory (Block, 1973; Constantinople, 1973; Rebecca, et al., 1976) and feminist expectations (Bem, 1977; Kaplan & Bean, 1976). There are many implications of the androgyny concept for gender identity, although research has not been particularly oriented in this direction.

The history of androgyny research is less than a decade old, and the current status of this concept appears to be developing in an as-yet-unresolved battleground. This chapter does not attempt to review this voluminous and chaotic body of work but simply notes some of the trends.

Initially, several key theoretical articles appeared (Block, 1973; Carlson, 1971; Constantinople, 1973; Pleck, 1975; Rebecca, et al., 1976), and these were rapidly followed by the description of two measurement techniques, one developed by Bem (1974), the other by Spence, Helmreich, and Stapp[5] (1974). Both of these measures (the Bem Sex Role Inventory and the Personal Attributes Questionnaire) utilized self-descriptive adjectives, were particularly well-suited for group administration to college student populations and were easy to score. They were both based on the notion that masculinity and femininity should be assessed separately rather than in the bipolar manner earlier measures had proscribed (i.e., if you scored high on masculine, you were necessarily low on feminine). This separability made it possible to discover that a sizable proportion of college students described themselves in ways that utilized both masculine- and feminine-associated adjectives. The ease of administration of these tests, the interest in sex roles and new approaches, and the seeming advantages of androgynous personalities (i.e.,

---

[5]Other tests have also been offered, including one by Berzins, Juris, Welling, and Wetter (1978).

more flexible, more creative, better adjusted) all combined to make research on androgyny extremely appealing and increasingly popular. The number of studies in the area rose dramatically, albeit in a relatively atheoretical manner. These measures were administered in hundreds of studies to almost every conceivable group. After only 3 years of research, special issues of journals were devoted to the topic. Lenney (1979) described the field in the late 1970s as approaching a stormy adolescence.

This observation turned out to be prophetic. Since 1980, the number of critiques that have appeared about androgyny almost equalled the number of studies done earlier. Initial differences arose early between Bem and Spence on how androgyny should be operationally defined. Since that time, there have been controversies with regard to androgyny's psychometric properties (e.g., Bem, 1979; Myers & Gonda, 1982; Pedhazur & Tetenbaum, 1979; Taylor & Hall, 1982), its supposed mental health advantages (Silvern & Ryan, 1979; Taylor & Hall, 1982; Whitley, 1983; Wiggins & Holzmuller, 1981), and whether it relates to other aspects of gender roles (e.g., Ickes & Barnes, 1978; LaFrance & Carmen, 1980; Lippa & Beauvais, 1983). One of the original test designers (Spence, 1984) has suggested relabeling the categories of masculine and feminine, as well as divorcing the measure from anything having to do with gender identity or orientation in order to avoid "unintended and unwarranted surplus meaning" (p. 6), a somewhat strange suggestion from the author of a test constructed primarily on the basis of perceived sex differences in socially desirable traits. It has the quality of throwing out the proverbial baby with its bath water. Arguing for more complexity does not imply that these measures have nothing to do with gender roles. It is clear, however, that the prolific use of these tests has elicited a number of controversies that may well have the beneficial effect of forcing people to come up with new theoretical conceptualizations of gender roles if they do not first lead to the construct's ultimate demise.

Despite the multiple squabbles, the basic theoretical possibility of a non-pathological, non-sex-typed orientation remains exciting to a number of investigators. From the point of view of this chapter, it may represent an alternative way of viewing gender identity and to get away from dichotomous categories, whose pernicious effects have been noted by many investigators. Kessler and McKenna (1978), for example, state that "where there are dichotomies, it is difficult to avoid evaluating one in relation to the other, a firm foundation for discrimination and oppression" (p. 164). Intergroup conflict theory (Williams & Giles, 1978) and the work of Tajfel and his associates is also germane here. Individuals define themselves largely in terms of social groups, and comparisons between groups constitute basic social processes (Tajfel, 1981). Nevertheless, such comparisons serve to create psychological group distinctiveness, and evaluation appears to be an inherent part of this process (Tajfel, 1981). Even when people are classified into two distinct categories on the basis of completely arbitrary criteria, intergroup discrimination occurs that favors in-group members in the distribution of rewards (Tajfel & Billig, 1974). When societies have consistently conferred differential status and power on one group, such laboratory effects are magnified many times over.

Combining the considerations of this last portion with the developmental emphasis of the rest of the chapter, a significant question can be raised: Is it possible to raise androgynous children (in its broadest possible meaning), and if so, what would they be like?

Unfortunately, attempting an answer gets us immediately back to definitions. If one conceptualizes androgyny as a combination of male and female traits, activities, et cetera, then, clearly, children must learn the underlying concepts prior to combining them, and androgyny could be a later stage of development. If, however, one considers androgyny as gender-aschematic (Bem, 1981b)—that is, with gender irrelevant, then the pre-gender-identity state of the infant might, at least hypothetically, be maintained. Presumably, different types of socialization practices would be associated with each of these possibilities.

Most people (researchers included) are much more sanguine in considering the first possibility. Even hypothetically considering a society where gender categorization, as we know it, does not exist makes many people uncomfortable, and they skeptically reject it as a possibility. In a conclusion to their book about sex-role stereotypes in 30 countries, for example, Williams and Best (1982) state that although they are fully in favor of equality of opportunity, "there is too much biology, sociology, and history involved to make a unisex position a comfortable one for the women and men of tomorrow" (p. 308).

I believe that labeling such a hypothetical state of affairs as "unisex" immediately brings a negative bias to it. It is possible to conceptualize a society that de-emphasizes the psychological aspects of gender and instead pays more attention to other, perhaps more individualized characteristics of people. Gender will obviously exist as a biological variable, but it does not inexorably follow that societies must also be organized along the same pattern as our reproductive capacity. Even where gender does form an organizing principle, differences need not be overemphasized. In this regard, it is interesting to note that many centuries prior to psychological research on androgyny, many Asian religions suggested that the ideal state is one that contained a harmonious balance of masculine and feminine elements (e.g., Kushi, 1979; Veith, 1972).

In a courageous article, Bem (1983) has considered the practicalities involved in rearing gender-aschematic children. Her theory of gender schema suggests that in addition to learning content-specific information about gender, the child develops a cognitive structure that assimilates and processes all new information in terms of gender categories, even when it is ostensibly unrelated to reproductive differentiation. She cites a number of studies suggesting that perceptual, memory, and learning processes are affected by a gender schema, but she goes on to suggest that there is individual variability in the strength of this schema that affects such behavior. We have seen in this chapter why the gender schema is so salient in most people—there is scarcely an area of existence that cultures have not associated in some way with the gender dichotomy. Her recommendations for raising gender-aschematic children within a society that places heavy emphasis on gender categories include various methods of inoculation, the providing of androgynous models, and inhibition of cultural messages about gender. She also recommends providing alternative schemata such as stressing individual variability, cultural relativism, and perceptions of sexism.

Although this utopian vision clearly does not have universal appeal, there are a number of parents trying these and other strategies in an attempt to provide greater overlap of the two different worlds boys and girls grow up in. As noted earlier, our research (Katz & Boswell, 1985) indicates that such parents are not uniformly successful, in part because (1) subtle differential socialization may be present, even when unintended; (2) once the child develops gender identity, he or she seeks out differentiating activities and objects that maintain it; and (3) it is next to impossible for parents to control the many other influences that affect a child in the socialization process (e.g., Fagot, 1982) without harming the child in other ways.

I share some of the ideological views expressed by Bem and other feminist writers, including the need for developmentally early modification efforts if things are ever going to be changed. The notion that change is impossible just because things have always been that way appears to be a good example of mindlessness (see Langer, 1984). Until recently, we have never had test-tube babies, gene-splicing, or home computers either. Nevertheless, the process of gender identity acquisition, with its seemingly invariant development of differential sex roles, appears to be a deep-seated one developmentally, psychologically, and culturally; considerably more needs to be known about its variations before successful modification efforts can be utilized.

To many investigators, the deleterious consequences of the two-category system far outweigh the comfort involved in retaining the status quo. If the process is hard to change, however, perhaps we need to start with the content. We might begin by increasing people's awareness of the complexity of the gender concept, and the fact that most of its definitional correlates are not as dichotomous as they appear. Instead of exaggerating sex differences in children, we might do better to consider the enormous overlap and not define maleness or femaleness as antithetical. Instead of "vive la différence," we might more seriously consider "vive la similitude."

References

Angelino, H., & Shedd, C. L. (1955). A note on berdache. *American Anthropologist, 57,* 121–126.

Bardwick, J. M. (1971). *Psychology of women: A study of bio-cultural conflicts.* New York: Harper & Row.

Barnett, R. C., & Baruch, G. K. 1977, March. *Women in the middle years: An overview and critique.* Paper presented at the Society for Research in Child Development, New Orleans.

Barry, R. J. (1980). Stereotyping of sex role in preschoolers in relation to age, family structure and parental sexism. *Sex Roles, 6*(6), 795–806.

Beere, C. A. (1979). *Women and women's issues: A handbook of tests and measures.* San Francisco, CA: Jossey-Bass.

Bem, S. L. (1974). The measurement of psychological androgyny. *Journal of Consulting and Clinical Psychology, 42,* 155–162.

Bem, S. L. (1975). Sex-role adaptability: One consequence of psychological androgyny. *Journal of Personality and Social Psychology, 31,* 639–693.

Bem, S. L. (1977). Probing the promise of androgyny. In A. G. Kaplan & J. P. Bean (Eds.), *Beyond sex role stereotypes: Readings toward a psychological androgyny.* Boston: Little, Brown.

Bem, S. L. (1979). Theory and measurement of androgyny: A reply to the Pedhazur-Tetenbaum and Locksley-Colten critiques. *Journal of Personality and Social Psychology, 37*(6), 1047–1054.

Bem, S. L. (1981a). Gender schema theory: A cognitive account of sex typing. *Psychological Review, 88*(4), 354–364.

Bem, S. L. (1981b). The BSRI and gender schema theory: A reply to Spence and Helmreich. *Psychological Review, 88*(4), 369–371.

Bem, S. L. (1983). Gender schema theory and its implications for child development: Raising gender-aschematic children in a gender-schematic society. *Signs: Journal of Women in Culture and Society.* Vol. 8, no. 4, 598–616.

Bernard, L. C. (1981). The multidimensional aspects of masculinity–femininity. *Journal of Personality and Social Psychology, 41*(4), 797–802.

Berzins, J. I., Welling, Martha A., & Wetter, Robert E. A new measure of psychological androgyny based on the Personality Research Form. *Journal of Consulting and Clinical Psychology,* 1978, 46(1), 126–138.

Best, D. L., Williams, J. E., Cloud, J. M., Davis, S. W., Robertson, L. S., Edwards, J. R., Giles, H., & Fowles, J. (1977). Development of sex-trait stereotypes among young children in the United States, England, and Ireland. *Child Development, 48*(4), 1375–1384.

Birns, B. (1976). The emergence and socialization of sex differences in the earliest years. *Merrill-Palmer Quarterly, 22*(3), 229–254.

Blakemore, J. E. O., LaRue, A. A., & Olejnik, A. B. (1979). Sex-appropriate toy preferences and the ability to conceptualize toys as sex-role related. *Developmental Psychology, 15*(3), 339–340.

Block, J. H. 1973, June. Conceptions of sex roles: Some cross-cultural and longitudinal perspectives. *American Psychologist,* 512–526.

Block, J. H. (1978). Another look at sex differentiation in the socialization behaviors of mothers and fathers. In J. Sherman & F. L. Denmark (Eds.), *The psychology of women: Future directions of research.* New York: Psychological Dimensions.

Boswell, S. L. 1979, March. *Sex roles, attitudes and achievement in mathematics: A study of elementary school children and Ph.D's.* Paper presented at the Society for Research on Child Development, San Francisco, CA.

Brown, L. M., & Weinraub, M. 1981, April. *Sibling status: Implications for sex-typed toy preferences and awareness of sex-role stereotypes in two to three-year old children.* Paper presented at the Society for Research in Child Development, Boston.

Burton, R., & Whiting, J. (1961). The absent father and cross-sex identity. *Merrill-Palmer Quarterly, 7,* 85–95.

Carlson, R. (1971). Sex differences in ego functioning. *Journal of Consulting and Clinical Psychology, 37,* 267–277.

Chodorow, N. (1974). Family structure and feminine personality. In M. S. Rosaldo & L. Lamphere (Eds.), *Woman, culture and society.* Stanford, CA: Stanford University Press.

Condry, J., & Condry, S. (1976). Sex differences: A study of the eye of the beholder. *Child Development, 47*(3), 812–819.

Connor, J. M., & Serbin, L. A. (1977). Behaviorally based masculine and feminine activity preference scales for preschoolers: Correlates with other classroom behaviors and cognitive tests. *Child Development, 48*(4), 1411–1416.

Constantinople, A. (1973). Masculinity–femininity: An exception to a famous dictum. *Psychological Bulletin, 80,* 389–407.

Crandall, V. C. (1969). Sex differences in expectancy of intellectual and academic reinforcement. In C. P. Smith (Ed.), *Achievement-related motives in children.* New York: Russell Sage Foundation.

Diamond, M. (1965). A critical evaluation of the ontogeny of human sexual behavior. *The Quarterly Review of Biology, 40,* 147–175.

Dinnerstein, D. (1976). *The mermaid and the minotaur: Sexual arrangements and the human malaise.* New York: Harper and Row.

Downs, A. C., & Langlois, J. H. (1979). Fathers as socialization agents of sex-typed play behaviors in young children. Unpublished manuscript, University of Texas, Austin, TX.

Edgerton, R. B. (1964). Pokot intersexuality: An East African example of the resolution of sexual incongruity. *American Anthropologist, 66,* 1288–1299.

Ehrhardt, A. (1979). Prenatal sex hormones and the developing brain: Effects on psychosexual differentiation and cognitive function. *Annual Review of Medicine, 30,* 417–430.

Eisenberg-Berg, N., Boothby, R., & Matson, T. (1979). Correlates of preschool girls' feminine and masculine toy preferences. *Developmental Psychology, 15*(3), 354–355.

Emmerich, W., Goldman, K. S., Kirsh, B., & Sharabany, R. (1977). Evidence for a transitional phase in the development of gender constancy. *Child Development, 48,* 930–936.

Ernster, V. L. (1975). American menstrual expressions. *Sex Roles, 1,* 3–13.

Fagot, B. (1974). Sex differences in toddlers' behavior and parental reaction. *Developmental Psychology, 10,* 554–558.

Fagot, B. (1977, March). *Sex determined parental reinforcing contingencies in toddler children.* Paper presented at the biennial meeting of the Society for Research in Child Development, New Orleans.

Fagot, B. I. (1978a). The influence of sex of child on parental reactions to toddler children. *Child Development, 49,* 459–465.

Fagot, B. I. (1978b, April). *The consequences of same-sex, cross-sex and androgynous preferences.* Paper presented at the annual meeting of the Western Psychological Association, San Francisco.

Fagot, B. I. (1979, June). *Play styles in early childhood: Continuity and change as a function of sex.* Paper presented at the meeting of the International Society for the Study of Behavioral Development, Lund, Sweden.

Fagot, B. I. (1982). Sex role development. In Ross Vasta (Ed.), *Strategies and techniques of child study.* New York: Academic Press, 273–303.

Fagot, B. I. (1983). Adults as socializing agents. In T. Field (Ed.), *Handbook of human development* (pp. 304–315). New York: Wiley.

Feldman, H. (1974). Changes in marriage and parenthood: A methodological design. In Peck & Senderowitz (Eds.), *Pronatalism: The myth of mom and apple pie* (pp. 206–226). New York: Crowell.

Feldman, S. S., Biringen, Z. C., & Nash, S. C. (1981). Fluctuations of sex-related self-attributions as a function of stage of family life cycle. *Developmental Psychology, 17,* 24–35.

Feldman, S. S., Nash, S. C., & Cutrona, C. (1977). The influence of age and sex on responsiveness to babies. *Developmental Psychology, 13*(6), 675–676.

Fischer, J. L., & Narus, L. R., Jr. (1981). Sex-role development in late adolescence and adulthood. *Sex Roles, 7*(2), 97–106.

Flerx, V. C., Fidler, D. S., & Rogers, R. W. (1976). Sex-role stereotypes: Developmental aspects and early interaction. *Child Development, 47,* 998–1007.

Fling, S., & Manosevitz, M. (1972). Sex typing in nursery school children's play interests. *Developmental Psychology, 7,* 146–152.

Forgey, D. G. (1975). The institution of Berdache among the North American Plains Indians. *Journal of Sex Research, 11*(1), 1–15.

Franck, K., & Rosen, E. (1949). A projective test of masculinity/femininity. *Journal of Consulting Psychology, 13,* 247–256.

Freud, S. (1927). Some psychological consequences of the anatomical distinction between the sexes. *International Journal of Psychoanalysis, 8,* 133–142.

Frueh, T., & McGhee, P. E. (1975). Traditional sex-role development and amount of time spent watching television. *Developmental Psychology, 11,* 109.

Gagnon, J. H. (1974). Scripts and the coordination of sexual conduct. In J. K. Cole & R. Dienstbier (Eds.), *Nebraska symposium in motivation, 1973.* Lincoln, NE: University of Nebraska.

Gilligan, C. (1977). In a different voice: Women's conceptions of self and of morality. *Harvard Educational Review, 47*(4), 481–517.

Gold, D. & Berger, C. (1978). Problem-solving performance of young boys and girls as a function of task appropriateness and sex identity. *Sex Roles, 4*(2), 183–193.

Green, R. (1974). *Sexual identity conflict in children and adults.* New York: Basic Books.

Green, R., & Money, J. (Eds.) (1969). *Transsexualism and sex reassignment.* Baltimore, MD: The Johns Hopkins Press.

Greif, E. 1979, March. *Sex differences in child–parent conversations: Who interrupts whom?* Paper presented at the meeting of the Society Research in Child Development. San Francisco, CA.

Hartup, W. W. (1976). Peer interaction and the behavioral development of the individual child. In Schopler & Reichler (Eds.), *Psychopathology and child development.* New York: Plenum.

Haugh, S. S., Hoffman, C. D., & Cowan, G. (1980). The eye of the very young beholder: Sex-typing of infants by young children. *Child Development, 52,* 598–600.

Hemmer, J., & Kleiber, D. (1981). Tomboys and sissies: Androgynous children? *Sex Roles, 7*(12), 1205–1212.

Hetherington, E. M. (1965). A developmental study of the effects of sex of the dominant parent of sex-role preference, identification and imitation in children. *Journal of Personality and Social Psychology, 2,* 188–194.

Hill, J. P., & Monks, F. J. (Eds.) (1977). *Adolescence and youth in prospect.* Atlantic Highlands, NJ: Humanities Press.

Hill, W. (1935). The status of the hermaphrodite and transvestite in Navaho culture. *American Anthropologist, 37,* 273–279.

Hines, M. (1982). Prenatal gonadal hormones and sex differences in human behavior. *Psychological Bulletin, 92*(1), 56–80.

Hoffman, L. W. (1977). Changes in family roles, socialization and sex differences. *American Psychologist, 32,* 644-657.

Huston, A. C. (1983). Sex-typing. In P. Mussen (Ed.), *Handbook of child psychology* (4th ed., Vol. 4) (pp. 387-468). New York: Wiley.

Hyde, J. S., & Phillis, D. E. (1979). Androgyny across the life span. *Developmental Psychology, 15*(3), 334-336.

Ickes, W., & Barnes, R. D. (1978). Boys and girls together and alienated: On enacting stereotyped sex roles in mixed-sex dyads. *Journal of Personality and Social Psychology, 36*(7), 669-683.

Imperato-McGinley, J., Guerrero, L., Gautier, T., & Peterson, R. E. (1974). Steroid 5-reductase deficiency in man: An inherited form of male pseudohermaphroditism. *Science, 186,* 1213-1215.

Inhelder, B., & Piaget, J. (1958). *The growth of logical thinking: From childhood to adolescence.* New York: Basic Books. (translated by A. Parsons & S. Milgram).

Jacklin, C., & Maccoby, E. (1978). Social behavior at thirty-three months in same-sex and mixed-sex dyads. *Child Development, 49,* 557-569.

Kagan, J. (1964). Acquisition and significance of sex-typing and sex-role identity. In M. L. Hoffman & L. W. Hoffman (Eds.), *Review of child development research* (Vol. 1). New York: Russell Sage Foundation.

Kandel, D. B. 1981, April. *Peer influence in adolescence.* Prepared for presentation at the biennial meeting of the Society for Research in Child Development, Boston.

Kaplan, A., & Bean, J. (Eds.) (1976). *Beyond sex role stereotypes: Readings toward a psychology of androgyny.* Boston: Little Brown.

Katz, P. A. (1976). The acquisition of racial attitudes in children. In P. A. Katz (Ed.), *Towards the elimination of racism.* New York: Pergamon Press.

Katz, P. A. (1979). The development of female identity. *Sex Roles, 5*(2), 155-178.

Katz, P. A., & Boswell, S. L. (1981). *Correlates of sex-role flexibility in children.* Final Report to the National Institute of Mental Health, Grant No. MH29417.

Katz, P. A., & Boswell, S. L. (1984). Sex-role development and the one-child family. In T. Falbo (Ed.), *The single-child family.* New York: The Guilford Press.

Katz, P. A., & Rank, S. A. (1981, April). *Gender constancy and sibling status.* Paper presented at the meeting of the Society for Research in Child Development, Boston.

Kessler, S. J., & McKenna, W. (1978). *Gender: An ethnomethodological approach.* New York: Wiley.

Key, M. R. (1977). The role of male and female in children's books—dispelling all doubt. In E. M. Hetherington & R. D. Parke (Eds.), *Contemporary readings in child development.* New York: McGraw-Hill.

Kohlberg, L. A. (1966). A cognitive-developmental analysis of children's sex-role concepts and attitudes. In E. E. Maccoby (Ed.), *The development of sex differences.* Stanford, CA: Stanford University Press.

Komarovsky, M. (1973). Presidential address: Some problems in role analysis. *American Sociological Review, 38,* 649-662.

Kuhn, D., Nash, S. C., & Brucken, L. (1978). Sex role concepts of two- and three-year olds. *Child Development, 49,* 445-451.

Kushi, M. (1979). *The book of Do In: Exercise for physical and spiritual development.* Tokyo, Japan: Japan Publications, Inc.

Kutner, N. G., & Levinson, R. M. (1978). The toy salesperson: A voice for change in sex-role stereotypes? *Sex Roles, 4*(1), 1-8.

LaFrance, M., & Carmen, B. (1980). The nonverbal display of psychological androgyny. *Journal of Personality and Social Psychology, 38,* 36-49.

Lamb, M. E. (Ed.) (1981). *The role of the father in child development.* New York: Wiley.

Lamb, M. E., & Roopnarine, J. L. (1979). Peer influences on sex-role development in pre-schoolers. *Child Development, 50*, 1219-1222.

Langer, E. (1984). Playing the middle against both ends: The usefulness of adult cognitive activity as a model for cognitive activity in childhood and old age. In S. Yussen (Ed.), *The growth of reflection*. New York: Academic Press.

Lazowick, L. M. (1955). On the nature of identification. *Journal of Abnormal Psychology, 51*, 175-183.

Lenney, E. (1979). Androgyny: Some audacious assertions towards its coming of age. *Sex Roles, 5*, 703-718.

Lerner, R. M., Orlos, J. B., & Knapp, J. R. (1976). Physical attractiveness, physical effectiveness and self-concept in late adolescence. *Adolescence, 11*(43), 313-326.

Levitin, T. E., & Chananie, J. D. (1972). Responses of female primary school teachers to sex-typed behaviors in male and female children. *Child Development, 43*, 1309-1316.

Lewis, M. (1972). Parents and children: Sex-role development. *School Review, 80*(2), 229-240.

Lewis, M., & Brooks, G. (1975). Infants' social perception: A constructivist's view. In L. B. Cohen & P. Salapasck (Eds.), *Infant perception: From sensation to cognition* (Vol. 2). New York: Academic Press.

Lewis, M., & Cherry, L. (1977). Social behavior and language acquisition. In M. Lewis & L. Rosenblum (Eds.), *Interaction, conversation and the development of language: The origins of behavior* (Vol. 2). New York: Wiley.

Lewis, M., & Goldberg, S. (1969). Perceptual-cognitive development in infancy: A generalized expectancy model as a function of the mother-infant interaction. *Merrill-Palmer Quarterly, 15*(1), 81-100.

Lewis, M., & Weinraub, M. (1979). Origins of early sex-role development. *Sex Roles, 5*(2), 135-153.

Lippa, R., & Beauvais, C. (1983). Gender jeopardy: The effects of gender, assessed femininity and masculinity, and false success/failure feedback on performance in an experimental quiz game. *Journal of Personality and Social Psychology, 44*(2), 344-353.

Loeb, R. C., & Horst, L. (1978). Sex differences in self- and teachers' reports of self-esteem in preadolescents. *Sex Roles, 4*(5), 779-788.

Lott, B. (1978). Behavioral concordance with sex-role ideology related to play areas, creativity and parental sex-typing of children. *Journal of Personality and Social Psychology, 36*, 1087-1106.

Luria, Z., & Rose, M. D. (1979). *Psychology of human sexuality*. New York: Wiley.

Maccoby, E. E., & Jacklin, C. N. (1974). *The psychology of sex differences*. Palo Alto, CA: Stanford University Press.

Marcus, H., Crane, M., Bernstein, S., & Sikadi, M. (1982). Self-schemes and gender. *Journal of Personality and Social Psychology, 42*(1), 38-50.

Masters, J. C., & Wilkerson, A. (1976). Consensual and discriminative stereotypy of sex-type judgments by parents and children. *Child Development, 47*, 208-217.

Masters, W. H., & Johnson, V. E. (1966). *Human sexual response*. Boston: Little, Brown.

McArthur, L., & Eisen, S. (1976). Television and sex-role stereotyping. *Journal of Applied Social Psychology, 6*, 329-351.

Minuchin, P. P., & Shapiro, E. K. (1983). The school as a context for social development. In P. Mussen (Ed.), *Handbook of child psychology* (4th ed., Vol. 4). New York: Wiley.

Mischel, W. (1966). A social-learning view of sex differences in behavior. In E. E. Maccoby (Ed.), *The development of sex differences*. Stanford, CA: Stanford University Press.

Mischel, W. (1969). Sex typing and socialization. In P. Mussen (Ed.), *Carmichael's manual of child psychology* (3rd ed., Vol. 2). New York: Wiley.

Money, J. (1968). Psychologic approach to psychosexual misidentity with elective mutism: Sex reassignment in two cases of hyperadrenocortical hermaphroditism. *Clinical Pediatrics, 7*(6), 331–339.

Money, J., & Brennan, J. G. (1968). Sexual dimorphism in the psychology of female transsexuals. *Journal of Nervous and Mental Disease, 147*(5), 487–499.

Money, J., & Erhardt, A. A. (1972). Developmental differentiation. In *Man and woman, boy and girl*. Baltimore: The Johns Hopkins University Press.

Money, J., Hampson, J. G., & Hampson, J. L. (1955). Hermaphroditism: Recommendations concerning assignment of sex, change of sex, and psychologic management. *Bulletin of the Johns Hopkins Hospital, 97*(4), 284–300.

Money, J., Hampson, J. G., & Hampson, J. L. (1957). Imprinting and the establishment of gender role. *A.M.A. Archives of Neurology and Psychiatry, 77*(3), 333–336.

Money, J., & Primrose, C. (1968). Sexual dimorphism and dissociation in the psychology of male transsexuals. *Journal of Nervous and Mental Disease, 147*, 472–486.

Mortimer, M. (1979). Sex stereotyping in children's books. *Australian Journal of Early Childhood, 4*(4), 4–8.

Moss, H. A. (1967). Sex, age, and state as determinants of mother–infant interaction. *Merrill-Palmer Quarterly, 13*, 19–36.

Mullis, I. V. S. (1975). *Educational achievement and sex discrimination.* Paper prepared by the National Assessment of Educational Progress, Denver, CO.

Myers, A. M., & Gonda, G. (1982). Utility of the masculinity–femininity construct: Comparison of traditional and androgyny approaches. *Journal of Personality and Social Psychology, 43*(3), 514–522.

Neugarten, B. (1968). Women's attitudes toward the menopause. In B. Neugarten (Ed.), *Middle age and aging*. Chicago: University of Chicago Press.

Nilsen, A. P. (1977). Alternatives to sexist practices in the classroom. *Young Children, 32*(5), 53–58.

Parke, R. D., & O'Leary, S. E. (1976). Family interaction in the newborn period: Some findings, some observations and some unresolved issues. In K. Riegel & J. Meachan (Eds.), *The developing individual in a changing world* (Vol. 2). The Hague: Mouton.

Parsons, J. E., Kaczala, C. M., & Meece, J. L. (1982). Socialization of achievement attitudes and beliefs: Classroom influences. *Child Development, 53*, 322–339.

Pedhazur, E. J., & Tetenbaum, T. J. (1979). Bem Sex Role Inventory: A theoretical and methodological critique. *Journal of Personality and Social Psychology, 37*(6), 996–1016.

Peterson, C., & McDonald, L. (1980). Children's occupational sex-typing. *Journal of Genetic Psychology, 136*(1), 145–146.

Pleck, J. H. (1975). Masculinity–femininity: Current and alternate paradigms. *Sex Roles, 1*(2), 161–178.

Pleck, J. (1981). *The myth of masculinity.* Cambridge, MA: The MIT Press.

Rebecca, M., Hefner, R., & Oleshansky, B. (1976). A model of sex-role transcendence. *Journal of Social Issues, 32*(3), 197–206.

Rheingold, H. C., & Cook, K. V. (1975). The contents of boys' and girls' rooms as an index of parents' behavior. *Child Development, 46*, 459–463.

Roberto, L. G. (1983). Issues in diagnosis and treatment of transsexualism. *Sex Roles, 12*(5), 445–473.

Rossi, A. S. (1968). Transition to parenthood. *Journal of Marriage and the Family, 30*, 26–39.

Rubin, J., Provenzano, F., & Luria, Z. (1974). The eye of the beholder: Parents' views on sex of newborns. *American Journal of Orthopsychiatry, 44*(4), 512–519.

Sanday, P. R. (1981). *Female power and male dominance: On the origins of sexual inequality.* London: Cambridge University Press.

Schwartz, L. A., & Markham, W. T. (1985, in press). Sex stereotyping in children's toy advertisements. *Sex Roles,* Vol. 12, 1/2, 157–170.

Seavy, C. A., Katz, P. A., & Zalk, S. R. (1975). Baby X: The effect of gender labels on adult responses to infants. *Sex Roles, 1*(2), 103–109.

Serbin, L. A., & Connor, J. M. (1979, March). *Environmental control of sex-related behaviors in the preschool.* Paper presented at the Society for Research in Child Development, San Francisco.

Sherif, C. W. (1980, September). *Needed concepts in the study of gender identity.* Presidential address to Division 35, Annual Convention of the American Psychological Association, Montreal.

Sidorowicz, L. S., & Lunney, G. S. (1980). Baby X revisited. *Sex Roles, 6*(1), 67–74.

Silvern, L. (1977). Children's sex-role preferences: Stronger among girls than boys. *Sex Roles, 3*(2), 159–171.

Silvern, L. (1978). Masculinity–femininity in children's self-concepts: The relationship to teachers' judgments of social adjustment and academic ability, classroom behaviors, and popularity. *Sex Roles, 4*(6), 929–949.

Silvern, L. E., & Ryan, V. L. (1979). Self-rated adjustment and sex-typing on the Bem Sex-Role Inventory: Is masculinity the primary predictor of adjustment? *Sex Roles, 5*(6), 739–764.

Slaby, R. G., & Frey, K. S. (1975). Development of gender constancy and selective attention to same-sex models. *Child Development, 46,* 849–856.

Smith, C., & Lloyd, B. (1978). Maternal behavior and perceived sex of infant: Revisited. *Child Development, 49,* 1263–1265.

Spence, J. T. (1982). Comments on Baumrind's "Are androgynous individuals more effective persons and parents?" *Child Development, 53,* 76–80.

Spence, J. T. (1984). Masculinity, femininity and gender-related traits: A conceptual analysis and critique. *Progress in Experimental Personality Research, 13,* 2–97.

Spence, J. T., & Helmreich, R. (1978). *Masculinity and femininity.* Austin, TX: University of Texas Press.

Spence, J. T., Helmreich, R., & Stapp, J. (1974). The Personal Attributes Questionnaire: A measure of sex-role stereotypes and masculinity–femininity. *JSAS Catalog of Selected Documents in Psychology, 4,* 127.

Spence, J. T., Helmreich, R., & Stapp, J. (1975). Ratings of self and peers on sex-role attributes and their relation to self-esteem and conceptions of masculinity and femininity. *Journal of Personality and Social Psychology, 32,* 29–39.

Sprafkin, J. N., & Liebert, R. M. (1978). Sex-typing and children's television preferences. In G. Tuchman, A. K. Daniels, & J. Benet (Eds.), *Hearth and home: Images of women in mass media.* New York: Oxford University Press.

St. Peter, S. (1979). Jack went up the hill . . . but where was Jill? *Psychology of Women Quarterly, 4*(2), 256–260.

Stoller, R. J. (1968). *Sex and gender* (Vol. 1). New York: J. Aronson.

Storms, M. D. (1979). Sex-role identity and its relationships to sex-role attributes and sex-role stereotypes. *Journal of Personality and Social Psychology, 37*(10), 1779–1789.

Stunkard, A., & Mendleson, M. (1967). Obesity and the body image: Characteristics of disturbances in the body image of some obese persons. *American Journal of Psychiatry, 123,* 1296–1300.

Sutton-Smith, B., & Rosenberg, B. G. (1960). Manifest anxiety and game preferences in children. *Child Development, 31,* 307–311.

Tajfel, H. (1981). *Human groups and social categories: Studies in social psychology.* Cambridge, England: Cambridge University Press.

Tajfel, H., & Billig, M. (1974). Familiarity and categorization in intergroup behavior. *Journal of Experimental Social Psychology, 10,* 159–170.

Taylor, M. C., & Hall, J. A. (1982). Psychological androgyny: Theories, methods, and conclusions. *Psychological Bulletin, 92*(2), 347–366.

Thoman, E. B., Leiderman, H., & Olson, J. P. (1972). Neonate–mother interaction during breast-feeding. *Developmental Psychology, 6*(1), 110–118.

Thompson, S. K. (1975). Gender labels and early sex-role development. *Child Development, 46,* 339–347.

Ullian, D. Z. (1976). The development of conceptions of masculinity and femininity. In B. Lloyd & J. Archer (Eds.), *Exploring sex differences.* New York: Academic Press.

Unger, R. K. (1979). *Female and male: Psychological perspectives.* New York: Harper & Row.

Urberg, K. A. (1979). Sex role conceptualizations in adolescents and adults. *Developmental Psychology, 15*(1), 90–92.

Urberg, K. A., & LaBouvie-Vief, G. (1976). Conceptualizations of sex roles: A life span developmental study. *Developmental Psychology, 12,* 15–23.

Veith, I. (1972). *The yellow emperor's classic of internal medicine.* Berkeley and Los Angeles, CA: University of California Press.

Vreogh, K. (1971). The relationship of birth order and sex of siblings to gender role identity. *Developmental Psychology, 4,* 407–411.

Weinraub, M., Brown, L., Sockloff, A., Ethridge, T., Gracely, E., & Myers, B. (1984). The development of the sex role stereotypes in the third grade: Relationship to gender labeling, gender identity, sex-typed toy preference and family characteristics. *Child Development, 55*(4), 1493–1503.

Weitz, S. (1977). *Sex roles: Biological, psychological and social foundations.* New York: Oxford University Press.

Whitley, B. E., Jr. (1983). Sex role orientation and self-esteem: A critical meta-analytic review. *Journal of Personality and Social Psychology, 44*(4), 765–778.

Wiggins, J. S., & Holzmuller, A. (1981). Further evidence on androgyny and interpersonal flexibility. *Journal of Research in Personality, 15,* 67–80.

Will, J. A., Self, P. A., & Datan, N. (1976). Maternal behavior and perceived sex of infant. *American Journal of Orthopsychiatry, 46,* 135–139.

Williams, J. E., & Best, D. L. (1982). Retrospect and prospect: A broader view. In J. E. Williams & D. L. Best (Eds.), *Measuring sex stereotypes: A thirty-nation study* (pp. 303–309). Beverly Hills, CA: Sage Publications.

Williams, J., & Giles, H. (1978). The changing status of women in society: An intergroup perspective. In H. Tajfel (Ed.), *Differentiation between social groups: Studies in the social psychology of intergroup relations.* London: Academic Press.

Worell, J. (1981). Life-span sex roles: Development, continuity and change. In R. Lerner & N. Busch-Rossnagel (Eds.), *Individuals as producers of their development.* New York: Academic Press.

Yarrow, L. J., Rubenstein, J. L., Pederson, F. A., & Jankowski, J. J. (1972). Dimensions in early stimulation and their differential effects on infant development. *Merrill-Palmer Quarterly, 18,* 205–218.

Yorburg, B. (1974). *Sexual identity: Sex roles and social change.* New York: Wiley–Interscience.

Zalk, S. R., & Katz, P. A. (1978). Gender attitudes in children. *Sex Roles, 4*(3), 349–357.

Three

Gender Stereotypes

RICHARD D. ASHMORE
FRANCES K. DEL BOCA
ARTHUR J. WOHLERS

Introduction

What is a man? What is a woman? Table 1 presents the "answers" to these questions that emerge from the large body of work on gender stereotypes. As can be seen, the extant literature suggests that conceptions of women and men take the form of two attribute lists (one male, one female). The present chapter takes a critical look at the currently dominant "list approach." In addition, we offer a general conceptual framework as a guide for future research and theory on gender stereotypes.

Psychologists and others interested in how women and men are construed have focused on two major issues: (1) the content of beliefs regarding the sexes, and (2) the relative desirability of attributes ascribed to one or the other gender. Although these two phenomena are clearly related, they are conceptually distinguishable and are treated separately in the present volume. This chapter is concerned with the *substantive content* of beliefs about women and men—that is, gender *stereotypes*; Chapter Four focuses on how the sexes and issues pertinent to female–male relations are *evaluated*—that is, gender-related *attitudes*.

We begin by reviewing the extant literature. This survey is not exhaustive. That is, not all studies concerning gender (or sex-role) stereotypes are covered. It is, however, representative. Because the overwhelming majority of empirical studies have focused on gender stereotype assessment by means

THE SOCIAL PSYCHOLOGY OF FEMALE-MALE RELATIONS   69

TABLE 1

The Gender Stereotypes . . . Or Are They?

Men are . . .	Women are . . .
Able to separate feelings from ideas[c]	Affected[a]
Active[c]	Affectionate[a]
Acts as a leader[c]	Amiable[b]
Adventurous[a,c]	Anxious[b]
Aggressive[a,c]	Appreciates art and literature[c]
Ambitious[a,c]	Appreciative[a]
Assertive[a]	Attractive[a]
Autocratic[a]	Aware of the feelings of others[c]
Boastful[a]	Careless[b]
Calm[b]	Catty[b]
Coarse[a]	Cautious[b]
Commanding[b]	Cautious about social standards[b]
Competitive[c]	Charming[a]
Confident[a,b]	Chatterers[b]
Courageous[a]	Clothes conscious[b]
Cruel[a]	Complaining[a]
Daring[a]	Courteous[b]
Decisive[b]	Deferent[b]
Deeper thinkers[b]	Dependent[a,b]
Dependable[b]	Desire for own family[b]
Determined[b]	Does not use harsh language[c]
Direct[c]	Dreamy[a]
Disorderly[a]	Emotional[a]
Dominant[a,b,c]	Excitable[a]
Easily influenced[c]	Expresses tender feelings easily[c]
Enterprising[c]	Express feelings[b]
Faster thinkers[b]	Feminine[a]
Feelings not hurt easily[c]	Fickle[a]
Forceful[a]	Flighty[b]
Handsome[a]	Flirtatious[a]
Hides emotions[c]	Frivolous[a]
Independent[a,b,c]	Fussy[a]
Jolly[a]	Gentle[a,c]
Knows the way of the world[c]	Guilty[b]
Larger[b]	Helpless[b]
Late[b]	High-strung[a]
Leaders[b]	High voice[b]
Likes math and science[c]	Hypocritical[b]
Logical[a,c]	Indecisive[b]
Loud[a]	Interested in own appearance[c]
Makes decisions easily[c]	Kind[b]
Makes own decisions[b]	Less able to reason[b]
Masculine[a]	Less responsible[b]
Mature[b]	Love of children[b]

TABLE 1 (Continued)

Men are . . .	Women are . . .
Never cries[c]	Make little use of IQ[b]
Not concerned about appearance[c]	Maternal[b]
Not dependent[c]	Meek[a]
Not excitable in a minor crisis[c]	Mild[a,b]
Not sentimental[b]	Nagging[a]
Not uncomfortable about being aggressive[c]	Neat in habits[c]
Objective[c]	Nervous[b]
Original[b]	Passive[b]
Poised[b]	Polite[b]
Rational[a]	Prudish[a]
Realistic[a]	Quiet[c]
Relaxed[b]	Rattlebrained[a]
Responsible[b]	Religious[c]
Resourceful[b]	Senseless prattle[b]
Robust[a]	Sensitive[a]
Rude[b]	Sentimental[a]
Self-confident[a,c]	Small[b]
Self-controlled[b]	Socially competitive[b]
Severe[a]	Soft-hearted[a]
Skilled in business[c]	Sophisticated[a]
Stable[a]	Strong need for security[c]
Steady[a]	Stupid[b]
Stern[a]	Submissive[a,b]
Strong[a,b]	Subject to change in emotions[b]
Superior[b]	Susceptible to emotional appeals[b]
Tactless[b]	Tactful[b,c]
Talks freely about sex with men[c]	Talkative[a,c]
Tall[b]	Talk too much[b]
Thinks men are superior to women[c]	Unfair[b]
Tough[a]	Want protection[b]
Unemotional[a,b,c]	Warm[b]
Unexcitable[a]	Weak[a,b]
Worldly[c]	Whiny[a]

[a]Part of the "focused sex stereotypes" identified by Williams and Bennett (1975) using the Adjective Check List. These are adjectives that at least 75% of both sexes agreed were typical of men or of women.
[b]Examples of responses to open-ended probe, "List 10 traits or characteristics of men and 10 traits or characteristics of women" (Sherriffs & McKee, 1957).
[c]The socially more desirable adjective of adjective rating scales for which 75% of the male and 75% of the female sample agreed the adjective was more likely to be found in an adult male (or adult female) (Rosenkrantz et al., 1968).

of self-report measures,[1] this review is organized in terms of the three major methods researchers have used to get subjects to divulge their beliefs about the sexes. A critical appraisal follows the discussion of the three approaches to sex stereotype assessment.

Once the existing research has been covered, a working conceptualization of gender stereotypes is presented. The starting point for the proposed framework is our belief that stereotypes (including gender stereotypes) and social cognition (a major topic in social psychology) are closely related. Work in social cognition can be partitioned into *structure* (e.g., How are personality impressions organized?) and *process* (e.g., How are impressions formed and altered?), and a structure-plus-process framework is proposed for work on gender stereotypes. We next review "new" research relevant to beliefs about the sexes that is made available by our working conceptualization. We close this section on structure by summarizing what is known about the substantive content of gender stereotypes and by suggesting what questions need to be asked. In the final section of the chapter we turn to process issues and consider how gender stereotypes are acquired, how they function in social interaction, and, finally, how they change.

Research Assessing Gender Stereotypes

The three major approaches to gender stereotype assessment can be ordered in terms of increasing constraint on the respondent: open-ended description, adjective checklist, and rating scales.[2] For each approach, the major pioneering program of research is described, and variations on the basic procedure are noted.

OPEN-ENDED DESCRIPTION

Open-ended assessments of gender stereotypes, where respondents are asked to describe their conceptions of males and females in their own words,

[1] A second popular research approach has been to content analyze the portrayal of the sexes on television, in magazines and newspapers, in school texts, and in a variety of other sources. Because the focus here is on the individual, this literature, which we view as providing evidence concerning cultural beliefs about men and women, is not analyzed.

[2] The present partitioning of sex stereotype measures is consistent with the organizational schemes used by other reviewers of this literature. Brannon (1978) concluded that the adjective checklist is the predominant means of assessing perceptions of the sexes. Beere (1979), while acknowledging considerable diversity in terms of specifics, divided measuring devices into those that require subjects to associate traits, occupations, et cetera, with males or females (which is the basic procedure of the adjective checklist) and those involving semantic differential scales (which are rating scales). Finally, Ruble and Ruble (1982) identify, as do we, open-ended, adjective checklist, and bipolar scale techniques, and add Likert-type measures.

have been relatively rare. Of those studies that have used an open-ended approach, the pioneering work of Sherriffs and McKee (1957) is the most often cited. Respondents in this study were instructed to "list 10 traits or characteristics of men and 10 traits or characteristics of women." This procedure yielded 1,427 "descriptive words, phrases, or sentences," which were sorted by the authors into 26 "psychologically meaningful" content categories (p. 456). Of the 26 categories, 23 comprised items assigned more often to one gender than to the other. Nine categories were designated as "masculine." In terms of the frequency with which items falling within these categories were ascribed to men, the most masculine categories were (in order) "Physical Attributes" (e.g., tall), "Ascendent" (e.g., dominant), "Responsible" (e.g., dependable), and "Independent" (e.g., makes own decisions). The most feminine of the 14 categories used more often to describe women were (again, in order) "Social Awareness" (e.g., clothes conscious), "Negative Affect or Behavior Toward Others" (e.g., catty), "Physical Attributes" (e.g., small), "Orientation to Home and Hearth" (e.g., maternal), and "Positive Affect or Behavior Toward Others" (e.g., amiable). Although some sex-of-subject differences occurred in the usage of the categories, male and female respondents showed considerable agreement about which attributes describe which sex.

In addition to specifying the content of gender stereotypes, Sherriffs and McKee were also interested in determining how each gender was evaluated vis-à-vis the other (i.e., in assessing *attitudes* toward the sexes). A subsample of the original group of subjects was asked at a later time to rate each of the characteristics produced by the open-ended instructions as favorable, neutral, or unfavorable (McKee & Sherriffs, 1957). Each description was then scored in terms of the number of positive and negative ratings it received. Several different analytic procedures produced a consistent set of results: Although both sexes were evaluated positively, men were regarded more favorably than women, especially by male subjects.

Although they are rare and infrequently cited, there have been other instances where investigators have used content analysis to summarize the results of open-ended assessments of how the sexes are perceived (e.g., Goodenough, 1957; MacBrayer, 1960). Most investigations, however, particularly more-recent ones, have used the open-ended approach, not to explicate the nature of gender stereotypes, but, rather, in the service of other aims—either as a first step in constructing a standardized measure of sex stereotypes (e.g., Rosenkrantz, Vogel, Bee, Broverman, & Broverman, 1968; Der-Karabetian & Smith, 1977) or of sex-role orientation (e.g., Bem, 1974), or as a means of comparing the results of different methodologies (e.g., Cowan & Stewart, 1977). Such research is discussed later in greater depth where appropriate.

Open-ended assessments of gender stereotypes have the advantage of imposing minimal constraint on subjects' responses—hence the alternate label, "free response." Because they allow respondents to describe their conceptions of the sexes in their own words, such procedures may come closest to representing how individuals actually think about women and men. The freedom enjoyed by subjects, however, poses problems for the investigator who must reduce or summarize the data collected. This is usually accomplished by means of a content analysis system. Because such schemes tend to be empirically derived—that is, they are developed to fit the data obtained in a particular investigation—comparisons across studies are difficult. Because such comparisons are necessary in order to test hypotheses regarding change over time or differences among respondent populations, a standard content analysis scheme for coding open-ended descriptors would be desirable. Generalized schemes for classifying both self-descriptions (e.g., Gordon's [1968] system for coding responses to the "Who Am I") and descriptions of others (see Hastie and Carlston, 1980, pp. 27–28) might be used as starting points. Because these analytic frameworks focus on types of descriptors (e.g., personality traits, social roles, physical characteristics) and not on content, it will be necessary to supplement these with rules for categorizing the content of open-ended responses. The categories identified by Sherriffs and McKee (1957) provide a first approximation in this regard.

ADJECTIVE CHECKLISTS

Adjective checklist assessments of gender stereotypes include procedures in which a list of descriptive statements, most often trait adjectives, is supplied by the investigator, and the subject's task is to indicate which items characterize men and which characterize women. By far the most extensive use of the adjective checklist for gender stereotype assessment is the program of research undertaken by Williams and his colleagues. Williams and Best (1982) describe the rationale for their choice of an assessment procedure as follows:

> The initial item pool was to be a large and diverse one descriptive of human personality, in general, rather than sex stereotypes, in particular; the item pool was to include both favorable and unfavorable traits in order to permit the assessment of positive and negative aspects of sex stereotypes; the method was not to require the assumption that masculinity and femininity are opposed concepts, and, thus, was to permit the assessment of androgyny; the method was to interface with previous research in personality and with personality theory; and the procedure was to be interesting to subjects and easily administered and scored. (Williams & Best, 1982, p. 21).

These criteria led them to use the Gough Adjective Check List (ACL), which contains 300 items and is usually used to assess personality.

The first gender stereotype study using the ACL was conducted by Williams and Bennett (1975). Subjects were told that the experimenters were interested in the typical characteristics of men and women and that, in our culture, some characteristics are more frequently associated with one sex than with the other. Respondents were instructed, "For each adjective you are to decide whether it is more frequently associated with men rather than women, or more frequently associated with women than men" (Williams & Bennett, 1975, p. 329).

The traits that were assigned to each gender by at least 75% of respondents of both sexes were used to define the *focused* male and female stereotypes. Thirty-three adjectives met this criterion for the male stereotype, and 30 for the female stereotype. In order to construct personality profiles of the stereotypic male and female, the focused stereotype for each sex was elaborated by including traits that had been assigned to either gender by at least 60% of the total sample. The *expanded* male stereotype then comprised 98 terms and the "expanded female stereotype," 83. When compared with the ACL standard norms, the expanded version of the male stereotype was found to be atypically low in "nurturance," "abasement," "deference," "affiliation," and "intraception." Conversely, it was found to be atypically high in terms of "autonomy," "aggression," and "exhibitionism." The expanded female stereotype was atypically low on "dominance" and high on "succorance" and "abasement." Based on the ACL evaluative classification of the traits, the focused stereotype for the male was found to be more favorable than that for the female, but the reverse was true for the expanded stereotypes.

Noting that the relative judgment method used in the Williams and Bennett study may have exaggerated relatively minor differences in trait attribution to males and females, Williams and Best (1977) employed a between-subjects design in a second investigation of gender stereotypes with the ACL. Each respondent was requested to describe one sex only. Instructions were altered accordingly, "For each adjective, you are to decide whether or not it is descriptive of men [women] in general" (p. 103). When the item scores obtained in the Williams and Bennett (1975) and Williams and Best (1977) studies were standardized and a correlation computed, the resulting coefficient for the two sets of ratings was .78. The authors concluded that the results produced by the two methods (relative vs. absolute judgments) were highly similar. Using data from both studies, a single standardized Sex Stereotype Index (SSI) score was derived for each trait, indicating the degree to which the adjective was associated with female versus male.

To further investigate the connotative meaning of gender stereotypes, SSI scores were correlated with activity and potency ratings (obtained from independent samples of college students) of the 300 ACL items (Best, Williams,

& Briggs, 1980). Significant correlations were obtained for both dimensions of meaning ($r = .35$ and $.31$ for activity and potency, respectively). On the basis of these results and an earlier finding of no relationship between SSI scores and trait favorability (Williams & Best, 1977), the investigators concluded, "that any assertion of greater 'social desirability' for the male stereotype [is] based on its 'greater activity' and not, as is often supposed, on its greater 'favorability' " (Best et al., 1980, p. 735).

Williams and his colleagues have extended their initial research with the ACL in two major directions. First, they have developed a gender stereotype measure suitable for use with preschool and early school-age children (the Sex Stereotype Measure or SSM). Second, Williams, Bennett, and Best (1975) have investigated cross-cultural variations in how females and males are perceived. Using the ACL and the SSM, they have assessed the conceptions of the sexes held by young adults and by children in 30 nations on five continents. Considerable similarity in views of the sexes has been found to exist across the societies studied (Williams & Best, 1982).

Although Williams and his associates have done the most to develop the adjective checklist technique, variants on this basic methodology have been exceedingly popular throughout the history of research on gender stereotypes. Virtually all of the earliest studies that appear in the literature used this procedure to investigate the pervasiveness of stereotypic conceptions of the sexes. Despite differences in subject populations, it was consistently concluded that most attributes of personality are seen as sex-linked (e.g., Sherriffs & Jarrett, 1953) and that widespread agreement exists about which characteristics are associated with which sex (e.g., Fernberger, 1948).

Subsequent research using the adjective checklist method has focused more on specifying the content of gender stereotypes and on comparing the favorability of attributes comprised by the stereotypes of each sex. In their comparative investigation of various assessment procedures, Sherriffs and McKee (1957) administered Sarbin's 200 adjectives to respondents using two different sets of instructions. Subjects were first provided with two trait lists and for each asked to "check those adjectives which are in general true of men (women)" (pp. 451–452). When they had completed both lists, they were given a third list and asked to "indicate for *each* adjective whether it is more true of men (M) or women (W)" (p. 452). Sherriffs and McKee found that both procedures yielded similar results in terms of stereotype content; however, the results with the forced-choice procedure appeared to exaggerate the findings obtained under the unforced-choice instructions.

The results of the unforced-choice procedure were used to examine the substantive content of gender stereotypes. Adjectives that were ascribed significantly more often ($p < .05$) to one sex than to the other defined the stereotype of that sex. According to the authors' own "reasonable grouping," the positive male stereotype included traits reflecting (1) "a straight-forward, uninhibited style"; (2) "rational competence and ability"; and (3) "action, vigor, and effectiveness." The positive female stereotype, on the other hand, contained qualities expressing (1) "social skills and grace"; (2) "warmth and emotional support"; and (3) "a concern for the significant, spiritual implications of experience" (pp. 452–454). The negative traits that were ascribed to each sex tended to be "mild exaggerations" of the desirable ones.

In contrast with the open-ended approach, the adjective checklist method imposes an important constraint on subjects—they are asked to indicate their beliefs about the sexes using words and phrases supplied by the investigator. This constraint has several positive implications:

1. Attribute vocabularies can be constructed such that they overcome known response biases (e.g., the avoidance of negative traits in describing others).
2. Response protocols are relatively easy to score and summarize.
3. Comparisons between individual subjects and across samples of respondents are facilitated.
4. For certain checklists such as the ACL, results of stereotype studies can be related to research on personality assessment.

This final point leads to the most important consideration in adjective checklist methodology—how to select the set of attributes. McKee and Sherriffs (1957) suggested two possible strategies. The investigator could attempt to obtain a representative sample of all items for which there are perceived gender differences or, alternatively, could select a pre-existing list of characteristics containing as many significant aspects of personality as possible. These are, in fact, the approaches that have been used. Der-Karabetian and Smith (1977), for example, chose the first option and developed an adjective checklist based on an open-ended procedure specifically designed to elicit perceptions of gender differences. With respect to the second alternative, extant devices used in gender stereotype research include the Edwards Personality Inventory (Lunneborg, 1970) and the Rokeach Value Survey (Unger & Siiter, 1974) as well as the ACL and Sarbin's attribute list.

RATING SCALES

This category of gender stereotype assessment techniques includes all procedures that make use of rating scales. Rather than making categorical judgments, subjects are required to rate the *degree* to which attributes (usually traits) are characteristic of each gender or the *extent* to which females and males differ in terms of their possession of particular attributes.

Virtually all research using this method of assessment has been stimulated by the initial work of Rosenkrantz and his colleagues (Rosenkrantz et al., 1968). The work of these investigators has been the most influential in the gender stereotype literature, and the Sex-Role Stereotype Questionnaire (SRSQ), the rating scale used in their research, is the most widely used instrument in the field.

The development of the SRSQ is described in Rosenkrantz et al. (1968). An initial pool of items was generated by means of an open-ended request to subjects to, "list behaviors, attitudes, and personality characteristics which they considered to differentiate men and women" (p. 287). Using the criterion that an attribute be used more than once, 122 items were obtained for inclusion in the "Stereotype Questionnaire." These items were arranged in the form of 60-point rating scales (e.g., *easily influenced–not easily influenced*), and a new sample of subjects was instructed, "Imagine that you are going to meet a person for the first time and the only thing you know in advance is that the person is an adult male (female)." Respondents rated first one sex, then the other, on the same set of items (order of presentation was counterbalanced), indicating the extent to which they expected each to characterize the adult male (masculinity response) and the adult female (femininity response). Those items for which 75% of the respondents of both sexes agreed that one pole of the scale characterized one gender more than the other were designated as "stereotypic." Forty-one of the 122 items met this criterion. Mean differences between masculinity and femininity responses for all of these items were found to be highly significant ($p < .001$). Significant differences at the .05 level of probability in both samples were obtained for an additional 48 items. These were termed "differentiating."

The authors of the Rosenkrantz et al. (1968) study extended their research efforts with the newly developed measure, and five separate studies involving the same group of investigators appeared in 1970. Responses on the SRSQ were related to the self-concepts of parents of college students (Rosenkrantz, Vogel, & Broverman, 1970), ideal conceptions of sex roles (Elman, Press, & Rosenkrantz, 1970), judgments of mental health (Broverman, Broverman, Clarkson, Rosenkrantz, & Vogel, 1970), maternal employment (Vogel, Broverman, Broverman, Clarkson, & Rosenkrantz, 1970), and ideal future family size (Clarkson, Vogel, Broverman, Broverman, & Rosenkrantz, 1970). The results of these investigations were summarized in a 1972 review article (Broverman, Vogel, Broverman, Clarkson, & Rosenkrantz, 1972).

Broverman and her associates reached three major conclusions based on research with the SRSQ:

1. There is wide consensus concerning the content of gender stereotypes across groups that differ in terms of sex, age, religion, marital status, and educational level.

2. Attributes associated with men are more positively valued than those
   ascribed to women.
3. Positively valued masculine traits entail "competence, rationality and
   assertion," while positively valued feminine traits reflect "warmth
   and expressiveness" (p. 61).

With regard to the conclusion that sex stereotypes are widely shared, it is
important to note that most of the investigations reported by this group of
collaborators have involved college students. Although the ranges they
report in terms of the ages and educational levels of respondents are impressive, the variability with respect to different demographic characteristics
was probably most evident in their one relatively small sample of noncollege
respondents (Rosenkrantz et al., 1970). Further, actual statistical comparisons were only made for six age-by-sex categories. Consensus with
respect to other demographic variables (e.g., marital status) was inferred
from the distribution of levels of the other variables in the six categories actually compared (e.g., most of the younger respondents were single while the
older subjects tended to be married).

In terms of relative evaluation of the male and female stereotypes, the
assertion of the investigators is somewhat misleading. It is true that there are
more male-valued than female-valued items among the 41 designated as
stereotypic. However, both sexes tended to be rated in positive terms (i.e.,
the mean femininity and masculinity responses fell on the socially desirable
side of most scales), and the mean favorability rating of male-valued items
was not significantly different from that for female-valued items
(Rosenkrantz et al., 1968).

The third conclusion concerning the substantive content of gender
stereotypes appears to be based primarily on separate factor analyses of
masculinity and femininity responses computed for two samples of male and
female respondents. According to the authors, two major factors were obtained in all four analyses: one comprising items for which the male pole had
been judged as more desirable, the other containing those items for which the
feminine pole had been rated more favorably. The investigators interpret
these results to mean that the stereotypic items of the SRSQ consist of two
orthogonal domains: male-valued attributes and female-valued characteristics. Although the analytical details are not reported, it appears as if the
authors' summary conclusion may be somewhat overdrawn. According to
the initial SRSQ study (Rosenkrantz et al., 1968), respondents tend to rate
both genders toward the more desirable pole, irrespective of whether an item
was male-valued or female-valued, a finding that seems somewhat at odds
with the conclusion that the sexes are seen to possess two completely different sets of traits.

In addition to its originators, many other investigators have used the
SRSQ either in the original or in an adapted form (e.g., with a different

response format, with an abbreviated set of items). For example, Ellis and Bentler (1973) used a 55-item abridged version of the SRSQ to assess the relationships among gender stereotypes, traditional sex-role standards (behavior deemed appropriate for one sex as opposed to the other), and a number of personality variables. In another study, O'Leary and Depner (1975) developed a 21-item measure based on the SRSQ and compared ratings of self and ideal other.

Spence, Helmreich, and Stapp (1974) used the SRSQ as a starting point for the development of a measure of self-perception of masculinity–femininity, the Personal Attributes Questionnaire (PAQ). In addition to developing a new instrument, they sought to obtain normative data for the SRSQ itself and to examine possible differences in scale ratings as a function of variations in target description. Subjects were given the 122 SRSQ items plus an additional 16 items devised by the researchers and asked to provide ratings under three conditions. One group of respondents received the standard SRSQ instructions and rated the *typical adult* male and female. Two other groups described the *typical college student* of each sex and the *ideal* male and female. Mean differences in ratings of the male and female under each of the conditions were compared. Significant differences were obtained for a larger number of items in the typical adult than in the typical college student condition. Significant differences occurred in both conditions for samples of subjects of each sex on 66 items. Of these, 55 were chosen for inclusion in the PAQ.

For those items comprised by the PAQ, ratings of the ideal male and female were compared with stereotypic responses. Items were designated as "male-valued" if ratings of both the ideal male and the ideal female were in the stereotypically masculine direction. Similarly, female-valued items were defined as those for which ideal ratings of both sexes were in the feminine direction. According to the authors, the 23 male-valued items are, in terms of content, predominantly instrumental in character, whereas the 18 items designated as female-valued are expressive.

In comparison with the adjective checklist procedure, rating scales require subjects to make more precise judgments about how personal attributes apply to the sexes—that is, to indicate the degree to which each sex possesses each characteristic rather than simply its presence or absence. In addition to greater precision of measurement, this approach has the advantage of making it easier to see how one sex is perceived relative to the other. In common with adjective checklists, however, rating-scale procedures require the investigator to select an attribute vocabulary. Most researchers have solved this problem by using all or a subset of the traits generated in the initial investigation of Rosenkrantz and his colleagues (Rosenkrantz et al., 1968). This raises the question as to whether this attribute list is valid for this purpose, particularly because it was compiled in the late 1960s (see Beere, 1983, p. 130).

A problem with rating-scale procedures arises from the need to have two scale end-points for each attribute item. To date, this issue has not been explicitly discussed in the gender stereotype literature. In constructing the SRSQ, Rosenkrantz et al. (1968) converted 122 descriptors into 122 rating scales with two labeled end-points. The items composing the instrument are described as "bipolar," but many are, in fact, unipolar (e.g., timid–not timid). It would seem desirable to be consistent in the use of one or the other type of scale. And, whichever format is preferred, relevant findings in the semantic differential literature should be used as a guide in item design and scale construction (see Heise, 1969).

GENDER STEREOTYPE RESEARCH: A PROGRESS REPORT

In this section, we take a critical look at the extant literature on sex stereotypes. We begin by considering the nature of what has been done—the heavy emphasis on empirical work and the concomitant lack of theory. Next, attention is focused on inconsistencies in results across investigations. Finally, we examine methodological factors that may contribute to variations in research findings. In so doing, we consider what respondents are asked to describe, how they are asked to perform their task, and how investigators analyze the raw data subjects provide.

What's Been Done?

A very large literature on gender stereotypes has amassed since the early 1970s. This work has been almost exclusively empirical, with scant attention paid to conceptual and theoretical issues (see Beere, 1983; Ruble & Ruble, 1982). There has been very little discussion of what a gender stereotype is or of what alternative definitions of the concept might be, and there has been almost no consideration of the theoretical status of the construct. This lack of attention to conceptual–theoretical issues has had two important implications.

First, the term, *sex* (or *sex-role*) *stereotype*, has been used very loosely. Investigators have tended to invoke the concept of gender stereotypes as an explanatory variable without actually assessing stereotypic beliefs (see Brannon, 1978; Ruble & Ruble, 1982). For example, studies of evaluation bias have used sex stereotypes to "explain" differential evaluations of identical work (e.g., essays, paintings) ascribed to females and males. While such an explanation is plausible, there are alternatives (e.g., a perceiver may downgrade a woman's achievement because of a negative attitude toward females without endorsing a full set of beliefs about the personality traits and other qualities of women).

Second, in the absence of explicit theorizing, an implicit or only partially articulated paradigm has guided research. Elsewhere, we have labeled this shared perspective a "sociocultural orientation" (Ashmore & Del Boca, 1981; Del Boca & Ashmore, 1980a). According to this underlying framework, sex stereotypes are part of a society's nonmaterial culture. It is assumed that gender stereotypes are acquired through socialization and that they influence perception of self and others. Within this paradigm there has been a rough division of labor: Sociologists have attempted to document cultural sex stereotypes by means of content analyses of portrayals of women and men in the media and other channels of socialization (e.g., school curricula); psychologists have assessed these same presumed stereotypes through the responses of individuals and sought to relate stereotypic beliefs to aspects of the individual's personality.

Although seldom noted, the most often cited studies in psychology were conducted by researchers interested in personality. This is evidenced by the fact that in all three aforementioned programs of research, self-descriptions of subjects were obtained in addition to descriptions of male and female stimulus targets. It is also noteworthy that two of the prototypic investigations were published in "personality journals" (Sherriffs & McKee, 1957, in the *Journal of Personality*; Rosenkrantz et al., 1968, in the *Journal of Consulting and Clinical Psychology*); the third study was published in *Sex Roles*, a multidisciplinary, rather than a social psychology, journal. Further, the rationale for the use of the ACL provided by Williams and Best (1982) quoted earlier (i.e., "the method was to interface with previous research in personality and with personality theory" [p. 21]) makes it evident that the authors of the third prototypic study were also concerned with personality issues.

The personality orientation of researchers has had two significant implications. First, it has impacted the nature of the questions asked in investigations of gender stereotypes (e.g., Are therapists' judgments of mental health influenced by sex stereotypes? To what extent are self-conceptions of the sexes similar to gender stereotypes?). And second, it has influenced the methodologies used to address these questions (e.g., the use of self-report personality inventories to assess stereotypes; the heavy use of trait adjectives in attribute vocabularies used to measure stereotypes). The role that gender plays in the psychological development of the individual is certainly an important topic (one that is treated in depth in Chapter Two of the present volume). We believe, however, that the emphasis on personality in sex stereotype research has had the unintended side effect of diverting attention away from social psychological issues and methods.

Inconsistencies in Research Findings

The preceding review points to three major goals of gender stereotype research: determining the degree to which characteristics associated with females and males are differentially evaluated, delineating the content of sex stereotypes, and documenting the pervasiveness of beliefs about the sexes.

Virtually all investigators have sought to determine the comparative favorability of the stereotypes for each sex. Most have concluded that the male stereotype is more positively evaluated than the female stereotype (e.g., McKee & Sherriffs, 1957; Broverman et al., 1972). The evidence, however, is much more equivocal than most secondary sources suggest. Because this issue is discussed in depth in Chapter Four, here we simply remind the reader that different methods of comparing stereotype favorability have produced different results. Recall, for example, that although a higher proportion of the male than of the female stereotypic attributes identified by Rosenkrantz and his collaborators (Rosenkrantz et al., 1968) were found to be socially desirable, no difference was obtained when *mean* favorability scores for male-valued and female-valued traits were compared.

What is the content of gender stereotypes? As Table 1 indicates, sex stereotypes as revealed by popular assessment devices are lists of short verbal descriptions of personal attributes. A number of investigators have attempted to summarize these lists. The most popular description of male and female stereotypes has been in terms of the "instrumental–expressive" distinction (e.g., Spence et al., 1974). Other labels have been used (e.g., "competence, rationality, and assertion" and "warmth and expressiveness" [Broverman et al., 1972]; "agency and communion" [Eagly & Steffen, 1984]), often interchangeably (e.g., Spence & Helmreich, 1978). It can be questioned whether these summary labels are, in fact, equivalent.

The issue of stereotype content is closely related to the question of how that content is cognitively represented. The structure of gender stereotypes has been characterized in terms of bipolar *dimensions* of personality (e.g., the Dominance–Submission classification used by Goodenough, 1957), *categories* of attributes associated with one or the other sex (e.g., instrumental and expressive [Spence et al., 1974]), or as a mixture of the two (e.g., in addition to the Dominance–Submission dimension, Goodenough [1957] used the category, "Childbearing"). At this point we simply note the variety of different findings concerning the content and structure of gender stereotypes. These topics are discussed in depth later in the chapter.

Most researchers have concluded that gender stereotypes are pervasive. Typically, this conclusion has been based either on (1) data suggesting that few characteristics or categories of attributes are *not* more often associated with one sex than the other (e.g., Sherriffs & McKee, 1957), or (2) data indicating that large percentages of respondents endorse particular stereotypic beliefs (e.g., Broverman et al., 1972). Although gender stereotypes may be pervasive, the existing research has not adequately established this often-cited conclusion.

With respect to the first type of data described, not all studies obtain convincing results. Some authors fail to employ any statistical criteria in assessing the perception of sex differences (e.g., Sherriffs & McKee, 1957). Others do not always replicate earlier findings (e.g., Cowan & Stewart, 1977).

With regard to data indicating that gender stereotypic beliefs are widely shared, most studies have used fairly homogeneous samples of respondents (usually college students). We have already commented on the data relevant to Broverman et al.'s (1972) statement on this point. We add here two further observations. First, subgroup *differences* (e.g., male vs. female, college students vs. their parents) are not uncommon in the literature. Second, and more importantly, researchers have seldom used methods that provide strong evidence about pervasiveness or consensus across perceivers. The overwhelming majority of samples used by psychologists have been based on convenience, and, because college students are readily available to professors, they are the most often queried. Because parents of college students are also relatively convenient, they are often used in studies aimed at documenting the widespread acceptance of stereotypic beliefs (e.g., Broverman et al., 1972). Although the use of samples of college sophomores (and, in this case, their parents) is an easy (and, thus, common) criticism of psychological research, it is necessary to reiterate here. Documenting the pervasiveness of gender stereotypes requires methods that permit the comparison of subgroups within the general population of interest (for most researchers this appears to be adult Americans).

Sample surveys, in which respondents are selected in such a way that the resulting sample is representative of some clearly specified universe of people, can provide direct evidence concerning the pervasiveness of stereotypes. While acknowledging the shortcomings of survey research (e.g., it is expensive), we urge greater consideration of this methodological tool. We make two specific suggestions: (1) An effort should be made to include items pertinent to gender stereotypes in the General Social Survey and other regularly conducted surveys of samples of respondents representative of adult Americans. (2) Researchers should consider using small-scale telephone surveys, which are relatively inexpensive, to assess beliefs about the sexes (see Del Boca, 1982, for an example).

Problems of Method

As the preceding discussion illustrates, there is more inconsistency among the findings in the gender stereotype literature than most secondary sources indicate. Some of this inconsistency can be attributed to methodological factors: (1) overreliance on a single approach to assessment; (2) variations in the implementation of this approach.

The open-ended, adjective checklist, and rating scale are all self-report measures. And, as generally used, they are highly obtrusive—it is clear to respondents that sex stereotypes are being assessed (see Beere, 1979; 1983). As a consequence, the popular methods of assessing gender stereotypes are susceptible to systematic distortion by such factors as demand characteristics and social desirability responding. The direction of such distortion will depend on a variety of factors, including the nature of the assessment setting (e.g., gender, age, and other characteristics of the researcher, gender composition of the group tested) and local norms.

There has been considerable variation in the manner in which the self-report approach has been implemented. Studies differ in terms of what subjects are asked to describe, how they go about their task, and in how their responses are analyzed. While all studies of gender stereotypes ask subjects to describe a "male" and/or a "female" stimulus, the actual targets used in research differ in a number of ways that are likely to influence the results obtained. A few studies have used the abstract concepts, "masculinity" and "femininity." Many more studies have asked subjects to describe two groups, "men" and "women"; still others request descriptions of particular exemplars of these categories (e.g., the "typical adult male [female]") or ask respondents to create their own individual targets in response to cues such as, "Imagine you are going to meet someone for the first time, and the only thing you know in advance is that he (she) is an adult" (Cowan & Stewart, 1977, p. 207). Compounding the problem is the fact that use of particular types of targets tends to be confounded with response format. For example, group labels are more likely to be used in studies involving an adjective checklist (e.g., Sherriffs & McKee, 1957; Williams & Bennett, 1975), while prototypes (typical instances) are more common in research that employs adjective rating scales. Just what effect such variations in task might have is not entirely clear. The potential for some systematic effect, however, is illustrated by Spence et al.'s (1974) finding that subjects responded less stereotypically to "typical college student" than to "typical adult." Further, there is evidence from Cowan and Stewart (1977) that subjects conjure up a wide variety of different stimuli (e.g., parents, authority figures, media personalities, girlfriends, and boyfriends) when asked to imagine that they are about to meet a male or female stranger.

Related to the issue of target specification is another aspect of the instructional set given to subjects. Some investigators have used instructions that encourage respondents to describe culturally shared stereotypes of the sexes (e.g., Lunneborg, 1970; Williams & Bennett, 1975). Others apparently attempt to elicit the subject's own personal beliefs about women and men. One might expect to observe greater consensus with the former strategy than with the latter.

In addition to differences in *what* subjects are asked to describe, there are also variations in *how* they go about this task. One major difference among methodologies is the degree to which they constrain the subject's response. One form that such constraint takes, the response format, was used to organize the preceding literature review. What is the effect of using an open-ended, adjective checklist, or rating scale procedure? Two studies have attempted to directly compare the effects of using different response formats. Sherriffs and McKee (1957) compared results obtained with open-ended and adjective checklist procedures and argued that they produced consistent results. In a more-recent investigation, Cowan and Stewart (1977) compared all three techniques and concluded that the different assessment procedures produced dramatically different results. Less stereotyping was obtained with the open-ended format than with either of the other two methods. In general, it appears that the more constraints placed on the respondent, the more "stereotyped" the data obtained. Because most gender stereotype research has used methods that constrain subjects, it might be argued that the pervasiveness of gender stereotypes that most writers cite is artifactually inflated.

In addition to influencing the amount of stereotyping that occurs, differences in response format also affect the content of stereotypes revealed. Subjects may simply not think of particular attributes at the time of testing when responding to an open-ended request. Conversely, vocabularies of preselected attributes may not include some important dimensions of person perception. Content categories pertinent to sexuality and intimate female–male relations (e.g., "Sexual Awareness," Sherriffs & McKee, 1957) and to physical appearance emerge in open-ended assessments, yet none of the studies that uses an investigator-provided attribute list identifies these as important components of beliefs regarding women and men. Thus, one benefit of using a nonconstraining open-ended procedure may be the identification of content relevant to the perception of a particular group that tends not to be included in personality inventories.

That major gender stereotype assessment procedures such as the SRSQ and ACL do not include contents that seem to be quite important for male–female relations leads to a broader question: What are the constituent elements of stereotypes? Most research to date has used trait adjectives. Elsewhere (Ashmore & Del Boca, 1979, 1981), we have argued that thinking about women and men involves more than personality traits. Deaux (1982, 1984) and her associates (Deaux and Lewis, 1983) have begun a line of gender stereotype research in which they assess role behaviors, occupations, sexual orientation, and physical appearance as well as traits. They find that not only are these components measureable, but also they are only loosely interconnected.

We believe that this is an important research innovation and that this multicomponent approach to sex stereotypes can be fruitfully extended. As a step in this direction we draw on Huston (1983), who has identified five categories of content pertinent to gender, and Hastie and Carlston (1980), who summarize taxonomies of person descriptors. The components studied by Deaux and her colleagues have parallels in both of these classification systems. In addition, Huston (1983) distinguishes "stylistic and symbolic content" (e.g., gestures, nonverbal behavior), and Hastie and Carlston (1980) include "attitudes, feelings, and beliefs." With respect to this latter type of person information, Birnbaum, Nosanchuk, and Croll (1980) found that preschoolers associated angry faces with males and happy, sad, and fearful facial expressions with females.

In addition to variations in materials and procedures that potentially produce inconsistencies in the gender-stereotype literature, differences in the processing of data, once collected, have implications for research results. Both the content and pervasiveness of gender stereotypes will be affected by the criteria that the researcher establishes for defining the stereotype. These criteria have in practice been highly variable. In some cases, investigators have simply relied on an inspection of the data (e.g., Sherriffs & McKee, 1957); more often, they have established a statistical criterion. Often, frequency of attribution is the sole decision rule. Frequencies required for inclusion of individual items in the stereotype of one or the other sex have ranged from 40% (e.g., Cowan & Stewart, 1977) to 75% (e.g., Rosenkrantz et al., 1968). In some cases, frequencies are computed for the total sample of respondents (e.g., the expanded stereotypes compiled by Williams & Bennett, 1975); in others, the frequency criterion must be met for different subgroupings of the total sample, usually for both male and female subjects (e.g., the "focused stereotypes" defined by Williams & Bennett, 1975). In addition to absolute frequency, the degree to which traits are differentially ascribed to the two sexes has been used as a criterion, sometimes in combination with a frequency requirement as well. Clearly, the less stringent the criteria employed, the more elaborated will be the stereotypes delineated.

Just as we urged development of a standard content analysis scheme for analysis of open-ended data, we propose that standard decision rules be established for defining sex stereotypes. We suggest the multiple cut-points of 33% to 50% of respondents (a sizeable minority of the sample endorsed the item), 50% to 67% (a simple majority endorsed the item), and 67% to 100% (a clear or strong majority felt the descriptor was sex stereotypic).

In summary, two basic problems of measurement have been identified–

over-reliance on self-report procedures, and variations in targets, instructions, and data analysis. We do not urge abandonment of self-report approaches. Rather, we suggest that gender stereotypes be assessed by multiple methodologies and that greater attention be paid to less-obtrusive assessment techniques. Concerning the variations on the currently dominant self-report approach, research explicitly assessing the influence of such variations is needed. The methodological problems discussed here and by other reviewers (cf. Beere, 1979, 1983; Brannon, 1978; Ruble & Ruble, 1982) are important and must be addressed. Our prescription for this area of work, however, is not simply "Do better research." Rather, we believe that more attention to theory is needed and that, in fact, addressing conceptual issues will improve the quality of research.

A Cognitive–Social-Psychological Framework for the Construct, Gender Stereotype

In the preceding section, the accumulated evidence concerning the three major approaches to assessing gender stereotypes was summarized and critiqued. One could stop at this point because this represents a relatively accurate overall picture of extant knowledge concerning how the sexes are perceived. The overarching goal of the present volume, however, is to critically analyze existing concepts and approaches. Because research on gender stereotypes has been instrument-driven and there has been a paucity of conceptual elaboration (cf. Deaux, 1982), such an analysis must involve consideration of broader theoretical issues. To this end, in this section, a cognitive–social-psychological framework for the construct, gender stereotype, is outlined; the remainder of the chapter is devoted to elaborating this framework and demonstrating its heuristic value.

GENDER STEREOTYPE, DEFINED

Gender-stereotype researchers have shown a surprising lack of concern with defining their central construct. Explicit definitions are seldom offered, and when they are, they often occur in parenthetical phrases (cf. Ashmore & Del Boca, 1979). Most researchers have used the term, "sex-role stereotype," not "sex stereotype" or "gender stereotype." We have used and will continue to use the latter pair of terms. Both theoretical treatments (however informal) and measurement operations focus on beliefs about men and women and not about sex roles (cf. Ashmore & Del Boca, 1979, p. 221; Brannon, 1978).

To obtain a generic definition of *sex stereotype*, we inspected the gender and ethnic stereotype literatures (which are clearly the two largest bodies of research and theory concerned with stereotypes) and found four points of agreement.

1.   A stereotype is a cognitive construct. That is, a stereotype is a belief, judgement, perception, expectation, attribution, or assumption. We prefer the term, *belief*, because it is the most general and the most free of excess connotations.

2.   A stereotype is a belief about what members of a particular group are like. Because target groups are socially defined, the term, *social category*, is used to designate the stereotyped object (i.e., group of people). And, *personal attribute* is used to indicate the content of stereotypes. Such content is not limited to personality traits (though these are the most often studied) but, rather, includes other types of personal information (e.g., physical characteristics, expected behaviors) as well.

3.   A stereotype is most often considered a set of beliefs rather than a single belief (see, however, Brigham [1971] regarding ethnic stereotypes and Spence, Helmreich, & Stapp [1974] concerning gender stereotypes).

4.   Although not clear in most definitions of gender stereotypes, many ethnic stereotype workers argue, and we agree, that stereotypes are structured sets of beliefs (cf. Cauthen, Robinson, & Krauss, 1971; Funk, Horowitz, Lipschitz, & Young, 1976; Jones & Ashmore, 1973).

On the basis of these common denominators, we proposed that gender stereotypes be defined as "the structured sets of beliefs about the personal attributes of women and men" (Ashmore & Del Boca, 1979, p. 222).

This generic definition hides three areas of disagreement: the first largely from the ethnic stereotype literature, the other two from definitions of gender stereotype (cf. Ashmore & Del Boca, 1979, 1981). Some workers define ethnic stereotypes as *"bad"* (because they are said to be "incorrect," "overgeneralized," "learned by faulty reasoning," or "rigid"). This notion of badness is not included in the preceding definition for two related reasons: (1) The alleged reasons for stereotypes being bad are best considered as hypotheses or questions for research (e.g., how exactly are beliefs about social categories learned?), not as points of definition. (2) To define stereotypes as bad implies that stereotypes and stereotyping are aberrant or bizarre cognitive structures and processes, and this, in turn, cuts off stereotype research from work on "normal" cognitive activities.

The second area of disagreement revolves around the issue of characteristic versus differentiating attributes. Most gender-stereotype researchers are concerned with perceived *differences* between women and men, whereas ethnic stereotype work is directed at documenting the attributes thought to be *typical* of members of various ethnic groups. This is an important and complicated issue (see Ashmore & Del Boca, 1981, pp. 19–21). Here, we simply note our hunch that stereotypes contain both characteristic and differentiating attributes. How exactly these two types of attributes are represented in memory is a thorny conceptual issue. And, the relative mix of these in various stereotypes is an important empirical question.

The final area of disagreement is more apparent than real. Most gender stereotype workers and most sociologists regard stereotypes as *shared* beliefs. Many psychologists regard stereotypes as "pictures in the head," that is, as *individual-level* phenomena. We believe that both camps are correct and that the issue is really one of level of analysis. We and others (see Ashmore & Del Boca, 1981, p. 19) have urged distinguishing personal (individual-level) from cultural (group-level) stereotypes. Here *stereotype* will be used to mean *personal stereotype*.

SOCIAL COGNITION AND SOCIAL INTERACTION

The personality slant of much extant sex stereotype research has the advantage of highlighting the role of gender in identity formation (see Katz, this volume). However, other functions of stereotypes have not been fully explored. It is particularly important for the present volume to emphasize the cognitive–social psychological functions of gender stereotypes. To this end, Figure 1 depicts a prototypic situation involving two people. This focus was chosen because the unique perspective of social psychology is concerned with the thoughts, feelings, and behavior of the individual in social interaction. As noted in Chapter One, individuals are always embedded in larger social contexts (e.g., families, cultures); these are omitted from the figure simply for clarity of presentation.

The two major components of Figure 1 are the Target and the Actor. The cognitive function of gender stereotypes is embedded in the complex set of cognitive structures (Long-term social memory) and processes (Attention through Response selection) depicted for the Actor. Stereotypes are assumed to be similar to other types of "knowledge" represented in memory—they serve to summarize and organize what the individual has learned about social groups. The social function of gender stereotypes involves both the Actor and the Target. Sex stereotypes not only summarize knowledge about women and men, but they also influence the Actor's (perceiver's) impressions of, and guide her/his behavior toward, specific women and men. In Figure 1, gender stereotypes in Long-term social memory shape how information concerning the Target is processed (e.g., What aspects of the Target's appearance and behavior are attended to or noticed?), which, in turn, influences the Actor's impression of the Target and ultimately how the Actor behaves toward the Target.

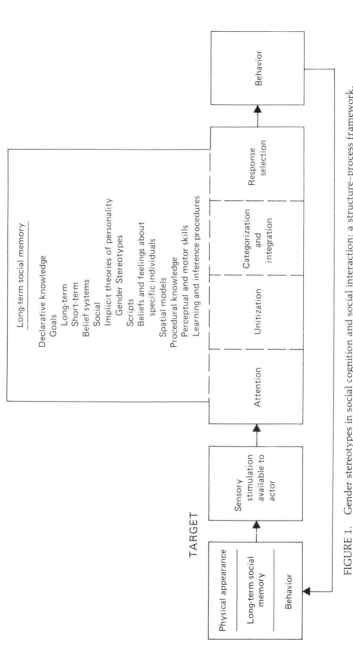

FIGURE 1. Gender stereotypes in social cognition and social interaction: a structure–process framework.

The framework proposed in Figure 1 is similar to and, in fact, draws from several general social cognition models (especially Hastie & Carlston, 1980). It is different, however, in two important respects. First, the present model is of social cognition in social interaction. Most social cognition models describe only what happens in the head of the perceiver. They begin with a vaguely defined input (information or stimulus) and end with a judgment or impression. In the present framework, another person is the Target. And, the Target is assumed to be every bit as much a cognitive creature as the Actor. Thus, the Target has Long-term social memory, including goals such as trying to make sense out of the Actor and trying to present a particular view of self. These and other goals are likely to influence which aspects of the Target's physical appearance and behavior are made public—that is, are accessible to the Actor. Second, the present model includes the Actor's behavior and how this feeds back to impact the Target. Thus, just as the arrows from left to right indicate that the Target influences the Actor, the right-to-left arrow at the bottom of the figure depicts the influence of the Actor on the Target.

In sum, it is here proposed that gender stereotypes be considered within a cognitive–social psychological framework that focuses on the cognitive activities of individuals in mutually influencing social interaction. In describing the utility of this framework, we draw on the emerging field of social cognition. As noted in Chapter One, we do not regard "social cognition" as referring only to work that applies the theory and methods of cognitive psychology to social objects and phenomena. Rather, we take a catholic view of the field, utilizing work based on a wide variety of theoretical and empirical approaches.

For the sake of clarity of presentation it is possible to distinguish structure and process as the two fundamental issues of social cognition. *Structure* refers to the question of how social information or knowledge is internally represented. *Process* denotes three interrelated topics: How are internal representations acquired? How does internally represented knowledge influence the processing of "new" social information? When and why do internal representations change? The structure and process aspects of gender stereotypes are taken up, in turn, in the next two sections of the chapter.

The Structure of Gender Stereotypes

Although a wide variety of models of long-term memory have been proposed, most researchers would probably agree with the following definition, "the 'repository' of our more permanent knowledge and skills" (Bower, 1975, p. 57). There is also considerable agreement, at least at the most general level, about the contents of long-term memory, and these are depicted in Figure 1. Two basic types of content are distinguished: declarative knowledge (*knowing that*, or the set of things one takes to be true and that can most often be verbalized, e.g., "Raspberries are expensive") and procedural knowledge (*knowing how*, also termed *cognitive skill*, which often cannot be verbalized) (cf. Anderson, 1980, pp. 222–226). Declarative knowledge is emphasized here because gender stereotypes are considered to be part of an individual's stock of "facts" (not necessarily veridical but beliefs that the perceiver regards as true). Declarative knowledge is partitioned into goals, belief systems, and spatial models. The last of these, spatial models, comprises the knowledge the individual has about various physical spaces. No more is said about spatial models; they are included primarily for completeness. Goals and belief systems, however, are quite important to understanding how the sexes are cognized.

Goals are things that the individual values and strives toward. Rokeach (1973) distinguishes terminal from instrumental values. The former refer to desired end-states that can never be realized but can be striven for (e.g., a world of beauty, a world at peace). Instrumental values are desired ways of behaving (e.g., being polite or creative). In Figure 1, two types of goals have been differentiated on the basis of time frame—long-term and short-term (e.g., our major short-term goal is to complete this chapter; one of our long-term goals is to be respected scholar-researchers). Goals are hypothesized to be important determinants of beliefs about the sexes, especially in shaping what types of women and men are perceptually distinguished (e.g., a 15 year-old boy, one of whose goals is to date, may discriminate girls very precisely along a physical attractiveness continuum, hence the notion of "a 10" . . . and lesser values).

The third and final type of declarative knowledge is belief systems. Most cognitive psychologists would use the term, *knowledge*, or *world knowledge*, and, in their general model of social cognition, Hastie and Carlston (1980) label this as, "general social knowledge." We follow Norman (1981b) in preferring *belief system* because this rubric stresses the organized nature of the stored knowledge and because it more clearly links individual belief systems with shared or cultural systems of belief.

The types of belief systems listed in Figure 1 are not exhaustive and are slanted toward thinking about women and men. In earlier treatments, we rephrased the preceding generic definition of gender stereotypes in implicit personality theory (IPT) terms as, "*The structured sets of inferential relations that link personal attributes to the social categories female and male*" (Ashmore & Del Boca, 1979, p. 225; italics in original) and suggested that "sex stereotypes—and, by extension, beliefs about ethnic groups and other social categories—are but one aspect of an individual's overall cognitive scheme for making sense out of other people (i.e., one aspect of the individual's 'implicit personality theory')" (Ashmore, 1981, p. 40). While retaining this basic IPT formulation, we add to it by suggesting that other types of knowledge are important to understanding how women and men are cognized.

In addition to implicit theories, there are three other types of belief systems relevant to thinking about men and women—social belief systems, scripts, and beliefs and feelings about specific individuals. Social belief systems are quite similar to implicit theories; both, in fact, can be thought of as *schemas*, "large complex units of knowledge that organize much of what we know about general categories of objects, classes of events, and types of people" (Anderson, 1980, p. 128). The term, *implicit theories*, is used to refer to generalized or abstract knowledge structures about people, what they are made of, how they develop and change, how and why they break down (cf. Wegner & Vallacher, 1977). There are other schemas, here termed, *social belief systems*, that may be relevant to perception of the sexes. Just as we have beliefs about people (which are clearly pertinent to the present topic) and about physical nature (e.g., "it is possible to walk on an asphalt road but not on water or a cloud," which are generally not relevant), we have belief systems concerned with society, and these indirectly involve men and women. For example, from approximately the mid-1800s until quite recently, mainstream American culture specified that the family comprised the father, who was the provider, a wife, who nurtured, and children, who—depending on family circumstance and child gender—either helped with family maintenance or simply grew up (cf. Bernard, 1981). This view of the family was not held by all Americans, not even all white middle-class Americans. It was, however, widely shared and has obvious implications for how the sexes are perceived. In addition to beliefs about the family, people have organized knowledge structures concerning economics, politics, and so on, and these may implicate the sexes.

The final two types of belief systems, scripts, and beliefs and feelings about specific individuals are specific rather than general. *Scripts* are expected action sequences in specific settings. That is, a script is a "coherent sequence of events expected by an individual, involving him either as a participant or an observer" (Abelson, 1976, p. 33). Most importantly for present purposes, scripts have slots and roles specifying who or what kind of person can fill each slot. For example, at least until the mid-1970s in American society, the "opening-a-door-for-another" script specified that if a man and a woman approached a door together he would open it, and she would precede him through it.

The final type of belief system, *beliefs and feelings about specific women and men*, is quite similar to Hastie and Carlston's (1980) "Event Memory," which they hypothesize "to serve as a storehouse for descriptions of temporally located events and individuals" (p. 8). (The other belief systems here distinguished would be seen by these authors as part of what they term "Conceptual Memory.") Individuals are here stressed over events simply because the present focus is on thinking about people. We highlight three things about beliefs and feelings about specific women and men. First, there are separate storage areas in long-term memory for the social categories men and women (and gender subtypes) and for specific women and men (cf. Higgins, Kuiper, & Olson, 1981, p. 399). An important implication of this is that an individual's gender stereotypes may be inconsistent with his or her ideas about specific females and males. Second, while separate, these are interrelated and interconnected. Specific women and men may figure prominently in the cognitive representation of social categories—for example, Bo Derek may, for some men, be the prototype for "beautiful women." Third, it is assumed that beliefs and feelings about specific individuals are organized, probably in a variety of different ways—for example, temporally (when met, what period of life known), degree of acquaintance (by reputation, acquaintance, friend, intimate), feeling tone (uncomfortable–comfortable), social category (female–male, black–white).

In summary, gender stereotypes have been placed in the context of social cognition and social interaction. Sex stereotypes are part of long-term social memory. More specifically, stereotypic conceptions of the sexes are regarded to be part of an individual's implicit theory of personality. In addition to gender stereotypes, there is considerable other knowledge pertinent to male–female relations in long-term social memory. This knowledge is embedded, often implicitly, in social belief systems, scripts, and beliefs and feelings about specific individuals. Though these various types of gender knowledge, including stereotypes, are interrelated, they are separate. For example, in the opening-the-door script, the man does not (necessarily) open the door because his female stereotype specifies that women are too weak or incompetent to open doors. Rather, the script is an overlearned sequence of behaviors that is engaged by situational cues and is most often performed "mindlessly."

EXPANDING THE GENDER-STEREOTYPE LITERATURE

At the outset, it was indicated that a large number of gender stereotype studies have been conducted. Why, then, should the literature be expanded? We do not mean doing more research of the same type. Rather, we draw on our methodological critique of the extant studies and our proposed cognitive–social-psychological framework to propose two new directions in research. The first is a call to develop methods for exploring the aforementioned various types of gender knowledge. The second new direction involves using person perception research methods to assess, in a relatively unobtrusive fashion, beliefs about men and women. This approach is described in some depth because it follows directly from the proposed conceptual framework and, at the same time, addresses a major methodological problem of the existing assessment procedures.

Self-report instruments such as the SRSQ are highly obtrusive and, as a consequence, subject to conscious and nonconscious distortion. Thus, it is necessary to develop less reactive ways of assessing beliefs about the sexes. Such techniques are available, and two are discussed here. One advantage of couching gender stereotypes in terms of social cognition is that the methods employed in this field become available to those concerned with female-male relations. Rosenberg and Sedlak (1972) distinguish two basic approaches to uncovering and representing implicit theories of personality —trait inference and personality description. These same approaches can be used to assess beliefs about the sexes. And, trait inference and personality description tasks focus the respondent's attention on drawing inferences from small amounts of information about a target or accurately describing a specific person not on revealing one's beliefs about the sexes. From the subject's perspective, then, these are not measures of gender stereotypes and, as a consequence, they are less reactive than the methods considered thus far.

In order to illustrate the trait inference approach to gender stereotype assessment, Del Boca and Ashmore (1980b, Study One) conducted an extended replication of Asch's (1946) *warm–cold* experiment. Subjects were asked to form an impression of either a man or a woman who was said to possess a set of intellectually positive or negative attributes (e.g., *intelligent* vs. *unintelligent*) and to be either *warm* or *cold*. The male target was perceived to be higher in intellectual desirability (e.g., *scientific–unscientific*), the female higher on communion (e.g., *generous–selfish*), with no sex of target effect for potency, social desirability, or agency. In addition to these sex stereotype effects, there were very strong differences in impression as a function of the trait information provided. In fact, it appeared that the trait information, which was extreme, visually salient, and stressed in the instructions, may have swamped the effect of sex of target. Thus, a second experiment was conducted in which sex was manipulated in the context of traits that are less evaluatively polarized. Again, the male target was seen as higher in intellectual desirability. The male target was also rated higher in potency (e.g., *weak–strong*); no differences were found for social desirability, activity, and agency. Taken together, the two studies suggest that females and males are seen to be different along a continuum that combines intellectual desirability and potency, with males perceived as hard-headed and interpersonally dominating (or controlling) and females regarded as soft-hearted and interpersonally submissive (or controlled).

Although not phrased as trait inference assessments of gender stereotypes, there have been a relatively large number of studies conducted in which sex of target is manipulated and subjects' impressions recorded. To date, the accumulated literature shows that "sex makes a difference" (Wallston & O'Leary, 1981), but the difference is not simple. The next generation of research in this area will need to more carefully specify the nature of other information about the target, as well as the conditions and context of the impression-formation situation.

Although the trait-inference approach has the advantage of being relatively unobtrusive, it has the disadvantage of not being especially useful in representing stereotypes as *structured* sets of beliefs. The second major IPT method, personality description, can provide information on cognitive structure. In the personality description approach, subjects are asked to describe people using any of a variety of procedures (e.g., open ended, checklist). On the basis of these descriptions, dissimilarity scores are calculated between all pairs of descriptors under the assumption that descriptors assigned to the same target are psychologically similar or close, whereas items seldom used to describe the same person are psychologically dissimilar or distant. The resulting dissimilarity matrix is then used as input to various multivariate computerized algorithms that seek to uncover and represent in some easy-to-comprehend fashion the underlying structure in the data. Two of the most commonly used methods of analysis are multidimensional scaling and hierarchical clustering (cf. Rosenberg & Sedlak, 1972). The multidimensional scaling algorithm seeks to position the descriptors as points in a multidimensional (usually Euclidian) space so that the distance between descriptors is the best possible fit to the input dissimilarity data. As a consequence, scaling is quite good at representing the overall structure of a set of descriptors.

Hierarchical clustering seeks to partition the descriptors into relatively homogeneous groups (clusters) which are, in turn, combined to form higher-order groupings, until at the conclusion of the algorithm, all items are collapsed into one cluster. Clustering represents the descriptors in terms of a tree diagram. Because the clustering algorithm begins by placing highly similar descriptors together and then building on these initial groupings, it is very useful for uncovering local structure within the "big picture" revealed by scaling (cf. Ashmore, 1981, pp. 42–43).

To demonstrate the utility of the personality-description approach, Ashmore and Tumia (1980) asked subjects to describe people, using 66 trait adjectives drawn from previous person perception research. Dissimilarity scores were calculated and inputted to multidimensional scaling. A two-dimensional configuration accounted quite well for the dissimilarity data. One dimension could be called "social evaluation," anchored at one end by such good social traits as *warm* and *sociable* and at the other end by bad social attributes (e.g., cold). Roughly orthogonal to the social-evaluation dimension was potency (i.e., soft–hard). Thus, subjects seemed to organize the descriptors, and presumably the people described by them, in terms of two relatively unrelated cognitive distinctions: social good–bad and soft–hard. After subjects had completed the person-description task, Ashmore and Tumia asked them to indicate the sex of each person they had described. Thus, it was possible to assess whether the descriptors were assigned consistently to one sex or the other. And they were. Men were more often described by hard traits (e.g., practical, critical) and women by soft traits (e.g., sentimental, wavering). In fact, the cognitive distinctions soft–hard and female–male were almost coterminous. This basic finding, which is quite consistent with the results from the trait inference approach, was replicated using a new sample of subjects and a different vocabulary (cf. Ashmore, 1981).

The dissimilarity data in each personality-description study was also used as input to the hierarchical clustering algorithm. For both data sets, there were clusters of items that were used consistently by subjects to describe one sex or the other. These clusters are interpreted as evidence of gender subtypes. That is, they indicate that subjects not only distinguish the general categories female and male but also discriminate types of women and types of men. Considering both studies, there is evidence that male college students (but not females) distinguish an "outgoing" type of woman (e.g., sociable, cheerful) and a "hardworker" type of man (e.g., determined, persistent). Females (but not males) identify a "weak woman" subtype. Both sexes have a "nurturant woman" type (e.g., trusting, patient, sympathetic).

What We Know and Need to Know about the Structure of Gender Stereotypes

Because most research has focused on assessment, there is a considerable amount of information on the content of gender stereotypes. There are, however, many loose ends concerning how the sexes are perceived. In this section, two important structure topics, both involving a mix of "known" and "need-to-know," are discussed: (1) the overall content and structure of gender stereotypes, and (2) gender subtypes.

The Overall Content and Structure of Gender Stereotypes

Much stereotype research has been aimed at documenting that particular lists of personality traits are perceived to be characteristic of men and of women. As noted, however, not all workers have been content to establish lists of sex stereotypes. They have gone beyond the list approach by attempting to describe in some summary fashion the content or meaning of stereotypic conceptions and have sought to demonstrate how the male and female stereotypes are related. Clearly the most popular has been to adopt or slightly modify Parson's instrumental–expressive distinction. Further, it is usually concluded that instrumentality and expressiveness are orthogonal dimensions. We would argue that this is not the whole story.

Our basic argument is quite simple—the preceding summaries ignore the dark side of gender stereotypes.[3] The pictures of both sexes are positive; they differ only in how men and women are good. We would argue on both logical and empirical grounds that stereotypes do not contain only positive elements. On logical grounds the evaluative dimension (from good to bad) is simply too ubiquitous an aspect of human thinking–feeling (cf. Osgood, May, and Miron, 1975; White, 1980) not to be involved in beliefs about the sexes. On empirical grounds, two quite independent lines of research are most relevant—the aforementioned open-ended study by Sherriffs and McKee (1957) and our own multidimensional scaling work. In a follow-up to the former study, McKee and Sherriffs (1957) asked subjects to rate each descriptor as favorable, neutral, or unfavorable. Consistent with the decision of many workers to accentuate the positive, both men and women were regarded favorably. That is, the descriptors generated as characteristic of each sex were seen as more favorable than unfavorable. However, congruent with the present position, there were plenty of unfavorable attributes thought to characterize women and men.

The multidimensional scaling analysis of each of our two person description studies revealed that a two-dimensional configuration adequately captured the information in the dissimilarity data and that the structure of the configuration could be interpreted in terms of two roughly orthogonal continua—social good–bad and female–male. The former was quite close to good–bad (generalized Evaluation or E) and the latter close to soft–hard

---

[3]Workers who use the instrumental–expressive distinction are not unaware of negative attributes in sex stereotypes. Rather, by using these positive labels, they wish to emphasize that beliefs about the sexes are related to sex roles or "shoulds" for men and women (see Spence, Deaux, & Helmreich, 1985).

(Potency or P), which are the first two dimensions consistently revealed in semantic differential research (cf. Osgood, May, & Miron, 1975).

These multidimensional scaling results suggest two conclusions about the overall structure and content of gender stereotypes. First, beliefs about the sexes can be placed in the context of a fairly general model of person perception involving two orthogonal dimensions, which for the moment are referred to as Evaluation and Potency.[4] This conclusion is supported by semantic differential research. The adjective pair, masculine–feminine consistently loads high on the Potency factor (and not on Evaluation or the third semantic differential factor, Activity). More directly pertinent, man and male differ most radically from woman and female on the Potency dimension. All four terms are rated high on Activity, and all four are positively evaluated, with the female terms rated somewhat higher (cf. Snider & Osgood, 1969).

The proposed general model is also consistent with results obtained from more traditional methods of gender stereotype assessment. Best, et al. (1980) correlated E, P, and A ratings of Gough's adjectives with their sex stereotype index (SSI). Evaluation and SSI were essentially uncorrelated, but the latter was significantly correlated with P and A ($r = .31, .35$, respectively). Best et al. (1980) conclude that Activity is the core affective meaning of gender stereotypes. We believe that, while the sexes may be perceived to differ along an active–passive continuum, the accumulated evidence supports Potency as the more central differentiation.

Second, a point that has been touched on, but that deserves independent emphasis, men and women are perceived to differ in terms of hard–soft or strong–weak (P) but not good–bad (E). This seems inconsistent with the often-reached conclusion that the male stereotype is more positive than the female stereotype. The discrepancy, however, is more apparent than real. If the *average* evaluative scale score of the descriptors in the male stereotype are compared with the *average* value of the female stereotype items, there is not a significant difference. However, the number of positive attributes thought to characterize men is greater than the number of socially desirable items in the female stereotype.

The foregoing suggests that the overall content and structure of gender

---

[4]This two-dimensional framework is based on aggregate data, and it is assumed that the two cognitive distinctions we have identified make sense to the modal subject (cf. Funk et al., 1976). However, because wide individual differences are expected, variations on this framework are necessary (see Ashmore, 1981, pp. 72–73). Further, the elements of this general model are personality descriptors. Deaux and Lewis (1985) do find that within the trait domain, the male and female stereotypes are negatively correlated. However, this bipolar structure does not hold for other stereotype components (e.g., occupations) in their data.

stereotypes can be summarized as female = soft and male = hard where hard–soft serves to define the bipolar potency dimension of IPT. Are views of the sexes reducible to P? Yes and no. On the affirmative side, the potency dimension is a cultural metaphor for gender, and it is a "metaphor we live by" (Lakoff & Johnson, 1980). Males are perceived as hard objects ("hard as a rock") and as such they "affect," "impact," "intrude," "don't change," "don't afford comfort," and "can hurt." Females are thought of as soft objects ("soft as a flower"); they are "affected," "impacted," "intruded," and they "change," "afford comfort," and "can soothe."

In addition to being a cultural metaphor, Potency serves as a surrogate for two highly correlated dimensions: dominance versus submission and controlling versus controlled. Adapting and extending White's (1980) argument, these dimensions "reflect inferences about the way others will act and expectations about the likely course of interpersonal relations" (Ashmore, 1981, p. 72). Specifically, male is associated with dominance (males are expected to lead) and controlling (males control others and themselves, e.g., their emotions); female is associated with submission (dependent) and controlled (by others and their emotions, e.g., excitable in a minor crisis). Thus, dominance/controlling versus submission/controlled, with P as its surrogate, encode broad yet behaviorally relevant assumptions about the sexes.

Though the present summary has much to recommend it, there are several loose ends. Most important from our point of view is that the male = hard versus female = soft summary is incomplete and to a degree misleading. It is incomplete because it leaves out the very important domain of sexuality. The major sex-stereotype assessment devices and our own person perception approach convey very little about women and men as sexual beings. In part, this is because describing others in sexual terms often involves so-called "dirty words" and such words are most likely to be expressed in speech (rather than in writing) and in informal (rather than formal) settings. A related reason is the concern with personality traits as the major (almost the sole) building block of stereotypes. In addition to adjectives, people can be described with nouns. The use of nouns to categorize raises the possibility that perceivers partition the overarching categories female and male into subcategories, and that these are named with nouns. We turn now to this issue.

Types of Women and Men

Although most research to date has been aimed at demonstrating two different gender stereotypes (one male, the other female), there is reason to believe that perceivers distinguish different categories or types of women and men. Most of the work to be cited in this section has not been regarded by the researcher or others as concerned with sex stereotypes. It is, however, relevant to how the sexes are cognized and, thus, should be brought into the gender stereotype literature.

On logical grounds, it is not functional for an individual to ignore (not "see") differences within each gender. Women and men are large and heterogeneous categories. Within each category, there are subcategories created by demographic variables (e.g., age, race, region, socioeconomic status) that cross-cut gender. And, women and men do not fill simple, nonoverlapping roles (see Staines & Libby, this volume). If stereotypes are to be at all functional (i.e., if they are to summarize knowledge about and guide behavior toward a social category and its members), then individuals must distinguish gender subtypes. This does not mean that the two categories are accurately perceived or that attributes associated with gender subtypes are valid.

There is a considerable amount of work relevant to gender subtypes that combines logical with empirical analysis. Psychoanalytic theorists (e.g., Lifton, 1967), historians (e.g., Hunter, 1976), sociologists (e.g., Komarovsky, 1946), and journalists (e.g., Goodman, 1979) have used a variety of procedures to identify types of men and women. Three points about these analyses deserve emphasis. First, the types distinguished vary considerably in terms of degree of abstractness (from Klein's [1950] "mother" and "courtesan" to the "hard-to-get woman" of Walster, Walster, Piliavin, & Schmidt [1973]).

Second, most of the work has been directed at subtypes of women. This differential emphasis is one manifestation of the overall pattern (noted in Chapter One) of researchers and lay persons seeing women as either the "problematic" category or as the group ignored in the past. Either point of view leads to concern about the study of women.

Third, the content of male and female types identified in previous research is instructive. Our reading of subtype names derived from work directly concerned with identifying types of women and men and from other research that focused on social types more generally (cf. Heise, 1979; Klapp, 1972) suggests that three categories capture the underlying meanings of the terms "traditional" (e.g., "nurturer" and "working man"), "nontraditional" (e.g., "women's libber" and "modern man"), and "sexual." The first two make sense—people need to have a vocabulary for describing both what is established and what is problematic or changing. The sexual category demonstrates a major blind spot in existing gender stereotype research: Sexuality is certainly relevant to female–male relations, but it is absent from most gender stereotype lists, especially those derived from adjective checklists and rating scales.

Concerning empirically derived gender subtypes, there are but two lines of research[5]—our own work (described earlier) utilizing hierarchical clustering analysis of person description data and the "folk model approach to the study of gender knowledge" undertaken by Holland and Davidson (1983). Guided by a cognitive anthropological perspective, they used a two-step procedure to explore "American folk models of gender." First, respondents were asked to name types of males and females. Second, a reduced-yet-representative set of female and male types was derived from the interview data. The female types were presented to male respondents and the male types to females, who were asked to sort them into piles on the basis of similarity. As with the sorting task data described earlier, dissimilarity scores were calculated and used as input to a multidimensional scaling program.

Although the results are complicated, it is possible to phrase the following summary: Females apparently distinguish male types in terms of (1) a good–bad dimension ("boyfriend" vs. "nurd" and "prick"); (2) a difference between men who do versus do not stress sex differences ("Don Juan" vs. "boy"); (3) a distinction between overt and not overt sexuality ("gays" vs. "guys"). The female types also seemed to be organized in terms of three distinctions: (1) likeable types (e.g., "honey") versus unlikeable ones, where the latter could be partitioned into those who are overly dependent (e.g., "airhead") or domineering (e.g., "bitch"); (2) attractive, good-to-be-seen-with women (e.g., "fox," "doll") versus those not to be seen with (e.g., "slut"); (3) a sexy–not sexy dimension (with negative types such as "whore" similar to the positive "fox" in being sexy, whereas "dog" and "down-to-earth girl" were not seen as sexy). While this is an initial investigation, it clearly suggests that people can and do distinguish gender subtypes and that these are cognitively organized. Further, the types and organizing dimensions used by this young adult sample are heavily laced with sexuality.

With few exceptions (e.g., Kutner & Brogan, 1974), this theme of sexuality has been ignored by psychologists concerned with gender stereotypes. It has not, however, been ignored by linguists, especially feminist linguists. There is, in fact, a large literature on how language denigrates women, and work on sexual female subtype names is an important part of this literature (cf. Thorne & Henley, 1975). For example, Schulz (1975) has identified 1000 English words that subcategorize women in sexual terms. Two directions for the social psychological analysis of sexuality and gender stereotypes seem

[5]Rosch's work on natural object categories, especially the notion of a basic level of categorization, has sparked interest among person-perception researchers (e.g., Brewer, Dull, & Lui, 1981). There has been speculation about a basic level for beliefs about the sexes (e.g., Taylor, 1981), and Deaux, Winton, Crowley, and Lewis (in press) have collected relevant data. Their results, however, were not positive. Further, the logic of a basic level of categorization for social objects is questionable (cf. Lingle, Altom, & Medin, 1984).

necessary. First, we need to know which of the sexual subtypes identified by linguists are part of people's active vocabulary (i.e., which labels do people understand and use?) and how these are cognitively organized. One possibility is to have respondents use the Holland and Davidson (1983) sorting procedure, with type names identified by means of linguistic analysis. Second, we need to explore how gender subtype labels are used in everyday social interaction. This requires use of participant observation methods that are quite foreign to most psychologists. It may also be possible to create laboratory analogues of "bull sessions" or "locker-room" talk.

Two important questions remain for a cognitive–social–psychological analysis of gender subtypes: How are they represented in long-term social memory? How do they develop and why do they change? Holland and Davidson (1983) depicted gender subtypes as points in multidimensional space. There are problems with this way of representing cognitive structure (cf. Lingle, Altom, & Medin, 1984). Our approach, relying on clustering analysis, also has drawbacks.

The use of hierarchical clustering to identify gender subtypes implies that the varieties of men and women perceptually distinguished by observers are neatly subsumed under the overarching categories men and women. Whereas nonsocial natural categories generally can be organized in terms of clear semantic hierarchies (e.g., animal can be partitioned into mammals, etc., with mammals further subdivided into humans, etc.), this is not the case with social categories (cf. Holyoak & Gordon, 1984; Lingle et al., 1984). One problem is overlapping categories—for example, in Holland and Davidson's scaling of male types, "brain" and "sissy" are not close in space and are not likely to fall into the same cluster, yet it is possible for a target to be both a "brain" and a "sissy." Another problem is that gender subtypes do not always resemble the general categories of which they are supposedly a part. For example, the category female is regarded as soft, submissive, and controlled, but a "castrating bitch" is certainly none of these things. Two directions seem possibly fruitful in addressing these issues: (1) Construing nonfitting types as violations of particular expectations and describing how fitting types can be transformed to arrive at the nonfitting ones. For example, *aggressiveness* and *assertiveness*, which are expected in a man, are encoded as such; in a woman, however, they are unexpected and may be transformed in two ways—made extreme ("She doesn't just want to have power; she wants to render me powerless") and made negative (*aggressiveness* becomes *interpersonally violent*). (2) Developing clustering algorithms that do not produce a single hierarchy with strict set-inclusion relations. Shepard and Arabie's (1979) ADCLUS is one such method that represents similarity data in terms of overlapping, nonhierarchical clusters.

There is one final question about gender subtypes: How are they to be accounted for? It is possible that the process of creating subtypes can be understood in terms of summarizing "what is" and "what should be," on the one hand, and explaining anomalous and threatening events on the other. We have argued (Ashmore, 1981; Ashmore & Del Boca, 1979) that personal goals play a major role in determining what types a person distinguishes. For example, a grade school teacher who must maintain classroom order as well as teach intellectual skills probably distinguishes several different types of disruptive boys—"normal–rambunctious," "can't sit still," "hyperactive," "delinquent." This "is/should be" approach is complemented by Taylor's (1981, see especially pp. 106–107) accounting for gender subtypes in terms of responses to individuals who do not fit expectations based on the broad categories female and male: "Disconfirmations simply provide a basis for splitting off a new stereotype, not revising an old one" (p. 106). For example, while males are expected to be strong and aggressive, a perceiver who encounters a man who behaves in a consistently weak and nonaggressive manner may account for this by categorizing the target person as a "wimp" or "sissy."

In addition to using this "is/should be" framework to predict what types exist and emerge as new situations arise, we suggest a conceptual issue that requires attention. Basically, this is the question of how new types (occasioned by disconfirming individuals or changing societal conditions) are integrated into existing belief systems. Taylor (1981) implies that these new types are simply added to some sort of a list. In other words, an individual's gender belief system gets bigger as subtypes are created. Holland and Davidson (1983) take an almost opposing approach—"the folk model has a capacity for absorbing new subtypes . . . Because of this capacity . . . the folk model of gender is likely to be quite stable" (p. 29, mimeo). In Piagetian terms, Taylor emphasizes accommodation (really a form thereof), whereas Holland and Davidson stress assimilation. The process of generating and maintaining gender subtypes is probably some complex mixture of accommodation (i.e., modifying existing belief systems in the light of new information) and assimilation (i.e., making new instances fit with existing structures). The preceding notion of transformations may be a useful way of conceptualizing this assimilation–accommodation process.

The Process Issues of Gender Stereotypes

The bulk of gender stereotype research, which has been concerned with content and measurement, has contributed substantially to our understanding of how the sexes are perceived. It is our belief, however, that a greater emphasis on process issues would bring significant dividends. To this end, we have added the present section. Much of the work to be covered is not labelled as gender stereotype; rather, it has in most cases been produced by researchers concerned with other issues, ranging from very applied questions (e.g., "Does TV influence viewers?") to basic work on social perception and stereotyping. The process-oriented approach of these workers can improve research and theory explicitly concerned with stereotypic conceptions of the sexes. And, in turn, process models will become enhanced by coming to grips with specific real-world instances of stereotyping. The review of process questions is organized in terms of the life history of gender stereotypes held by an individual: (1) How are beliefs about the sexes acquired? (2) How are gender stereotypes used in day-to-day functioning, especially in interpersonal relations? (3) How are stereotypic conceptions changed?

THE ACQUISITION OF GENDER STEREOTYPES

Surprisingly little is known about how children learn gender stereotypes. There is research directed at assessing at what ages children know various things about gender—for example, At what age do children correctly label self and others in terms of gender? (cf. Del Boca & Ashmore, 1980a; Huston, 1983; Ruble & Ruble, 1982). There is also work indicating that parents, teachers, pediatricians, and other adults who interact with children have different beliefs about boys and girls. And, there is evidence that adults treat boys and girls differently (see Block, 1976, 1979, and Katz, this volume, but also Maccoby & Jacklin, 1974, for a dissenting view). Finally, a large number of investigators have documented that the cultural representations (in books and newspapers, on billboards and television shows) of the sexes are not the same and that often men and women are portrayed in line with traditional roles. Certainly these and other literatures are relevant to the acquisition of stereotypes, but very little research has been directed at the learning process itself. Why?

There are two major reasons for the paucity of work on stereotype acquisition. First, such research is difficult to conduct. For example, the researcher needs to assess not only parents' beliefs (or television portrayals or . . .), but also how these are conveyed to the child, how the child decodes the message, how the particular message of interest interacts with other inputs, and finally what the child comes to believe. (Finding a means of assessing what the child [especially the very young child] believes is often a very difficult task.) Further, longitudinal research seems the design of choice, and yet such work is extremely complicated and time consuming under the best of circumstances.

Second, we conjecture that most researchers have not studied acquisition directly because they feel they know the answer already. As noted, most sex-stereotype research has been guided by a sociocultural orientation. According to this perspective, individuals learn stereotypes during socialization. Parents, teachers, the media, and so on are all said to "teach" culture. How exactly this is done is seldom addressed. This blindness about culture is not just the case among gender-stereotype workers. Schwartz (1978) has argued persuasively that cultural anthropologists themselves have failed to adequately address the issue of how culture is acquired.

Although there is little acquisition research to report, there are three developments that promise future dividends. First, family researchers are increasingly adopting a cognitive and systems orientation to their subject matter (see Ashmore & Brodzinsky, in press; Bacon & Ashmore, in press). That is, the traditional paradigm, which assumed that parents (largely by rewards and punishments and modelling) "taught" things to children who over time "developed," is being replaced by a conceptual framework that stresses the mutual influence of all family members (e.g., children can shape parents) and the cognitive activities of all family members. This framework seems especially suited to fostering the needed research on how the family socializes gender stereotypes in children.

The second potentially important development is a coming of age of television research. Until the 1970s, work concentrated on the audience (Who watches TV?), content (What do they see?), and, to a lesser extent, effects (Are they influenced by what they see?). While such research continues, since the mid-1970s, there has been a movement toward a concern with process issues. Actually two movements are identifiable.

One, termed the "uses and gratifications approach," seeks to explicate the factors that shape viewer preferences (Why do people watch what they do?). Although there are many valid criticisms of the implementation of this approach (cf. Dorr, 1982, pp. 73–75), the basic premise, that viewers are active "choosers" regarding television content and that such choosing can be linked to psychological factors (e.g., "Goals" in Figure 1), is sensible and is likely to lead to informative research.

The second approach, which might be termed the "cognitive-processing perspective" (Collins, 1982, p. 9), is concerned with the process of learning from television. Workers taking this approach seek to understand how what the perceiver brings to viewing situations (essentially long-term social memory, including goals, belief systems, and skills) interacts with what is portrayed to produce "learning." This direction is certainly congruent with our view of (wo)man's cognitive side. There is also increasing appreciation by some television researchers that TV watching does not occur in a vacuum. In particular, the influence of television content will depend on the social environment surrounding the viewer (cf. Hawkins & Pingree, 1982).

To date, these advances in television research have not had much impact on workers concerned with the medium and male–female relations. "Content analyses abound" (Greenberg, 1982, p. 181), and the following seem legitimate conclusions: (1) Male characters outnumber females by about 3 to 1, and this has not changed much since the 1950s. The male to female ratio varies as a function of show type, with situation comedies and soap operas the most egalitarian (1:1 ratios) and detective–police dramas and Saturday a.m. cartoons most male dominated (ratios of 5:1 and 4:1, respectively). (2) Male characters are associated with the world of work (about ⅔ of TV's women are "unemployed"), whereas female characters are associated with the family (women are more likely to play central roles in family dramas). (3) Male characters are seen to have the following traits: rational, smart, powerful, stable, tolerant; female characters are seen to be attractive, happy, warm, sociable, peaceful, fair (cf. Greenberg, 1982).

The effects of television viewing are considerably less clear. Greenberg (1982) concludes that higher amounts of watching TV are associated with more sex stereotyping. Hawkins and Pingree (1982, see especially Footnote 5, p. 238) seem to agree with this conclusion; but, of the three studies summarized by these researchers, one (by Gerbner & Signorelli, 1979) found that amount of TV viewing and sexism were negatively related in some demographic subgroups. Further, in the only published longitudinal study of television exposure and female–male beliefs, Morgan (1982) found that amount of TV viewing was predictive of sex-role stereotypes (his index contained both gender stereotype and gender-related attitude items from the present perspective) for adolescent females but not males. In sum, the differential portrayal of the sexes (especially the greater prominence of males) seems clear, but whether TV content affects individual beliefs and how this occurs remain open issues (cf. Huston, 1983). The aforementioned emerging process-oriented approaches to TV viewing might well help to fill in these relatively unknown areas.

The third and final current development that may be useful in conceptualizing and studying the learning of sex stereotypes is the turning toward acquisition issues by cognitive social psychologists (cf. Higgins et al., 1981; Holyoak & Gordon, 1984). At present, most of this is in the form of speculation and not completed and replicated empirical research. We note just one example. Holyoak and Gordon (1984) argue that social cognition is particularly concerned with social interaction and interpersonal behavior (in contrast with cognitive psychology's focus on the cognitive task performance of a single, isolated individual). As a consequence, they suggest that much of importance in social cognition is likely to be "domain specific." Thus, gender stereotype research should be especially concerned with "learnings about sex" that are specific to certain types of men and women, to particular settings or contexts, and so on. Much of this learning is likely to be stored in terms of scripts and beliefs and feelings about specific women (men) rather than directly as part of gender stereotypes.

GENDER STEREOTYPES AND INTERPERSONAL RELATIONS

Once learned, how do gender stereotypes and other gender knowledge stored in long-term memory influence interpersonal behavior? In seeking to answer this question we are concerned with *stereotyping*: "the operation of stereotypes in the perception of people and interpersonal events" (Ashmore & Del Boca, 1979, p. 235), or "how and when stereotypes are applied in social interaction" (Taylor, 1981, p. 83). To structure this discussion, we refer the reader to Figure 1, where the process of stereotyping is depicted as the flow of information from the left to the right side of the figure. It is important to stress that the cognitive processes identified in Figure 1 (from Attention to Response selection) are not conceived as separate and sequential stages. Rather they are interrelated and can occur in parallel; the left-to-right ordering is intended to depict a modal sequence, not a strict set of steps.

Our discussion of gender stereotypes in the process of social interaction begins by focusing on the target. Earlier, we noted one very important implication of explicitly including the target in the diagram—the target is an active cognizer who has goals and purposes and can choose to make certain thoughts, feelings, and behaviors either easier or more difficult for the actor to see. A second reason for including the target and stimuli available to the actor is that we do not believe that perceivers must always contend with weak and chaotic stimulus displays or that information processing necessarily involves giving meaning to essentially meaningless stimuli. Quite simply, there is an external reality. McArthur and Baron (1983) quite correctly note that this fact has been ignored by most social cognition workers. McArthur and Baron (1983) provide a detailed and reasoned analysis of what is to be gained by explicitly considering what is out there.

Turning to the actor (or perceiver), the first factor to be considered is attention. The external environment, especially the social component, is simply too complex for the perceiver to take in everything. Thus, perception is inherently selective, and *attention* describes this process of selection. Attention is influenced by both perceiver and target factors. Essentially, characteristics of the target that make it the figure against the ground draw attention. For example, intense (a man who talks loudly and makes emphatic gestures) or changing (a woman who is in constant motion) stimuli command attention (McArthur, 1982). In a series of experiments, Taylor (1981) has shown that a solo (e.g., a single woman in a group of men) is attention grabbing. McArthur (1982) identifies two perceiver variables affecting attention—expectancy and arousal. One is more likely to attend to expected events (up to some threshold, cf. Hastie, 1981). Increasing physiological arousal tends to reduce the field of attention. This has potentially important implications for relationships between individual men and women. Sexual attraction involves often intense physiological arousal, and it is under such conditions that attention is most narrow and perception the least discriminating (hence, in part, the notion that "love is blind").

A second important aspect of the actor's information processing is *unitizing*. Perceivers do not see a continuous through-time display. Rather, incoming stimuli are partitioned into meaningful events. To date, most research on social event perception has been directed at single actors doing relatively simple actions (cf. Newtson, 1976). Even in such situations, however, there is evidence that perceiver factors (e.g., differences in perceptual goals, subjective importance of perceived action) influence the behavior segmentation process. With respect to female–male relations, it will be important to assess how various types of gender knowledge influence how the behavior of individual women and men, as well as the sexes in interaction, is partitioned into meaningful units.

The *"Categorization and integration"* box in the figure stands for a set of interrelated cognitive activities. Three of these are crucial to gender stereotyping: *categorization* (identifying an individual as a man or woman and as a member of a particular gender subtype); *inference* (on the basis of category membership drawing conclusions about what the target is like); and *attribution* (using a target's gender categorization to explain or account for his/her behavior). (These activities are described in some depth by Ashmore & Del Boca, 1979.)

The final cognitive subprocess is *response selection*. Basically, this involves translating "thinking-about" into behavioral intention and overt action. Although cognitive psychologists are just beginning to address this issue, Norman's (1981a) "activation-trigger-schema system" (ATS) model, which is built around the assumption that sensorimotor schemas control action, is congruent with the general cognitive framework here suggested and may be a useful guide to research. Response selection is emphasized for two primary reasons:

1. The actor may form a positive impression of another (the target) and may have the short-term goal of getting to know the target better, but may not be able to select a behavior appropriate to this impression and goal. Either because of the absence of the necessary sensorimotor schemas or the motor skill to enact these, there can be a disjuncture between cognition and action. The clumsy adolescent boy who cannot seem to do the right thing around girls is one example of this.

2. When using closed-ended procedures to assess gender and other stereotypes, the response categories provided by the researcher may not coincide with the subjects' cognitive categories. This possibility suggests greater use of open-ended procedures to establish pools of items. Even in doing this, however, it should be kept in mind that subjects (hopefully) aim to select and provide responses that they think the researcher will correctly understand. (See Wyer and Carlston, 1979, for a more general discussion of this point.) Thus, open-ended work will need to take into consideration who the audience is, the context of the response, and form of the response.

In addition to identifying various cognitive activities central to the gender stereotyping process, we note two general issues regarding stereotypes in action. First, gender stereotypes are not applied in a simple fashion to every female and male target encountered. In short, perceivers do not simply consider the target's gender in forming an impression and deciding how to behave. Certainly, gender does make a difference, but in summarizing person perception research on the role of gender in the impression formation process, Wallston and O'Leary (1981) remark, "While main effects are frequently found in studies using only social category information, interactions with sex are more common where additional information is provided" (p. 12). Further, other information can overshadow or swamp target gender effects (e.g., Del Boca & Ashmore, 1980b). The next stage in research on how target gender interacts with other information is to move closer to real-world contexts where both perceiver and target are "doing something" rather than the typical impression-formation paradigm, where the subject's only task is to figure out what the (usually hypothetical) target is like.

In this regard the following list of variables might be considered:

1. **Degree of prior acquaintance**. With increasing acquaintance with another, it is likely that knowledge about them is organized in terms of a person node (Ostrom, Pryor, & Simpson, 1981) and that thinking and behaving may be guided more by person than by social category information.

2. **Degree of structural interdependence**. For simplicity, it can be assumed that such interdependence is bipolar, ranging from extreme positive or promotive interdependence (e.g., two soldiers in the same foxhole in a war), through noninterdependence (e.g., two people at a bus station who are sitting on different benches waiting for different buses), to extreme negative interdependence (e.g., two soldiers in different but physically close foxholes fighting for opposing armies). Positive interdependence pushes toward positive sentiment and

negative interdependence toward negative sentiment (cf. Ashmore & Del Boca, 1976).

3. **Power.** It is clearly adaptive for the low power person to be more "perceptive" than the high power individual (cf. McArthur & Baron, 1983).

4. **Context.** The sex ratio in a particular situation influences attention and impression formation (cf. Taylor, 1981). Also, the type of activity is likely to be important. Although activities differ in a variety of ways, the distinction, formal–intimate (cf. Triandis, 1971), is most important for the present discussion. In formal activities with unknown others it is likely that social-category information (e.g., gender) is particularly important in shaping impressions and behavior.

5. **Target and perceiver characteristics.** Because these have been discussed earlier, we do not comment further.

The second general issue about stereotypes in action is the self-fulfilling prophecy or behavioral confirmation. As a general phenomenon (cf. Jones, 1977) and as manifested in male–female relations (e.g., Skrypnek & Snyder, 1982), it has clearly been demonstrated that one's expectations can influence one's behavior so that the other behaves in such a way as to confirm the initial expectation. Again though, there is need for next-generation research that goes beyond demonstrations. One strategy is to develop models of stereotypes and interpersonal behavior in specific real-world domains. Ruble and Ruble (1982) have done just this for gender stereotypes as a factor in performance evaluation in industrial–organizational settings. A second approach is to investigate responses to inconsistent information. Most social cognition work has emphasized the assimilation function of cognition (congruent events are "seen," incongruent events are misinterpreted or not seen). Obviously, this is oversimplified. Hastie (1981) suggests a curvilinear relation between congruence of an event with a schema and memory for the event, with best memory for highly congruent and highly incongruent events. His model (and posited underlying mechanisms) make considerable sense. To be useful to the gender stereotype researcher, however, we need to know how the model fares in situations where discrepancies are not nearly so salient and extreme as those studied by Hastie to date.

STEREOTYPE CHANGE

The consideration of responses to disconfirming evidence leads to the question of stereotype change. The results of a small number of studies suggest that exposing children to counterstereotypical models (e.g., a woman behaving in a masculine manner) can reduce sex stereotyping (cf. Huston,

1983, pp. 425–426).[6] This research, however, provides little insight into the process of stereotype change. And, there is almost no research to report on the question, How and why do stereotypes change? (see, however, Weber & Crocker, 1983). This lack of research can be traced to two quite divergent sources. Stereotype researchers often assume that stereotypes are rigid and unalterable. Given this assumption, studying stereotype change makes no sense. On the other hand, the cognitive social psychologists concerned with stereotypes, as noted earlier, stress how information is assimilated to schemas and, as a consequence, underplay how cognitive structures accommodate to external reality (cf. Higgins et al., 1981, p. 399, Footnote 1).

Concluding Note

The preceding brief discussion of stereotype change provides a nice lead-in to this concluding section. We began this chapter with a somewhat negative evaluation of the extant literature. We questioned the list approach to gender stereotypes and were critical of the three self-report methodologies that dominate the field. This somber beginning, however, was followed by an extended discussion of what might be (in contrast with what is).

What future directions do we see as most likely to be fruitful? (1) relatively less reliance on a small set of self-report measures to document the content of sex stereotypes; (2) more conceptual and empirical work on the various types of gender knowledge (especially how beliefs about specific women and men articulate with beliefs about gender categories); (3) greater emphasis on how gender knowledge is represented in memory (especially the structural properties of such knowledge); (4) more attention to process issues. This last direction is really a very large and diverse set of possibilities. Basically, it is our hope that the social cognition researcher, whose primary interest is basic principles of thinking about people and events, will move closer to the real world of women and men interacting in an established and important societal context, and, in turn, that those primarily concerned with gender

---

[6]There have also been a small number of studies that have attempted to assess the impact of changing societal conditions (e.g., the rise of the Women's Movement, increased labor-force participation by women) by comparing responses to stereotype measures at two points in time (e.g., 1957 and 1978, Werner and La Russa [1984]). It is generally concluded in such work that perceptions of the sexes change little in the face of apparently significant and relevant changes in societal arrangements (see Spence et al., 1985). Although this conclusion may be valid for the content of stereotypic conceptions (see, however, Werner and La Russa, 1984, on the methodological shortcomings of most of the work), there is reason to believe that there has been considerable change regarding evaluation. Werner and La Russa found that in 1978, the female stereotype contained more positive and fewer negative attributes than the male stereotype, whereas 20 years earlier, the relative proportions had been reversed.

stereotypes will take advantage of research and theory in social cognition to provide more insight into the major process questions: How are gender stereotypes learned? How do they influence interpersonal behavior? How are they changed? This moving together, which we feel is already occurring, will enhance our understanding of both the basic principles of social cognition and the nature of relations between the sexes.

Acknowledgments

The preparation of this chapter was aided by the following individuals: Margaret A. McManus and Dieter Papke assisted with both library research and typing of initial drafts; Pat Freeman and Mary Anne Grandinetti typed the semifinal and final drafts; Michael P. Johnson, Margaret A. McManus, and David S. Titus read and commented on the semifinal draft. We gratefully acknowledge their help.

References

Abelson, R. D. (1976). Script processing in attitude formation and decision making. In J. S. Carroll & J. W. Payne (Eds.), *Cognition and social behavior*. Hillsdale, NJ: Erlbaum, 33–46.

Anderson, J. R. (1980). *Cognitive psychology and its implications*. San Francisco, CA: W. H. Freeman and Co.

Asch, S. E. (1946). Forming impressions of personality. *Journal of Abnormal and Social Psychology, 41,* 258–290.

Ashmore, R. D. (1981). Sex stereotypes and implicit personality theory. In D. L. Hamilton (Ed.), *Cognitive processes in stereotyping and intergroup behavior*. Hillsdale, NJ: Erlbaum.

Ashmore, R. D., & Brodzinsky, D. M. (Eds.) (in press). *Thinking about the family: Views of parents and children*. Hillsdale, NJ: Erlbaum.

Ashmore, R. D., & Del Boca, F. K. (1976). Psychological approaches to understanding intergroup conflict. In P. A. Katz (Ed.), *Toward the elimination of racism*. New York: Pergamon Press.

Ashmore, R. D., & Del Boca, F. K. (1979). Sex stereotypes and implicit personality theory: Toward a cognitive-social psychological conceptualization. *Sex Roles, 5,* 219–248.

Ashmore, R. D., & Del Boca, F. K. (1981). Conceptual approaches to stereotypes and stereotyping. In D. L. Hamilton (Ed.), *Cognitive processes in stereotyping and intergroup behavior*. Hillsdale, NJ: Erlbaum.

Ashmore, R. D., & Tumia, M. (1980). Sex stereotypes and implicit personality theory. I. A personality description approach to the assessment of sex stereotypes. *Sex Roles, 6,* 501–518.

Bacon, M. K., & Ashmore, R. D. (in press). A consideration of the cognitive activities of parents and their role in the socialization process. In R. D. Ashmore & D. M. Brodzinsky (Eds.), *Thinking about the family: Views of parents and children*. Hillsdale, NJ: Erlbaum.

Beere, C. A. (1979). *Women and women's issues: A handbook of tests and measures*. San Francisco, CA: Jossey-Bass.

Beere, C. A. (1983). Instruments and measures in a changing, diverse society. In B. L. Richardson & J. Wirtenberg (Eds.), *Sex role research: Measuring social change.* New York: Praeger Publishers.

Bem, S. L. (1974). The measurement of psychological androgyny. *Journal of Consulting and Clinical Psychology, 42,* 165–172.

Bernard, J. (1981). The good-provider role: Its rise and fall. *American Psychologist, 36,* 1–12.

Best, D. L., Williams, J. E., & Briggs, S. R. (1980). A further analysis of the affective meanings associated with male and female sex-trait stereotypes. *Sex Roles, 6,* 735–746.

Birnbaum, D. W., Nosanchuk, T. A., & Croll, W. L. (1980). Children's stereotypes about sex differences in emotionality. *Sex Roles, 6,* 435–443.

Block, J. H. (1976). Issues, problems, and pitfalls in assessing sex differences: A critical review of *The psychology of sex differences. Merrill-Palmer Quarterly, 22,* 283–308.

Block, J. (1979, September). Socialization influences on personality development in males and females. Paper presented at the 87th Convention of the American Psychological Association, New York.

Bower, G. H. (1975). Cognitive psychology: An introduction. In W. K. Estes (Ed.), *Handbook of learning and cognitive processes* (Vol. 1): *Introduction to concepts and issues.* Hillsdale, NJ: Erlbaum.

Brannon, R. (1978). Measuring attitudes (toward women, and otherwise): A methodological critique. In J. Sherman & F. Denmark (Eds.), *Psychology of women: Future directions in research.* New York: Psychological Dimensions, Inc.

Brewer, M. B., Dull, V., & Lui, L. (1981). Perceptions of the elderly: Stereotypes as prototypes. *Journal of Personality and Social Psychology, 41,* 656–670.

Brigham, J. C. (1971). Ethnic stereotypes. *Psychological Bulletin, 76,* 15–38.

Broverman, I. K., Broverman, D. M., Clarkson, F. E., Rosenkrantz, P. A., & Vogel, S. R. (1970). Sex-role stereotypes and clinical judgments of mental health. *Journal of Consulting and Clinical Psychology, 34,* 1–7.

Broverman, I. K., Vogel, S. R., Broverman, D. M., Clarkson, F. E., & Rosenkrantz, P. S. (1972). Sex-role stereotypes: A current appraisal. *Journal of Social Issues, 28,* 59–78.

Cauthen, N. R., Robinson, I. E., & Krauss, H. H. (1971). Stereotypes: A review of the literature 1926–1968. *Journal of Social Psychology, 84,* 103–125.

Clarkson, F. E., Vogel, S. R., Broverman, I. K., Broverman, D. M., & Rosenkrantz, P. S. (1970). Family size and sex-role stereotypes. *Science, 167,* 390–392.

Collins, W. A. (1982). Cognitive processing in television viewing. In D. Pearl, L. Bouthilet, & J. B. Lazar (Eds.), *Television and behavior: Ten years of scientific progress and implications for the 80's* (Vol. II). Washington, DC: U.S. Government Printing Office.

Cowan, M. L., & Stewart, B. J. (1977). A methodological study of sex stereotypes. *Sex Roles, 3,* 205–216.

Deaux, K. (1982, August). Sex as a social category: Evidence for gender stereotypes. Paper presented at the Annual Convention of the American Psychological Association, Washington, DC.

Deaux, K. (1984). From individual differences to social categories: Analysis of a decade's research on gender. *American Psychologist, 39,* 105–116.

Deaux, K., & Lewis, L. L. (1983, May 12). Assessment of gender stereotypes: Methodology and components. Purdue University.

Deaux, K., & Lewis, L. L. (1984). The structure of gender stereotypes: Interrelationships among components and gender label. *Journal of Personality and Social Psychology 46,* 991–1004.

Deaux, K., Winton, W., Crowley, M., & Lewis, L. L. (in press). Level of categorization and content of gender stereotypes. *Social Cognition.*

Del Boca, F. K. (1982). A test of three explanations of attitudes toward public policy concerning sexual equality: Self-interest, prejudice against women, and symbolic sexism. Unpublished doctoral dissertation, Rutgers—The State University of New Jersey, New Brunswick.

Del Boca, F. K., & Ashmore, R. D. (1980a). Sex stereotypes through the life cycle. In L. Wheeler (Ed.), *Review of personality and social psychology* (Vol. 1). Beverly Hills, CA: Sage Publications.

Del Boca, F. K., & Ashmore, R. D. (1980b). Sex stereotypes and implicit personality theory II: A trait-inference approach to the assessment of sex stereotypes. *Sex Roles, 6,* 519–535.

Der-Karabetian, A., & Smith, A. (1977). Sex-role stereotyping in the United States: Is it changing? *Sex Roles, 3,* 193–198.

Dorr, A. (1982). Television and affective development and functioning. In D. Pearl, L. Bouthilet, & J. B. Lazar (Eds.), *Television and behavior: Ten years of scientific progress and implications for the 80's* (Vol. II). Washington, DC: U.S. Government Printing Office.

Eagly, A. H., & Steffen, V. J. (1984). Gender stereotypes stem from the distribution of women and men in social roles. *Journal of Personality and Social Psychology, 46,* 735–754.

Ellis, L. J., & Bentler, P. M. (1973). Traditional sex-determined role standards and sex stereotypes. *Journal of Personality and Social Psychology, 23,* 28–34.

Elman, J., Press, A., & Rosenkrantz, P. (1970). Sex roles and self-concepts: Real and ideal. *Proceedings of the 78th Annual Convention of the American Psychological Association,* pp. 455–456.

Fernberger, S. W. (1948). Persistence of stereotypes concerning sex differences. *Journal of Abnormal and Social Psychology, 43,* 97–101.

Funk, S. G., Horowitz, A. D., Lipshitz, R., & Young, F. W. (1976). The perceived structure of American ethnic groups: The use of multidimensional scaling in stereotype research. *Sociometry, 39,* 116–130.

Gerbner, G., & Signorelli, N. (1979). Women and minorities on television. Unpublished manuscript, Annenberg School of Communications, University of Pennsylvania, Philadelphia.

Goodenough, E. W. (1957). Interest in persons as an aspect of sex difference in the early years. *Genetic Psychology Monographs, 55,* 287–323.

Goodman, E. (1979). *Turning Points.* New York: Fawcett Crest.

Gordon, C. (1968). Self conceptions: Configurations of content. In C. Gordon & K. J. Gergen (Eds.), *The self in social interaction.* New York: Wiley.

Greenberg, B. S. (1982). Television and role socialization: An overview. In D. Pearl, L. Bouthilet, & J. B. Lazar (Eds.), *Television and behavior: Ten years of scientific progress and implications for the 80's* (Vol. II). Washington, DC: U.S. Government Printing Office.

Hastie, R. (1981). Schematic principles in human memory. In E. T. Higgins, C. P. Herman, & M. P. Zanna (Eds.), *Social cognition: The Ontario Symposium* (Vol. 1). Hillsdale, NJ: Erlbaum.

Hastie, R., & Carlston, D. (1980). Theoretical issues in person memory. In R. Hastie, T. M. Ostrom, E. B. Ebbeson, R. S. Wyer, Jr., D. L. Hamilton, & D. E. Carlston (Eds.), *Person memory: The cognitive basis of social perception.* Hillsdale, NJ: Erlbaum.

Hawkins, R. P., & Pingree, S. (1982). Television's influence on social reality. In D. Pearl, L. Bouthilet, & J. B. Lazar (Eds.), *Television and behavior: Ten years of scientific progress and implications for the 80's* (Vol. II). Washington, DC: U.S. Government Printing Office.

Heise, D. R. (1969). Some methodological issues in semantic differential research. *Psychological Bulletin, 72,* 406–422.

Heise, D. R. (1979). *Understanding events: Affect and the construction of social action.* Cambridge: Cambridge University Press.

Higgins, E. T., Kuiper, N. A., & Olson, J. M. (1981). Social cognition: A need to get personal. In

E. T. Higgins, C. P. Herman, & M. P. Zanna (Eds.), *Social cognition: The Ontario symposium*. Hillsdale, NJ: Erlbaum.

Holland, D., & Davidson, D. (1983). *Labeling the opposite sex: Metaphors and themes in American folk models of gender*. Unpublished manuscript, University of North Carolina, Chapel Hill.

Holyoak, K. J., & Gordon, P. C. (1984). Information processing and social cognition. In R. S. Wyer, Jr., T. K. Srull, & J. Hartwick (Eds.), *Handbook of social cognition*. Hillsdale, NJ: Erlbaum.

Hunter, J. E. (1976). Images of women. *Journal of Social Issues, 32*, 7–17.

Huston, A. C. (1983). Sex-typing. In P. H. Mussen (Ed.), *Handbook of child psychology* (4th ed.) (Vol. 4). New York: Wiley.

Jones, R. A. (1977). *Self-fulfilling prophecies: Social, psychological and physiological effects of expectancies*. Hillsdale, NJ: Erlbaum.

Jones, R. A., & Ashmore, R. D. (1973). The structure of intergroup perception: Categories and dimensions in views of ethnic groups and adjectives used in stereotype research. *Journal of Personality and Social Psychology, 25*, 428–438.

Klapp, O. E. (1972). *Heroes, villains, and fools*. San Diego, CA: Aegis Publishing Company (originally by Prentice Hall, 1962).

Klein, X. U. (1950). The stereotype of femininity. *Journal of Social Issues, 6*, 3–12.

Komarovsky, M. (1946). Cultural contradictions and sex roles. *American Journal of Sociology, 52*, 182–189.

Kutner, N. G., & Brogan, D. (1974). An investigation of sex-related slang vocabulary and sex-role orientation among male and female university students. *Journal of Marriage and the Family, 36*, 474–484.

Lakoff, G., & Johnson, M. (1980). *Metaphors we live by*. Chicago: The University of Chicago Press.

Lifton, R. J. (1967). Woman as knower: Some psychohistorical perspectives. In R. J. Lifton (Ed.), *The woman in America*. Boston: Beacon Press.

Lingle, J. H., Altom, M. W., & Medin, D. L. (1984). Of cabbages and kings: Assessing the extendability of natural object concept models to social things. In R. S. Wyer, Jr., T. K. Srull, & J. Hartwick (Eds.), *Handbook of social cognition*. Hillsdale, NJ: Erlbaum.

Lunneborg, P. W. (1970). Stereotypic aspect in masculinity–femininity measurements. *Journal of Consulting and Clinical Psychology, 34*, 113–118.

MacBrayer, C. T. (1960). Differences in perception of the opposite sex by males and females. *Journal of Social Psychology, 52*, 309–314.

Maccoby, E. E., & Jacklin, C. N. (1974). *The psychology of sex differences*. Stanford, CA: Stanford University Press.

McArthur, L. Z. (1982). Judging a book by its cover: A cognitive analysis of the relationship between physical appearance and stereotyping. In A. Hastorf & A. Isen (Eds.), *Cognitive Social Psychology*. New York: Elsevier.

McArthur, L. Z., & Baron, R. (1983). Toward an ecological theory of social perception. *Psychological Review, 90*, 215–238.

McKee, J. P., & Sherriffs, A. C. (1957). The differential evaluation of males and females. *Journal of Personality, 25*, 356–371.

Morgan, M. (1982). Television and adolescents' sex role stereotypes: A longitudinal study. *Journal of Personality and Social Psychology, 43*, 947–955.

Newtson, D. (1976). Foundations of attribution: The perception of ongoing behavior. In J. H. Harvey, W. J. Ickes, & R. F. Kidd (Eds.), *New directions in attribution research* (Vol. 1). Hillsdale, NJ: Erlbaum.

Norman, D. A. (1981a). Categorization of action slips. *Psychological Review, 88*, 1–15.

Norman, D. A. (1981b). Twelve issues for cognitive science. In D. A. Norman (Ed.), *Perspectives on cognitive science*. Norwood, NJ: Ablex.

O'Leary, V. E., & Depner, L. E. (1975). College males' ideal female: Changes in sex-role stereotypes. *Journal of Social Psychology, 95*, 139–140.

Osgood, C. E., May, W. H., & Miron, M. S. (1975). *Cross-cultural universals of affective meaning*. Urbana, IL: University of Illinois Press.

Ostrom, T. M., Pryor, J. B., & Simpson, D. D. (1981). The organization of social information. In E. T. Higgins, C. P. Herman & M. P. Zanna (Eds.), *Social cognition: The Ontario symposium* (Vol. 1). Hillsdale, NJ: Erlbaum.

Rokeach, M. (1973). *The nature of human values*. New York: The Free Press.

Rosenberg, S., & Sedlak, A. (1972). Structural representations of implicit personality theory. In L. Berkowitz (Ed.), *Advances in experimental social psychology* (Vol. 6). New York: Academic Press, pp. 235–247.

Rosenkrantz, P., Vogel, S. R., Bee, H., Broverman, I. K., & Broverman, D. M. (1968). Sex-role stereotypes and self concepts in college students. *Journal of Consulting and Clinical Psychology, 32*, 287–295.

Rosenkrantz, P. S., Vogel, S. R., & Broverman, I. K. (1970, April). Sex Role Perceptions and the Generation Gap. Paper presented at the Eastern Psychological Association Meeting, Atlantic City, NJ.

Ruble, D. N., & Ruble, T. L. (1982). Sex stereotypes. In A. G. Miller (Ed.), *In the eye of the beholder: Contemporary issues in stereotyping*. New York: Praeger.

Schulz, M. R. (1975). The semantic derogation of women. In B. Thorne & N. Henley (Eds.), *Language and sex: Difference and dominance*. Rowley, MA: Newbury House.

Schwartz, T. (1978). The acquisition of culture. Paper presented at the Center for Psychosocial Studies, Chicago.

Shepard, R. N., & Arabie, P. (1979). Additive clustering: Representation of similarities as combinations of discrete overlapping properties. *Psychological Review, 86*, 87–123.

Sherriffs, A. C., & Jarrett, R. F. (1953). Sex differences in attitudes about sex differences. *Journal of Psychology, 35*, 161–168.

Sherriffs, A. C., & McKee, J. P. (1957). Qualitative aspects of beliefs about men and women. *Journal of Personality, 25*, 451–464.

Skrypnek, B. J., & Snyder, M. (1982). On the self-perpetuating nature of stereotypes about women and men. *Journal of Experimental Social Psychology, 18*, 277–291.

Snider, J. G., & Osgood, C. E. (1969) (Eds.), *Semantic differential technique: A sourcebook*. Chicago: Aldine.

Spence, J. T., Deaux, K., & Helmreich, R. L. (1985). Sex roles in contemporary American society. In G. Lindzey & E. Aronson (Eds.), *Handbook of social psychology* (3rd ed.). New York: Random House.

Spence, J. T., & Helmreich, R. L. (1978). *Masculinity and femininity*. Austin: University of Texas Press.

Spence, J. T., Helmreich, R., & Stapp, J. (1974). The personal attributes questionnaire: A measure of sex role stereotypes and masculinity–femininity. *Catalog of Selected Documents in Psychology, 4*, 43–44.

Taylor, S. E. (1981). A categorization approach to stereotyping. In D. L. Hamilton (Ed.), *Cognitive processes in stereotyping and intergroup behavior*. Hillsdale, NJ: Erlbaum.

Thorne, B., & Henley, N. (1975). Difference and dominance: An overview of language, gender, and society. In B. Thorne & N. Henley (Eds.), *Language and sex: Difference and dominance*. Rowley, MA: Newbury House.

Triandis, H. C. (1971). *Attitude and attitude change*. New York: Wiley.

Unger, R. K., & Siiter, R. (1974, April). Sex-role stereotypes: The weight of a "grain of truth." Paper presented at the Eastern Psychological Association Meetings, Philadelphia, PA.

Vogel, S. R., Broverman, I. K., Broverman, D. M., Clarkson, F. E., & Rosenkrantz, P. S. (1970). Maternal employment and perception of sex-role among college students. *Developmental Psychology, 3,* 384–391.

Walster, E., Walster, G. W., Piliavin, J., & Schmidt, L. (1973). Playing hard-to-get: Understanding an elusive phenomenon. *Journal of Personality and Social Psychology, 26,* 113–121.

Wallston, B. S., & O'Leary, V. E. (1981). Sex makes a difference: Differential perceptions of women and men. In L. Wheeler (Ed.), *Review of personality and social psychology* (Vol. 2). Beverly Hills, CA: Sage Publications.

Weber, R., & Crocker, J. (1983). Cognitive processes in the revision of stereotypic beliefs. *Journal of Personality and Social Psychology, 45,* 961–977.

Wegner, D. M., & Vallacher, R. R. (1977). *Implicit psychology.* New York: Oxford University Press.

Werner, P. D., & LaRussa, G. W. (1984). Persistence and change in sex role stereotypes. Manuscript submitted for publication.

White, G. M. (1980). Conceptual universals in interpersonal language. *American Anthropologist, 82,* 759–781.

Williams, J. E., & Bennett, S. M. (1975). The definition of sex stereotypes via the adjective check list. *Sex Roles, 1,* 327–337.

Williams, J. E., Bennett, S. M., & Best, D. L. (1975). Awareness and expression of sex stereotypes in young children. *Developmental Psychology, 11,* 635–642.

Williams, J. E., & Best, D. L. (1977). Sex stereotypes and trait favorability on the Adjective Check List. *Educational and Psychological Measurement, 37,* 101–110.

Williams, J. E., & Best, D. L. (1982). *Measuring sex stereotypes: A Thirty-nation study.* Beverly Hills, CA: Sage.

Wyer, R. S., & Carlston, D. E. (1979). *Social cognition, inference and attribution.* Hillsdale, NJ: Erlbaum.

Four

Gender-Related Attitudes

FRANCES K. DEL BOCA
RICHARD D. ASHMORE
MARGARET A. McMANUS

"Sugar and spice and everything nice;
That's what little girls are made of."

"Women may be whole oceans deeper than we are,
but they are a whole paradise better"[1]

Introduction

Is the female sex as unambiguously positive as these two pieces of cultural wisdom suggest? More importantly, are women (and girls) regarded as "good" by individual Americans and American culture at large? Most researchers, in fact, have concluded that the social category, *female*, is not positively evaluated, at least not relative to *male*. The present chapter is concerned with evaluative responses to, or attitudes toward, the sexes. It is organized much like the preceding chapter on stereotypes. The first section is an overview of the empirical research, which has focused on measuring attitudes (especially toward women or types of women) or demonstrating "evaluation bias" (usually against women). In the next major section, we present a conceptual framework for the social psychological analysis of

[1]From *The Ambassador* (Act III) by Pearl Craigie, cited in *The Quotable Woman, 1800–1975* (Partnow, 1977).

gender-related attitudes. The remaining two sections of the chapter take up, in turn, the content-structure and process issues of gender-related attitudes. In the former, an attempt is made to broaden the assessment procedures and attitude objects considered by researchers. The process section addresses three issues: the acquisition, the link to behavior, and the change of gender-related attitudes.

What's Been Done: Assessing Attitudes and Demonstrating Evaluation Bias

There has been both conceptual analysis of and empirical research on gender-related attitudes. However, the bulk of social psychological work has been empirical, and the present section is devoted to this research focus. The primary aim of most investigators has been the determination of how various gender-relevant targets are evaluated by respondents. The techniques employed by researchers have largely been limited to three basic types: stereotype assessment, Likert-type attitude scales, and the experimental manipulation of stimulus targets.

FAVORABILITY OF GENDER STEREOTYPES

As discussed in the preceding chapter, a major aim of most investigators of gender stereotypes has been to compare the relative favorability of the male and the female stereotype. It is important to note, however, that investigators have not typically phrased this goal in terms of measuring "attitudes" toward women and men or "prejudice against women." Their concern has been with assessing the social desirability of the attributes (most often personality traits) ascribed to each sex rather than individuals' evaluations of the social categories, female and male. The procedures used to delineate the content of sex stereotypes also provide attitudinal (i.e., evaluative) information; consequently, the prototypic investigations of gender stereotypes covered in Chapter Three are reviewed here as well.

In a companion paper to their classic investigation of the content of beliefs about men and women (Sherriffs & McKee, 1957), McKee and Sherriffs (1957) report the results of data analyses directed at determining the differential evaluation of the male and female stereotypes. As detailed in the preceding chapter, sex stereotypes were assessed by means of both an open-ended query and an adjective checklist. Subsequent to the original study, a subsample of the group of subjects who responded to the open-ended instructions was asked to rate as favorable, neutral, or unfavorable each *list* of male and female attributes that had been generated earlier. An independent sample of respondents rated each *item* on the adjective checklist "for its desirability or undesirability when applied to men and when applied to women" (McKee & Sherriffs, 1957, p. 360). Several different analyses of the two data sets produced consistent results: Both sexes were evaluated positively; men, however, were regarded more favorably than women, especially by male subjects.

Using Gough's Adjective Check List (ACL) as a means for assessing gender stereotypes, Williams and Bennett (1975) employed two different criteria to determine the content of beliefs regarding women and men. Those attributes that were assigned to one gender by 75% of the respondents of both sexes were used to define the *focused* male and female *stereotypes*; traits ascribed to either gender by at least 60% of the total sample were used to define a pair of *expanded stereotypes*.

Williams and his collaborators used three different approaches to examine the favorability of gender stereotypes. First, the focused and expanded stereotypes for each sex were compared using the ACL classifications of the traits as positive, negative, or neutral. An inconsistent pattern of results emerged: Whereas the focused male stereotype contained a higher proportion of desirable characteristics than that for the female, comparison of the two expanded stereotypes revealed a more favorable constellation of traits for the female (Williams & Bennett, 1975).

Second, each of the two expanded stereotypes was treated as a hypothetical person. Two sets of ACL scale scores were derived from the raw data, and the resulting stereotyped personality profiles were analyzed by a trained clinician. According to the clinical assessment, there is a "high degree of immaturity and psychological pathology evident in both and . . . the stereotyped male is even more disturbed than the stereotyped female" (Williams & Bennett, 1975, p. 335).

Third, favorability ratings of the 300 ACL attributes were obtained from a second sample of respondents. These were found to be uncorrelated ($r = -.07$) with scores on a bipolar index (female–male) of the degree to which each ACL attribute was associated with one or the other sex (Best, Williams, & Briggs, 1980). Based on the total pattern of findings obtained across studies, Williams and his colleagues concluded that the male and female stereotypes do not differ in social desirability.

A rather different conclusion was reached by the third group of investigators discussed in Chapter Three, the developers of the prototypic rating scale assessment technique, the Sex-Role Stereotype Questionnaire (SRSQ). Having identified a set of 41 gender-stereotypic items, Rosenkrantz and his associates (Rosenkrantz, Vogel, Bee, Broverman, & Broverman, 1968) attempted to assess differences in the favorability of the male and female stereotypes by asking a separate sample of respondents to indicate which of the two poles for each scale was the more socially desirable. A Social Desirability (SD) score was computed for each item based on the proportion of subjects designating the masculine pole as the more desirable. For 29 of the 41 stereotypic items, SD scores indicated that the masculine pole was evaluated more favorably. In a subsequent review article, this finding was interpreted as indicating, "that men and masculine characteristics are more highly valued in our society than are women and feminine characteristics" (Broverman, Vogel, Broverman, Clarkson, & Rosenkrantz, 1972, p. 65). No difference, however, was obtained when the *mean* SD score of the 29 male-valued items was compared with the mean score of the 12 items for which the feminine pole was judged as more desirable. Further, the average rating of both the male and female stimulus was on the positive side of the rating scales.

The foregoing summary of the major studies in the sex stereotype literature indicates that, despite frequent statements to the contrary, evidence is mixed regarding the differential evaluation of the female and male stereotypes. Different teams of researchers reach opposing conclusions. For example, Williams and his associates argue against, and Broverman and her collaborators argue for, the position that the male stereotype is more favorably evaluated than that for the female. Perhaps more importantly, the findings on which these conflicting conclusions are based are themselves equivocal; that is, alternative ways of analyzing *the same data* frequently produce different results.[2] Such disparities raise two questions. First, is there a systematic relationship between the means of analysis used and the findings that are obtained? More specifically, is one type of data analysis more likely than another to produce a result of difference (or no difference) in female and male stereotype favorability? Second, and more importantly, what is the most appropriate means of assessing the evaluative orientation reflected by a stereotype?

The answer to the first is, yes—there is an association between means of analysis and result. In the two most recent programs of research (i.e., Broverman and her associates with the SRSQ and Williams and his collaborators, using the ACL) the male stereotype is found to be more highly valued than that of the female only when a summative approach is used to determine stereotype favorability—that is, only when the total number of favorable attributes contained in the stereotype for each sex is compared. The results of using such a procedure are highly dependent on the number of

[2]McKee and Sherriffs (1957) are an exception: Regardless of the method of analysis, the male stereotype was more positively valued. However, a very careful replication of their adjective checklist procedure in 1978 revealed that the female stereotype was slightly more positive (Werner & La Russa, 1984).

items designated by the investigator as stereotypic (e.g., Williams and Bennett [1975] obtained different results for their focused and their expanded sex stereotypes). Comparison procedures that somehow correct for the number of items comprised by the male and the female stereotype have tended not to show a significant difference in the overall social desirability of the attributes ascribed to each sex. As noted earlier, for example, a statistically significant result was *not* obtained when *mean* SD scores for male-valued and female-valued traits were compared by Rosenkrantz and his colleagues (Rosenkrantz et al., 1968).

Given some connection between method and result, which procedure for determining stereotype favorability is the more defensible? One potentially fruitful approach to this question is to consult relevant studies in the field of person perception in social psychology. Such research indicates that *summative* procedures do not predict the favorability of a total personality impression as well as do *averaging* models (cf. Schneider, Hastorf, & Ellsworth, 1979, p. 180). This suggests that a comparison of mean favorability scores for stereotypic items would be a more appropriate method of determining gender stereotype evaluation than a comparison of the absolute numbers or proportions of desirable and undesirable traits attributed to each sex.

The foregoing analysis should not be construed as meaning that the relative elaboration of the two gender stereotypes in terms of number of component items is not significant. With few exceptions, researchers report that the male stereotype comprises a larger number of elements—and a larger number of favorable attributes—than does that for the female. One possible implication is that males are given a broader range of socially approved behavioral options than are females—that is, more ways in which they can be "good." If this is so, it certainly is a plus for males, and in this sense, the male stereotype *is* more positive than that for the female.

ATTITUDE SCALES

The most popular method of assessing gender-related attitudes is the Likert-type attitude scale (cf. Beere, 1979; Brannon, 1978). The best known and most widely used scale of this type is the Attitudes Toward Women Scale (AWS) devised by Spence and Helmreich (1972a). They began with a large pool of attitude statements, many of which were adapted from an instrument developed much earlier, the Kirkpatrick Belief–Pattern Scale for Measuring Attitudes toward Feminism (Kirkpatrick, 1936). Spence and Helmreich wrote additional "items describing roles and patterns of conduct in major areas of activity in which women and men were, in principle, capable of being granted equal rights" (p. 3). In its final form, the AWS consists of 55 statements with four response alternatives: Agree Strongly, Agree Mildly, Disagree Mildly, and Disagree Strongly. The authors group the items into six "more or less independent" categories: (1) Vocational, educational, and intellectual roles; (2) Freedom and independence; (3) Dating, courtship, and etiquette; (4) Drinking, swearing, and dirty jokes; (5) Sexual behavior; and (6) Marital relationships and obligations.

Normative data for the AWS were collected from two University of Texas student samples in 1971 and subsequently from a large sample of students' parents. Although some variations in results were reported, factor analyses of the data for the different normative samples revealed considerable stability in factor structure across groups (see, however, Brannon, 1978, p. 677). Other differences among samples, however, were observed. Students were found to be significantly more liberal than parents. For both generations, but particularly for the student samples, female respondents were found to be less traditional than males, although some interesting reversals to this trend emerged. Males in the student sample were significantly more "feminist" (i.e., more likely to endorse parity between the sexes) than their female counterparts on eight items concerning alimony, sexual behavior, dating, and courtship. Females in the parent sample were found to be more conservative than males primarily on items of propriety (e.g., swearing).

The AWS was initially developed for use in a study of interpersonal attraction (Spence & Helmreich, 1972a), and there are a number of published studies that examine the relation of AWS scores to judgments of likability for female stimulus targets who vary in systematic ways such as sex congruence of interests and level of competence (e.g., Spence & Helmreich, 1972b; Spence, Helmreich, & Stapp, 1975). However, the major use of the AWS has been in descriptive research aimed at assessing attitudes of new samples of respondents (e.g., Hotard & Anderson, 1974), correlating AWS scores with other variables (e.g., Albright & Chang, 1976), and/or examining change in gender-related evaluations over time (e.g., Helmreich, Spence, & Gibson, 1982).

Although gender-related attitude scales have been most often used since the early 1970s, it should be noted that interest in this topic began much earlier. Kirkpatrick's scale (1936) for assessing attitudes toward feminism was the first such instrument, and it has served as the primary item source in the development of the AWS and several other scales (cf. Beere, 1979). The construction of Likert-type attitude scales proliferated during the 1960s and 1970s. Although these scales have a wide variety of different labels (e.g., "attitudes toward women," "sex role traditionality," "feminism"), most contain items tapping a variety of topics and issues, responses to which are summed to yield a single score on a continuum variously described as traditional –nontraditional, conservative–liberal, sexist–egalitarian, antifeminist–pro-feminist (see Beere, 1979, p. 384; Brannon, 1978, p. 673). There are, in addition, measures that focus on "marital and parental roles," "employee roles" (especially women as managers, e.g., Peters, Terborg, & Taynor, 1974), and "somatic and sexual issues" (see Beere, 1979, Chapters 8, 9, and 11, respectively). The focus of most extant scales is on women and their behavior, though there are some exceptions. For example, a scale that directly parallels the AWS, the Attitudes toward the Male Role Scale (AMR), has been developed (Doyle & Moore, 1978).

Attitude scales are traditionally evaluated against the two yardsticks of reliability and validity. Although not equally true of all attitude scales with gender-relevant referents, most of the better-known measures have been constructed according to established guidelines that assure a relatively normal distribution of scores and an acceptable degree of internal consistency. However, the question of validity has received insufficient attention. For this reason, we examine this issue in some detail here, using the AWS—clearly one of the better scales in use—as a means of illustrating some of the potential problems that arise in instruments that measure attitudes pertaining to gender.

Both content and construct validity need to be considered in evaluating gender-related attitude scales. Central to both types of validity is the precise specification of the attitude object. Taking the AWS as a specific case, there is some ambiguity about what the intended attitude referent is. As noted earlier, many statements in the original item pool were adapted from a measure of attitudes toward feminism. The title of the instrument, the "Attitudes toward Women Scale," however, suggests that the target is the broad social category, women. The authors describe the scale as an "instrument to measure attitudes toward the rights and roles of women in contemporary society" and refer to subjects as "conservative" or "liberal" in their attitudinal orientation, implicitly equating attitudes toward women with attitudes toward women's roles. Accordingly, a "traditional" or "conservative" viewpoint is seen as indicative of a negative evaluation of women as a social group, while a "liberal" position is regarded as reflecting a favorable attitude. Attitudes toward women may be correlated with attitudes toward gender roles. However, "women" and "rights and roles of women" are not the same thing, and the question of how they are related is an empirical one.

For an attitude scale to be content valid, the constituent items must adequately represent the overall domain of interest. The final form of the AWS contains six categories of items. In content validity terms, the questions are Do these categories adequately cover the overall domain of the "rights and roles of women"? Does the relative number of items in each category correspond to the relative importance of each area? With regard to the first question, it is likely that potentially important rights and roles are not represented. In constructing the scale, Spence and Helmreich restricted item content primarily to elective behavior and areas of activity where women and men are, "in principle, capable of being granted equal rights" (Spence & Helmreich, 1972a, p. 3). Statements concerning the legal status of women and items appearing not to have relevance to men (e.g., statements concerning reproductive freedom) were intentionally excluded. Such omissions would seem to undermine the content validity of a measuring device concerned with attitudes toward women's rights and roles. Concerning the second question, two of the six content categories (i.e., "Vocational, educational, and intellectual roles" and "Marital relationships and obligations") comprise 34 of the 55 items on the total scale. Although these two topics are intuitively important for relations between the sexes, no rationale is offered for why they contribute disproportionately to the total scale score.

The issue of content validity is complicated further by assumptions regarding the directionality of particular items. According to the authors, the "profemale," "liberal," or "feminist" position on every issue is one that supports parity between the sexes. The liberal response, then, would be to endorse statements such as, "Divorced men should help to support their children but should not be required to pay alimony if their wives are capable of working," and "It is all right for wives to have an occasional, casual, extramarital affair." Item analyses might support this view, but, on a conceptual level, the point is arguable. Interestingly, these same items were among those for which college females in the normative samples scored as more traditional than their male counterparts. That men endorse such items because they evaluate women favorably or because they share feminist ideals seems debatable. One obvious alternative is that men agree with statements that they see as in their self-interest in their relations with women.

Construct validity, essentially establishing that one's scale measures what it is intended to measure and nothing else, involves two major steps: elaborating a nomological net and testing hypotheses derived from this (Cronbach & Meehl, 1955). A nomological net is a miniature "theory," which specifies hypothetical constructs, observable variables, and links between and among these. Once articulated, the researcher's theory must be tested. There are three major ways of empirically establishing construct validity: known groups, change over time, and correlation with other measures (cf. Carmines & Zeller, 1979).

Although some researchers have presented evidence about the validity of their scales, this is seldom done in accordance with the logic of construct validity. Constructors of gender-related attitude scales rarely articulate their theory (cf. Vaughter, 1983). With regard to the second step of construct validation, a narrow and unconvincing set of approaches has been used. We know of no published attempts to use change as evidence of construct validity. Some efforts have been made to use correlational data in this regard. However, as Brannon (1978, pp. 696–697) notes, in most such cases scores on one self-report attitude measure are correlated with responses to a second self-report instrument. This is not compelling evidence of validity because self-report measures share the same sources of invalidity (e.g., reactivity and concomitant susceptibility to conscious and nonconscious distortion). What is needed is evidence that attitude scales correlate with maximally different measures of the same construct (cf. Campbell & Fiske, 1959). Especially convincing would be demonstrations that scores on such scales covary with behavioral indices of gender-related attitudes (cf. Brannon, 1978, pp. 699–708).

To date, the known-groups approach to construct validity is the primary one utilized, and even here the validity evidence is neither clear nor compelling. Spence and Helmreich (1972a) for the AWS (and other researchers for their gender-related attitude scales) have implicitly assumed that men and women are known groups with respect to female–male issues and targets. More specifically, it has been assumed that women are more liberal in their sex-role attitudes than are men. The reasoning behind these assumptions has not been articulated, and there is contrary evidence (e.g., there has not always been a female–male difference in support for the Equal Rights Amendment). (See also Vaughter [1979] regarding the inappropriateness of using women and men as known groups for gender-related attitude scales.)

Although strong evidence that gender-related attitude scales measure what they purport to (i.e., convergent validity) is rare, demonstrations that these instruments do not measure extraneous variables (i.e., discriminant validity) is almost nonexistent. This state of affairs is particularly perplexing because such scales, as with most self-report measures, are highly obtrusive. There can be no doubt in respondents' minds that the AWS (and other such scales) are intended to measure something about their evaluative orientations toward women and men. On most college campuses, it is socially desirable to support sexual equality. Responses to the AWS and similar devices, then, are highly susceptible to systematic distortion in the direction of these norms. To the extent that such scales assess endorsements of socially desirable attitude positions rather than gender-related attitudes, they cannot be valid indicators. Thus, to demonstrate discriminant validity, it must be shown that the AWS and similar devices do not correlate with indices of social desirability responding. Paulus (1984) has identified two primary forms of social desirability responding—"self-deception" and "impression management"—and developed measures of both. Because Paulus's concepts roughly correspond to the nonconscious and conscious forms of faking on gender-related attitude scales identified by Beere (1979, p. 385), use of his scales may allow researchers to assess whether existing and proposed new instruments are contaminated by either type of social desirability responding.

EXPERIMENTAL DEMONSTRATIONS OF EVALUATION BIAS

One of the most frequently referenced articles in the large literature on male–female relations is Goldberg's (1968) demonstration of "women's prejudice against women." This study established a paradigm for investigating "evaluation bias": Gender of target persons is systematically varied in a context where other stimulus information is held constant; evaluations of the stimulus targets and/or their products (e.g., essays, art work) are assessed. Main effects for target sex or interactions of gender with other experimental manipulations (e.g., physical attractiveness) are taken as evidence of prejudice or discrimination against women.

In Goldberg's original investigation subjects (all female undergraduates) were instructed to critically evaluate a series of abridged articles selected from the professional literatures of six different fields. As determined by preliminary ratings, two fields were associated with males (law and city planning), two with females (education and dietetics), and two were judged to be neutral (art history and linguistics). For each article, gender was experimentally manipulated by changing the writer's first name (e.g., "John McKay" vs. "Joan McKay"). Goldberg hypothesized that articles would be judged less positively when attributed to a female author than when attributed to a male. Further, he predicted that this trend would be reversed or "greatly diminished" for those professional fields associated with women. Goldberg compared evaluative ratings of male and female authors and their essays for nine different response items and concluded, somewhat contrary to his original hypotheses, that women tend to consistently downgrade the work of members of their own gender, even in those fields traditionally reserved for them.

Because Goldberg's conclusions have been widely publicized and accepted by secondary sources, two problematic features of his research should be noted. First, the hypothetical authors differed in one additional respect beyond gender. In the questions used to assess respondents' evaluations of the writers and their work, sex-specific forms of address were used to convey gender, "Mr." for male authors and "Miss" for their female counterparts. Although the use of these terms may have had no impact on subjects' judgments, there is the possibility that this confounding variable contributed to the obtained differentials. For example, in addition to indicating gender, the title "Miss" may have suggested that the writer was a young and, hence, relatively inexperienced professional. Given that the subjects themselves were probably not well-equipped to evaluate the quality of the essays, in the absence of other information, the Mr. versus Miss variation might have produced a more negative judgment of the female authors' work.

Second, although Goldberg himself concluded that his subjects exhibited a generalized prejudice against women across academic fields, the results of his investigation are not entirely consistent with his conclusion. Female–male evaluative differentials were largest in those disciplines regarded as masculine. And, although males were evaluated more positively in the two feminine fields, these differences were not statistically significant (Goldberg, 1967). Thus, congruent with Goldberg's initial hypothesis (but not with his conclusion), evaluation bias *was* diminished in those professions associated with women.

Since Goldberg's original study, numerous investigators have used his basic experimental paradigm. Two separate categories of research within this tradition can be distinguished. First, many studies have attempted to test the limiting conditions of Goldberg's reported finding that, other things being equal, males are evaluated more favorably than females. A second set of investigations has focused on how gender and other characteristics of a prospective or actual employee influence job-related decisions such as hiring and promotion. For both types of research, it can be concluded that "while main effects are frequently found in studies using only social category information, interactions are more common where additional information is provided" (Wallston & O'Leary, 1981, p. 12). Three such variables have received considerable attention: (1) the sex congruence of the activity engaged in or the occupation applied for by the stimulus person, (2) the degree of competence demonstrated by the target, and (3) the physical attractiveness of the target.

Consistent with Goldberg's initial prediction (and, we would argue, with his results), hypothetical actors of either gender with sex-appropriate interests or occupations are evaluated more positively than identical counterparts in sex-inappropriate fields (see Arvey, 1979; Ruble & Ruble, 1982; Wallston & O'Leary, 1981). In terms of competence, *proven* ability (e.g., a blue ribbon painting) apparently attenuates and, in some cases, reverses evaluation bias (e.g., Pheterson, Kiesler, & Goldberg, 1971). (Nieva and Gutek [1980] reach a different conclusion with regard to the interaction of competence and target sex.) Similarly, more bias favoring the male is observed in hiring than in promotion decisions, where the target has presumably already demonstrated some competence by acquiring the position in the first place. Finally, gender of target has been found to interact with attractiveness. The nature of the interaction, however, is complex, and seems to depend on both other information about the stimulus person and the nature of the dependent variable. On the whole, however, it can be concluded that attractiveness manipulations have more impact on evaluations of female than male targets (see Wallston & O'Leary, 1981).

Although the approach introduced by Goldberg has clearly indicated that sex makes a difference in how individuals and their products are evaluated, two major questions can be raised about this research paradigm: Has the success of the method spoiled its utility? What social psychological variable(s) is (are) assessed when the approach is used? With respect to the first question, the evaluation bias paradigm is, in principle, less obtrusive or reactive than the aforementioned self-report attitude scales (cf. Beere, 1983, p. 131). In current practice, however, this may not be the case. Many attempts to replicate Goldberg's results have failed (cf. Allen, 1978, Chapter 6). Although there has been some debate about how such failures should be interpreted, most writers apparently trust the original phenomenon. The question then becomes whether the inability to reproduce Goldberg's findings results from *real* change over time in how females are evaluated relative to males or from an increase in the reactivity of the paradigm (cf. Allen, 1978, Chapter 6). As noted earlier, Goldberg's study was widely publicized; consequently, it may no longer offer an unobtrusive method for assessing attitudes. That is, subjects participating in research making use of the paradigm may discern the experimenter's intent and systematically distort their responses in the direction of egalitarian norms.

The second of the two preceding questions concerns what is assessed in the evaluation bias paradigm. Goldberg himself used the term *prejudice* in describing his results, and he subsequently developed an individual difference measure of prejudice against women, using the evaluation bias approach. Thus, from Goldberg's perspective, the evaluation bias paradigm taps an individual's internal predisposition to respond to women and men in a positive–negative fashion—that is, a gender-related *attitude*. Most researchers, however, appear to regard subjects' responses as samples of discriminatory *behavior* rather than as indices of attitude, behavior that is presumably influenced by attitude, but behavior none the less.

In our judgment, the behavioral interpretation seems the more justifiable. Research within this paradigm—at least as generally implemented—is probably best viewed as demonstrating an effect (i.e., gender-based behavioral discrimination) rather than as an attitude assessment. Although multiple response items are used, subjects in most studies evaluate a single stimulus target, and their responses are aggregated to test for the possibility of evaluation bias. Each respondent would need to evaluate multiple male and female targets in order to yield a reliable measure of the attitudes of individuals. Although multiple targets (usually a very small number) are sometimes used in research and could be the basis of measuring individual attitudes (see Goldberg, 1974), increasing the number of targets is likely to increase the reactivity of the procedure and, hence, undermine its validity as an attitude assessment device.

The attitude versus behavior interpretation of evaluation bias raises a broader question: How is research conducted within this paradigm best conceptualized? One explanation of differential evaluations of the sexes is negative attitudes toward women. An alternative view is that subjects may make use of a prototype-matching strategy when making judgments regarding the stimulus targets, the quality of their efforts, their suitability for various positions, and so on. For example, in evaluating a hypothetical target for a managerial position, respondents may ask themselves How close to the prototypic "good manager" is this particular person? Presumably, some combinations of attributes provide better "fits" than others. Renwick and Tosi (1978) asked subjects to evaluate the suitability for a managerial position of stimulus persons who varied in sex, marital status, and undergraduate and graduate educational background. A significant four-way interaction was obtained, with the most positively evaluated target being the male who was married with two children, an undergraduate business major and an MBA. Although subjects' judgments may have resulted from a complex combination of attitudes regarding gender, marital status, and educational background, a plausible alternative explanation is that the highest-rated candidate comes closest to the prototypic manager.

A Framework for Conceptualizing Gender-Related Attitudes

The accumulated research, though extensive and informative, suffers from a number of methodological problems. Addressing these problems (i.e., doing better research) is not enough, however. Scant attention has been paid to conceptual and theoretical issues (cf. Beere, 1979, 1983; Brannon, 1978; Vaughter, 1983). We agree with Vaughter (1983), who wrote, "we need to reach beyond psychometric improvements . . . it is recommended that we link our concern for measurement with a concern for theory development" (p. 145). As a step in this direction, a general conceptual framework for gender-related attitudes is proposed in this section.

In constructing the proposed framework, two questions are addressed: What is a gender-related attitude? How do gender-related attitudes fit within the cognitive-social psychological framework outlined in Chapter One and fleshed out in Chapter Three? In considering both questions, we draw on social-psychological theory and research on attitudes. Two distinct literatures were consulted: mainstream social-psychological analyses of attitudes, and work on intergroup attitudes (prejudice). Evaluative predispositions concerning the sexes are attitudes—hence the need to consider the former. Because relations between the sexes as broad overarching social categories are similar to relations between ethnic and national groups, intergroup attitude research is also relevant.

WHAT IS A GENDER-RELATED ATTITUDE?

This question can be partitioned into two parts: What is an attitude? How does one determine that it is gender related? Attitude is defined as "a general and enduring favorable or unfavorable feeling about an object or issue" (Cacioppo, Harkins, & Petty, 1981, p. 32). Three points about this definition require elaboration.

First, attitude is a hypothetical construct. That is, attitudes as "general feelings" are not directly observable and cannot be indexed by a single overt behavior. Attitudes do, however, predispose the individual toward action; hence, they are often termed "predispositions." As research and theory on the relation of attitude to behavior indicates, an attitude does not predispose a person to perform a *specific* action. Rather, positive attitudes incline the individual toward positive behaviors (e.g., to approach, to help), whereas negative attitudes predispose toward negative actions (e.g., to avoid, to hurt) (cf. Ajzen & Fishbein, 1977).

This leads to the second point requiring elaboration: An attitude is a positive–negative, pro–con, good–bad predisposition. In short, attitude is evaluative. It is assumed that the degree of positive–negative feelings about an object is, under most conditions, isomorphic with evaluation of the object (Fishbein & Ajzen, 1975, p. 11, Footnote 2; Osgood, 1969). The "under most conditions" is necessary because it is possible to imagine objects that make one feel good but that are evaluated negatively (cf. Ehrlich, 1973, p. 7).

Third, although affect is here regarded as the core of attitude, it is assumed that evaluations of an object are generally accompanied by beliefs about, and behavioral predispositions toward, that object. Thus, attitudes can be assessed by cognitive and conative, as well as by affective indicators (cf. Cacioppo et al., 1981; Ostrom, 1969).

Turning to the subset of evaluative responses of concern in the present chapter raises the question, What is a *gender-related* attitude? Attitudes toward men, toward women, and toward gender subtypes (e.g., women managers) are obviously gender-related, as are pro–con feelings about sex-role arrangements. And, as is clear from the preceding section, it is precisely these attitude objects that have received the most research attention.

Although determining gender-relatedness becomes a thorny issue as one moves beyond these obvious targets, it is a thorniness worth confronting for at least two reasons. First, as is discussed more fully subsequently, attitudes toward women and men and sex-roles are often part of larger belief systems that involve other issues (e.g., equal pay for equal work) and target groups (e.g., feminists). Second, there are public policy issues (i.e., laws and operating procedures of government agencies) that have implications for male–female relations, and, thus, attitudes toward these issues are gender related. How the policy issues are to be identified does not submit to an easy answer. On the one hand, our emphasis on cognition suggests that the individual is the final judge of gender relatedness. However, as a social being, (wo)man is enmeshed in society and, as a consequence, it is to be expected that there are shared definitions of gender relevance at the subgroup and societal level. And, because vocal social groups are important in setting the public agenda of issues, one way to begin an inventory of male–female issues is to inspect the policy statements of such groups. In the U.S., primary such groups (e.g., National Organization for Women—NOW) are concerned with women's rights and espouse what has been labelled "liberal feminism" (see Jaggar, 1977). Carroll (1980) identified the following issues as part of the liberal feminist agenda: the Equal Rights Amendment, abortion and the Human Life Amendment, government-funded child care facilities, social security for homemakers, equal credit/loan opportunities for both sexes, paid maternal leave, "protective" laws regarding women in industry, the burden of proof in rape cases, and exemption from combat of women in the Armed Forces. This list is not intended (by Carroll or us) to be exhaustive or definitive. Rather, these are among the set of issues that need to be considered in developing a more complete understanding of men's and women's evaluative orientations concerning relations between the sexes.

GENDER-RELATED ATTITUDES
WITHIN A COGNITIVE–SOCIAL PSYCHOLOGICAL FRAMEWORK

Earlier, we raised the question, How do gender-related attitudes fit within the cognitive–social psychological framework described earlier in this volume? To briefly review this framework, it is assumed that (wo)man is both a cognitive creature and a social being. (Wo)man the cognitive creature is an active information processor who seeks to make sense out of "external reality." (Wo)man is a social being in two basic senses: (1) (S)he is always embedded in a social context and thus must take into account the thoughts, feelings, and behaviors of others; (2) His/her current psychological makeup is shaped by past social learning (i.e., socialization).

Figure 1 in Chapter Three depicts the socialized adult actor in an interpersonal context. Past learning is assumed to be represented in Long-term social memory, which can be partitioned into declarative ("knowing that") and procedural ("knowing how") knowledge. Two types of declarative knowledge, goals and belief systems, are particularly important for male–female relations. Goals are what the individual strives for—for example, financial success, esteem from peers. Belief systems are organized sets of knowledge concerning some domain. For example, considerable research has been directed at assessing belief systems about people; this work, under the label, "implicit personality theory," was used in Chapter Three to conceptualize gender stereotypes.

In the present chapter, evaluative responses/positive–negative feelings are incorporated into the cognitive–social psychological scheme described in Chapter Three. That is, attitude is the degree of overall positive–negative feeling for or against an object as represented in Long-term social memory (see Chapter Three, Figure 1). Thus, with regard to the sexes, not only are beliefs about but also summary feelings for or against men and women stored in memory. And, though feelings and beliefs are related, it is assumed that the summary feeling is stored separately—that is, it is not generated from the beliefs each time the person makes a response (see Fiske & Linville, 1980; Lingle & Ostrom, 1981). Although the precise manner of this internal representation is unclear, it is useful to think of feelings as a distinct memory code from beliefs (i.e., propositional) and from images (i.e., pictorial) (see Ashmore & Del Boca, 1979; Zajonc, 1980).

As elements of Long-term social memory, attitudes not only summarize and organize past learning, they also influence current information processing and social behavior. That is, attitudes impact on the set of cognitive processes depicted at the bottom of Figure 1 in Chapter Three (i.e., attention, unitization, categorization and integration, and response selection) and ultimately on the overt response of the individual to other people, to social categories, and to a variety of other objects. In sum, the present cognitive–social psychological framework points both to content–structure issues (summarizing–organizing function) and to process issues concerning gender-related attitudes.

Content–Structure Issues
Concerning Gender-Related Attitudes

The issues of content and structure are intertwined and can be thought of collectively as the *what* of gender-related attitudes. In order to empirically study content–structure, the question of *how* must also be considered: How are gender-related attitudes to be assessed?

WHAT IS THE CONTENT–STRUCTURE
OF GENDER-RELATED ATTITUDES?

·Three approaches to this question can be identified: (1) tricomponential structure of attitude, (2) thematic content of verbal attitudes, and (3) attitudes within belief systems.

Tricomponential Structure of Attitude

One of the more popular approaches to the structure of attitudes has been to posit three components: affective, cognitive, and conative (cf. McGuire, 1969). As noted earlier, it is recognized that positive–negative feelings are generally accompanied by cognitions and behavioral intentions. Research on the covariation of the three components has produced mixed results; some studies yield "low-to-moderate intercorrelations" (cf. Ehrlich, 1973, p. 107), whereas others find .strong correlations (e.g., Ostrom, 1969). This variability suggests two as-yet-untried research directions.

First, individuals may differ in the degree to which thoughts, feelings, and behavioral intentions are integrated. Ehrlich (1973) has argued that only "well-formed" attitudes (where the three components are "balanced") are predictive of social behavior. The conditions under which males and females interact suggests that many gender-related attitudes are not likely to be well formed. Unlike other instances of intergroup relations, women and men experience high levels of "intergroup contact." Such contact occurs in a variety of settings and while enacting a diversity of roles, and individual men and women often form intimate relationships. This situation may make it particularly difficult for most people to develop and maintain well-formed gender-related attitudes. Thus, for example, an individual may accept a traditional negative stereotype of females (cognitive component) and, at the same time, be attracted to (affective component) and seek to interact with (conative component) many women.

Second, "individuals may vary in the degree to which an attitude component is dominant" (Ehrlich, 1973, p. 108). Of particular importance are attitudes based primarily on emotional experience. Sears (1983) and his colleagues use the term *symbolic predisposition* to refer to "strong affects that are conditioned to particular symbols, such as 'blacks,' 'America,' 'Democrat,' or 'Communism' " (p. 83). Often the groundwork for symbolic predispositions is established early in life when the child's intellectual machinery is not fully developed. Because learning about men and women begins very early in life (cf. Del Boca & Ashmore, 1980; Katz, this volume), it is likely that affective orientations toward the sexes may also be acquired early and that gender-related attitudes may, at least in part, be symbolic predispositions.

The three attitude components can themselves be further divided. Triandis (1971, pp. 51–54) has adapted Osgood, Suci, and Tannenbaum's (1957) Semantic Differential methodology to assess behavioral intentions. Factor analyses of responses to national groups (e.g., Portuguese) yield five dimensions of behavioral intentions: Respect (e.g., "ask for the opinions of"), Marital (e.g., "go on a date with"), Friendship (e.g., "gossip with"), Social distance (e.g., "prohibit from voting"), and Superordination (e.g., "command"). Although assessment of types of behavioral intentions regarding gender attitudes is an intriguing and potentially fruitful undertaking, simply using the extant Behavior Differential makes little sense. As Hacker (1951) noted over 30 years ago, marriage simply does not mean the same thing in male–female relations as it does in ethnic group relations.

The cognitive component of an intergroup attitude is often equated with the stereotype of the target group (cf. McGuire, 1969, p. 155). As noted in Chapter Three, gender stereotypes are not homogeneous with regard to content. It might be possible to systematically explore the evaluative components of beliefs about the sexes. Rosenberg's (1977) preliminary taxonomy of the evaluative contents of personality impressions (e.g., morality, social competence, intellectual ability) provides a starting point in this regard.

At a somewhat more speculative level, it might prove fruitful to decompose the affective component of gender-related attitudes. Although it is certainly useful to think of attitude as overall or summary pro–con feeling, it is likely that the attitude holder can discriminate the content as well as the valence of his/her feelings. At the negative end, for example, it seems plausible that a person could distinguish between objects that make him or her feel angry, afraid, or disgusted. Attitude researchers have not explored this line of reasoning (cf. Ehrlich, 1973, Chapter 4). This is unfortunate because one's behavior is likely to be quite different toward an object that arouses anger, another that elicits fear, and yet a third that produces disgust. Because women and men interact with one another in a wide variety of settings and roles, it is quite likely that attitudes toward the sexes are affectively complex.

Thematic Content of Verbal Attitudes

Probably the best self-report measure of whites' attitudes toward blacks, the Multiracial Attitude Inventory (MRAI), is based on the assumption that "among the domains of statements related to a given attitudinal object there exist subgroups of statements sharing among themselves a theme they share less strongly with other subgroups" (Brigham, Woodmansee, & Cook, 1976, p. 11). With regard to attitudes toward blacks, 12 themes have been identified. Some of these are specific to black–white relations (e.g., "Integration–Segregation Policy: Integration of the schools will be beneficial to both white and black children alike"), and others have quite different meaning in female–male versus black–white relations (e.g., *"Acceptance in Close Personal Relationships*: I would accept an invitation to a New Year's Eve party given by a black couple in their home") (Brigham et al., 1978, p. 11). However, other content clusters such as *Gradualism* (gradual vs. sudden change in racial status quo), *Acceptance in Status-Superior Relationships, Derogatory Beliefs,* and *Black Superiority* (overfavorableness to blacks, which is used as an index of social desirability) are likely to have parallels in gender-related attitudes.

The development of an analogue to the Multiracial Attitude Inventory would be a significant contribution to the gender-related attitude literature. An ideal starting point for such an instrument would be Brannon's (1978) "taxonomy of constructs concerning women," which identifies seven general content domains relevant to assessing attitudes toward women: (1) General (e.g., "What most women are like: personal trait-like qualities seen as general and nonsituational"); (2) Social–Interpersonal Responses to Women (e.g., "Support for chivalry and etiquette"); (3) Women and Marriage (e.g., "General desirability and naturalness of marriage to one member of the other sex"); (4) Having and Raising Children (e.g., "Belief in natural desire of all women to have children"); (5) Conflict of Career and Family (e.g., "Beliefs in the greater suitability of some careers than others for women"); (6) Discrimination Against Women (e.g., "Women in positions of power or leadership"); and (7) The Women's Movement (e.g., "Basic sympathy or hostility to perceived aims and goals of the movement") (Brannon, 1978, pp. 683–690). This taxonomy might be supplemented by asking activists (on both the pro- and antifeminist sides) to articulate what they regard as the major issues.

Attitudes within Belief Systems

How are individual attitudes related to one another and to other knowledge in Long-term social memory? Two seemingly incompatible conclusions arise from the work that has examined the relationship between evaluations of multiple attitude objects. On the one hand, some personality and social psychologists have found that many social attitudes are structured or organized in terms of liberalism–conservatism (Wilson, 1973) or radicalism–conservatism (Eysenck, 1954). That is, at least in England and the U.S., attitudes seem to come in bundles, with conservatives positively evaluating such diverse issues and objects as capital punishment, strong national defense, religion, and censorship, whereas liberals or radicals have negative attitudes about these issues. The opposing view has been most consistently championed by a political scientist, Converse (1964, 1970), who argues that the public policy attitudes of most Americans are not clearly and tightly organized.

We believe both sides are correct. Social attitudes are organized in Long-term social memory. A good cognitive creature (as *Homo sapiens* is) would have it no other way. However, there are many reasons to suspect that for most perceivers most of the time, attitudes are only loosely interconnected and would seldom meet the dictates of formal logic. What are these reasons? (1) (Wo)man is a limited information processor. Because our rationality is bounded, we often take cognitive shortcuts (termed "heuristics"), which, while serving us well most of the time, can lead us astray. (2) (Wo)man has other goals than being logical—for example, to be liked. (3) Most of our organized sets of beliefs and attitudes are held implicitly. We are seldom asked to explain and defend our belief systems and thus a great deal of illogic may be unnoticed. (4) Beliefs and attitudes about the same object are likely to be stored in memory in multiple ways.

What might some of these multiple ways be, especially with regard to gender-related attitudes? Building on Abelson (1968), Bem (1970) argues that much of our knowledge is represented in memory in the form of *opinion molecules*, which "are conversational units. They give us something to say when a particular topic comes up in conversation" (p. 39). An opinion molecule consists of "(1) a belief, (2) an attitude, and (3) a perception of social support for them" (p. 38). An example: "Abortion is murder. I'm completely against abortions. Everybody in my church feels the same way." Opinion molecules merit consideration for two reasons: (1) "Talking-about" is an important social behavior. It is particularly important for social scientists who use self-report methods for assessing social attitudes. (2) Knowledge stored as small, isolated opinion molecules allows for a considerable amount of inconsistency (because molecules about "logically related" topics are not connected).

In addition to being part of small, isolated opinion molecules, gender-related attitudes are also represented in memory as elements of more general belief systems. Vaughter (1979; 1983) suggests that one gender belief system, "sexism," is pervasive in American society. This belief system, which contains both nonconscious and conscious elements, is organized around the belief in male superiority. (See also Nemerowicz, 1979.) And, at least by implication and in relation to men, women are regarded as inferior. Thus, the sexist belief system involves prejudice against women. A variant—perhaps necessitated because men and women interact with one another on a regular and sometimes intimate basis—includes both positive and negative beliefs about women. Women, though weak, are valuable and should be protected (a chivalry component); at the same time, because they are naive and emotional, they should not be allowed to fill leadership positions (an open subordination component) (Nadler & Morrow, 1959).

In addition to this *prejudice perspective* (where gender-related attitudes are organized in terms of overall evaluations of the sexes), it is possible to identify two other approaches to social attitudes: self-interest and symbolic politics (cf. Del Boca, 1982). *Self-interest* is a dominant theoretical approach in political science. The underlying logic is quite simple: (Wo)man is a hedonistic creature. (S)he develops and maintains positive attitudes toward groups and public policies that promise personal material benefits and negative attitudes toward those that lead to personal costs.

In addition to the central issue of the role of self-interest as motivator of social attitudes, this perspective raises two important questions for gender-related attitudes: (1) How do men and women define self-interest? The basic self-interest position assumes that people correctly perceive their own *objective* self-interest and behave consistently in ways to advance that interest. Variants have been proposed that loosen the assumption of veridical perception. For example, the Marxist notion of false consciousness refers to the inability of people to perceive their self-interest. (2) How narrowly is the self in self-interest defined? The unmodified self-interest position takes the *individual* as the sole reference point: "What's in it for *me*?" Again, variants have been proposed: Self-interest has been seen as extending to one's family or even further to one's social category ("If it will benefit psychology professors, we're for it"). Do males and females think of social issues and public policies in terms of outcomes for them, for their loved ones, for their gender group?

Yet a third general approach to social attitudes can be identified: termed *symbolic politics*, this perspective is of a more recent origin. Most of the symbolic politics work to date has concerned racial issues and has been conducted by Sears and his colleagues (Kinder & Sears, 1981; McConahay & Hough, 1976; Sears & Kinder, 1971; Sears & McConahay, 1973). The notion of a "symbolic attitude" has been defined in several different ways. We regard a symbolic attitude toward a social category as based on a strong, general affective attachment to the societal status quo, together with the vague apprehension that the group in question (or some members of it) are threatening that status quo.[3] Applying this to female–male relations, symbolic sexism is "(1) a general, positive attachment to the political, economic, and social (including sexual) status quo, together with the belief that existing societal arrangements should be maintained; and (2) a vague apprehension

---

[3]This usage is not isomorphic with Sears' (1983) aforementioned definition of a symbolic predisposition. However, both Sears and we stress the importance of affect.

that public policies designed to promote sexual equality, somehow pose a threat to the status quo, and by implication, to those cherished values which serve to maintain the 'American way of life' " (Del Boca, 1982, pp. 19–20). In short, according to the symbolic politics perspective, attitudes toward gender-related issues and objects are organized in terms of perceived implications of these targets for the "American way of life."

OPERATIONALIZING GENDER-RELATED ATTITUDES

Having discussed the *what* of gender-related attitudes, we turn to the question of *how*: How should such attitudes be assessed? To date, a narrow set of research operations has been employed: stereotype assessment, attitude scales, and experimental studies of evaluation bias. Because all assessment procedures have built-in sources of invalidity (i.e., method variance), it is desirable to explore a wider range of methodologically dissimilar measurement techniques. To do this, we draw on the logic and specific recommendations of Cook and Selltiz (1964).

Cook and Selltiz's "multiple indicator approach to attitude measurement" is based on two premises. First, as noted earlier, attitudes can never be *directly* measured; as a consequence, all methods of assessment involve inferring an underlying attitude from observed behavior, be it a verbal report or some other judgment about or action toward the attitude object. And second, behavior with respect to an attitude target is influenced by two classes of variables in addition to the individual's attitude: other characteristics of the person (e.g., motivational state, other attitudes) and characteristics of the situation (e.g., expectations of others, potential consequences of various acts). Hence, it is advisable to use multiple measures in attitude research, preferably measures that differ in terms of the factors other than attitude that are likely to influence a behavioral response.

According to Cook and Selltiz, there are five major approaches to attitude measurement: self-report, objective task performance, observation of overt behavior, reactions to partially structured stimuli (projective techniques), and physiological indicators. Only the first three approaches are discussed here.[4] The logic of self-report measures is simple—what a person thinks or feels can be inferred from what she or he says. In the objective task-performance approach, subjects are asked to perform a task that involves

---

[4]Projective techniques are not often used in assessing attitudes, and such usage is problematic because of the unreliability of these techniques (see Cook & Selltiz, 1964). Physiological measures can only indicate extremity, not valence of attitude, and are both costly and unwieldy (see, however, Cacioppo & Petty, 1983).

material related to the attitude object. Such tasks "are presented as tests of information or ability, or simply as jobs that need to be done" (Cook & Selltiz, 1964, p. 50). The assumption underlying the use of this approach is that task performance will be influenced by attitude. Because attention is focused directly on the task rather than on the attitude object itself, the respondent is presumably unaware of the investigator's intent to measure her or his attitude. The behavior-to-attitude inference for the third approach identified by Cook and Selltiz (1964), observation of overt behavior, is straightforward—positive action toward an attitude object (e.g., helping) is indicative of a positive attitude toward the target, whereas negative behavior reflects a negative evaluation.

Traditional gender-stereotype assessment techniques and attitude scales fall into the category of self-report measures. As discussed earlier, such methods are highly reactive because the subject is fully aware of the investigator's purpose. Experimental demonstrations of evaluation bias can be seen as objective task measures (see, however, our discussion of evaluation bias in an earlier section of this chapter). Although such assessment procedures generally have the advantage of being unobtrusive, the widespread use of the Goldberg paradigm may have negated this plus-point in current practice. Collectively, then, extant measures of gender-related attitudes may share a source of invalidity—obtrusiveness with possible conscious and nonconscious distortion of response. Thus, it is necessary to supplement current methods with indicators that are less subject to this type of method variance.

Although self-report measures are subject to faking, they have the advantage of being efficient—a large amount of information can be obtained from an individual in a short span of time. This advantage has not been fully exploited. Further, many present applications of the self-report approach have not done the best possible job of answering the investigator's questions. Much extant research has been directed at description—essentially, what is the nature, distribution in the population, and stability over time of various gender-related attitudes?

As noted in Chapter Three, the reliance on convenience samples (most often college students, sometimes their parents) severely restricts the generalizability of descriptive research. Sample surveys, in which respondents are selected in such a way that the resulting sample is representative of some clearly specified universe of people, solve the generalizability problem and, thus, are ideally suited to provide descriptive data. Is there survey data concerning gender-related attitudes? Yes, and it is of three varieties: questions asked by commercial pollsters such as George Gallup, surveys explicitly concerned with women or women's issues (the series of four surveys in 1970, 1972, 1974, and 1980 sponsored by Virginia Slims is the most prominent), and modules of relevant questions included in the General Social Survey and other omnibus surveys. (All involve samples representative of adult Americans and door-to-door interviewing.)

Although useful for illuminating some aspects of public opinion relevant to gender, the commercial polls conducted by Gallup and the series of surveys sponsored by Virginia Slims are not optimal for social scientists concerned with gender-related attitudes. In large part, this is because questions or entire surveys of gender-related attitudes occur only (or primarily) when female–male relations are somehow problematic (e.g., during or immediately following war). In addition, more questions are about women than men. In part to overcome the problem of noncomparability of items across time, the General Social Survey was established by the Russell Sage Foundation and the National Science Foundation in 1972 and has been conducted regularly since. In addition to demographic items, there are questions on race relations, the family, politics, crime, health, leisure, and miscellaneous issues. The General Social Survey contains two items assessing attitudes toward traditional sex roles. There are also three items relevant to women in politics.

In sum, there are survey data on gender-related attitudes available for analysis. Although existing data have limitations, they can be fruitfully analyzed to reveal trends in attitude change over time. For example, Mason, Czajka, and Arber (1976), using poll data from several different sources, investigated the extent of change in attitudes toward women's roles over the course of a decade. Thus, despite some of the shortcomings of the existing data base, survey methodology holds considerable promise for future research. Because large-scale face-to-face surveys are expensive, we would recommend smaller-scale telephone surveys as a compromise between these and the convenience samples often studied by researchers interested in gender-related attitudes (see Del Boca [1982] for an example).

The second type of approach to attitude assessment is objective task performance. Most of the specific procedures discussed by Cook and Selltiz (1964) involve inferring attitude on the basis of systematic bias in information processing (e.g., learning, memory, logic) of materials regarding the attitude object. Although such an inference is not always unambiguous, such procedures might be fruitfully explored by workers concerned with gender-related attitudes. Another possibility is the personality description method of assessing implicit personality theory that was described in depth in Chapter Three. Because the subject is describing personalities or, more often, specific individuals known to him or her, the respondent is unlikely to view the task as an attempt on the part of the researchers to assess his or her attitude toward a social category. Further, this technique provides a more reliable attitude indicator than the evaluation-bias paradigm because the individual describes many different representatives of the attitude object class rather than responding to one or a small number of stimulus targets.

The third and final class of attitude indicators identified by Cook and Selltiz (1964) is observation of overt behavior. We join other commentators (Beere, 1983; Brannon, 1978; Vaughter, 1983) in urging greater attention to behavioral measures by male–female relations researchers. Such measures have the clear advantage of indexing attitude via actions that the subject him/herself regards as having consequences. In addition, indicators based on overt behavior are generally less reactive and, as a consequence, less susceptible to social-desirability responding than self-report measures.

Brannon (1978) has identified five "generic behavioral measures": "signing one's name to a document," "donating money to a cause," "buying cause-related materials," "volunteering time to a cause," "observation of routine interactional behavior," (pp. 704–706). The first four seem well suited to assessing evaluative orientations toward public policies (e.g., signing vs. not signing a petition urging passage of the ERA) and activist organizations (e.g., donating money or volunteering time to Phyllis Schlafly's Eagle Forum). Observation of routine interactional behavior provides a means of measuring attitudes toward individuals and social categories.

A particularly important aspect of routine social interactions is nonverbal behavior, and both Brannon (1978), with regard to attitudes toward women, and Crosby, Bromley, and Saxe (1980), concerning ethnic prejudice, identify nonverbal behavior as a possible indicator of evaluative predisposition. Although nonverbal behavior offers some interesting possibilities for research on gender-related attitudes, two cautions are in order. First, it is generally assumed by both researchers and the lay public that nonverbal behaviors are relatively automatic or uncontrolled responses to people and events (Schneider, Hastorf, & Ellsworth, 1979). Such behaviors, however, can be under conscious control and, hence, susceptible to a variety of influences, including the desire to present a particular image of self.

Second, there are problems in interpreting the meaning of various nonverbal indicators. The same nonverbal behavior can be interpreted in multiple ways and, more importantly, the different meanings attached to various behaviors point to rather different attitudinal orientations. Male-to-female touch, for example, has been viewed both as an indicator of attraction and as a means of maintaining status differentials between the sexes (see Henley, 1977). If touch is viewed as indicative of affection, one would infer a positive attitude; if it is seen as a gesture of dominance, the inference might be that the actor regards the target as inferior. Future research might be directed at explicating the personal and situational variables that determine when nonverbal behaviors signal a positive–negative or upper–lower status orientation of an actor toward a target.

Nonverbal behavior does not, of course, exhaust the possibilities with respect to this class of attitude indicators. Cook and Selltiz (1964) suggest two additional possibilities. Sociometric choices provide a means of assessing attitudes with respect to social categories. And, investigators can observe behavior in situations where respondents are asked to role-play a part in a staged social interaction. How the individual enacts a particular work or family role might be observed, as might responses to others who play complementary roles.

Process Issues Concerning Gender-Related Attitudes

In the preceding section, we discussed how conceiving of gender-related attitudes in the context of a cognitive–social psychological framework and as related to attitude research in basic social psychology suggests a broader perspective on the interrelated questions of *what* and *how*. We now turn from content–structure to process issues—the acquisition of gender-related attitudes, attitudes in action, and changing attitudes toward the sexes and related issues. As was the case with sex stereotypes (Chapter Three, this volume), there is not a great deal of directly relevant work on these topics. There is, however, research and theory in the attitude literature of basic social psychology, and especially in the intergroup conflict area, that suggest directions for future research.

THE ACQUISITION OF GENDER-RELATED ATTITUDES

Social scientists concerned with intergroup conflict have stressed the need to explicitly address the level-of-analysis problem (cf. Sherif and Sherif, 1965). With regard to ethnic group conflict, there are societal-level theories (which aim to explain how members of a society or community come to share a norm of outgroup hostility) and individual-level theories (designed to account for how individuals within societies become prejudiced) (cf. Ashmore & Del Boca, 1976). Because the aim of this volume is to move toward a *social psychology* of female–male relations, the focus here is on the individual level. First, theories that purport to identify causes of intergroup attitudes are presented. Second, we chart the course of the acquisition and maintenance of gender-related attitudes in the developing individual.

Individual-Level Theories

Although all such theories seek to explain how individuals acquire negative intergroup beliefs, attitudes, and behavior, they vary considerably in terms of emphasis on individual versus social-context factors. Three groupings are distinguishable: (1) *Intrapersonal*—explanations are phrased in terms of the personality, cognition, or motivation of the individual; (2) *Interpersonal*—explanatory variables are transactions between the individual and other specific individuals (e.g., parents) or between the individual and societal institutions (e.g., schools, media); (3) *Intergroup*—individual thought, feeling, and behavior are traced to relations between social groups.

The most well-known of the intrapersonal explanations derive from Freudian theory. There are a wide variety of psychoanalytic explanations of intergroup conflict; for present purposes, however, these can be partitioned into psychoanalytic reductionism and psychosocial theories of prejudice (cf. Billig, 1976, Chapters 2–5). Psychosocial theories are interpersonal explanations and are discussed later. According to psychoanalytic reductionists, prejudice can be traced to unconscious instincts, especially the aggressive instinct, or to aggressive impulses aroused by frustration. One way to protect the self against these instincts or impulses is to displace aggression onto some outgroup. The individual can also defend against aggressive feelings by projecting them onto outgroup members (e.g., "They want to rule the world").

Although psychoanalytic reductionism can be criticized on both conceptual (e.g., How exactly are particular outgroups selected as targets for displacement and projection?) and empirical (e.g., the evidence for frustration as a cause of prejudice is skimpy) grounds (cf. Ashmore & Del Boca, 1976), this perspective does raise two intriguing points concerning the etiology of gender-related attitudes. First, Freudian approaches feature sexual as well as aggressive impulses and the channeling of the sexual or libidinal instinct is regarded as a source of considerable frustration and a major factor in personality development. Because sexuality is important to both the gender identity of individual men and women and to the close relationships between women and men (see Chapters 2 and 5, this volume), it seems likely that the individual's coping with sexual issues will be related to his/her evaluative responses to the sexes and other gender-relevant issues. Thus, it seems advisable in future attitude research to seek to understand the nature of this relationship.

Second, psychoanalytic approaches stress the importance of infancy and early childhood and of parent–child relationships in personality development. And, in fact, there are several psychoanalytically inspired explanations of traditional or negative attitudes toward women that take as their starting point the fact that women are the child's primary caretaker (cf. Del Boca & Ashmore, 1980; Pleck, 1978; Stockard & Johnson, 1979). Basically these explanations assume that the young child experiences his/her mother as all-powerful and monolithic and as a source of considerable pain as well as pleasure. According to Dinnerstein (1976), the all-powerful and all-encompassing mother is not seen by the child as a "human" or a "person"; this sets the stage for a negative attitude. Lerner (1974) argues that negative attitudes toward women result from a defensive reversal of the early extreme dependency of the child on the mother.

The theories focusing on the early mother–child relationship have not received much attention from empirical researchers. This is unfortunate because mother and father are the child's earliest exemplars of the social categories, female and male, and it seems plausible that perceptions and evaluations of parents should be related to sex stereotypes and gender-related attitudes. There is a literature on children's perceptions of parents, but this work is seldom conceived of in terms of the child's overall "learning about sex" (see, however, Del Boca & Ashmore, 1980, pp. 167–168). We urge that this connection be made and that work on children's "perceptions" of parents include feelings as well as traits because the former may be less obtrusive and closer to the spirit of the psychoanalytic formulations.

In sharp contrast to such theories is Tajfel's (1969) analysis of the "cognitive aspects of prejudice." Tajfel placed *categorization*—the partitioning of objects into categories or classes on the basis of perceived similarity-dissimilarity—at the heart of his cognitive approach and made two claims. First, he argued that categorization of both nonsocial and social (e.g., people) objects leads perceivers to underestimate within-category variability and to overestimate between-category variability. Quite simply, once formed, categories lead us to "see" category members as more similar to one another than they actually are and to "see" members of different categories as more dissimilar than, in fact, they are. This enhancement-of-contrast effect has been supported by subsequent research (cf. Ashmore & Del Boca, 1976, pp. 88–90), and both Taylor (1981) and Wilder (1981) have successfully extended the basic categorization notion, thereby providing support for Tajfel's first claim.

His second assertion is even more directly relevant to the issue of intergroup attitudes. Tajfel suggested that intergroup bias may be "a direct product of the categorization process . . . that the mere existence of different social groups is sufficient to foster biased behavior. In particular, persons favor groups of which they are members (ingroups) at the expense of groups to which they do not belong (outgroups)" (Wilder, 1981, p. 228). Three major explanations of ingroup bias have been offered: cultural norm (people, at least in Western culture, are socialized to favor the ingroup), social identity (people favor the ingroup in order to establish and maintain a positive social identity), cognitive differentiation (people favor the ingroup as a means of maintaining the cognitive differences between the two groups). These explanations are complementary. The point to be stressed here is that the third hypothesis, for which Wilder (1981) has found support, traces intergroup discrimination (and perhaps prejudice) to the basic cognitive activity of categorization.

A final intraindividual explanation of prejudice is Rokeach's Belief Congruence theory (Rokeach, Smith, & Evans, 1960). Offered originally as an alternative to race prejudice, Rokeach argued that negative intergroup attitudes and behavior are based on assumed differences in belief (e.g., "I'm god-fearing; they're heathens"), not race per se. This proposition generated considerable research; the formulation has been criticized (see Ashmore & Del Boca, 1976) and Rokeach (1980) has responded to the critiques. Although the notion of belief prejudice has not been applied to male–female attitudes, there is reason to consider the application of Rokeach's proposition to gender-related attitudes. The sexes are socialized to have different interests and goals (see Chapter Two, this volume). It is, thus, not unlikely that the sexes may have conflicting beliefs (e.g., the much-popularized football widow) and that these contribute to less-than-positive intergroup attitudes.

Turning to interpersonal approaches to intergroup conflict, the first type of explanation, "psychosocial theories of prejudice," builds on the same basic Freudian assumptions as the psychoanalytic reductionists but adds consideration of social factors. Clearly, the major such theory is *The Authoritarian Personality* (Adorno, Frenkel-Brunswik, Levinson, & Sanford, 1950). The core of the theory is that harsh, punitive, status- and power-oriented parental child-rearing practices produce a personality syndrome that predisposes the child to acceptance of an antidemocratic or authoritarian ideology (which includes prejudice against minorities). Thus, the psychodynamic roots of the formulation are clear in the importance attached to parental treatment and the linking of ideology (including prejudice) to underlying personality needs (via such defense mechanisms as projection and displacement). At the same time, it was recognized by Adorno and his colleagues that personality dynamics do not cause ideologies and that antidemocratic ideologies depend on social and economic factors.

It is possible to discern three paths from authoritarianism to gender-related attitudes. First, the authoritarian channels his/her aggressive impulses not against parents and other authority figures but against relatively defenseless minority groups. To the extent that women are seen as such a group they become a target for displaced aggression. Second, authoritarianism includes a rigid adherence to traditional values. Because female subservience is part of such values, a condescending view of women would result. This connection is described by Altemeyer (1981) in his updated and revised (i.e., nonpsychodynamic) version of right-wing authoritarianism. Third, as Pleck (1978) notes, an authoritarian upbringing can lead the individual to be overly concerned with proper sexuality and fear of cross-sex identification. As a defense against such identification the other sex could be derogated.

Whereas psychoanalytic reductionists and the authors of *The Authori-*

tarian Personality placed heavy emphasis on the id and the superego (respectively), many later psychoanalytic workers focused on the ego. For example, Bettelheim and Janowitz (1964) wrote, "The search for identity, and with it the search for ego strength and personal control, might very well involve as a detour the desire to find one's identity, or to strengthen it, through prejudice" (p. 57). Although not from a psychodynamic perspective, Ehrlich (1973) has proposed a "principle of self-congruity," in which a negative self-concept is hypothesized to predispose the person to negative other-attitudes and ethnic prejudice. This principle has received some empirical support (cf. Ashmore & Del Boca, 1976, pp. 84–85). Pleck (1978) has also identified low self-esteem as a possible cause of men's traditional attitudes toward women. The small number of studies relevant to this variant of the more general proposition, however, yield mixed results.

The second interpersonal approach to explaining ethnic prejudice focuses not on personality dynamics, but on how societal factors combine with (wo)man's propensity to seek causal attributions to lead whites to infer that blacks are "bad." As naive scientists, humans seek to account for their own and others' actions. Behavior can be attributed either to factors internal to the actor (e.g., ability) or motivation or to external factors (e.g., task difficulty). In short, behavior can, via attribution processes, lead to conclusions about a person's or group's ability and motivation. Whites learn about blacks primarily through the mass media, where blacks more often than whites appear as athletes, entertainers, as unemployed, on welfare, and as criminals. Because of the high societal value placed on individualism, Americans are predisposed to make internal attributions. As a consequence, whites conclude that blacks, because of either ability or motivation, are disposed to be successful as athletes and entertainers but also to be stupid or lazy ("Why else would they be unemployed and on welfare?").

The attributional approach has not yet been applied to the question of how gender-related attitudes are acquired and maintained.[5] Even though men and women have greater and more-varied contact than blacks and whites, it is still true that the "reality" of American society is that men more often occupy positions of power and prestige. Thus, assuming an inclination toward internal attributions, it is not unlikely that Americans infer that men are superior to women in either ability or effort, or more generally that men are better.

The third and final interpersonal explanation of intergroup attitudes places the most emphasis on society relative to the individual. According to this view, an individual's ethnic attitudes are learned just as are other aspects

---

[5]There is, however, considerable work on differential attribution as a function of sex of target. (See Wallston & O'Leary, 1981, pp. 23–28, for a review.)

of one's culture. That is, acquiring prejudice is part of the socialization process and it is maintained in adulthood by conformity pressures. The socialization–conformity explanation has considerable intuitive appeal and is supported by empirical data (cf. Ashmore & Del Boca, 1976; Ehrlich, 1973). As
noted in the previous chapter, however, exactly how children learn society's
prejudices from parents, schools, and other socialization agents is seldom
directly studied.

In addition to the intrapersonal and interpersonal approaches, it is possible to account for prejudice in terms of the relations between social groups.
At the risk of oversimplification, two such schools of thought can be identified: one seeks to account for negative intergroup attitudes in terms of objective conflict between groups for scarce resources and the other stresses the
role of nonobjective symbolic factors in intergroup conflict (cf. Ashmore &
Del Boca, 1976; Austin & Worchel, 1979; Coser, 1956). These approaches,
of course, correspond directly with the aforementioned self-interest and
symbolic politics belief systems.

Del Boca (1982) tested these two explanations and a third (prejudice
against women) as determinants of support for/opposition to two public
policies concerned with gender equality—the ERA and the Human Life
Amendment. Two studies were conducted—a telephone survey of a representative sample of New Jersey adults and in-person interviews with middle-
class suburban women. Though complex, it is possible to summarize the
findings of the two studies as follows.

1.   In the pitting of the three explanations against one another, there was
no clear winner. Depending on the sex of the respondent and the policy issue,
each factor was able to account for (in a multiple regression analysis) a
significant portion of the variance in policy attitude.
2.   Attitude toward the women's liberation movement, which could not
be subsumed under any of the three explanations, was a major predictor of
support for/opposition to the two policy issues.
3.   There was preliminary evidence for three causal chains: (1) Males' attitudes toward the ERA were best accounted for by prejudice against
women. Prejudice impacted both directly on policy position and indirectly
by influencing attitude toward the women's movement which, in turn, influenced policy attitude. (2) For females' attitudes toward the ERA, the pattern was quite complex, with two chains discernible—one from symbolic
sexism to policy position and one from prejudice against women through attitude toward the women's liberation movement to ERA attitude. (3) For
females' HLA attitudes, there was a simple path from one aspect of symbolic
sexism (attachment to traditional American values) to policy attitude. In
sum, attitudes toward gender-related public policies are multiply deter-

mined, and different causal chains are discernible as a function of subject sex and policy issue.

Gender-Related Attitudes through the Life Cycle

The preceding review of theories of prejudice has pointed to a variety of factors that may be implicated in the development of gender-related attitudes. Here, we summarize and provide a second way of organizing these by looking at the role that different factors might play over the life course of a single individual. Katz (Chapter Two, this volume) divides the life cycle into four major developmental periods: infancy, early and middle childhood, adolescence, and adulthood. In general, intrapersonal, interpersonal, and intergroup explanations of attitudes involve factors that have their maximal impact on the individual at different, yet overlapping, points in this sequence.

In terms of intrapersonal explanations, psychoanalytic reductionists emphasize events that occur very early in life. Dinnerstein, for example, focuses on the mother–child relationship during infancy; more orthodox Freudians underscore the significance of the Oedipal (preschool) period. According to these and other psychoanalytic writers, the early experiences of the individual will have a lasting impact on the way in which he or she orients toward other people and toward social categories, including women and men.

Interpersonal theories, on the other hand, involve factors that have a somewhat later time of onset and extend over a longer span of time. In particular, the socialization and conformity approach to intergroup attitudes points to a variety of different sources of information about men, women, and gender relations over the life course. Infancy is primarily a period of child care rather than socialization. With the beginning of childhood, however, systematic and conscious efforts are made to teach the child the ways of his/her culture. As agents of socialization, parents are particularly influential during the childhood period, with peers, school, and the mass media becoming increasingly important as the individual progresses through childhood and adolescence.

Finally, the intergroup approach focuses attention on the nature of interdependence between the social categories, male and female, and the degree and quality of contact that occurs between and among women and men. In childhood, boys and girls tend to play in same-sex groups (Schofield, 1982), and these groups are relatively independent (i.e., a time of "separate-but-equal"?). Sex segregation of play continues in adolescence, but boys and girls increasingly interact with one another as individuals. In adulthood, the sexes find themselves in both integrated (e.g., the family) and segregated (e.g., the workplace) settings. Also, with more-recent efforts to change the gender status quo (e.g., the ERA) and increasing participation of women in spheres traditionally reserved for men, the relation of women to men as social categories and the proper role of each within society has become problematic. Thus, for many adults of both sexes, the matter of personal and group self-interest and the perception that certain changes in female–male relations threaten cherished values have come to the fore.

GENDER-RELATED ATTITUDES AND BEHAVIOR

Earlier, we were critical of the predominance of self-report measures of gender-related attitudes and urged greater emphasis on behavioral indicators. This was intended, in part, to increase the accuracy of assessment (by reducing the obtrusiveness of the measuring device) and as a means of assessing the validity of existing measures. Here, we suggest two other ways in which behavior should be of interest to the researcher concerned with attitudes and male–female relations. These are phrased as questions: When, how, and why do gender-related attitudes correspond with behavior? What behaviors ought one be concerned with in female–male relations?

The Attitude–Behavior Link

Although some sociologists had long been critical of the assumption that attitudes are good predictors of behavior (e.g., LaPiere, 1934), it was not until Wicker's (1969) review article that most social psychologists became aware of the weakness of the evidence concerning the attitude–behavior link. This challenge to a long-held assumption stimulated a considerable amount of conceptual and empirical work, and since the mid-1970s, a great deal has been learned about when, how, and why attitudes influence behavior (cf. Ajzen & Fishbein, 1977; Cialdini, Petty, & Cacioppo, 1981; Deutscher, 1973; Fishbein & Ajzen, 1975; Schuman & Johnson, 1976; Zanna, Higgins, & Herman, 1982). What has been learned can be partitioned into methodological and conceptual lessons (see Cooper & Croyle, 1984).

Two methodological points deserve emphasis: reliability and congruence of the attitude and behavior measures. It is an assessment truism that an unreliable indicator will not correlate well with other measures. A second such truism is that reliability increases with the number of items. Yet, much of the research assessing the attitude–behavior correlation has used single-item measures, especially single-item measures of behavior. The second methodological point has been championed by Ajzen and Fishbein (1977), who argue (and provide considerable evidence to support this argument) that an attitude measure will predict a behavioral index best when the two assessments are congruent with regard to action, target, context, and time. Concern with the generality or specificity of the target is particularly important for researchers studying gender-related attitudes. Quite simply, for example, attitude scales that assess attitude toward traditional sex-role arrangements (a very general attitude object) will not be good predictors of pro–con behavior toward a female manager (a very specific attitude object).

A major conceptual lesson has been the demonstration of multiple pathways to action. Bentler and Speckart (1979) have shown that a person's behavior is not only influenced by his/her attitude, but also by past behavior (a "habitual" component). Abelson (1982) has argued that attitudes predict behavior only when the situational context pushes or allows the person "to respond in terms of her personal values and beliefs" (p. 133). Such contexts, which are termed "individuated," are not as common as one might expect. Rather, often, "behavior is controlled by a particular script for which the attitude in question is not relevant to its action rule" (p. 135). Taking an example from male–female relations, a waiter in a restaurant may present an ordered bottle of wine to the male rather than the female customer not because of a negative attitude toward women but because this action is part of a sequence of scripted behavior. It is quite likely that a great deal of interaction between the sexes is scripted rather than individuated (i.e., attitude driven).

What Behaviors?

A second question can be asked about gender-related attitudes in action: What behaviors are most important to understand and predict? There is probably widespread agreement that action that directly or indirectly hurts or harms another should be the focus. For the sake of discussion, we distinguish a continuum of such behavior from (1) direct individual-to-individual harm-doing, through (2) an individual hurting another as an agent of an organization or within a business-as-usual context, to (3) an individual supporting societal-level arrangements that put social groups at a disadvantage.

Even though little boys are presumably taught not to hit little girls (cf. Maccoby & Jacklin, 1974, pp. 238–239), women (along with the elderly and children) are frequent victims of violent crime (Siegel, 1983, p. 1269). Of particular significance for male–female relations is what has been termed "private violence," or "what people who know each other, even profess to love each other, do to each other" (Andersen, 1983, p. 18). Relative to men, women are disproportionate victims of such violence as spouse battering, marital rape, and incest. The foregoing forms of interpersonal aggression are most often treated as abnormal, and explanations are sought in terms of deviant personalities and traumatic life events. Certainly, these behaviors are statistically abnormal and much family violence can be traced back to the victimization in childhood of the aggressor (Straus, Gelles, & Steinmetz, 1980). However, we think it would be a mistake to ignore the possibility that gender-related attitudes might not be implicated in male–female interpersonal harm-doing. This suggestion is the individual-level complement of feminist analyses that trace violence against women to societal arrangements concerning the sexes (e.g., Schwendinger & Schwendinger, 1983).

The second type of behavior involves an individual harming another, but the context is quite different from that surrounding most private violence—the situation is "business as usual" and the person inflicting the harm is often a professional who is acting as a legitimate authority within an organization. We note two examples. First, therapists' behavior toward their clients, from diagnosis to treatment, is obviously important to the psychological health and personal development of the patients. There has been much written about the sex bias of many personality theories and the differential treatment of men and women. The empirical research on this latter topic is far from clear (cf. Hare-Mustin, 1983, pp. 594–595). In part, the unclarity of findings has resulted from researchers expecting, and thus looking for, simple effects (e.g., more-negative diagnoses of women). Three points from the preceding review suggest that complex rather than simple outcomes are to be expected: (1) A major conclusion from the evaluation-bias literature is that interactions, not gender-of-target main effects, are the rule; (2) There are many gender-related attitudes (not simply a pro–con orientation toward women) that might be implicated in a therapist's actions toward a client (e.g., attitude toward traditional gender roles); (3) The linking of a clinician's attitude to behavior depends on a variety of personal and situational variables.

Second, another example of business-as-usual harm-doing is personnel decisions in business and industry. Such decisions can be partitioned into questions of getting a job and issues of job assignment, conditions of work, and promotions. Differential treatment concerning the former is *access discrimination*, while the term *treatment discrimination* is used to denote differential treatment once a person has been hired. As in the case of therapists' judgments, a considerable amount of research has been done, but the findings are not clear. For example, Nieva and Gutek (1980) concluded that there is considerable antifemale evaluation bias against women, whereas Landy and Farr (1980) concluded that there is not a consistent gender-of-ratee effect in performance evaluations. These contrasting conclusions can, in part, be traced to the fact that these reviewers were looking at somewhat different literatures. On the other hand, however, we again suggest that part of the problem may be that researchers are looking for simple gender-of-target effects when, as the preceding review of evaluation-bias work indicates, there is much reason to believe that these are not common.

The final type of behavior of consequence for relations between the sexes is the individual's support for/opposition to public policies concerning gender equality. Although not all would agree, we feel that, on balance, current laws and government procedures favor males. Thus, the promoting of gender equality requires changing public policies to improve women's rights. The ERA and the Human Life Amendment are public policy issues with opposing implications for women's rights. As the preceding discussion of Del Boca (1982) indicated, gender-related attitudes clearly have an impact on support for and opposition to these proposed constitutional amendments.

CHANGING GENDER-RELATED ATTITUDES

We address two different questions about the process issue of change: Are gender-related attitudes changing? Can programs be designed for successfully changing gender-related attitudes?

Intuitively, it seems that gender-related attitudes must be changing. The world that American men and women inhabit seems much changed over the past decade or two and it seems logical that people's thoughts and feelings would have changed too. And, there is some evidence for altered evaluations. In a late-1970s replication of a major gender stereotype study done in the 1950s (McKee & Sherriffs, 1957), Werner and LaRussa (1984) found considerable stability in the substantive content of beliefs about the sexes, but a major change in evaluation—the female stereotype, which had been much less positive than that of the male in 1957 was slightly more favorable in 1978. Using national survey data, Mason, Czajka, and Arber (1976) found a decline in sex-role traditionalism between 1964 and 1974. And, Spence, Deaux, and Helmreich (1985) report a major shift toward modern (vs. traditional) responding on the AWS between 1972 and 1976, but little change from 1976 to 1980.

Although this pattern is not surprising, we raise three concerns regarding the question, Are attitudes changing? First, most extant measures are highly reactive and the liberalization of attitudes may reflect changing norms rather than altered evaluations or feelings. Changing norms are not unimportant; norms, as well as attitudes, influence behavior. In seeking to account for apparently higher levels of antiblack prejudice revealed by unobtrusive versus self-report measures, Crosby et al. (1980) drew on Kelman's (1961) distinction between compliance and internalization: "whites today are complying with the norms of nondiscrimination but . . . they have not yet internalized unprejudiced values" (p. 559). A parallel disjuncture may be true in current male–female relations.

Second, any consideration of change leads to the need to distinguish three types of time effects—period, age, and cohort (cf. Sears, 1983, p. 82). A period effect is true of all people (in a given society) alive at a particular time (e.g., almost all adult Americans can remember where they were when they learned that John Kennedy was assassinated). An age effect is specific to a particular age or point in the life cycle (e.g., college-student norms are applicable only to people attending college and this most often occurs in young adulthood). A cohort effect describes similarity among people born at a particular time (e.g., the Depression generation). If gender-related attitudes are changing, what kind of effect is it?

Third, what gender-related attitudes are changing? There are a variety of attitude objects, and it is possible, indeed likely, that change in opinion is not uniform across targets. Our hunch is that the greatest change has occurred for questions concerning gender equality as a value. That is, Americans are more likely today than a few decades ago to endorse equal job, economic, and political opportunity for women (e.g., "equal pay for equal work") and to oppose sex discrimination (e.g., reserving industrial or political leadership positions for men).

The second general question about "changing attitudes" concerns social engineering: Can programs be designed to promote change in intergroup attitudes? Since the early 1970s, a large number of women's studies courses and consciousness-raising groups have been implemented to effect such change. The evidence about the effectiveness of these courses is uncertain, in part because program evaluation has often been a low priority goal. Bagenstos and Millsap (1983) offer a number of suggestions about how to improve the evaluation of these educational efforts.

A major approach to changing ethnic prejudice goes under the rubric, "the contact hypothesis" (Amir, 1969, 1976; Ashmore, 1970). According to this hypothesis, intergroup prejudice is reduced by intergroup contact that is (1) equal status, (2) cooperative, (3) supported by authorities, and (4) at least initially, successful. There is evidence supporting the hypothesis, and it has been the basis of several successful curriculum interventions in multi-ethnic schools (e.g., Aronson, Blaney, Stephan, Sikes, & Snapp, 1978). The contact hypothesis has important implications for gender-related attitudes. Occupational segregation helps maintain traditional attitudes and desegregation of jobs can change such attitudes. But, this is most likely under the aforementioned set of conditions (see also Pleck, 1978), and it is not always certain that business and government officials take these conditions into consideration.

Where Do We Go from Here?

To date, most research has focused on assessment of gender-related attitudes and demonstrating evaluation bias. This concentration on measurement and documentation of an effect makes sense—one must be able to measure or demonstrate the existence of something before moving on to other questions about that something. We feel, however, that now is the time to move on to a second generation of work on gender-related attitudes. The following suggestions are made in this regard. First, as an extension of the existing measurement focus, we urge assessing a wider variety of constructs, with a wider variety of methods. Second, we propose greater attention to theory. Especially important are the questions, What are gender-related atittudes? How are they integrated with the individual's overall social knowledge? Third, we recommend greater attention to process issues. The next generation of research could very profitably be directed at the trio of such issues—causes, in action, and change.

Our fourth and final recommendation is that we need to put the pieces back together. In this volume (and elsewhere) identity, stereotypes, and attitudes are treated separately. There is much to recommend this strategy, but it is time to systematically interrelate these constructs.

References

Abelson, R. P. (1968). Computers, polls, and public opinion—some puzzles and paradoxes. *Transaction, 5*, 20–27.

Abelson, R. P. (1982). Three modes of attitude–behavior consistency. In M. P. Zanna, E. T. Higgins, & C. P. Herman (Eds.), *Consistency in social behavior: The Ontario Symposium* (Vol. 2). Hillsdale, NJ: Erlbaum.

Adorno, T. W., Frenkel-Brunswik, E., Levinson, D. J., & Sanford, R. N. (1950). *The authoritarian personality.* New York: Harper & Row.

Ajzen, I., & Fishbein, M. (1977). Attitude–behavior relations: A theoretical analysis and review of empirical research. *Psychological Bulletin, 84*, 888–918.

Albright, G., & Chang, F. (1976). An examination of how one's attitudes toward women are reflected in one's defensiveness and self-esteem. *Sex Roles, 2*, 195–198.

Allen, B. P. (1978). *Social behavior: Fact and falsehood.* Chicago: Nelson Hall.

Altemeyer, R. A. (1981). *Right-wing authoritarianism.* Winnipeg: University of Manitoba Press.

Amir, Y. (1969). Contact hypothesis in ethnic relations. *Psychological Bulletin, 71*, 319–342.

Amir, Y. (1976). The role of intergroup contact in change of prejudice and ethnic relations. In P. A. Katz (Ed.), *Towards the elimination of racism.* New York: Pergamon Press.

Andersen, K. (1983, September 5). Private violence. *Time*, 18–19.

Aronson, E., Blaney, N., Stephan, C., Sikes, J., & Snapp, M. (1978). *The jigsaw classroom.* Beverly Hills, CA: Sage Publications.

Arvey, R. D. (1979). Unfair discrimination in the employment interview: Legal and psychological aspects. *Psychological Bulletin, 86*, 736–765.

Ashmore, R. D. (1970). The causes and cures of prejudice. In B. E. Collins, *Social psychology*. Reading, MA: Addison-Wesley.

Ashmore, R. D., & Del Boca, F. K. (1976). Psychological approaches to understanding intergroup conflict. In P. A. Katz (Ed.), *Towards the elimination of racism*. New York: Pergamon Press.

Ashmore, R. D., & Del Boca, F. K. (1979). Sex stereotypes and implicit personality theory: Toward a cognitive–social psychological conceptualization. *Sex Roles, 5*, 219–248.

Austin, W. G., & Worchel, S. (Eds.) (1979). *The social psychology of intergroup relations*. Monterey, CA: Brooks/Cole.

Bagenstos, N. T., & Millsap, M. A. (1983). Evaluation issues in women's studies. In B. L. Richardson & J. Wirtenberg (Eds.), *Sex role research: Measuring social change*. New York: Praeger.

Beere, C. A. (1979). *Women and women's issues: A handbook of tests and measures*. San Francisco: Jossey-Bass.

Beere, C. A. (1983). Instruments and measures in a changing, diverse society. In B. L. Richardson & J. Wirtenberg (Eds.), *Sex role research: Measuring social change*. New York: Praeger.

Bem, D. J. (1970). *Beliefs, attitudes, and human affairs*. Belmont, CA: Brooks/Cole Publishing Co.

Bentler, P. M., & Speckart, G. (1979). Models of attitude–behavior relations. *Psychological Review, 86*, 452–464.

Best, D. L., Williams, J. E., & Briggs, S. R. (1980). A further analysis of the affective meanings associated with male and female sex-trait stereotypes. *Sex Roles, 6*, 735–746.

Bettelheim, B., & Janowitz, M. (1964). *Social change and prejudice*. New York: The Free Press.

Billig, M. (1976). *Social psychology and intergroup relations*. New York: Academic Press.

Brannon, R. (1978). Measuring attitudes toward women (and otherwise): A methodological critique. In J. A. Sherman & F. L. Denmark (Eds.), *The psychology of women: Future directions in research*. New York: Psychological Dimensions.

Brigham, J. C., Woodmansee, J. J., & Cook, S. W. (1976). Dimensions of verbal racial attitudes: Interracial marriage and approaches to racial equality. *Journal of Social Issues, 32*, 9–21.

Broverman, I. K., Vogel, S. R., Broverman, D. M., Clarkson, F. E., & Rosenkrantz, D. S. (1972). Sex-role stereotypes: A current appraisal. *Journal of Social Issues, 28*, 59–78.

Cacioppo, J. T., Harkins, S. G., & Petty, R. E. (1981). The nature of attitudes and cognitive responses and their relationship to behavior. In R. E. Petty, T. M. Ostrom, & T. C. Brock (Eds.), *Cognitive responses in persuasion*. Hillsdale, NJ: Erlbaum.

Cacioppo, J. T., & Petty, R. E. (Eds.) (1983). *Social psychophysiology: A sourcebook*. New York: Guilford.

Campbell, D. T., & Fiske, D. W. (1959). Convergent and discriminant validation by the multitrait–multimethod matrix. *Psychological Bulletin, 56*, 81–105.

Carmines, E. G., & Zeller, R. A. (1979). *Reliability and validity assessment*. Beverly Hills, CA: Sage Publications.

Carroll, S. J. (1980, August). *Women as candidates: Campaigns and elections*. Unpublished doctoral dissertation, Department of Political Science, Indiana University.

Cialdini, R. B., Petty, R. E., and Cacioppo, J. T. (1981). Attitude and attitude change. *Annual review of psychology*. Palo Alto, CA: Annual Reviews.

Converse, P. E. (1964). The nature of belief systems in mass publics. In D. E. Apter (Ed.), *Ideology and discontent*. New York: The Free Press.

Converse, P. E. (1970). Attitudes and non-attitudes: Continuation of a dialogue. In E. R. Tufte (Ed.), *The quantitative analysis of social problems*. Reading, MA: Addison-Wesley.

Cook, S. W., & Selltiz, C. (1964). A multiple-indicator approach to attitude assessment. *Psychological Bulletin, 62*, 36–55.

Cooper, J., & Croyle, R. T. (1984). Attitudes and attitude change. *Annual review of psychology*. Palo Alto, CA: Annual Reviews.

Coser, L. A. (1956). *The functions of social conflict*. Glencoe, IL: The Free Press.

Cronbach, L. J., & Meehl, P. E. (1955). Construct validity in psychological tests. *Psychological Bulletin, 52*, 281–302.

Crosby, F., Bromley, S., & Saxe, L. (1980). Recent unobtrusive studies of black and white discrimination and prejudice: A literature review. *Psychological Bulletin, 87*, 546–563.

Del Boca, F. K. (1982). *A test of three explanations of attitudes toward public policy concerning sexual equality: Self-interest, prejudice against women, and symbolic sexism*. Unpublished doctoral dissertation, Rutgers University.

Del Boca, F. K., & Ashmore, R. D. (1980). Sex stereotypes through the life cycle. In L. Wheeler (Ed.), *Review of personality and social psychology* (Vol. 1). Beverly Hills, CA: Sage Publications.

Deutscher, I. (1973). *What we say/what we do*. Glenview, IL: Scott, Foresman and Co.

Dinnerstein, D. (1976). *The mermaid and the minotaur: Sexual arrangements and human malaise*. New York: Harper & Row.

Doyle, J. A., & Moore, R. J. (1978). Attitudes toward the male's role scale (AMR): An objective instrument to measure attitudes toward the male's sex role in contemporary society. Abstracted in the *JSAS Catalog of Selected Documents in Psychology, 8*(2), 35.

Ehrlich, H. J. (1973). *The social psychology of prejudice*. New York: Wiley.

Eysenck, H. J. (1954). *The psychology of politics*. London: Routledge and Kegan Paul.

Fishbein, M., & Ajzen, I. (1975). *Belief, attitude, intention, and behavior: An introduction to theory and research*. Reading: MA: Addison-Wesley.

Fiske, S. T., & Linville, P. W. (1980). What does the schema concept buy us? *Personality and Social Psychology Bulletin, 6*, 543–557.

Goldberg, P. A. (1967, April). *Misogyny and the college girl*. Paper presented at the Eastern Psychological Association Convention, Boston.

Goldberg, P. (1968). Are women prejudiced against women? *Trans-action, 5*, 28–30.

Goldberg, P. A. (1974). Prejudice toward women: Some personality correlates. *International Journal of Group Tensions, 4*, 53–63.

Hacker, H. (1951). Women as a minority group. *Social Forces, 30*, 60–69.

Hare-Mustin, R. T. (1983). An appraisal of the relationship between women and psychotherapy: 80 Years after the case of Dora. *American Psychologist, 38*, 593–601.

Helmreich, R. L., Spence, J. T., & Gibson, R. H. (1982). Sex-role attitudes: 1972–1980. *Personality and Social Psychology Bulletin, 8*, 656–663.

Henley, N. M. (1977). *Body politics*. Englewood Cliffs, NJ: Prentice-Hall.

Hotard, S., & Anderson, J. (1974). Demographic and attitudinal correlates of attitudes toward women. Paper presented at the 20th meeting of the Southeastern Psychological Association.

Jaggar, A. (1977). Political philosophies of women's liberation. In M. Vetterling-Braggin, F. A. Elliston, & J. English (Eds.), *Feminism and philosophy*. Totowa, NJ: Littlefield, Adams & Co.

Kelman, H. C. (1961). Processes of opinion change. *Public Opinion Quarterly, 25*, 57–78.

Kinder, D. R., & Sears, D. O. (1981). Prejudice and politics: Symbolic racism versus racial threats to the good life. *Journal of Personality and Social Psychology, 40*, 414–431.

Kirkpatrick, C. (1936). Content of a scale for measuring attitudes toward feminism. *Sociology and Social Research, 20*, 512–526.

Landy, F. J., & Farr, J. L. (1980). Performance rating. *Psychological Bulletin, 87*, 70–107.

LaPiere, R. T. (1934). Attitudes vs. actions. *Social Forces, 13*, 230–237.

Lerner, H. E. (1974). Early origins of envy and devaluation of women: Implications for sex role stereotypes. *Bulletin of the Menninger Clinic, 38*, 538–553.

Lingle, J. H., & Ostrom, T. M. (1981). Principles of memory and cognition in attitude formation. In R. E. Petty, T. M. Ostrom, and T. C. Brock (Eds.), *Cognitive responses in persuasion*. Hillsdale, NJ: Erlbaum.

Maccoby, E. E., & Jacklin, C. N. (1974). *The psychology of sex differences*. Stanford, CA: Stanford University Press.

Mason, K. O., Czajka, J. L., & Arber, S. (1976). Change in U. S. women's sex-role attitudes, 1964-1974. *American Sociological Review, 41*, 573-596.

McConahay, J. B., & Hough, J. C. (1976). Symbolic racism. *Journal of Social Issues, 32*, 23-45.

McGuire, W. J. (1969). The nature of attitudes and attitude change. In G. Lindzey & E. Aronson (Eds.), *The handbook of social psychology* (2nd ed.). Reading, MA: Addison-Wesley.

McKee, J. P., & Sherriffs, A. C. (1957). The differential evaluation of males and females. *Journal of Personality, 25*, 356-371.

Nadler, E. B., & Morrow, W. R. (1959). Authoritarian attitudes toward women, and their correlates. *Journal of Social Psychology, 49*, 113-123.

Nemerowicz, G. M. (1979). *Children's perceptions of gender and work roles*. New York: Praeger.

Nieva, V. F., & Gutek, B. A. (1980). Sex effects on evaluation. *Academy of Management Review, 5*, 267-276.

Osgood, C. E. (1969). On the whys and wherefores of E, P, and A. *Journal of Personality and Social Psychology, 12*, 194-199.

Osgood, C. E., Suci, G. J., & Tannenbaum, P. H. (1957). *The measurement of meaning*. Urbana, IL: University of Illinois Press.

Ostrom, T. M. (1969). The relationship between the affective, behavioral, and cognitive components of attitude. *Journal of Experimental Social Psychology, 5*, 12-30.

Partnow, E., (Ed.) (1977). *The quotable woman, 1800-1975*. Los Angeles: Corwin Books.

Paulus, D. L. (1984). Two-component models of socially desirable responding. *Journal of Personality and Social Psychology, 46*, 598-609.

Peters, L. H., Terborg, J. R., & Taynor, J. (1974). Women as managers scale (WAMS): A measure of attitudes toward women in management positions. *JSAS Catalog of Selected Documents in Psychology*, Ms. #585.

Pheterson, G. I., Kiesler, S. B., & Goldberg, P. (1971). Evaluation of the performance of women as a function of their sex, achievement, and personal history. *Journal of Personality and Social Psychology, 19*, 114-118.

Pleck, J. H. (1978). Males' traditional attitudes toward women: Conceptual issues in research. In J. A. Sherman & F. L. Denmark (Eds.), *The psychology of women: Future directions in research*. New York: Psychological Dimensions.

Renwick, P. A., & Tosi, T. (1978). The effects of sex, marital status, and educational background on selection decisions. *Academy of Management Journal, 21*, 93-103.

Rokeach, M. (1980). Some unresolved issues in theories of beliefs, attitudes, and values. In H. E. Howe (Ed.), *Nebraska symposium on motivation*. Lincoln: University of Nebraska Press.

Rokeach, M., Smith, P. W., & Evans, R. I. (1960). Two kinds of prejudice or one? In M. Rokeach (Ed.), *The open and closed mind*. New York: Basic Books.

Rosenberg, S. (1977). New approaches to the analysis of personal constructs in person perception. In J. Cole (Ed.), *Nebraska symposium on motivation*. Lincoln: University of Nebraska Press.

Rosenkrantz, P. S., Vogel, S. R., Bee, H., Broverman, I. K., & Broverman, D. M. (1968). Sex-role stereotypes and self-concepts in college students. *Journal of Consulting and Clinical Psychology, 32*, 287-295.

Ruble, D. N., & Ruble, T. L. (1982). Sex stereotypes. In A. G. Miller (Ed.), *In the eye of the beholder: Contemporary issues in stereotyping*. New York: Praeger.

Schneider, D. J., Hastorf, A. H., & Ellsworth, P. (1979). *Person perception* (2nd ed.). Reading, MA: Addison-Wesley.

Schofield, J. W. (1982). *Black and white in school: Trust, tension or tolerance.* New York: Praeger.

Schuman, H., & Johnson, M. P. (1976). Attitudes and behavior. *Annual review of sociology.* Palo Alto, CA: Annual Reviews.

Schwendinger, J. R., & Schwendinger, H. (1983). *Rape and inequality.* Beverly Hills, CA: Sage.

Sears, D. O. (1983). The persistence of early political predispositions: The roles of attitude object and life stage. In L. Wheeler & P. Shaver (Eds.), *Review of personality and social psychology* (Vol. 4). Beverly Hills, CA: Sage Publications.

Sears, D. O., & Kinder, D. R. (1971). Racial tensions and voting in Los Angeles. In W. Z. Hirsch (Ed.), *Los Angeles: Viability and prospects for metropolitan leadership.* New York: Praeger.

Sears, D. O., & McConahay, J. B. (1973). *The politics of violence: The new urban blacks and the Watts riot.* Boston: Houghton Mifflin.

Sherif, M., & Sherif, C. W. (1965). Research on intergroup relations. In O. Klineberg & R. Christie (Eds.), *Perspectives in social psychology.* New York: Holt, Rinehart and Winston.

Sherriffs, A. C., & McKee, J. P. (1957). Qualitative aspects of beliefs about men and women. *Journal of Personality, 25,* 451–464.

Siegel, M. (1983). Crime and violence in America: The victims. *American Psychologist, 38,* 1267–1273.

Spence, J. T., Deaux, K., & Helmreich, R. L. (1985). Sex roles in contemporary American society. In G. Lindzey & E. Aronson (Eds.), *Handbook of social psychology* (3rd ed.). New York: Random House.

Spence, J. T., & Helmreich, R. (1972a). The Attitudes towards Women Scale (AWS). *JSAS Catalog of Selected Documents in Psychology, 2.*

Spence, J. T., & Helmreich, R. (1972b). Who likes competent women? Competence, sex-role congruence of interests, and subjects' attitudes toward women as determinants of interpersonal attraction. *Journal of Applied Social Psychology, 2,* 197–213.

Spence, J. T., Helmreich, R., & Stapp, J. (1975). Likability, sex-role congruence of interest, and competence: It all depends on how you ask. *Journal of Applied Social Psychology, 5,* 93–109.

Stockard, J., & Johnson, M. M. (1979). The origins of male dominance. *Sex Roles, 5,* 199–218.

Straus, M., Gelles, R., & Steinmetz, S. (1980). *Behind closed doors: Violence in the American family.* Garden City, NY: Anchor Books.

Tajfel, H. (1969). Cognitive aspects of prejudice. *Journal of Social Issues, 25,* 79–97.

Taylor, S. E. (1981). A categorization approach to stereotyping. In D. L. Hamilton (Ed.), *Cognitive processes in stereotyping and intergroup behavior.* Hillsdale, NJ: Erlbaum.

Triandis, H. C. (1971). *Attitude and attitude change.* New York: Wiley.

Vaughter, R. M. (1979). Evaluating measures of sexism. *JSAS Catalog of Selected Documents, 9.* Ms. #1915.

Vaughter, R. M. (1983). All things being equal, a behavior is superior to an attitude: Studies of sex-typed and sex-biased attitudes and behaviors. In B. L. Richardson & J. Wirtenberg (Eds.), *Sex role research: Measuring social change.* New York: Praeger.

Wallston, B. S., & O'Leary, V. E. (1981). Sex makes a difference: Differential perceptions of women and men. In L. Wheeler (Ed.), *Review of personality and social psychology* (Vol. 2). Beverly Hills, CA: Sage Publications.

Werner, P., & LaRussa, G. W. (1984). Persistence and change in sex-role stereotypes. Manuscript submitted for publication.

Wicker, A. (1969). Attitudes versus actions: The relationship of verbal and overt behavioral responses to attitude objects. *Journal of Social Issues, 25,* 41–78.

Wilder, D. A. (1981). Perceiving persons as a group: Categorization and intergroup relations. In D. L. Hamilton (Ed.), *Cognitive processes in stereotyping and intergroup behavior.* Hillsdale, NJ: Erlbaum.

Williams, J. E., & Bennett, S. M. (1975). The definition of sex stereotypes via the Adjective Check List. *Sex Roles, 1,* 327–337.

Wilson, G. D. (Ed.) (1973). *The psychology of conservatism.* New York: Academic Press.

Zanna, M. P., Higgins, E. T., & Herman, C. P., (Eds.) (1982). *Consistency in social behavior: The Ontario Symposium* (Vol. 2). Hillsdale, NJ: Erlbaum.

Zajonc, R. B. (1980). Feeling and thinking: Preferences need no inferences. *American Psychologist, 35,* 151–175.

Part Two

GENDER AND INTERPERSONAL RELATIONSHIPS

Five

Women and Men
in Personal Relationships

TED L. HUSTON
RICHARD D. ASHMORE

Introduction

This chapter marks a transition in the book from a focus on gender and the individual to an analysis of the ways men and women involve themselves in their interpersonal relationships. The present chapter is concerned with relationships that are considered intimate, or personal, in nature. National surveys suggest that adults' sense of their well-being depends in large measure on the quality of their social bonds (Campbell, 1981; Freedman, 1978). Moreover, the strivings that count most to people generally have to do with establishing and maintaining intimate relationships (Klinger, 1977).

The contemporary importance of close, personal relationships may reflect, in part, the difficulty persons have in achieving rewarding and durable alliances (Levinger, 1977). Men and women no longer live out most of their adult lives in the context of a particular marriage relationship. People marry later and divorce more often than in earlier times, and women outlive men by an average of approximately 8 years. About a third of all adults are single at any particular time.

Writings on life-style and life-course draw attention to the varied interpersonal worlds within which individuals live as they move through their lives.

THE SOCIAL PSYCHOLOGY OF FEMALE-MALE RELATIONS   **167**

Safilios-Rothschild (1981), recognizing this diversity, argues that social scientists interested in relationships should start with individuals, map all of their interpersonal ties, and then examine over time the ways in which the ties are intertwined. Such research would no doubt point to the continued centrality of marriage in the lives of most adults. Most individuals spend a large part of their adult years either being married, seeking marriage, or getting over a divorce. When individuals move toward and into marriage, friends and kin generally recede into the background; friends and kin often become prominent again with divorce or the death of a spouse (Johnson, 1982; Milardo, Johnson, & Huston, 1983; Rands, 1980; Shulman, 1975; Slater, 1963).

The concentration of scholarly work mirrors the normative importance of particular types of relationships during different periods of the lifespan (Huston & Levinger, 1978). Romance is typically studied among teenagers and young adults; friendship among the yet-to-be-married and formerly married; marriage among adults of all ages (even though the majority of the studies are of relatively young couples); and kin relationships in connection with major life transitions (such as becoming a parent, divorcing, or being widowed).[1]

The terms, *close relationship* and *personal relationship*, which are here used interchangeably, identify associations that are commonly thought to be informal, intense, diversified, cooperative, and friendly (Wish, Deutsch, & Kaplan, 1976). The adjectives *close* and *personal*, as well as *intimate* (see Brehm, 1985), also have been used as synonyms for relationships that are viewed as loving, trusting, deep, romantic, enduring, committed, or cohesive (Huston & Burgess, 1979). The idea of a close bond also has been taken to refer to ties that are psychologically important—that is, alliances that have a strong and sustained impact on the participants' sense of their identity and well-being (McCall, 1974). Associations that are ephemeral, limited to routine activities at work, or circumscribed by restrictive role requirements are not regarded as close or personal in nature. (This does not mean that role considerations are absent from personal relationships or that the same relationship cannot be viewed from either a personal or a role perspective [compare, for example, the treatment of marriage in this and the next chapter by Staines and Libby].)

---

[1]Blumstein and Schwartz (1983) have noted that "gay couples have been even more invisible in American life than have gay individuals" (p. 44). The lack of attention to homosexual relationships is beginning to be remedied, the best evidence of which is a recent issue of the *Journal of Homosexuality*, edited by Peplau and Jones (1982), which is primarily devoted to homosexual relationships.

Close relationships are distinguishable from other liaisons in that they involve frequent, diverse, and strong behavioral interdependence that lasts over a long period of time (Kelley, Berscheid, Christensen, Harvey, Huston, Levinger, McClintock, Peplau, & Peterson, 1983). Such interdependence gives rise to occasions when the individuals' interests compete, and, thus, it is not surprising that partners in close relationships are more likely than those involved in loose alliances to experience conflict, frustration, and anger. In fact, vulnerability, ambivalence, and hostility are more apt to be felt in close involvements than in more casual liaisons (Argyle & Furnham, 1983; Kelley et al., 1983; Lewin, 1940).

This chapter is concerned with those close personal relationships that men and women create from late adolescence into old age. Although these include the friendships that individuals move into, nurture, and sometimes allow to wither away, the focus here is on romantic and marriage relationships. The existing literature comparing women and men in personal relationships is piecemeal and diverse, and it cuts across a variety of topical areas and levels of explanation. Furthermore, much of the work is atheoretical, and there has not always been available a comprehensive framework within which to describe and analyze interpersonal interaction and social relationships. The next section of the chapter attempts to remedy both of these shortcomings, first by discussing theories pertinent to understanding male–female personal relationships and then by presenting a descriptive–analytic model for studying them.

Much of the writing on close personal relationships goes no farther than to describe male–female differences in interpersonal patterns, thus leaving the impression that such patterns reflect differences in the psychological, or even genetic, makeup of men and women. The middle section of the chapter takes up conceptual and methodological issues pertaining to seeing sex as a cause of relational phenomena, first in terms of the notion that men and women are subject to dissimilar cultural forces (both at any particular time and across the life span), and then in terms of the view of gender as a construct denoting a bundle of correlated dispositions (e.g., values, expectations) and situational contexts (e.g., work role, power) that combine to account for the development of gender-differentiated relational patterns. A central goal of this chapter is to broaden the causal net used to analyze gender-related patterns by explicating the ways in which the partners' interdependence, and the circumstances surrounding their particular relationship, account for differences in relationships.

The final part of the chapter critically analyzes the extant research on women and men in personal relationships, using the ideas developed in the initial sections of the chapter.

Toward a Framework for the Social-Psychological Analysis
of Personal Relationships

THEORETICAL PERSPECTIVES PERTINENT
TO UNDERSTANDING MEN AND WOMEN IN CLOSE RELATIONSHIPS

Many researchers have taken the salutatory step of studying close personal relationships directly, and where possible in vivo, but much of this
work is descriptive, with little attention to theory development and few attempts to tie the analysis of relationships explicitly to other work on sex and
gender (cf. Deaux, 1985, p. 70). Thus, as a first step in building a conceptual
framework for the social psychological analysis of women and men in personal relationships, it is necessary to consider theories pertinent to
understanding sex differences in interpersonal conduct, especially those that
bear on behavior in close heterosexual relationships. Although such theories
can be categorized in a number of different ways, the assumed ultimate
causal nexus of sex differences is particularly important. The theories germane to male–female relationships can be grouped into clusters that fall at
different points along an individual–societal continuum—at one extreme are
explanations of sex differences in terms of biological propensities; at the
other, female–male differences in behavior are traced to cultural arrangements.

Hinde (1984), after reviewing the cross-cultural and social psychological
literatures on gender differences in behavior concludes that the patterns are
generally consistent with principles of evolutionary biology. Hinde's
analysis includes (but is not restricted to) sociobiological ideas about sex differences, which argue that humans evolved in ways that tend to maximize
the likelihood that their individual genes will survive (Mellen, 1981;
Symons, 1979). Men are seen as having a biological stake in having sexual
relationships whenever they have the chance and, at the same time, trying to
control the availability of their sex partners to others. Reproductive success
for women, in contrast, depends on (1) selecting the best possible mate in
terms of genetic makeup, and (2) maximizing the likelihood that their offspring will survive to maturity.

Chodorow (1974) takes an opposing position to that of sociobiologists.
She argues that the continuity across generations in the nearly universal differences that distinguish men and women in personality and roles have to do
not with anatomy but rather with the greater responsibility and involvement
women have had in rearing children. Male and female children experience
different social environments when they are young, and, as a consequence,
"feminine personality comes to define itself in relation and connection to
other people more than masculine personality does" (p. 43).

The idea that through socialization boys and girls learn to orient themselves differently to others is carried further by Gilligan (1982) who believes that men and women come to hold fundamentally different world views. Men are oriented toward separation and individuation; women toward connection and fellowship. Gilligan's ideas are consistent with those of symbolic interactionists, whose writings can be taken to suggest that through socialization men and women develop identities that differ in the way that they view themselves in relation to others (McCall & Simmons, 1978; Stryker, 1980).

Although Hinde, Chodorow, and Gilligan differ in the emphasis they place on the biological versus experiential factors that might account for gender differences, they agree in seeing the behavioral propensities of individuals as primary causes of why men and women behave differently. Although Hinde, on the one hand, and Chodorow and Gilligan, on the other, present logical analyses, their arguments are difficult to test empirically, and the extant evidence suggests that men and women are minimally different in their *propensities* to behave in particular ways (cf. Deaux, 1984; Maccoby & Jacklin, 1974; however, see Block, 1976).

Another approach to theorizing about sex differences in terms of individual propensities is exemplified by Parsons and Bales (1955), who argue that the very nature of group interaction creates a necessity for role specialization (see also Burke, 1967, 1968). They suggest that it is difficult in a group for one person to be effective when fulfilling roles as both the task leader and the social leader. They also assert that the flexibility of the adult personality is limited, thus making it difficult for any one individual to switch back and forth between instrumental and expressive modes. Traditional sex roles, they argue, are adopted because they are functional, given the beneficial consequences of role specialization for group effectiveness and morale. Moreover, the differentiation of the instrumental and expressive roles along gender lines encourages children to identify with their same-sex parent, which, following psychoanalytic theory, they presume to be healthy. The premises that underlie Parsons and Bales's (1955) theory have been put to considerable test and generally have not been supported (see Peplau, 1983; Waxler & Mishler, 1970; see also Ickes, 1981, for reviews). Instrumentality and expressiveness can be effectively combined in the same individual; people often change from one mode to another, depending on the requirements of the situation; and groups appear to function better when members are able to be alternate instrumental and expressive behaviors (Ickes & Barnes, 1978).

Several theories attempt to bridge the dispositional and interpersonal factors that account for the emergence of gender-correlated differences in behavior in personal relationships. Social learning theory (e.g., Jacobson &

Margolin, 1979) and symbolic interactionism (e.g., McCall & Simmons, 1978) postulate that dispositions to act in particular ways develop as a consequence of the kinds of behaviors that have been modeled and reinforced. Men and women may be disposed to enact gender-appropriate behaviors because they have different socialization histories. Gender differences emerge to the extent that enacting gender stereotypical behavior is more self rewarding and more apt to be responded to favorably by others than behavior that is inconsistent with sex stereotypes. Sex-typing in personality and interests acquired through socialization affects the types of behavior men and women introduce in interaction and their reactions to each other's behavior. A highly sex-typed man, for example, may attempt to direct matters in a relationship, but whether he persists, according to social learning theory, depends on the woman's reaction. The response of the woman, assuming she is also sex-typed, will reinforce the man's agentic behavior, and thus enhance gender differences in their relationship.

Social exchange theories (Blau, 1964; Homans, 1961; Thibaut & Kelley, 1959) share with social learning formulations a concern with the regulatory implications of the affective consequences of behavior. However, exchange theories, as they have evolved, have become increasingly different in drawing attention to the idea that participants in relationships are not simply reacting to the pattern of affect that results from interaction, but also that each participant has goals (both for self and for other) and that each is able to anticipate the consequences with regard to goals of various combinations of behavior.

Formulations which suggest that complementary differences in personality and role expectations result in gender differences in relational patterns generally develop their rationale using principles derived from exchange theory (Tharp, 1963; Winch, 1958, 1967). Complementary propensities are viewed as more likely to be mutually rewarding than are other combinations of propensities (see Levinger & Rands, 1985, for further explication of the logic behind these theories). Thus, male–female differences in propensities are thought to provide the psychological context for the emergence of sex-typed behavior patterns in relationships.

The more cognitive reformulations of exchange theory emphasize the idea that individuals can and do weigh the outcomes that accrue to their partner. Individuals are assumed to do so, however, only to the extent that they believe it is in their own long-term interest (Kelley, 1979). It follows, then, that gender differences in attention to the partner's outcomes will occur only insofar as the long-term consequences of so doing are different for men and women. This view contrasts with Gilligan's suggestion that women, by virtue of their socialization, are more inclined than men to give weight to their partner's outcomes without necessarily calculating the long-term benefits for themselves of so doing.

In turn, Gilligan's view also contrasts with Hatfield's (Hatfield, Utne, & Traupmann, 1979) application of equity theory, which assumes that men and women use the same standard to evaluate the pattern of outcomes that result from their association. According to the equity principle, individuals are satisfied with their relationship to the extent that there is a *balance* for partners in the proportion of contributions (inputs) to profits (outcomes). Gilligan, however, would argue that equity is primarily a male criterion, and that women, who are oriented to restoring and maintaining a sense of community in relationships, will ignore issues of equity when applying them would serve to separate individuals.

Exchange theory draws attention to the fact that individuals function within a web of interdependent relationships. How partners behave and relate to one another may be affected by the impressions they make on persons outside the relationship (Ridley & Avery, 1979). In contexts in which traditional sex-role values are espoused, for example, men and women may enact such roles even though they may be uncomfortable doing so. Men may be motivated to be directive in order to maintain their position within the community and, in their view, their status in the eyes of friends, kin, or coworkers. Similarly, women may wish not to embarrass their husbands, or risk being seen as bossy or controlling. In other subcultures, populated by persons with nontraditional sex-role ideas, the reactions (both real and anticipated) may be very different, and thus encourage deviation from the style of interaction traditionally scripted for men and women.

Exchange theory is one of several psychological frameworks that recognize that the patterns of behavior within relationships are related to the way in which the partners participate in the larger culture. On the one hand, the status (acceptance) that one receives from others is affected by how these others view the nature of the focal relationship. On the other, the status positions that individuals occupy in the larger culture relate to the partners' resources and the opportunities they can draw on in the relationship. Exchange theory has been used to interpret how the differential access of men and women to economic resources (e.g., Blood & Wolfe, 1960) and their relative social status (Berger, Rosenholtz, & Zelditch, 1980) might affect the balance of power in close relationships. The data regarding the importance of resources in accounting for power indicate that asymmetries in resources are reflected in asymmetries in power (see Huston, 1983). The work of Berger et al. (1980) and Meeker and Weitzel-O'Neill (1977) suggests that gender (and other culturally based status characteristics) affects interaction because participants have different scripts or expectancies for high- and low-status individuals. High-status people are expected to take the lead; they are given more opportunities to make a contribution; and their contributions are more often supported by others. The idea developed by Berger et al. (1980) that social status outside a group causes differences in how group members behave in the group does not imply that ascribed status is more important than achieved status as a determinant of group processes. In most societies, the opportunities for economic advancement are greater for men, and men, therefore, have more of an opportunity to earn economic status. At the same time, the economic resources that women bring to a relationship compared to men appear to affect their power, except in societies that are strongly patriarchal (Rodman, 1972).

While exchange theory suggests how societal factors can be transformed into forces that influence relationships (see also Guttentag & Secord, 1983), role theory (Rodgers, 1973; Staines & Libby, Chapter Six, this volume; Turner, 1970) offers a more fully societal-level account of men and women in relationships. In its most extreme form, role theory regards individuals as filling slots and enacting required behaviors regardless of their individual wants. An important extension of the role notion is provided by adding a life-cycle perspective, which emphasizes that individuals move into and out of particular roles as they pass through major life stages.

The preceding theories or frames of reference have been introduced to account for gender-correlated differences in interaction, especially those in close heterosexual relationships. They have been employed here as interpretive nets rather than as tools to generate specific hypotheses. Biologically oriented theorizing (e.g., Hinde, 1984; Mellen, 1981; Symons, 1979) stands alone in taking a position regarding the specific nature of the gender differences that ought to be identifiable. The other theories, though varying in their emphasis on the psychological, the interpersonal, and the sociocultural levels of explanation, have two important common features: (1) they are relativistic in the sense that cultural milieus are assumed to both cause and to reflect gender differences in relationships; and (2) they assume that the categories of causes themselves are causally intertwined. Thus, social norms, socialization histories, sex-role attitudes, behavioral propensities, and subjective and overt reactions to particular behaviors are seen as part of a complex web of interconnected causes. Such a state of affairs suggests that the choice of a frame of reference for viewing gender differences should be seen as a starting point on a journey toward what may turn out to be an ever-changing destination. As is argued here in Part II, theoretical progress in this area will depend, in large measure, on whether models can be articulated that tie specific attributes of social systems, interpersonal networks, and particular attributes of partners to specific interpersonal patterns in close relationships.

INTERACTION, INTERDEPENDENCE, AND RELATIONSHIPS

A Descriptive-Analytic Model

This section offers a fine-grained descriptive–analytic model that centers on interaction and that highlights interdependence through time. Early interpersonal attraction work focused on static stimulus characteristics (e.g., a photograph of a pretty face) and individuals meeting for the first time. Although many researchers have recognized the limitations of this stranger paradigm and turned to real-world liaisons, there has not always been a systematic and rigorous framework available for describing and analyzing such relationships. Kelley and his colleagues (1983) have given us the needed conceptual–methodological apparatus. Interaction and interdependence are central in this model. A concrete sequence of interaction can be used to delineate the features of relationships that might differentiate the behavior and the psychological experiences of men and women during interaction.

The following details of the interaction are derived from reports about the first outing, or "date," of a couple interviewed extensively as part of a longitudinal study of courtship and marriage (Huston, McHale, & Crouter, 1985). The sequence of events shown in Figure 1 reportedly occurred shortly after the couple—whom we shall call Russell and Denise—had sat down for dinner. The beginning of the outing had gone well. Russell had come to the evening with the hope that Denise would take a liking to him, and by the

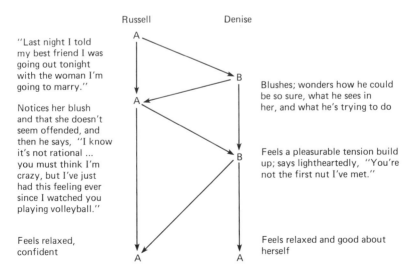

FIGURE 1.   Illustrative interaction sequence.

time they sat down for dinner he had sensed that his hopes were being realized.

The sequence shown in the figure begins with Russell's declaration that he
had told his best friend the previous evening that he was going out with the
woman he was going to marry. His comment initiates a chain of interconnected reactions and actions. Denise blushes, and a number of thoughts flash
through her head: "How could he be so sure?" "What does he see in me that's
so special?" "Why is he telling me this?" Russell, having noticed Denise
blush, and feeling relieved that she did not seem to be offended by his
boldness, continues: "I know it's not rational . . . You must think I'm crazy,
but I've just had this feeling ever since I watched you playing volleyball."
Denise feels a pleasurable tension as she hears this. To break the tension, she
humors him, and they move on to another topic of conversation, feeling
relaxed.

This description of the interaction episode necessarily focuses on only a
subset of the psychological and interpersonal events that could be identified.
Nonetheless, it can be used to draw attention to some key distinctions.

1. Overt behavior that has influence on the other (interpersonal events)
   can be distinguished from covert activity (subjective events). Thoughts,
   intentions, attributions, physiological processes, and feelings are
   linked within each participant. The arrows drawn between Russell
   and Denise illustrate the idea of social influence.
2. Influence can be immediate or delayed, and it can be reflected in
   behavior, physiological activity, and cognition. Russell's declaration is
   shown to produce a number of reactions on the part of Denise. Moreover, Russell's boldness was instigated, in part, by the interpersonal
   events that preceded the segment of interaction portrayed in the figure.
3. Overt behavior can be broken down into verbal behavior and nonverbal behavior.
4. Events communicate at several levels simultaneously, and various
   types of events can occur together. Thus, for example, persons can
   think one thing and say another; paraverbal and nonverbal cues may
   be consistent with or contrary to one another; and listeners can frown,
   smile, or respond in other ways while a speaker talks.
5. Some properties of relationships are reflected in particular actions and
   reactions exhibited during a single social interaction (e.g., emotions,
   modes of influence); other properties require attention to longer sequences of interaction (e.g., resolution of conflict); and still others refer
   to patterns that are reflected in or carry over from one episode to
   another (e.g., problem solving and the implementation of a solution).

It is characteristic of close relationships that the behavior of each partner often has multiple, delayed, and contingent effects on the other. Russell's disclosure, when coupled with his later efforts to elicit commitment from Denise, combine to make Denise cautious about revealing her feelings to him. Events evident in any specific social encounter may vary depending on the immediate goals of the partners and the functions that the interaction serves in the relationship. The segment of interaction portrayed in Figure 1 has a playful, recreational overtone, but serious business is being transacted. Concerns having to do with impression management, attraction, and attractiveness are in the foreground. Other interactions that subsequently take place between Russell and Denise will involve conflict of interest, the exchange of mundane information, the development of relationship norms, as well as confrontation with and avoidance of personal and relationship crises.

Table 1 summarizes representative research that has examined sex differences in the ways men and women involved in close relationships interact.

TABLE 1

Illustrative Findings Regarding Sex Differences in Social Interaction in Close Relationships

Finding	Type of data
Wives disclose more personal feelings and opinions than husbands when asked to talk about both intimate and nonintimate topics (Morton, 1978).	Observational
Women are more likely than men to disclose their fears (Rubin, Hill, Peplau, Dunkel-Schetter, 1980).	Self-Report
Women ask more questions, show greater support, and are more skilled at using "mm's" and "oh's" to indicate interest during conversation (Fishman, 1978).	Observational
Women in close relationships express approval through nonverbal channels during conflict more than men (Lochman & Allen, 1979).	Observational
Men involved in heterosexual relationships use direct (telling, asking, talking to the partner) and bilateral (bargaining and efforts at persuasion) tactics more than women in order to get their way. Women use indirect (suggestions, hints, withdrawal) tactics more than men (Falbo & Peplau, 1980).	Self-Report
Men conversing with women talk more and interrupt more (Zimmerman & West, 1975).	Observational
Women in close relationships are reported to cry, sulk, and criticize men for their lack of consideration and insensitivity; men are reported to show anger, to reject tears, and to call for a logical and nonemotional approach to dealing with the problem. Men are also *reported* to be more inclined to give reasons for delaying the discussion (Kelley, Cunningham, Grisham, LeFebvre, Sink, & Yablon, 1978).	Self-Report

The studies summarized cover the types of data that have been gathered and illustrate typical findings. One way to group the documented sex differences in interaction in personal relationships is in terms of two conceptually distinct dimensions: The first of these is variously referred to as power, dominance, status, and equality–inequality. The second concerns issues of affection, nurturance, and caring (cf. Brown, 1965; Carson, 1969; Wish et al., 1976). In close heterosexual relationships, the nature and patterning of activity can be directed by either the man or the woman, and the affective tone of interaction can be either warm or hostile. Two examples follow: the third finding in the table—that women show greater support in conversations—indicates that women more than men are oriented toward keeping conversation smooth and positive; the final finding listed shows husbands to be more likely to engage in behaviors that are simultaneously negative and dominating.

The patterns shown in the table are generally consistent with sex stereotypes and fit traditional ideas about sex roles—that is, men engage in more instrumental–assertive behavior, while women are higher in expressive-nurturant actions. The tabled findings should not be taken to suggest, however, that men and women behave and respond in distinctively different ways; most of the differences are small. Moreover, with few exceptions (e.g., Falbo & Peplau, 1980), investigators have examined features of social interaction independently of one another. The temptation to assume that the differences are intercorrelated and reflect the organizational structure of close relationships should be resisted. Some models of the cause of sex differences suggest a common origin for most differences; others see various aspects of relationships as being influenced by a variety of forces, with the forces themselves being only moderately correlated, if at all.

The base of data also warrants considerable caution for other reasons in drawing conclusions about the pervasiveness of sex differences in close relationships.

1. Few aspects of interaction have been studied to the point where it is possible to determine the extent to which the findings are generalizable. The participants in research typically have been young, college-educated couples. The homogeneity of the couples used makes it difficult to identify causal conditions associated with particular gender patterns (see section on causal contexts, this chapter).
2. Studies showing no sex differences are less likely to be published than those showing sex differences (see Maccoby & Jacklin, 1974).
3. Much of the data about sex differences are based on reports provided by the individuals involved. When participants are asked to generalize about interactional patterns, it is not clear whether they accurately

remember what has happened (Harvey, Christensen, & McClintock, 1983; Huston & Robins, 1982). Reports may be biased by sex stereotypes or sex-role attitudes held by participants.

4. Observational data about sex differences may be affected by the stereotypes of observers as well as by the self-presentational concerns of the men and women being observed (cf., O'Rourke, 1963).

The Objective Side of Relationships: The Behavioral Organization of Close Relationships

Relationships generally begin in the context of either instrumental or recreational pursuits. Individuals meet in offices, in classrooms, at churches and other places of worship, in nightclubs, at family social gatherings, at parties. With time, many relationships become increasingly differentiated. For example, those originally confined to work settings spill over into leisure activities. Personal relationships are usually distinguished from others by the greater variety of activities couples pursue together, as well as by the extent to which each partner depends on the other's instrumental performance (e.g., income-producing activity, household work).

Focusing on close heterosexual relationships, sociologists have attempted to differentiate marriages by reference to the patterns of instrumental and leisure activities couples pursue together and apart. As early as 1945, Burgess and Locke identified two types of marriages: the institutional and the companionate. The institutional type was said to be characterized by traditional roles, with the husband being the breadwinner and the wife the homemaker; spouses in such marriages pursue their own leisure interests, with husbands often doing things with friends and wives with kin. Spouses in companionate marriages, by contrast, adhere less strongly to traditional role prescriptions and they tend to center their leisure time primarily around each other.

It is arguable whether traditionalism and companionship covary in the way Burgess and Locke (1945) suggest. The important lesson, however, to be gleaned for our purpose from Burgess and Locke's analysis—and similar ones carried out by others (Bernard, 1964; Bott, 1957; Cuber & Harroff, 1965; Young & Wilmott, 1973)—is that close relationships can be characterized not only in terms of the interpersonal events that take place when the partners are together but also by reference to the types of activities couples do together and apart.

Two papers published in the early 1950s by Paul Herbst were seminal in shaping our view of the behavioral organization of marriage (or any close personal male–female relationship). Herbst (1952, 1953), drawing on Lewinian thought, described marriage and other family relationships in terms of the "behavioral fields" of family members, with each of these fields conceived in terms of recurrent individual and joint activities. Patterns of activity, when considered in conjunction with the more detailed information about patterns of interpersonal events shown in Table 1, provide the basis for developing portraits of the behavioral topography of personal relationships. The use of the term "topography" represents an attempt to capture the idea of the behavioral structure of relationships and the interrelationships of the behavioral features.

Table 2 shows the types of activities that can be used to differentiate marriage relationships. Two primary categories were identified by following the logical groupings that have guided research and by including distinctions that seem important in understanding how men and women differentially involve themselves in their marriages. The first category, *instrumental activities*, can be broken down into paid labor and work inside and around the house. The second dimension of behavioral organization is *leisure* or *recreational activity*. As can be seen in the table, each type of activity can be done by the partners either alone or together. The table draws attention to a number of ways to describe the activities of marriage partners in relation to one another. The distinction between institutional and companionate marriages, noted earlier, is made partly on the basis of the sex-typing of husband–wife activities and the extent to which they pursue leisure activities together. Measures derived from the kind of data presented in the table have

TABLE 2

The Behavioral Organization of Marriage

	Activity done	
Type of activity	Alone	Together
Instrumental (work)		
Paid employment	Number of hours; work schedule; nature of work	Extent of joint income producing work (e.g., small business owners)
At home	Total amount of time; extent to which husbands and wives carry out masculine and feminine sex-typed household tasks; extent of liking or disliking of tasks carried out	Amount of joint work carried out at home; extent to which joint work centers on feminine or masculine sex-typed tasks
Leisure (recreation)	Extent of leisure; sex-typing of leisure	Amount of joint leisure; sex-typing of joint leisure activities

been the focus of considerable research (which we summarize in the section on marriage).

Table 2 also raises a number of issues about the gender-related patterning of marriage. How do couples determine which household tasks each partner will do? In what way is their negotiation process influenced by factors that the partners bring to their relationship (e.g., sex-role attitudes), as well as by current circumstances surrounding the marriage (e.g., employment status of husband and wife)? The same questions of which activities are selected and what forces have an impact on the decision-making process can be asked with regard to leisure.

The Subjective Side of Relationships: Summary Evaluations of the Partner and the Relationship

During interaction, as was noted earlier, partners experience, suppress, attempt to modify, and express affect. There is a second aspect of affect in relationships: the summary affective judgments or evaluations—variously termed "liking," "love," "attraction," and "satisfaction"—that individuals make about their partner and the relationship itself.

The emotional (transient affective) experiences and the evaluative judgments individuals make about partners and relationships are undoubtedly related. It is possible, in principle, to measure attraction in terms of the extent to which particular affective states occur as the result of relationships (Berscheid, 1985). Positive emotions connote attraction; negative ones hostility. Particular kinds of attraction are also distinguishable, in part, by emotions. Love and passion are differentiable from liking by reference to the nature of the affective experiences that individuals report having. If we can take at face value verbal reports, the affective experiences associated with love are different for men and women—women are more likely to report feelings of euphoria, giddiness, and having difficulty concentrating (Dion & Dion, 1973, 1976; Kanin, Davidson, & Scheck, 1970).

The complex patterns of interdependence that characterize personal relationships inevitably result in the individuals having a history of both positive and negative emotional experiences with each partner. The measures that have been used to assess attraction and satisfaction, however, generally place individuals on a single unidimensional continuum. Participants in close relationships are asked to rate the extent to which they like (Rubin, 1970), love (Lowman, 1980; Rubin, 1970) or trust (Larzelere & Huston, 1980) one another. For premarital dating couples, liking, loving, and trusting have been found to be modestly intercorrelated, with the intercorrelations between liking and loving generally being higher for men than for women (Cunningham & Antill, 1981; Rubin, 1970).

The measures of the various forms of attraction differ in the extent to which the items tap beliefs, evaluations, and behavioral propensities. Rubin's (1970) liking scale includes items that require individuals to rate the extent to which the target person is mature, admirable, intelligent, and has good judgment. The love scale items pertain primarily to the affective responses that the relationship can elicit (e.g., feeling possessive, believing it would be hard to get along without the partner), and ideas about the partners' behavioral dispositions toward each other (e.g., to help the partner in need). These measures, then, ask for more than purely evaluative/affective judgments. Rather, the judgments carry implications about interpersonal antecedents and behavioral consequences.

The same is true, but even more so, when measures of marital satisfaction are examined (e.g., Locke & Wallace, 1959; Spanier, 1976). These measures primarily assess satisfaction by reference to specific behavior patterns (Norton, 1983). The Spanier (1976) measure of dyadic adjustment, for example, requires respondents to rate the extent to which they are happy in their relationship, but most of the items pertain to judgments of the degree to which partners agree on how to handle various matters, the amount of conflict they experience, the frequency with which the partners kiss, how often they confide in each other, and the extent to which they engage in outside interests together. These judgments can hardly be viewed as evaluative, *in and of themselves*. Most of the questions pertain to observable behavior patterns. Sex differences, were they to be found, would be difficult to interpret without performing some kind of item-by-item analysis of responses. The more general point, however, is that most writers have measured attraction and satisfaction in such a way as to prevent the exploration of their interpersonal antecedents and consequences without risking circular reasoning.

The Causal Contexts of Gender-Related Patterns in Personal Relationships

Before using the frameworks offered in the preceding section to analyze and critique extant work on women and men in personal relationships, it is necessary to address the question: How should one seek to understand and account for gender-related patterns in intimate heterosexual relationships? In the past, this would have seemed to be a silly question to most researchers as well as to most laypersons—"Men (women) do this because they are men (women)." If pushed, the explanation of sex differences in behavior (whether or not in the context of a personal relationship) would have been in terms of genetic or biological factors, or traits and role expectations acquired through socialization.

Without disputing the importance of either the nature or the nurture explanations (each is actually a family of explanations), it is here suggested that to understand how women and men behave in relationships, one must consider the context in which gender-related patterns develop in particular relationships (see also Unger, 1979, and Deaux, 1985, on sex and gender as explanatory variables). By *context* is intended the material and social elements and the relations among these elements within which a given relationship is embedded. Contexts vary along a continuum from the very immediate and local (i.e., the people and things immediately surrounding a particular woman and man) to the very general, apparently diffuse, yet all-encompassing society. Contexts are important in understanding gender-related patterns because they often provide opportunities or resources, on the one hand, and constraints, on the other, that can cause sex differences in behavior and experience even when the propensities (whether determined by nature or nurture) of individual men and women are only slightly different, or even when there is no difference.

Consideration of immediate contexts is temporarily postponed, and we turn now to the cultural context of close relationships. How the male and female members of a married couple behave will, on average, be different in a society where the majority of married women are homemakers (as was true in the United States just two generations ago) compared with one where a majority of married women do engage in paid employment (as is true today). Societal conditions in this case confound biological sex with employment status. To the extent that sex covaries with a package of culturally determined factors, all pushing in a particular direction (e.g., giving the male more resources and opportunities), it is likely that men and women will behave quite differently and that gender-related patterns in relationships will be easily identified.

This line of reasoning has a number of very important implications, both for men and women in relationships and for researchers studying this phenomenon. When societal patterns are such as to make the life situations of most men quite different from those of most women, this is likely to be associated with clear and widely shared cultural norms and values supporting these patterns, and these, in turn, will be taught to the young. In such homogeneous cultures, children develop competencies and expectations that tend to replicate cultural patterns.

On the other hand, when societal patterns are not homogeneous, when a variety of different conditions exist for members of both sexes, this would seem to offer both benefits and costs for individual women and men and couples. On the positive side, the existence of diversity increases options. Under these circumstances, couples may move toward social contexts that support their relationship, and, thus, they may actually help construct a causal context that pushes them in directions that are consistent with their desires.

Societal-level heterogeneity of conditions for the sexes also raises some possible costs (at least in the short run)—individuals may find themselves balancing conflicting expectations, and their behavior may change to some extent in response to the expectations of the members of the groups within which they find themselves. Thus, for example, a husband and wife may act more like a traditional couple in some settings than in others. Further, they may, at times, be confused about how they should behave given the situation and others present. Finally, if a particular husband and wife are not able to see and mutually understand how their individual and joint conduct varies with the social context, it can lead to conflict between the partners.

There are two interrelated implications of the cultural context of relationships for researchers. First, sex differences in behavior in close relationships are more likely to be found in field studies than in laboratory investigations, which frequently control all but a few of the factors that operate in natural settings to enhance sex differences (cf. Deaux, 1985).[2]

The second research implication is that homogeneous societal conditions conceal, whereas changing conditions help reveal, the cultural causes of gender differences. When homogeneous patterns within a culture are anchored in strong and long-standing cultural traditions, it is difficult for scholars to identify the social forces involved in maintaining the patterns. Lewin's (1951) advice to social scientists that the best time to study something is when it is changing reflects the idea that the strength of various forces, whether they be psychological or environmental, is seen most clearly when forces are pitted against one another. A society undergoing change generally becomes more pluralistic in regard to its norms and behavior, and there is more of an opportunity to examine the interplay among forces than is the case when patterns in a society are stable.

In addition to broad societal factors, the activities of men and women in close relationships must be understood in terms of a complex set of interwoven forces that are more immediate to the interactants. This point can be appreciated by examining a concrete situation:

> It is 4:30 Monday afternoon. Don arrives home, tired after a full day of work. He sits down to read the newspaper, feeling uneasy. He is used to having his wife, Rhonda, home after work, but last week she took a job as a bank teller. Now, she doesn't get home until 5:30; sometimes it's even later. As the time approaches 5:00, Don begins to feel a tug toward

---

[2]Laboratory research, however, can also accentuate sex differences by "forcing" couples to deal with issues that in their day-to-day life they can avoid or by selecting tasks that are not representative of those that the couple ordinarily confronts.

the kitchen, where he knows the morning dishes have been left. There is no doubt in his mind that he will do them, even though he feels revulsed at the thought of the sour smell of the dried egg he imagines he will have to scrub off the fry pan. Washing dishes isn't his idea of man's work, but last week he discovered that Rhonda strongly disagrees, and now that they both work he really can't argue with her. Rhonda had put up a fuss both times he forgot to do them last week. The night after he had agreed to do the dishes, he left the pots and pans for her, hoping that she would be pleased with his efforts and explaining that he wasn't sure how to proceed with them. Although she was gratified, she was also happy to show him how to scrub them.

The vignette illustrates matters of key importance in analyzing gender-related aspects of relationships. The most general point that can be made using the vignette is that the action of the husband—his movement toward the kitchen to do the dishes—is anchored in a combination of psychological and environmental *forces that exist in the field* at the time he takes action (Lewin, 1951). He may not be conscious of all these forces; in fact, the self-consciousness of his behavior in the vignette can be taken to result from the conflicting nature of the forces toward and away from action.

The forces operating in a particular relational context also may reflect the aforementioned cultural factors, and, moreover, the forces that account for the actions and reactions of partners at a particular time may be stable or transient, and they may be general or specific to the particular situation. Perhaps more importantly, relational behaviors are caused by multiple forces, which are complexly interwoven and highly context specific (cf. Swann, 1984). For expository purposes, however, it is useful to examine separately the elements that when combined produce particular behavioral patterns in a particular situation.

The *psychological orientations* of actors are properties of individuals that serve as rudders, both directing their behavior and their response to the behavior of the others with whom they become involved. Three components of psychological orientations particularly germane to understanding gender differences can be distinguished as follows: (1) the beliefs a person has about what he or she and the other *ought* to do; (2) what the individual likes or *wants* to do; and (3) the extent to which the person has the *competence*, or the ability, to perform a particular behavior. Although these orientations are relatively stable, they should not be confused with traits, which are generalized propensities to act in certain ways across a variety of targets and situations. Rather, psychological orientations are enacted within particular relationships and can be modified significantly through interaction in relationships.

The differentiation of these components has important implications because they are not always aligned within a particular individual. Don's psychological orientations pull him in many directions. His conception of marital roles tells him that washing dishes is women's work, but he recognizes that his view is anchored in assumptions he makes about work roles that are no longer pertinent to his current situation. His idea of what he ought to do is different this week from the week before. It reflects a combination of values he has internalized, the changed work status of his wife, and the negotiations he had with her during the previous week regarding their respective roles.

Individuals may be drawn toward behaving in particular ways because of what they want to do, or like to do, or away from the behavior because they find it aversive. Several aspects of the vignette give clues to Don's distaste for doing dishes: he read the paper first; imagined the sour smell of the dried eggs on the fry pan; and he left the pans hoping that Rhonda would scrub them.

Although performing some activities (or actions) may be either intrinsically rewarding or unpleasant, the affective consequences of action may vary, depending on the person, the context, and the like. Individuals may *want* to behave in ways that are not personally pleasing for at least two important reasons. Sometimes an action may change the environment in ways that are pleasing, as when Don's cleaning up the dishes makes his home more pleasant. A critical part of the causal context in this example is the undone dishes, which stimulate action not because Don enjoys doing dishes, but rather because accomplishing this task results in desirable consequences (i.e., a nicer home environment). The immediate audience and the larger interpersonal context provide a second important reason why an individual may enact behavior that is not intrinsically rewarding. Indeed it is in the nature of personal relationships that often what each individual wants to do reflects an awareness and concern for its impact on the partner. Men and women in close relationships, thus, may do what they do not because they find it personally rewarding, but because they want to please their partner (for any of a number of reasons). In sum, then, the meaning partners attach to behavior, and hence its symbolic importance, depends on both the environmental and the relational context within which it occurs.

The third component of an individual's psychological orientation has to do with the person's competence, or skill. Individuals who are otherwise motivated to perform in a particular way may fail to do so because they are not sure what to do or how to go about doing something. The role that gender differences in skill may have in accounting for behavior patterns has received little attention. It has been suggested, however, that men and women may have different areas of expertise and that these differences have an impact on the outcome of social influence processes (Peplau, 1983).

The importance of skill as a determiner of patterns of behavior around the house of men and women has been explored in the first author's own work. In one study, it was found that spouses who felt skilled at performing tasks around the home traditionally done by members of the other sex were more involved in carrying out such tasks (Atkinson & Huston, 1984). Similarly, men who felt that they would be skilled at child care prior to becoming fathers subsequently became more involved in carrying out such responsibilities once their baby was born (McHale & Huston, 1984). Both of these studies found self-reported skill to be a stronger correlate of involvement than either sex-role attitudes, masculinity, or femininity. The important point not to be lost here is that gender differences in skill may be at least as important in accounting for some behavioral patterns in close relationships as sex-role ideology or personality attributes.

The three components of an individual's psychological orientation—feelings of obligation, wanting, and a sense of competence—partly reflect the socialization histories of that individual. The preceding analysis underlines that these differences also develop and are altered as a result of the individual's participation in a particular relationship. Thus, although men and women come to their relationships with beliefs about roles, dispositions to act and react in particular ways, and with a package of skills, these initial attributes are often modified through interaction. Couples create new understandings, their motivations to behave in particular ways become stronger or weaker, and individuals acquire, sharpen, or lose their sense of skill with regard to particular matters.

Moreover, the attributes and circumstances that affect one type of behavior or response may not be generalizable to others. It is likely, for example, that the causes of division of labor are different from the causes of sex differences in recreational pursuits, which, in turn, are different from the antecedents of why men and women act differently from one another during conflict. It is also undoubtedly true that many causes of sex differences in relationships result from the interplay of the attributes of the partners in combination with the larger circumstances within which their relationships are embedded. Each individual in a relationship provides a context for the other, and both partners are influenced, individually and jointly, by events outside the relationship that impinge on them. Progress toward understanding the role of gender in close relationships requires researchers to begin to examine what it is about being a man or a woman that is relevant to the kinds of circumstances they find themselves in, the attributes they develop, and the relevance of these to their behavior.

A Critical Analysis of the Accumulated Literature on Women and Men in Personal Relationships

This section presents an analysis of the natural history of heterosexual relationships, beginning with dating and courtship, and then turning to work on men and women in marriage. (See Peplau and Gordon, 1985, for a somewhat more general discussion of men and women in close relationships.)

DATING AND COURTSHIP

The research on the growth of romantic relationships has focused on initial attraction and the development of love, and mate selection. Our focus in examining this research is on studies that reveal the possible multiple causes of gender differences in premarital relationships.

The Initiation of Dating Relationships

A number of studies have shown that men and women are drawn to physically attractive dating partners (see Adams, 1982; Berscheid, 1985). Most of this work has examined the relationship between physical appearance and attraction in situations in which individuals are given information (e.g., a picture) or where an encounter between two individuals is set up by the researcher. The studies do not explore the impact of physical attractiveness on the day-to-day social lives of men and women, however. The influence of physical attractiveness on the development of relationships can best be appreciated by recognizing that individuals often have to take some initiative in getting them started. Reis and his colleagues (Reis, Wheeler, Spiegel, Kernis, Nezlek, & Perri, 1982) had individuals, rated for physical attractiveness, keep daily records of their social interactions for about 2 weeks. They found that physical attractiveness in men was related to the overall extent of their involvement with women. Physically attractive men initiated more contact with women, and they rated their heterosexual contacts as more meaningful and mutually disclosing. Moreover, subsequent analyses showed that the relationship between men's physical attractiveness and their involvement with women is mediated by their self-confidence.

Contrary to beliefs pervasive in popular culture, but consistent with predictions derived from earlier research (Berscheid, Dion, Walster, & Walster, 1971; Huston, 1973), Reis et al. (1982) found physical appearance in women to be unrelated to the frequency and extent of their involvement with men. Research conducted during the 1970s provides a partial explanation of these findings (Berscheid et al., 1972; Huston, 1973; Kiesler & Baral,

1970). These studies suggested that even though men are highly attracted to beautiful women, they seek the companionship of women of lesser attractiveness because they anticipate a better chance of being accepted. Reis et al. (1982) provided data that fit this explanation and expand upon it. They found that physically attractive women are less socially assertive (perhaps because they have less of a need to be) and less trusting of men (perhaps because they are more likely to feel they have been exploited by men in the past).

Physical attractiveness in women was related to the extent to which women were self-disclosing and found their interactions with men pleasant, however. Physically attractive women may have pleasant contacts because they have greater freedom to socialize with rewarding partners, and because they may feel they have more personal control over their social time. Reis et al. note that when men interact with physically attractive women—women whom they stereotype as possessing a number of desirable personal qualities (cf. Adams, 1982)—they behave in ways so as to induce women to confirm their favorable expectations (Snyder, Tanke, & Berscheid, 1977). This suggests that men may be more likely to court beautiful women, and hence draw them out. A study by Andersen and Bem (1981) indicates that women interacting with attractive men also court the men; moreover, they also found that the tendency to treat physically attractive individuals more favorably was stronger for sex-typed men and women.

As the preceding discussion indicates, men, in general, initiate cross-sex contacts more directly than women, and they seem to be drawn to women who are both desirable to them and likely to accept their overtures. Factors affecting the likelihood women will initiate contact with men have not been the subject of much investigation. Because making verbal overtures is still considered by many to be more the business of men than of women (Remoff, 1984), it seems likely that women who are nontraditional in sex-role attitudes would be more likely than traditional women to directly express an interest in establishing contact with men. It is also possible, as data from the Reis et al. (1982) study suggest, that women who are generally assertive may be particularly apt to initiate cross-sex contact, and that women may tend to approach men who are somewhat unsure of themselves. There is a need to look at subcultural and age, or life-stage, differences in regard to the initiation of relationships. For example, it may be that among middle-aged previously married individuals, women take more of an initiative in beginning relationships.

Traditional sex-role perceptions place women in the position of controlling their relationships by manipulating their personal attractiveness and by selectively signaling men of their interest in them (Remoff, 1984). The ways in which either women or men manage impressions in dating situations have not been the subject of systematic research. Laboratory experiments, however, have shown that men prefer a woman who shows an interest in them and not in dating others, rather than the woman who is consistently "hard to get" (Forsyth & Clark, 1975; Walster, Walster, Piliavin, & Schmidt, 1973). Certainly, in vivo research is needed on how exactly women signal that they are "hard to get" or interested (in being approached by a particular male).

It would be important to consider how a female who "asks out" a male or signals her interest in being approached is perceived. Ashmore et al. (Chapter Three, this volume) have suggested that perceivers distinguish various gender subtypes and that sexuality is a significant consideration in the perceptual partitioning of the overarching social categories, *male* and *female*. Given traditional gender norms regarding dating and courtship, which specify that men ask and women say "yes" or "no," a woman who takes the initiative or even signals her interest may be seen by the male recipient as forward or perhaps categorized as a "loose woman," "on the make," or even "an easy lay." If this is the case, it would have important implications for the male's behavior and ultimately the length and quality of their interaction.

A laboratory experiment by Abbey (1982) suggests that men and women might disagree about the meaning of a female's intended signal, "I'm interested (in your approaching me)." In viewing a brief videotape of a young man and woman talking, men "saw" much more sexual interest and invitation (on the part of both the male and female actors) than did women. In short, it appears that men (or American college-age men) perceive more sexual content in social behavior than do women. If so, and particularly if men see women as more sexually interested than they are, it could have significant implications for the initiation and early stages of heterosexual interactions.

Love and Commitment

Having established a relationship, the members of the couple must assess how they feel overall about one another, and this raises the question of love. Interestingly, a number of studies have shown that young adult men are more ready to fall in love than similarly aged women. Men score higher on scales measuring romanticism (Fengler, 1974; Hobart, 1958; Knox & Sporakowski, 1968; Rubin, 1970; Rubin, Peplau, & Hill, 1981; see Cunningham & Antill, 1981, for an exception to the generalization), and they report higher levels of love early in relationships (Burgess & Wallin, 1953; Cate, Huston, & Nesselroade, 1985; Kanin, Davidson, & Scheck, 1970).

The reasons for these sex differences have not been explored empirically. One speculation is that traditional role patterns force women to commit their affection more slowly because they need to be more attentive than men to attributes that are unlikely to be evident during the early stages of their relationships (Rubin, Peplau, & Hill, 1981). This explanation fits other data that suggest that men place more importance on physical attractiveness and sociability than women (both of which can be assessed early in relationships) (Adams, 1982; Hudson & Henze, 1969); women, in contrast, value intellectual and economic competence more than men (Burchinal, 1964; Hudson & Henze, 1969; Laner, 1977; Langhorne & Secord, 1955). In addition, men's role as initiator increases the likelihood that they will be more enamored early in their relationships than women. Men may also fall in love more quickly than women because men have greater influence on the recreational activities couples do (see Peplau, 1979), and hence they may direct the couple to activities that are more enjoyable to themselves than to their partner. Further, it is possible that women are more responsive than men, and, thus, they may be more likely to behave in ways that induce feelings of love. Finally, men may have a tendency to "fall in love" because it increases the likelihood that a sexual relationship will develop. Peplau, Rubin, and Hill (1977) have found that men place more importance on sex than love in dating (whereas the reverse is true for women). Men still appear to push for sex earlier than women, and women are more likely than men to require affectional involvement prior to becoming sexually involved (Hinde, 1984; Peplau et al., 1977). Men see love as more casual, playful, and erotic than women, who are more apt to emphasize issues of pragmatics, rapport, dependency, and self-fulfillment than men (Hatkoff & Lasswell, 1979).

A major question for those concerned with understanding the course of heterosexual personal relationships is, How do two "dating" individuals come to be a married couple? A considerable amount of conceptual and empirical work—much under the rubric of mate selection—has addressed this question.

The most well-known models of mate selection suggest that commitment evolves as the partners discover areas of compatibility (Kerckhoff & Davis, 1962; Murstein, 1970; Winch, 1958; 1967). These models assume that the behavior of men and women in dating relationships reflects stable dispositions, values, and desires regarding roles, and that some combinations of psychological and role attributes are more likely than others to lead to mutually rewarding interaction. The following data, however, call into question the assumption that individuals interested in attracting a partner, or maintaining a love relationship, behave only or primarily in accordance with generalized, stable dispositions. While men and women in premarital relationships do behave differently, this pattern may be more traceable to expectations about how one's behavior will be received than to personality dispositions.

The writings of Jones and his colleagues (Jones, 1964; Jones & Pittman, 1982; Jones & Wortman, 1973) provide leads regarding the interpersonal contexts that are apt to stimulate sex differences in self-presentation. The first consideration is the extent to which individuals have a stake in producing a favorable reaction (Jones & Pittman, 1982). Particularly important in this regard is the aforementioned evidence suggesting that men fall in love faster than women; moreover, an additional body of data shows that the person who is more in love in a relationship is less powerful (Peplau, 1979). These findings, when considered together, suggest that early in relationships, men may be more motivated than women to behave in ways calculated to make a good impression. Some indirect support for this comes from a study (Huston, Surra, Fitzgerald, & Cate, 1981) showing that in the early stages of romantic relationships, men are more active in doing things that serve to maintain the relationship (such as talking about it and trying to resolve problems).

The second set of considerations identified by Jones and Pittman (1982) has to do with men's and women's beliefs about how persons of the other sex will respond to them, depending on how they present themselves. In choosing how to put forward a positive view of self to someone of the other sex, gender stereotypes and sex-role expectations are likely to be quite important. Further, beliefs about what women and men are like and how they should behave may be incorporated into, or implicit in the *scripts* (conceptual representations of stereotyped event sequences [Abelson, 1981]) that men and women carry around in their heads about female–male encounters. For example, Skrypnek and Snyder (1979) asked men to divide gender-linked tasks between themselves and a partner, leading half the men to believe their partner was a man and the other half to think their partner was a woman. All the partners were in fact female. The men generally assigned male sex-typed tasks to themselves and female sex-typed tasks to their partners when they were led to believe that they were paired with a woman. No such tendency was found when they thought their partner was a man. Next, women were told the outcome of their partners' division and were asked to also divide the tasks. They tended to choose the feminine tasks for themselves more when their partner had previously been led to believe they had been paired with a woman rather than a man. This study shows how initial scripts (in this case, men do male tasks and women do female tasks), many of which might be held nonconsciously, may come to structure relationships.

In addition to nonconsciously held scripts, female–male dating interactions are quite likely influenced by strategic attempts by one or the other partner to create a favorable impression. This, of course, raises the question of what would create a positive impression in a member of the other sex. Studies in which men and women are asked to guess what members of the other sex regard as ideal for their own sex suggest that men are relative accurate (in guessing that women want a degree of expressiveness in the ideal man), but women wrongly (given males' ratings of the ideal woman as the criterion) perceive that men want them to be more oriented to domestic matters (cf. Spence, Deaux, & Helmreich, 1985). If so, women—if they are attracted to a man—may be presenting a more home-oriented view of self than, in fact, is attractive to men. (It should be kept in mind, however, that college-age males may be less than honest in describing their ideal female.)

The preceding analysis suggests that many men and women take a relative pragmatic approach to premarital relationships—they consider before they act how well their behavior will go over, and they are motivated to do things that please the would-be lover (cf. Zanna & Pack, 1975). The idea that people take such a pragmatic approach is consistent with the results of nearly 3 decades of research that have produced thin evidence, at best, to support the notion that the extent of compatibility in the personal attributes (personality, values, role concepts) partners bring to relationships play a significant role in accounting for mate selection (see Levinger, 1983; Levinger & Rands, 1985, for reviews).

Further, compatibility theory, as a general model, is based on assumptions that are not tenable, under most circumstances.

1. The model assumes an open marketplace, with each individual being able to select a partner from an array of possibilities. The preceding discussion of the importance of physical attractiveness for men's attraction to women and occupational status and money for women's evaluation of men suggests that the marketplace is better for some (wealthy men and beautiful women) than for others.

2. Compatibility theory assumes that the field of potential partners is diverse with regard to attributes important to matching. This may not be the case for those living in culturally homogeneous areas or who, for other reasons, are cut off from others.

3. It is assumed that the behavior of the partners in courtship is anchored in stable psychological attributes. As has been noted, this is simply not the case, at least for some people. And, it takes only one partner to have strategic or pragmatic concerns to sabotage the opportunity for compatibility testing to operate.

In sum, courtship for most people seems not to be a process of assessing whether the other has stable dispositions that fit one's own, but rather a complex interactional phenomenon in which what the person brings to the developing relationship is just one input, which in concert with the broader societal context and emergent relational properties, shapes the course of premarital relationships.

MARRIAGE

The goal of this section is to provide an overview and critique of research and theory as it bears on two issues. The first of these has to do with analyzing the causes of gender-related patterns in the *organization of behavior* in marital relationships. This review follows the categories of activities identified in Table 2—instrumental activities are considered first, followed by leisure. The second topic has to do with the connection between the behavioral organization of marriage and the *subjective assessments* men and women make about it and their partner.

Causes of the Behavioral Organization of Marriage

The first aspect of the behavioral organization of marriage, *instrumental activity*, has been analyzed primarily in terms of work roles and the beliefs that men and women have about sex roles. The fact that husbands participate in the paid labor force more than wives and that wives carry out most of the work around the house has been well documented, as is the upswing, particularly since World War II, in the proportion of women employed in the work force (Degler, 1980; Geerkin & Gove, 1983; Waite, 1981). There appears to have been a subtle shift in the division of labor in the house over the past couple of decades, with the change being as great for couples where the wives do not work outside the home as when wives do hold an outside job (Duncan & Duncan, 1975; Pleck & Rustad, 1980).

As noted in Table 2, tasks can be differentiated in terms of whether they are performed traditionally by wives, by husbands, or by either spouse. This distinction is important because husbands' and wives' performance of tasks is affected by different factors, and these factors depend on the sex-typing of the task. Thus, the following review of the literature is focused on studies that have broken instrumental tasks down in terms of sex-typing.

The work roles of husbands and wives have been the object of considerable research on sex-segregation in household task performance. The bulk of this work has examined variations in the work hours of wives rather than husbands. The most general conclusion that can be reached is that wives' employment is more strongly connected to their own rather than their husbands' household behavior, and that the effect of wives' employment is primarily evident with regard to feminine sex-typed tasks (Atkinson & Huston, 1984; Beckman & Houser, 1979; Blood & Wolfe, 1960). The more hours wives are employed, the less "women's" work they do around the house. At the same time, wives' employment is related to more traditionalism with regard to patterns of husband–wife participation in "masculine sex-typed" tasks (Atkinson & Huston, 1984; Hoffman, 1960). Most of these tasks are not done frequently, and, thus, the work patterns of the spouses are unlikely to exert a press on either spouse to get involved.

Studies of the impact of the work involvement of husbands on division of labor in marriage are rare, the assumption apparently being that employment status is less likely to vary for men than for women. Blood and Wolfe (1960), however, did examine this issue and found that, when wives were employed and husbands not employed, men reportedly were more involved in feminine sex-typed household tasks. In couples in which working men were married to women who were employed full-time, the husbands reportedly did relatively fewer feminine sex-typed tasks.

The conceptual framework presented earlier—which suggests that the broad societal and immediate interpersonal contexts must be considered in analyzing relational phenomena—points to the need for research that goes beyond employment status and work hours. Men and women may have different motives for working, and employment may be caused by, and perhaps confounded with, other psychological and social factors that bear on household task performance (see also Bronfenbrenner & Crouter, 1982; Kanter, 1977; Moen, 1982; Pleck, 1977). Couples may work the same shift, or different shifts (Nock & Kingston, 1984); the jobs men and women hold may be of similar or different prestige levels, or one partner may bring in more income than the other (Blood & Wolfe, 1960); individuals may work for different reasons, some of which have to do with their sense of identity; work demands may be more important to one or the other of the spouses; and work settings can differ in the kinds of moods they generate in workers (Crouter, Huston, & Robins, 1982).

This explication serves to draw attention to a variety of causal paths that link individuals to work, and work to marriage. They suggest that stable psychological orientations may draw individuals into the work force and that these same orientations may also affect behavior in the marriage. They draw attention to how work hours and work shifts may affect husbands' and wives' opportunities for involvement (recall the implications of Rhonda's arriving home after Don for Don's participation in housework). They show the possible importance of power and exchange (Blood & Wolfe, 1960). And, finally, they point to how emotions generated at work (e.g., fatigue, depression, anxiety, arousal) might carry over into the home, and affect the activities of the worker at home.

The influx of women into the work force appears to be tied, in part, to cultural changes in sex-role attitudes. Women who work are less traditional than other women in sex-role attitudes (Mason & Bumpass, 1975),[3] and it is possible that sex-role attitudes and work roles operate together to affect household task performance. Studies have shown that spouses' beliefs about sex-role issues are tied to reports about division of labor (Beckman & Houser, 1979; Geerken & Gove, 1983; Hoffman, 1960; Nickols & Metzen, 1982), but most of these studies have not partialed out employment status. The exception is a study by Atkinson and Huston (1984), which showed that, for wives, sex-role attitudes predicted division of labor less strongly when the employment hours of husbands and wives relative to one another was taken into account. Beckman and Houser (1979) considered only couples in which both spouses were employed outside the home and found that wives' sex-role attitudes predicted their reports of division of labor, but only for a subset of the couples in which the wives held professional positions. Among such women, nontraditional attitudes were reported to be related to husbands being more involved, comparatively, in feminine sex-typed tasks; sex-role traditionalism was also related to women's reports of involvement in masculine sex-typed tasks—the more nontraditional, the more involvement.

The pattern of behavior associated with nontraditional sex-role attitudes suggests that deviation from a traditional sex-role ideology is associated with a more laissez-faire attitude about housework (Atkinson & Huston, 1984). Perhaps, nontraditional women are disinclined to perform "women's work," and men holding such attitudes are less likely to try to push them to do such work. The less-traditional men, nonetheless, do not seem any more inclined than others to step in and do the feminine sex-typed work themselves. Moreover, it appears that such men are less apt to take on responsibilities at home usually done by men; wives who are less traditionally inclined, however, do more of the masculine sex-typed tasks.

The idea that instrumental household tasks represent work—and perhaps more importantly "women's work"—probably accounts, at least in part, for the lack of attention given by researchers to other components of psychological orientations—such as women's and men's likes and dislikes, or their sense of their skill at performing tasks around the house—as determinants of the performance of such tasks. Further, to the authors' knowledge, research has not been carried out that examines task segregation in relationships by reference to the extent to which particular men and women enjoy specific tasks or find them unpleasant.

The possibility that men and women may feel more skilled at some tasks than others is suggested by White and Brinkerhoff (1981), who found that

---

[3]The direction of causality in this instance is not clear. There is reason to believe that going to work for a woman is both caused by and a cause of nontraditional sex-role attitudes.

boys and girls are assigned chores on the basis of their sex appropriateness. Their study suggests one basis for the finding that men and women feel almost uniformly highly skilled in tasks traditionally assigned to their own sex; they vary within sex, however, in their sense of skill with regard to performing tasks traditionally assigned to the other sex (Atkinson & Huston, 1984).[4] Men's and women's perceived skill was a very strong predictor of the extent to which they crossed over and performed tasks traditionally done by members of the other sex (Atkinson & Huston, 1984). A parallel study, using the subsample of the couples from the Atkinson and Huston (1984) study, found that men's sense of their skill before they became fathers strongly predicted their subsequent level of involvement in child care activity (McHale & Huston, 1984).

The observations made in this section, once again, draw attention to the importance of going beyond a single class of variables—in this case, the explanatory focus of most research has centered around work, with work being viewed primarily in terms of employment status and work hours—to a consideration of how work is related to individual dispositions and to relational phenomena and how these interrelated factors have an impact on doing household tasks.

Companionship and *leisure* are here treated together, but it is important to recognize that married couples do both instrumental and recreational activities together. A study (Huston, McHale, & Crouter, 1985) has shown that from 2 months into marriage to a year later couples do fewer activities together, both of a leisure and instrumental nature. The drop in leisure involvement is greater than it is for shared instrumental activities, the result being that marriage relationships move from being primarily recreational to being more like a working partnership over the first year. The overall extent of companionship in marriage as it changes over longer periods of time has not been examined.

The impact of work roles on companionship has received little attention, a state of affairs that stands in stark contrast to research on division of household labor. The exception to this generalization is a study by Robinson (1977), which found that when husbands and wives with preschool-aged children both worked full-time, wives spent an average of about 2 hours a day less than either husbands or homemakers in leisure. The consequences of work roles on the extent and nature of husband–wife companionship, however, have yet to be systematically explored. Thus, for example, we do

---

[4]We do not mean to imply that perceived skill is either fixed or necessarily objective. Men and women can learn to be quite adept at tasks traditionally done by the other sex. And, individuals can be mistaken about their ability to do certain things or they may deliberately mislead their spouse about their skills.

not know whether dual-worker (or dual-career) couples spend less time in leisure together, or whether they do different kinds of activities in their leisure time.

The institutional and companionate marriage patterns described earlier and in Table 2 differentiate couples in terms of the extent to which the partners do things jointly, or separately. Sex-role attitudes and sex-typing in personality are strongly implicated in theoretical writings as causes of levels of companionship in marriage (see Peplau, 1983, for a review). To the authors' knowledge, however, the impact these factors have on the extent to which couples pursue leisure activities together has not been directly investigated. That some of the items on sex-role attitude scales pertain to leisure pursuits suggests recreational activities may be seen as differentially appropriate for men and women. Boys and girls are brought up in somewhat different leisure worlds, with boys being exposed more to sports and outdoor activities, and girls being more likely to be given props (e.g., dolls) that stimulate imaginative play (see A. Huston, 1983, for a review of the socialization of leisure interests). These early learning experiences no doubt produce in men and women some differences in their likes and dislikes, as well as differences in the skills and knowledge they have relevant to pursuing and enjoying particular activities. These factors, all of which bear on issues of whether husbands and wives are likely to be psychologically oriented toward pursuing particular activities, may have a powerful effect on the extent and nature of the leisure time couples spend together.

While the recreational interests and skills that men and women bring to marriage are doubtless important, the earlier analysis of causal contexts suggests that what leisure activities married men and women do and whether they do them alone or together is heavily dependent on emergent relational phenomena. This point is made by Carlson (1979), who states:

> When an individual marries and subsequently establishes a family, he may no longer be able to carry out as many of his own desires and wishes as before. The background factors which before may have accurately predicted his behavior are now altered through a decision-making process which includes his spouse and other members of the family as well as kinship reference groups on both sides of the family. He may now modify his own recreational activities in light of the desires and wishes of other family members. (p. 448)

Gender differences in leisure interests and preferences are well documented (A. Huston, 1983). It is, thus, not surprising that when couples are asked to identify sources of marital conflict, disagreements having to do with leisure and companionship come out close to the top of the list (Blood & Wolfe, 1960; Gottman, 1979; Kelley, Cunningham, & Stambul [cited in Kelley, 1979]). The disagreements may pertain to whether to pursue activities alone or together, the timing of leisure, or the choice of recreational

activities. Most researchers would probably begin to account for such conflict in terms of the partner's individual likes and dislikes. But the framework
presented earlier in this chapter highlights the need to consider, among other
things, how the feelings partners have for one another can be more important than their personal preferences regarding leisure pursuits.

The scholar interested in pursuing factors affecting husband–wife leisure
patterns has a number of relevant theories on which to draw. Thibaut and
Kelley's (1959) theory of interdependence would suggest that leisure patterns
develop out of the partners' explorations of the actual (or anticipated) affective consequences for each of the partners that result from the pursuit of particular leisure activities, alone and together. Exchange theories draw attention to matters of power, resources, networks, and dependency, all of which
may affect how conflicts regarding companionate activities are resolved
(Blau, 1964; Homans, 1961). Social-learning theory views attraction toward
or away from leisure with the partner as caused by a more general attraction
toward or aversion from the partner (Wills, Weiss, & Patterson, 1974). Symbolic interactionism, with its focus on matters of identity, directs attention
to the psychological investment individuals have in particular activities.
Finally, one or another spouse may be oriented toward subordinating his or
her interests, either because the individual is strongly in love, or because he
or she has internalized a set of values dictating that such subordination is appropriate.

Marital Satisfaction

The literature on marital satisfaction is voluminous (cf. Lewis & Spanier,
1979). Few studies, though, have explored the ways in which the behavioral
organization of marriage might be related differently to satisfaction for
husbands and wives. The present review highlights such research and addresses two interrelated issues: (1) sex differences in the *content* of partner's
behavior as related to satisfaction, and (2) how the *patterning* of activity
(e.g., task segregation) has an impact on evaluations of the marriage and
spouse.

First, husbands' marital satisfaction is more affected by their wives' performance of instrumental activity at home than by the extent to which their
wives are affectionate toward them; the reverse pattern is found for wives'
evaluations of their husbands (Wills et al., 1974). Wives' satisfaction is also
related to the stability of their husbands' employment, and the amount of income the husband's employment produces, but the reverse is not true for
husbands' satisfaction and wives' employment, at least not consistently so
(Lewis & Spanier, 1979). These findings are in line with what would be expected assuming husbands and wives hold traditional sex-role attitudes (i.e.,

men are satisfied if their wives enact well the traditional female role by being affectionate and taking care of the house, while women are pleased with their marriage when husbands are successful in providing financial support, a key element of the male role). Research is needed, however, that directly tests whether the pattern is, in fact, due to husbands and wives using sex-role attitudes to evaluate each others' behavior. Further, the issue of exactly how sex-role orientations provide a filter through which behavior is interpreted must be addressed. The point is that the interaction–interdependence model and the aforementioned notion of causal contexts suggest that gender-related patterns are likely to be due to multiple, interacting factors. In the present instance, the sex differences in correlates of satisfaction suggest that sex-role orientations that are widely shared in society and that individual men and women bring to their relationships are responsible for their evaluations. The line of reasoning advanced in this chapter leads to suggesting the direct testing of rather than assuming of this causal explanation.

Second, there is a debate among researchers about whether sex segregation of activities (instrumental and leisure) in a marriage is promotive of harmony (see Parsons & Bales, 1955) or discord (see Komarovsky, 1976). The available evidence is mixed, and, thus, does not allow us to choose the more-accurate position. The muddiness of the findings may, in part, be explicable in terms of the logic presented earlier in this chapter (see especially sections on interaction and on causal contexts). To regard single features of relationships as isolated causes of other features of relationships is not likely to be productive. In considering how satisfied she is with her spouse and marriage, a wife may take into account in evaluating her husband's performance with regard to the household tasks not only the extent of his involvement but also such matters as the amount of time he works for pay outside the home, the understandings the two of them have developed concerning how much he should be involved in home maintenance, her sense of his skill in doing household work, and her perception of her husband's involvement compared with that of other men in similar circumstances.

Third, conflict is somewhat more strongly related (inversely) to wives' feelings of love for their partners than vice versa (Huston et al., 1985; Kelly, Huston, & Cate, 1985). The reasons for this are not clear, but it may be a consequence of the greater power men as compared to women have in marriage (see Huston, 1983, for a review), coupled with the tendency of men to be more conflict avoidant than women (Kelley et al., 1978). Such a response to conflict on the part of men may protect their power advantage, as Goode (1982) has suggested, but the cost of such means of control may be a corresponding loss of affection.

The foregoing list of gender-related patterns in marital satisfaction raises the broader question, How are we to account for the way in which husbands and wives calculate summary evaluations of their spouse and their marriage? A number of social-psychological theories bear on this question. Before discussing particular models, a caveat is in order. All of these models assume that individuals make judgments about the satisfactoriness of relationships on the basis of their reflections about the pattern of events that result from the relationship over an extended period of time. Obviously, such a cognitive frame of reference is not always used, particularly when individuals are under considerable stress (Kelley, 1982).

One set of explanations, the justice-oriented models, presume that individuals can make and do make distinctions between the amount of reward, the extent to which each individual has contributed to the relationship, the needs of the partners in comparison to one another, and the extent to which each partner derives benefits from the association. Moreover, they assume that these judgments can be separated and made dispassionately. Because the attempt is made to predict satisfaction from decisions about matters of fairness, the assumption must also be made that the judgments can be reasonably assumed to cause satisfaction, rather than vice versa (Huston & Burgess, 1979). On logical grounds there is reason to question the tenability of these assumptions (e.g., it is likely that, at least under certain circumstances, a spouse will overestimate or overstate his/her inputs).

Hatfield and her colleagues (Hatfield, Utne, & Traupmann, 1979) suggest that men and women apply a single universal standard—that of equity—to evaluate fairness in marriage. Equity is said to prevail when the ratio of the partners' contributions (inputs) to rewards (outcomes) is equal. If one partner contributes more, according to the equity principle, that partner will expect a proportionate advantage in rewards received. Others (e.g., Deutsch, 1975; Lerner, 1974), however, have suggested that it is in the very nature of intimate relationships that partners seek to equalize the benefits or outcomes (i.e., they seek equality rather than equity). The equity principle, if applied consistently, would lead to the resources of the partners becoming increasingly different with time and, as a consequence, make it increasingly difficult for the partners to maintain the mutual respect necessary for intimacy to be sustained (Deutsch, 1975). Several reports testing the equity principle seem to show that equity predicts marital satisfaction for both men and women (see Utne, Hatfield, Traupmann, & Greenberger, 1984). A study by Cate, Lloyd, Henton, and Larson (1982) stands alone in pitting reward, equality, and equity against one another as correlates of satisfaction. Cate et al. (1985), using premarital rather than married couples, showed that judgments of equity and equality covary and that the perceived rewardingness of the relationship was more strongly correlated with relationship satisfaction than perceived equality which, in turn, was a stronger correlate than equity.

Fairness, it turns out, is an elusive concept, and a difficult one to study, partly because it is undoubtedly true that what seems just to people is not always a matter of ethics, but rather one of self-interest. To the extent that it is in the interest of men and women to adopt different rules of justice, or different criteria for calibrating such things as contributions, needs, and the like, it can be expected that they will do so. Men, for example, may push for equity because they have had the power to create a context where the contributions they provide are seen as more valuable than those contributed by women. Women in the past may have bought into such a framework because of their economic dependency on men (Walster & Walster, 1975).

It is also likely that persons in close relationships are stimulated to consider issues of equity when they are dissatisfied, particularly when they believe they have options other than remaining in the relationship. Thus, to the extent that the marriage market is better for men than for women during middle age, we might see middle-aged men being inclined to encourage the application of a principle of equity because it is to their personal advantage to do so. Similarly, women who are in the dependent position may argue for equality, either because it serves their individual interests or because they believe it serves the interests of women, in general.

These observations suggest that we need to work toward understanding the circumstances that affect the weight that individuals give to different ways of evaluating their relationships. It is no doubt the case that most individuals, at one time or another, evaluate their personal relationship by reference to matters of rewards, costs, equity, equality, and relative need. It is in the nature of intimate relationships, according to a number of writings (e.g., Clark & Mills, 1979; Deutsch, 1975; Kelley, 1979), that the partners place concern for the welfare of each other above abstract rules of justice. Further, the conceptual framework advanced earlier in the chapter highlights the fact that figuring costs and rewards and calculating satisfaction occurs in the context of a particular relationship and that relationships are embedded in and shaped by their interpersonal and societal contexts.

Concluding Comments

In this chapter, social-psychological theories and an interaction–interdependence framework have been used to analyze men and women in personal relationships. The present focus on courtship and marriage of heterosexual couples needs to be expanded to include the full range of personal relationships women and men enter into, maintain, and dissolve in adulthood. That is, it is necessary to analyze same- and other-sex friendships and same-sex intimate relationships (see Footnote 1).

.The general logic presented in this chapter provides a conceptual approach and an agenda for research on these and other personal relationships. Thus, the basic line of reasoning of the chapter is reiterated here. Although researchers of necessity must analyze relationships at narrowly defined times and must identify certain features as independent variables and others as dependent variables, much extant research and theory assumes the following model of the course of intimate heterosexual relationships: Individual males and females bring a set of stable personal dispositions to potential relationships; these are fully and honestly displayed; and mates are selected after testing for compatibility of personal dispositions. Once married, couples work out (or fail to) an arrangement concerning instrumental activities, and the success in doing this determines marital satisfaction, which, in turn, shapes leisure and companionship (e.g., satisfied couples do things together; dissatisfied ones do not).

The framework advocated here, in contrast, suggests that close relationships and the way in which men and women experience them and behave in them are best thought of in terms of patterns of interaction and interdependence. The relational patterns are shaped by men's and women's dispositions and perceptions, but the dispositions themselves are drawn out and altered as a result of the character of the relationship. Also, individuals, their personal relationship, the immediate interpersonal context of their relationship, and the broader societal context are all interconnected and evolve through time.

References

Abbey, A. (1982). Sex differences in attributions for friendly behavior: Do males misperceive females' friendliness? *Journal of Personality and Social Psychology, 42*, 830–838.

Abelson, R. P. (1981). The psychological status of the script concept. *American Psychologist, 36*, 715–729.

Adams, G. R. (1982). The physical attractiveness stereotype. In A. G. Miller (Ed.), *In the eye of the beholder: Contemporary issues in stereotyping*. New York: Praeger.

Anderson, S. M., & Bem, S. L. (1981). Sex typing and androgyny in dyadic interaction: Individual differences in responsiveness to physical attractiveness. *Journal of Personality and Social Psychology, 41*, 74–86.

Argyle, M., & Furnham, A. (1983). Sources of satisfaction and conflict in long-term relationships, *Journal of Marriage and the Family, 45*, 481–493.

Atkinson, J., & Huston, T. L. (1984). Sex role orientation and division of labor early in marriage, *Journal of Personality and Social Psychology, 46*, 330–345.

Beckman, L. J., & Houser, B. B. (1979). The more you have the more you do: The relationship between wife's employment, sex-role attitudes, and household behavior. *Psychology of Women Quarterly, 4,* 160–174.

Berger, J., Rosenholtz, S. J., & Zelditch, M. (1980). Status organizing processes. In A. Inkeles, N. S. Smelser, & R. H. Turner (Eds.), *Annual Review of Sociology.* Palo Alto, CA: Annual Reviews.

Bernard, J. (1964). The adjustments of married mates. In H. T. Christensen (Ed.), *Handbook of marriage and the family.* Chicago: Rand McNally.

Berscheid, E. (1985). Interpersonal attraction. In G. Lindzey & E. Aronson (Eds.), *Handbook of Social Psychology* (3rd ed.). New York: Random House.

Berscheid, E., Dion, D. K., Walster, E., & Walster, G. W. (1971). Physical attractiveness and dating choice: A test of the matching hypothesis. *Journal of Experimental Social Psychology, 7,* 173–189.

Blau, P. M. (1964). *Exchange and power in social life.* New York: Wiley.

Block, J. (1976). Issues, problems, and pitfalls in assessing sex differences: A critical review of the psychology of sex differences, *Merrill-Palmer Quarterly, 22,* 283–300.

Blood, R. O., & Wolfe, D. M. (1960). *Husbands and wives: The dynamics of married living.* New York: Free Press.

Blumstein, P., & Schwartz, P. (1983). *American couples: Money, work, sex.* New York: William Morrow and Co.

Bott, E. (1957). *Family and social network.* London: Tavistock.

Brehm, S. S. (1985). *Intimate relationships.* New York: Random House.

Bronfenbrenner, U., & Crouter, A. (1982). Work and family through time and space. In S. Kamerman & C. Hayes (Eds.), *Families that work: Children in a changing world.* Washington, DC: National Academy of Sciences.

Brown, R. (1965). *Social psychology.* New York: The Free Press.

Burchinal, L. G. (1964). The premarital dyad and love involvement. In H. T. Christensen (Ed.), *Handbook of marriage and the family.* Chicago: Rand McNally.

Burgess, E. W., & Locke, H. J. (1945). *The family.* New York: American Book Co.

Burgess, E. W., & Wallin, P. (1953). *Engagement and marriage.* Philadelphia: Lippincott.

Burke, P. J. (1967). The development of task and social-emotional role differentiation, *Sociometry, 30,* 379–392.

Burke, P. J. (1968). Role differentiation and legitimation of task activity, *Sociometry, 31,* 404–411.

Campbell, A. (1981). *The sense of well-being in America: Recent patterns and trends.* New York: McGraw-Hill.

Carlson, J. E. (1979). The family and recreation: Toward a theoretical development. In W. R. Burr, R. Hill, F. I. Nye, & I. L. Reiss (Eds.), *Contemporary theories about the family* (Vol. 1). New York: Free Press.

Carson, R. C. (1969). *Interaction concepts of personality.* Chicago: Aldine.

Cate, R. M., Huston, T. L., & Nesselroade, J. R. (1985). Premarital relationships: Toward the identification of alternative pathways to marriage. *Journal of Social and Clinical Psychology.*

Cate, R. M., Lloyd, S., Henton, J. M., & Larson, J. (1982). Fairness and reward level as predictors of relationship satisfaction. *Social Psychological Quarterly, 45,* 177–181.

Chodorow, N. (1974). Family structure and feminine personality. In M. Z. Rosaldo & L. Lamphere (Eds.), *Women, culture, and society.* Stanford, CA: Stanford University Press.

Clark, M. S., & Mills, J. (1979). Interpersonal attraction in exchange and communal relationships, *Journal of Personality and Social Psychology, 37,* 12–24.

Crouter, A., Huston, T., & Robins, E. (1982, October). Bringing work home: Psychological spillover from work to the family. Paper presented at the annual meeting of the National Council on Family Relations, St. Paul, Minnesota.

Cuber, J. F., & Harroff, P. B. (1965). *The significant Americans: A study of sexual behavior among the affluent.* New York: Appleton-Century-Crofts.

Cunningham, J. D., & Antill, J. K. (1981). Love in developing relationships. In S. Duck & R. Gilmour (Eds.), *Personal relationships: Vol. 2: Developing personal relationships.* New York: Academic Press.

Deaux, K. (1984). From individual differences to social categories: Analysis of a decade's research on gender, *American Psychologist, 39,* 105–116.

Deaux, K. (1985). Sex and gender. *Annual Review of Psychology, 36,* 49–81.

Degler, C. (1980). *At odds: Women and the family in America from the revolution to the present,* New York: Oxford.

Deutsch, M. (1975). Equity, equality, and need: What determines which will be used as the bans of distributive justice? *Journal of Social Issues, 31,* 137–149.

Dion, K. L., & Dion, K. K. (1973). Correlates of romantic love, *Journal of Consulting and Clinical Psychology, 41,* 51–56.

Dion, K. L., & Dion, K. K. (1976). Love, liking and trust in heterosexual relationships. *Personality and Social Psychology Bulletin, 2,* 187–190.

Duncan, B., & Duncan, O. D. (1975). *Sex typing and social power,* New York: Academic Press.

Falbo, T., & Peplau, L. A. (1980). Power strategies in intimate relationships. *Journal of Personality and Social Psychology, 37,* 879–896.

Fengler, A. P. (1974). Romantic love in courtships: Divergent paths of male and female students. *Journal of Comparative Family Studies, 5,* 134–139.

Fishman, P. N. (1978). Interaction: The work women do. *Social Problems, 25,* 397–406.

Forsyth, D., & Clark, R. D. (1975). The effects of frustration and social desirability of heterosexual attraction. *Representative Research in Social Psychology, 6,* 114–118.

Freedman, J. (1978). *Happy people: What happiness is, who has it, and why.* New York: Harcourt Brace Jovanovich.

Geerken, M., & Gove, W. R. (1983). *At home and at work: The family's allocation of labor.* Beverly Hills, CA: Sage.

Gilligan, C. (1982). *In a different voice.* Cambridge, MA: Harvard University Press.

Goode, W. J. (1982). Why men resist. In B. Thorne & M. Yalom (Eds.), *Rethinking the family: Some feminist questions.* New York: Longman.

Gottman, J. (1979). *Marital Interaction.* New York: Academic Press.

Guttentag, M., & Secord, P. F. (1983). *Too many women? The sex ratio question.* Beverly Hills, CA: Sage.

Harvey, J., Christensen, A., & McClintock, E. (1983). Research methods. In H. H. Kelley, F. Berscheid, A. Christensen, J. Harvey, T. Huston, G. Levinger, E. McClintock, L. A. Peplau, & D. Peterson. *Close Relationships,* New York: Freeman.

Hatfield (Walster), E., Utne, M. K., & Traupmann, J. (1979). Equity theory and intimate relationships. In R. L. Burgess & T. L. Huston (Eds.), *Social exchange and developing relationships.* New York: Academic Press.

Hatkoff, T. S., & Lasswell, T. E. (1979). Male/female similarities and differences in conceptualizing love. In M. Cook (Ed.), *Love and attraction.* London: Pergamon.

Herbst, P. G. (1952). The measurement of family relationships. *Human Relations, 5,* 3–35.

Herbst, P. G. (1953). Analysis and measurement of a situation: The child in the family. *Human Relations, 6,* 113–140.

Hinde, R. A. (1984). Why do the sexes behave differently in close relationships? *Journal of Social and Personal Relationships, 1,* 471–501.

Hobart, C. W. (1958). The incidence of romanticism during courtship. *Social Forces, 36,* 362–367.

Hoffman, L. W. (1960). Effects of employment of mothers on parental power relations and the division of household tasks. *Marriage and Family Living, 22,* 27–35.

Homans, G. C. (1961). *Social behavior: Its elementary forms.* New York: Harcourt, Brace & World.

Hudson, J. W., & Henze, L. F. (1969). Campus values and mate selection: A replication. *Journal of Marriage and the Family, 31,* 772-775.

Huston, A. C. (1983). Sex-typing. In P. H. Mussen & E. M. Hetheringtom (Eds.), *Handbook of Child Psychology* (Vol. 4). New York: Wiley.

Huston, T. L. (1973). Ambiguity of acceptance, social desirability, and dating choice. *Journal of Experimental Social Psychology, 9,* 32-42.

Huston, T. L., & Burgess, R. L. (1979). Social exchange in developing relationships: An overview. In R. L. Burgess & T. L. Huston (Eds.), *Social exchange in developing relationships.* New York: Academic Press.

Huston, T. L., & Levinger, G. (1978). Interpersonal attraction and relationships. *Annual Review of Psychology, 29,* 115-156.

Huston, T. L., McHale, S. M., & Crouter, A. (1985). When the honeymoon is over: Changes in the marriage relationship over the first year. In R. Gilmour & S. Duck (Eds.), *The Emerging Science of Personal Relationships.* Hillsdale, NJ: Erlbaum.

Huston, T. L., & Robins, E. (1982). Conceptual and methodological issues in studying close relationships. *Journal of Marriage and the Family, 44,* 901-925.

Huston, T. L., Surra, C. A., Fitzgerald, N. M., & Cate, R. M. (1981). From courtship to marriage: Mate selection as an interpersonal process. In S. W. Duck & R. Gilmour (Eds.), *Personal Relationships: Vol. 2: Developing personal relationships.* London: Academic Press.

Ickes, W. (1981). Sex role influences in dyadic interaction: A theoretical model. In C. Mayo & N. Henley (Eds.). *Gender, androgyny, and nonverbal behavior.* New York: Springer.

Ickes, W., & Barnes, R. D. (1978). Boys and girls together—and alienated: On enacting stereotyped sex roles in mixed-sex dyads, *Journal of Personality and Social Psychology, 36,* 669-683.

Jacobson, N. S., & Margolin, G. (1979). *Marital therapy: Strategies based on social learning and behavior exchange principles.* New York: Brunner/Mazel Publishers.

Johnson, M. P. (1982). Social and cognitive features of the dissolution of commitment to relationships. In S. Duck & R. Gilmour (Eds.), *Personal Relationships: Vol. 4: Dissolution.* London: Academic Press.

Jones, E. E. (1964). *Ingratiation: A social psychological analysis.* New York: Appleton-Century-Crofts.

Jones, E. E., & Pittman, T. S. (1982). Toward a general theory of strategic self-presentation. In J. Suls (Ed.), *Psychological perspectives on the self* (Vol. 1). Hillsdale, NJ: Erlbaum.

Jones, E. E., & Wortman, C. (1973). *Ingratiation: An attributional approach.* Morristown, NJ: General Learning Press.

Kanin, E. J., Davidson, K. R., & Scheck, S. R. (1970). A research note on male–female differentials in the experience of heterosexual love. *Journal of Sex Research, 6,* 64-72.

Kanter, R. M. (1977). *Work and family in the United States: A critical review and agenda for research and policy.* New York: Russell Sage Foundation.

Kelley, H. H. (1979). *Personal relationships: Their structures and processes.* Hillsdale, NJ: Erlbaum.

Kelley, H. H. (1982). The causes of behavior: Their perception and regulation. In L. Festinger (Ed.), *Retrospections on social psychology.* New York: Oxford University Press.

Kelley, H. H., Berscheid, E., Christensen, A., Harvey, J. H., Huston, T. L., Levinger, G., McClintock, E., Peplau, L. A., & Peterson, D. R. (1983). *Close Relationships.* New York: W. H. Freeman and Company.

Kelley, H. H., Cunningham, J. D., Grisham, J. A., Lefebvre, L. M., Sink, C. R., & Yablon, G.

(1978). Sex differences in comments made during conflict in close relationships. *Sex Roles,* 4, 473–491.

Kelly, C., Huston, T. L., & Cate, R. M. (1985). Premarital relationships correlates of the erosion of satisfaction in marriage. *Journal of Social Personal Relationships.*

Kerckhoff, A. C. (1974). The social context of interpersonal attraction. In T. L. Huston (Ed.), *Foundations of interpersonal attraction.* New York: Academic Press.

Kerckhoff, A. C., & Davis, K. E. (1962). Value consensus and need complementarity in mate selection. *American Sociological Review, 27,* 295–303.

Kiesler, S. B., & Baral, R. L. (1970). The search for a romantic partner: The effects of self-esteem and physical attractiveness on romantic behavior. In K. L. Gergen & D. Marlowe (Eds.), *Personality and social behavior.* Reading, MA: Addison-Wesley.

Klinger, E. (1977). *Meaning and void: Inner experience and incentives in people's lives.* Minneapolis: University of Minneapolis Press.

Knox, D. H., & Sporakowski, M. J. (1968). Attitudes of college students toward love. *Journal of Marriage and the Family, 30,* 638–642.

Komarovsky, M. (1976). *Dilemmas of masculinity.* New York: Norton.

Laner, M. R. (1977). Permanent partner priorities: Gay and straight. *Journal of Homosexuality,* 3, 21–39.

Langhorne, M. C., & Secord, P. F. (1955). Variations in marital needs with age, marital status and regional locations. *Journal of Social Psychology, 41,* 19–38.

Larzelere, R. E., & Huston, T. L. (1980). The dyadic trust scale: Toward understanding interpersonal trust in close relationships. *Journal of Marriage and the Family, 42,* 595–604.

Lerner, M. J. (1974). Social psychology of justice and interpersonal attraction. In T. L. Huston (Ed.), *Foundations of interpersonal attraction.* New York: Academic Press.

Levinger, G. (1977). Reviewing the close relationship. In G. Levinger & H. L. Raush (Eds.), *Close relationships.* Amherst: University of Massachusetts Press.

Levinger, G. (1983). Development and change. In H. H. Kelley et al., *Close relationships.* New York: W. H. Freeman and Co.

Levinger, G., & Rands, M. (1985). Compatibility in marriage and other close relationships. In W. J. Ickes, (Ed.), *Compatible and Incompatible Relationships.* New York: Springer-Verlag.

Lewin, K. (1951). *Field theory in social science.* New York: Harper.

Lewin, K. (1940). The background of conflict in marriage. In M. Jung (Ed.), *Modern marriage.* New York: Crofts.

Lewis, R., & Spanier, G. (1979). Theorizing about the quality and stability of marriage. In W. R. Burr, R. Hill, F. I. Nye, & I. L. Reiss (Eds.), *Contemporary theories about the family.* New York: Free Press.

Lochman, J. E., & Allen, G. (1979). Elicited effects of approval and disapproval: An examination of parameters having implications for counseling couples in conflict. *Journal of Consulting and Clinical Psychology, 47,* 634–636.

Locke, H. J., & Wallace, K. M. (1959). Short marital adjustment and prediction tests: Their reliability and validity. *Marriage and Family Living, 21,* 251–255.

Lowman, J. (1980). Measurement of family affective structure. *Journal of Personality Assessment, 44,* 130–141.

Maccoby, E., & Jacklin, C. N. (1974). *The Psychology of Sex Differences,* Stanford, CA: Stanford University Press.

Mason, K. O., & Bumpass, L. L. (1975). U.S. women's sex role ideology, 1970. *American Journal of Sociology, 80,* 1212–1219.

McCall, G. J. (1974). A symbolic interactionist approach to attraction. In T. L. Huston (Ed.), *Foundations of interpersonal attraction.* New York: Academic Press.

McCall, G. J., & Simmons, J. L. (1978). *Identities and interactions: An examination of human associations in everyday life.* New York: Free Press.

McHale, S. M., & Huston, T. L. (1984). Men and women as parents: Sex role orientations, employment, and parental roles. *Child Development, 55,* 1349–1361.

Meeker, B. F., & Weitzel-O'Neill, P. A. (1977). Sex roles and interpersonal behavior in task-oriented groups, *American Sociological Review, 43,* 91–105.

Mellen, S. L. W. (1981). *The evolution of love.* San Francisco: W. H. Freeman.

Milardo, R. M., Johnson, M., & Huston, T. L. (1983). *Journal of Personality and Social Psychology, 44,* 964–976.

Moen, P. (1982). The two-provider family: Problems and potentials. In M. E. Lamb (Ed.), *Nontraditional families: Parenting and child development.* Hillsdale, NJ: Erlbaum.

Morton, T. U. (1978). Intimacy and reciprocity of exchange: A comparison of spouses and strangers. *Journal of Personality and Social Psychology, 36,* 72–81.

Murstein, B. I. (1970). Stimulus-value-role: A theory of marital choice. *Journal of Marriage and the Family, 32,* 465–481.

Nickols, S. Y., & Metzen, E. J. (1982). Impact of wife's employment upon husband's housework. *Journal of Family Issues, 3,* 199–216.

Nock, S. L., & Kingston, P. W. (1984). The family work day. *Journal of Marriage and the Family, 46,* 333–343.

Norton, R. (1983). Measuring marital quality: A critical look at the dependent variable. *Journal of Marriage and the Family, 43,* 141–151.

O'Rourke, J. F. (1963). Field and laboratory: The decision-making behavior of family groups in two experimental conditions, *Sociometry, 26,* 422–433.

Parsons, T., & Bales, R. F. (1955). *Family socialization and interaction processes.* New York: Free Press.

Peplau, L. A. (1979). Power in dating relationships. In J. Freeman (Ed.), *Women: A feminist perspective.* Palo Alto, CA: Mayfield.

Peplau, L. A. (1983). Roles and gender. In H. H. Kelley et al., *Close Relationships.* New York: W. H. Freeman.

Peplau, L. A., & Gordon, S. (1985). Women and men in love: Sex differences in close heterosexual relationships. In V. E. O'Leary, R. K. Unger, & S. B. Wallston (Eds.), *Women, gender and social psychology.* Hillsdale, NJ: Erlbaum.

Peplau, L. A., & Jones, R. W. (1982). Symposium on homosexual couples. *Journal of Homosexuality, 8*(2), 1–64.

Peplau, L. A., Rubin, Z., & Hill, C. T. (1977). Sexual intimacy in dating couples. *Journal of Social Issues, 33,* 86–109.

Pleck, J. (1977). The work–family role system. *Social Problems, 24,* 417–427.

Pleck, J., & Rustad, M. (1980). *Husbands' and wives' time in family work and paid work in the 1975-1976 study of time use.* Wellesley, MA: Wellesley College Center for Research on Women.

Rands, M. (1980). *Social networks before and after marital separation.* Unpublished doctoral dissertation, University of Massachusetts, Amherst.

Reis, H. T., Wheeler, L., Spiegel, N., Kernis, M. H., Nezlek, J., & Perri, M. (1982). Physical attractiveness in social interaction: II. Why does appearance affect social experience? *Journal of Personality and Social Psychology, 43,* 979–996.

Remoff, H. T. (1984). *Sexual choice: A woman's decision.* New York: Dutton.

Ridley, C. A., & Avery, A. W. (1979). Social network influence on the dyadic relationship. In R. L. Burgess & T. L. Huston (Eds.), *Social exchange in developing relationships.* New York: Academic Press.

Robinson, J. P. (1977). *How Americans use time: A social-psychological analysis.* New York: Praeger.

Rodgers, R. H. (1973). *Family interaction and transaction: A developmental approach.* Englewood Cliffs, NJ: Prentice-Hall.

Rodman, H. (1972). Marital power and the theory of resources in cultural context, *Journal of Comparative Family Studies, 3,* 50–69.

Rubin, Z. (1970). Measurement of romantic love. *Journal of Personality and Social Psychology, 16,* 265–273.

Rubin, Z., Hill, C. T., Peplau, L. A., Dunkel-Schetter, C. (1980). Self-disclosure in dating couples: Sex roles and the ethic of openness. *Journal of Marriage and the Family, 42,* 305–317.

Rubin, Z., Peplau, L. A., & Hill, C. T. (1981). Loving and leaving: Sex differences in romantic attachments. *Sex Roles, 7,* 821–835.

Safilios-Rothschild, C. (1981). Toward a social psychology of relationships. *Psychology of Women Quarterly, 5,* 377–384.

Shulman, N. (1975). Life cycle variation in patterns of close relationships. *Journal of Marriage and the Family, 37,* 813–821.

Skrypnek, B. J., & Snyder, M. (1979). *On the self-perpetuating nature of stereotypes about women and men.* Unpublished manuscript, University of Minnesota, Minneapolis.

Slater, P. E. (1963). On social regression. *American Sociological Review, 28,* 334–364.

Snyder, M., Tanke, E. D., & Berscheid, E. (1977). Social perception and interpersonal behavior: On the self-fulfilling nature of social stereotypes. *Journal of Personality and Social Psychology, 35,* 656–666.

Spanier, G. B. (1976). Measuring dyadic adjustment; New scales for assessing the quality of marriage and similar dyads. *Journal of Marriage and the Family, 38,* 15–28.

Spence, J. T., Deaux, K., & Helmreich, R. L. (1985). Sex roles in contemporary American Society. In G. Lindzey & E. Aronson (Eds.), *Handbook of social psychology* (3rd ed.) New York: Random House.

Stryker, S. (1980). *Symbolic interaction: A social structural approach.* Menlo Park, CA: Benjamin/Cummings.

Swann, W. (1984). Quest for accuracy in person perception: A matter of pragmatics. *Psychological Review, 91,* 457–477.

Symons, D. (1979). *The evolution of human sexuality.* New York: Oxford University Press.

Tharp, R. G. (1963). Psychological patterning in marriage. *Psychological Bulletin, 60,* 97–117.

Thibaut, J. W., & Kelley, H. H. (1959). *The social psychology of groups.* New York: Wiley.

Turner, R. H. (1970). *Family interaction.* New York: John Wiley & Sons.

Unger, R. (1979). Toward a redefinition of sex and gender. *American Psychologist, 34,* 1085–1094.

Utne, M. K., Hatfield, E., Traupmann, J., & Greenberger, D. (1984). Equity, marital satisfaction, and stability. *Journal of Social and Personal Relationships, 1,* 323–332.

Waite, L. J. (1981). U.S. women at work, *Population Bulletin, 26,* No. 2.

Walster, E., & Walster, G. W. (1975). Equity and social justice. *Journal of Social Issues, 31,* 21–43.

Walster, E., Walster, G. W., Piliavin, J., & Schmidt, L. (1973). "Playing hard-to-get": Understanding an elusive phenomenon. *Journal of Personality and Social Psychology, 26,* 113–121.

Waxler, N. E., & Mishler, E. G. (1970). Experimental studies of families. In L. Berkowitz (Ed.), *Advances in Experimental Social Psychology, 5,* 249–304.

White, L. K., & Brinkerhoff, D. B. (1981). The sexual division of labor: Evidence from childhood. *Social Forces, 60,* 170–181.

Wills, T. A., Weiss, R. L., & Patterson, G. R. (1974). A behavioral analysis of the determinants of marital satisfaction. *Journal of Consulting and Clinical Psychology, 42,* 802–811.

Winch, R. F. (1958). *Mate selection: A study of complementary needs.* New York: Harper & Bros.

Winch, R. F. (1967). Another look at the theory of complementary needs in mate selection. *Journal of Marriage and the Family, 29,* 756–762.

Wish, M., Deutsch, M., & Kaplan, S. J. (1976). Perceived dimensions of interpersonal relations, *Journal of Personality and Social Psychology, 33,* 409–420.

Young, M., & Willmott, P. (1973). *The symmetrical family.* New York: Pantheon.

Zanna, M. P., & Pack, S. J. (1975). On the self-fulfilling nature of apparent sex differences in behavior. *Journal of Experimental Social Psychology, 11,* 583–591.

Zimmerman, D. H., & West, C. (1975). Sex roles, interruptions and silences in conversations. In B. Thorne & N. Henley (Eds.), *Language and sex: Difference and dominance.* Rowley, MA: Newbury-House.

Six

Men and Women
in Role Relationships

GRAHAM L. STAINES
with the collaboration of PAM L. LIBBY

Introduction

This chapter analyzes the concept of *gender role* (or sex role) by presenting an alternative to the conventional interpretation of the concept. The traditional view posits two major gender roles (male and female), which apply to most, if not all, domains of life. The chapter refers to this traditional view as the *global* approach. By comparison, the alternative perspective on gender roles examines how the experience of major social roles that are enacted by both sexes (e.g., worker, spouse, and parent) varies as a function of gender. This revised approach thus emphasizes the differences between the experiences of male and female workers, husbands and wives, fathers and mothers. The chapter refers to this alternative view as the *social-role-specific* (or, more simply, the *role-specific*) approach.

The first section of the chapter addresses three basic conceptual issues. First, it explores the meaning of social role, by indicating some of the points on which role theorists agree, and by giving special attention to how theorists differ in formulating their conceptions of social roles. Second, having discussed social roles in general, this section of the chapter proceeds to an analysis of gender roles in particular. Third, this section introduces the three major social roles (worker, spouse, parent) on which the discussion of the role-specific approach is based.

THE SOCIAL PSYCHOLOGY OF FEMALE-MALE RELATIONS

The remaining portion of the chapter adopts a strategy of demonstration to establish the utility of the role-specific view of gender roles. It endeavors, that is, to indicate the value (and the limitations) of this alternative approach by showing what it can accomplish. Accordingly, this latter portion of the chapter is devoted to addressing three broad empirical questions about the trio of major social roles. The three questions, each of which is discussed in a separate section, are as follows: (1) How do the three roles *compare* on a variety of characteristics? (2) How do the three roles *interact?* (3) What are the *consequences* of roles for role incumbents? The final section of this chapter presents the conclusions arrived at using the role-specific approach to gender roles. In line with the volume's overall theme of female–male relations, it also explores the implications of the experiences that women and men have in major social roles for the social relationships between individual women and men.

The Concept of Social Role

Broad agreement exists among role theorists as to the general rationale for social roles. Most theorists would agree that social roles make sense from the perspectives of both society and the individual. From a societal standpoint, roles contribute to the differentiation, allocation, and coordination of human activities (Turner, 1968). Social roles also make sense from the standpoint of the individuals who participate in them. They essentially offer such individuals a potentially reasonable social exchange (Goode, 1960). In return for enacting one's own role (i.e., performing one's role duties), one receives the benefits of the performances of the complementary roles of others (i.e., the rights associated with one's role). In the analysis of the concept of social role, however, consensus among role theorists quickly breaks down (Pfohl, 1975). Three areas of disagreement are particularly salient for the present analysis.

EXPECTATIONS VERSUS BEHAVIOR

Role theorists differ over what emphasis to place on expectations as opposed to behavior. Before we can fully understand this difference of emphasis, however, we need to distinguish between two major types of expectations: prescriptive and predictive. *Prescriptive expectations* refer to people's beliefs about what behaviors should be performed (i.e., prescriptions) and also about what behaviors should be avoided (i.e., proscriptions). *Predictive expectations* refer to beliefs about what behaviors will occur or are likely to occur (i.e., predictions). In addition to and separate from the two types of expectations is the actual *behavior* that role incumbents perform.

Each of the concepts involving expectations or behavior raises the important issue of degree of consensus (or typicality). Prescriptive expectations, for example, may be widely shared among a social group or among society at large. When shared in this fashion they may also be referred to as *social norms* (Brown, 1965). Predictive expectations, when widely shared, come close to the notion of *cultural stereotypes* (Ashmore & Del Boca, 1979; Chapter Three, this volume), although the latter notion includes nonbehavioral attributes (e.g., physical characteristics) that the former excludes. Finally, certain patterns of behavior may also be widely exhibited (i.e., highly typical).

Differences can and do develop among what people feel a person should do (prescriptions), what they feel he or she will likely do (predictions), and what he or she actually does (behavior). But, interestingly, in many situations the foregoing three factors remain remarkably in line (Brown, 1965; Turner, 1968). When prescriptions, predictions, and behaviors are each marked by a high degree of consensus, the pressures for convergence among the three factors are greatly magnified.

The foregoing conceptual distinctions regarding expectations and behavior help clarify the differences among theorists concerning the definition of social role. Roles are most commonly defined in terms of shared prescriptions (Brown, 1965), but they may be defined in terms of shared predictions or widely exhibited patterns of behavior. Each definition has certain implications and, in some instances, limitations. Defining roles as prescriptions implies that, for some possible roles, prescriptions represent a null set. In the case of certain possible roles that meet with social disapproval (e.g., murderer), there are no prescribed behaviors. By comparison, defining roles as predictions ignores the fact that society takes a particular interest in certain behaviors (either prescribing or proscribing them, and providing sanctions to enforce behavioral compliance) and pays considerably less attention to other behaviors, even though both types of behaviors may be expected in the predicted sense. Finally, defining roles as typical patterns of behaviors is vulnerable to the objection that it ignores role theory's traditional emphasis on the sensitivity of behavior to social expectations, both prescriptive and predictive. In the absence of expectations, the concept of role adds little to the concept of behavior.

Rather than extend further the arguments about definitions of role, this chapter defines roles as the shared prescriptions (or norms) associated with a particular social category or position. It recognizes, nevertheless, that roles typically involve shared prescriptions, shared predictions, and typical behaviors; and that all components are worth studying jointly. Not all components enjoy equal importance, however. Prescriptions, which represent the essence of roles, and behavior deserve greater emphasis.

CONFORMITY VERSUS EMERGENCE

Social scientists (Nye & Gecas, 1976) have distinguished between the structuralist and symbolic interactionist approaches to role theory. The structuralist point of view treats roles as social givens (i.e., shared prescriptive expectations associated with social positions) and focuses on whether and how people conform to such normative expectations. The interactionist approach concentrates on how roles *emerge* in the first place and how they subsequently evolve. It views roles as emergent behavioral regularities (from which flow predictive expectations and, to a lesser extent and on a delayed basis, prescriptive expectations). The structuralist and interactionist orientations to roles clearly give different emphasis to expectation and behavior, with the structuralist point of view emphasizing expectation and the interactionist view emphasizing behavior.

The view adopted here is that, despite their differences, the two approaches each have something to contribute to the analysis of major social roles. The two approaches may thus be viewed as incomplete rather than incompatible. That is, some parts of major social roles (usually the broad guidelines) are fairly well defined; hence, conformity to normative expectations is an appropriate focus. Other parts of such roles (usually the specifics) are much less well defined and the process of elaborating, articulating, and modifying the role becomes an appropriate and salient issue. Unfortunately, available empirical research on gender roles comes disproportionately from the structuralist rather than the interactionist camp (Nye & Gecas, 1976).

CLUSTERS OF BEHAVIORS

Individual roles refer to clusters of behaviors (whether expected or actual) and human judgments are involved in deciding which behaviors get assigned to which roles. Not too surprisingly, different people cluster behaviors into roles differently. Social participants (i.e., actors), lay observers, and social scientists (especially role theorists) can and do arrive at different clusterings, and members of each category can disagree among themselves. One reason for disagreement concerns levels of aggregation because roles may be conceptualized at different levels of aggregation (or inclusiveness).

Decisions by social scientists about how to cluster behaviors into roles are not right or wrong in any absolute sense. Neither are they completely arbitrary. Instead, such decisions prove more appropriate or less appropriate for a particular purpose. The next part of this chapter explains how the issues of clustering behaviors into roles, and especially the matter of level of aggregation, are particularly central to the analysis of gender roles; and it criticizes the traditional approach to gender roles for selecting a level of aggregation that is too high.

The Concept of Gender Role

The concept of gender role (or sex role) raises all the issues implicit in the concept of social role plus additional ones as well (Angrist, 1969). Scholars have generally adopted one of two approaches to the conceptualization of gender roles, the traditional (or global) approach or the revised (or role-specific) approach.

According to the traditional approach, gender is a role; more accurately, it is two roles, male and female. In short, the traditional view assumes that gender roles are a subset of social roles but a subset that contains only two members. Based on the earlier discussion of expectation and behavior, three types of questions become salient for the traditional approach: (1) How do people feel that women and men should behave? (prescriptive expectations) (2) How do people feel that women and men do behave? (predictive expectations) (3) How do women and men in fact behave? (behavior). It is instructive to learn how sex-role researchers have divided their energies among these three questions. Many studies have investigated sex stereotypes (i.e., the predictive expectations in Question 2) and many others have investigated actual sex differences (i.e., the behavior in Question 3). Yet, as Pleck (1981a) has noted, researchers have devoted much less effort to studying sex-role norms (i.e., the prescriptive expectations in Question 1). In the context of social roles, prescriptions matter more than predictions, and thus the relative neglect of the normative dimension proves particularly regrettable and needs to be rectified in future research.

The revised (or role-specific) approach to studying gender roles examines social roles that are enacted by both sexes (e.g., worker, spouse, parent) and asks what difference gender of the incumbent makes (Lopata & Thorne, 1978). The issue thus converts from "How does gender define a subset of roles known as gender roles?" (traditional approach) to "How does gender affect the experiences of performing various social roles?" (revised approach). In particular, the revised approach holds that gender of incumbent can make a difference to the three role components discussed in conjunction with the traditional approach: shared prescriptive expectations, shared predictive expectations, and typical behavior. Obviously gender makes a difference to the experience of many, if not most, social roles, but it makes a much greater difference to some roles than to others. In a colloquial rather than a strict sense, the revised approach allows one to think of gender roles as those social roles substantially affected by the gender of the incumbent.

The definitional differences between the traditional (or global) and revised (or role-specific) conceptions of gender role have at least three important implications for research. The first two implications directly involve the issue of appropriate level of aggregation. In the first place, the traditional approach focuses on gender-related behaviors that apply generally to most, if not all, life situations and social roles, whereas the revised approach searches for gender-linked behavior patterns that may apply to only one major life role. Thus the revised approach may uncover situationally specific (or role-specific) sex differences that the traditional approach might overlook because of their lack of generality.

Second, the traditional approach has typically analyzed gender roles in terms of less-specific behavioral referents than those used by the revised approach. As noted in the previous point, the traditional approach searches out highly general gender-linked behavioral characteristics. It has generally done so in terms of global personality traits presented in the form of adjectival scales (e.g., aggressive–unaggressive, sensitive–insensitive). Such traits constitute somewhat diffuse behavioral tendencies or predispositions. Because the revised approach searches for gender-linked patterns in a narrower domain (namely, one specific role) it can examine more specific types of behaviors (e.g., number of hours spent with one's children), and its analysis and measurement of gender-linked differences in roles thus enjoy greater precision and clarity.

Third, the traditional approach to sex roles has been much more preoccupied with *relative* than with *absolute* levels of behavioral characteristics (Pleck, 1981a; Chapter Three, this volume); the revised approach has proven more open to considering absolute levels as well. When the two components of a basic dichotomy, male and female in the case of the traditional approach, are each interpreted as roles, it is not surprising that many theorists define them in terms of each other (e.g., male equals nonfemale) and thus concentrate on gender differences as the relativist criterion requires. By comparison, the revised approach depends less exclusively on the male–female polarity and, in practice, has allowed absolute as well as relative assessments of female and male experiences of social roles.

Scholars have taken different positions with regard to the two approaches to gender roles. Many researchers (especially psychologists) have adopted the traditional approach uncritically, ignoring its limitations, and have not even considered the alternative approach. A number of scholars (e.g., Lopata & Thorne, 1978) have taken strong exception to the traditional view that female and male constitute roles at all. Their objections to the notion of two basic gender roles vary considerably and depend in part on their particular definitions of social role, but they do include the charges that the behavioral expectations associated with gender are nonuniversal and diffuse (see the preceding Point 2 about the value of behavioral specificity). The position taken in this chapter, however, is not that the traditional (or global) approach is inherently wrong; we recognize that there are widely shared prescriptive (and proscriptive) expectations associated with gender.[1] Rather, we emphasize that the traditional approach's higher level of aggregation has the consequences outlined earlier that limit its value. Hence, we conclude that the role-specific approach has more to contribute to the present analysis of women and men in role relationships, and we adopt it in the remainder of this chapter.

Three Major Social Roles

This chapter applies the revised approach to gender roles to three major social roles: worker, spouse, and parent. The choice of these three roles proves easy to defend because of their overriding importance. Each role covers a wide range of human behaviors; each is performed by most people during much of their adult lives; each is considered highly salient by role incumbents; each exhibits both formal (or institutionalized) and informal components; and each is relatively distinct from the others. Considered jointly, the three roles account for a broad segment of human experience, yet they are sufficiently few in number to permit careful analytic comparisons.

Some additional discussion is needed to clarify the nature of the three roles selected here. In the first place, it is customary to divide them into an occupational role (worker) and two family roles (spouse, parent), and to view the occupational and family roles as operating in separate arenas. We would caution against too strong a bifurcation between work and family life, however. Instead, we emphasize that work is, at least in part, a family role and that family roles involve certain work-like activities.

A second point of clarification regarding the three roles concerns the dividing lines between them. Although, as noted, the three major social roles are relatively distinct, some ambiguities arise. Housework provides a case in point. It may be difficult to determine whether certain domestic chores (e.g., cooking, cleaning) belong to the spouse or to the parent role. Such chores exist when only the spouse role is operative but expand in scope when the parent role is added. In the case of women who lack paid employment, moreover, housework typically becomes the basis of the full-time housewife

[1]These widely held gender-related expectations (or gender-role norms) are one of the developmental antecedents of gender identity (see Katz, Chapter Two, this volume).

or homemaker role. How should the full-time housewife role be classified in terms of our trio of roles? Some investigators (e.g., Campbell, Converse, & Rodgers, 1976) have viewed the full-time housewife as a type of worker, although one who lacks financial remuneration. The notion that *housewife* may be regarded as a formal occupation supports their view (Arvey & Begalla, 1975). Without denying the obvious parallels between full-time housework and full-time employment, the current analysis regards the full-time housewife as enacting one form of the spouse and (frequently) parent roles, although it recognizes the difficulties in dividing all of the full-time housewife's activities between the spouse and parent roles.

Comparisons among Roles

This section of the chapter has two basic aims: first, to compare the three major social roles on a variety of characteristics; and, second, in line with the revised (or role-specific) approach to gender roles, to compare the sexes on each role characteristic for each role. To date, few investigators have attempted to compare the roles systematically. There is a need, therefore, to construct a list of relevant role characteristics, one that includes highly important characteristics, but also one that gives weight to those characteristics for which some comparative information is available (or at least feasible). The list generated in this chapter may be divided into two types of characteristics, the relatively objective (or publicly observable) and the relatively subjective (or private), although the distinction is not sharply drawn. The objective ones include extent of role participation, type of role activities, role status and prestige, and role power. The subjective characteristics include level of role satisfaction, type of role gratification, and degree of role involvement.

A surprising number of methodological problems confront any attempt based on existing studies to compare the characteristics of the three major social roles. Of particular concern is the reliance of most relevant studies on survey (or self-report) methodologies, although a minority of studies use observational and other strategies of measurement. Despite the obvious wisdom of relying on a combination of self-report and observational measures, we are compelled to depend heavily on survey data. We urge that future research right the current methodological imbalance.

Problems in providing information on the characteristics of the three roles do not stop with the general limitations of survey research. Because of the paucity of previous efforts to compare the roles systematically, available survey data rarely take the appropriate comparative form. Some of the problems concern survey sampling. Ideally, one wishes to compare representative samples of incumbents in each role (i.e., all workers versus all spouses versus all parents). Many studies, however, restrict analysis samples to some subtype of incumbents (e.g., employed persons only). Other methodological problems in comparing roles concern survey measures and question wording. The ideal is to have questions with parallel wording for the roles of worker, spouse, and parent. Few studies, however, display any commitment to parallel wording. Even with comparability as the explicit goal, constructing parallel wording (and, in the case of open-ended questions, parallel codes) can pose a serious challenge. In reality, frequently no wording exists for one of the three roles (e.g., parent), or a different type of wording exists for one of the roles (e.g., work), or the wording combines two roles into a larger role (e.g., marriage and parenthood become combined into a single family role), or the question itself compares two roles rather than having a separate question for each role.

Aside from the issue of role comparisons, this section of the chapter also has a second aim—namely, to compare the sexes on each role characteristic for each role. In accordance with the revised approach to gender roles, such comparisons indicate the extent and manner in which the experience of major social roles varies by gender. Methodological difficulties arise again in the attempt to assess sex differences in role characteristics. A major issue here is that real sex differences in subjective role characteristics tend to be quite small; hence, the imperfections of measures and the variations among samples give rise to inconsistent findings across studies. In addition, using items phrased in very general or global terms (e.g., overall role satisfaction) in order to facilitate across-role comparisons makes for smaller sex differences than are obtained for items with more specific content. On the other hand, because sex differences concern only one role at a time, one can make use of studies that have particular items available for only one or two of the roles.

OBJECTIVE ROLE CHARACTERISTICS

Extent of Role Participation

A variety of possible approaches exist for measuring the extent of role participation. One may examine the proportion of the total adult population that participates in the role. One might, for instance, ask about the proportion of the population that participates in the role at some point in their lives. Such data do not offer sharp comparisons among the roles and between the sexes, however, because the percentage of either sex who at some time participates in a given role tends to approach 100 (Glick, 1977). Alternatively, one might inquire about the proportion of the total adult population currently participating in the role. Certain data suggest that parenthood registers the highest rate of participation (77%, Veroff, Douvan, & Kulka, 1981), followed by marriage (66%, U.S. Bureau of the Census, 1980) and then work (63%, U.S. Bureau of the Census, 1980).

As an alternative to measuring the extent of role participation of the total adult population, one may concentrate exclusively on those individuals who presently enact the role. Measures of the role participation of incumbents generally adopt a short-term focus and consider a role occupant's degree of participation on a daily or at most weekly basis. Short-term measures of the participation of role incumbents raise two important issues—namely, the distinctions between time and activity and between absolute and proportional measures.

In the first place, the language of *time* (i.e., number of hours spent) allows researchers to ask how much of a person's normal life is devoted to each role. Time allocations are usually assessed by one of two self-report techniques: asking respondents to keep a detailed record of a day's time use in diary form (i.e., a time budget) for 1 or 2 specific days (the more-precise method) or requiring respondents to estimate the amount of time they typically devote to a role on a daily or weekly basis (the less-precise method). By way of comparison, one can ask respondents about the extent to which they are engaged in the *activities* associated with a role.

The second issue concerns *absolute* versus *proportional* (or *relative*) measures of participation (Pleck, 1983). Some researchers ask role incumbents about their absolute level of participation in a role. Other researchers ask respondents what proportion of a role they perform relative to their spouses (and possibly other members of the household). The two foregoing distinctions among short-term measures of the role participation of incumbents (i.e., time versus activity, absolute versus proportional) are, in principle, logically independent, and all four combinations are possible. In actual research, nevertheless, the two distinctions are highly correlated. Temporal measures tend to be absolute and measures of activity tend to be proportional.

In comparing the temporal–absolute and activity–proportional measures of role participation, we begin by noting certain characteristics they have in common. On the positive side, each type of measure readily permits comparison between the sexes. On a less-positive note, each type of measure involves certain conceptual ambiguities. In the case of the temporal–absolute measures, for example, it may be unclear which of two roles (e.g., marriage or parenthood) should lay claim to the time spent on a particular activity (e.g., preparing meals). In the case of activity–proportional measures, the presence of children, especially older children, may complicate the simple division of activities between husband and wife and require a three-way (or more) split.

Of the various differences between the temporal–absolute and activity-proportional measures, one factor favors the activity–proportional approach. People perform role tasks with varying degrees of efficiency, but only the activity–proportional approach takes this into account. In other words, this approach gives people credit only for their actual role-task accomplishments and not for time wasted or spent inefficiently. All other differences between the two types of measures of role participation, however, favor the temporal–absolute approach. The latter method enjoys much greater precision of measurement. Whereas time diaries measure down to the level of individual minutes, the activity–proportional method typically uses very crude rating scales with just a few, somewhat imprecise, scale points. In addition, the temporal–absolute measures prove sensitive to variations in the total amount of role activity, whereas the activity–proportional measures do not. A final and, in the present context, decisive advantage for the temporal–absolute measures concerns comparisons among roles. The temporal–absolute measures permit straightforward comparisons among contributions to various roles, but the activity–proportional measures founder on across-role comparisons because their meaning depends so heavily on what one's spouse does. Accordingly, the present review emphasizes data on absolute amounts of time allocated to roles.

Before reporting on actual time allocations, we note that time spent on the marital role has not been satisfactorily measured. Rarely have researchers attempted to assess the amount of time that spouses spend doing things together (marital interaction) or even the amount of time they spend in each other's presence (marital contact). Instead, researchers have contented themselves with finding out about time spent on housework, undoubtedly a less-central component of the marital role. It bears emphasis that our ignorance of the amount of time spent in the marital relationship represents a serious gap in existing knowledge.

The typical (though not universal) pattern is for time in the work role (Stafford, 1980) to exceed time spent on housework (Pleck, 1983), which in turn exceeds time devoted to the parental role (Pleck, 1983). We have converted the weekly figures on working hours to daily figures that disregard the distinction between working and nonworking days. In the case of men, the daily time allocations become 5.7 hours on work, 1.6 hours on housework, and .4 hours on parenting. Among women, the relevant figures are 4.4 hours on work, 3.4 hours on housework if working and 5.6 hours if not employed, and .8 hours on parenting if working and 1.7 hours if not.

Types of Role Activities

Given available data, it is not easy to compare work, marriage, and parenthood according to the types of activities that each role typically involves. Research has investigated the activities of each role but not in a common framework. Some partial comparisons have occasionally been attempted, however. The housework component of the spouse role corresponds roughly to certain paid occupations (e.g., domestic), and some researchers have viewed being a housekeeper as an occupation and compared it with other occupations (Arvey & Begalla, 1975). Similarly, portions of the parental role correspond roughly to certain standard occupations (e.g., child care worker, babysitter). What is lacking, however, is a systematic comparison of the three major social roles along a set of dimensions of activities (e.g., substantive complexity, degree of routinization, frequency of time pressure [Miller & Garrison, 1982]).

As a consequence, the present analysis is limited to comparisons between the sexes for each role, using different activity categories for each role. In the case of work, because men and women tend to work in different occupations, it is customary to divide occupations into three categories: typically male (i.e., those in which men predominate numerically by a large margin), typically female (those with high proportions of women), and mixed (those with the sexes represented in more-balanced numbers). According to McLaughlin's (1978) analysis of data from the Dictionary of Occupational Titles, the three categories of occupations differ in the types of activities they require of workers. Male occupations (e.g., carpenter, police officer) make the greatest demands for physical skill, strength, and working with things; intermediate demands for mental skill and manipulation of data; and relatively few demands for working with people. Female occupations (e.g., secretary, hairdresser) score high on interpersonal demands and low on other types of requirements. Mixed occupations (e.g., psychologist, statistician) demand high levels of mental skill, manipulation of data, and working with people, and low levels of other requirements. Insofar as men tend to work in typically male occupations and women in typically female occupations, therefore, the two sexes engage in different types of activities at work.

In the case of the two family roles, we focus on the amount of time men and women invest in different types of activities. In confining the analysis of activities in the marital role to housework, we overlook other significant marital activities but the requisitive data on time spent do not exist for these nonhousework activities. According to the most-recent time budget data available to us (Pleck, 1983), men and women allocate their housework time quite differently. Whereas women spend much of their time on frequent, repetitive, and routine tasks (e.g., cooking, cleaning, and laundry), men spend a large portion of their time on infrequent, irregular, and nonroutine housework and household activities (e.g., household repairs, paperwork, and family-related transportation and travel). Thus, the data on time allocated to housework tend to confirm the existence of typically male and typically female chores.

In the popular conception, types of parental activities do not divide along gender lines as readily as types of housework activities. Most people, that is, can identify typically male and female home chores but would have more trouble in separating male and female parental assignments. Time-budget data reported by Robinson (1977a), however, do point to sex differences in parental activities. Mothers spend much of their parental time on basic infant and child care; fathers spend a good deal of their parental time playing with their children. It is reasonable to conclude that sex differences in types of parental activities do exist but are probably less pronounced than for housework activities.

Role Status and Prestige

The present discussion uses the term *status* to designate the public esteem associated with occupancy of a role. Our society bestows considerable status on those who assume the roles of paid worker, spouse, or parent. Interestingly, very little research has been undertaken to compare the public esteem associated with being in each of the roles. Nor has research clarified whether and how such esteem varies according to the gender of the incumbent. One might, nonetheless, speculate that greater status is associated with being a male than a female worker, but the sex difference may reverse direction in the case of the two family roles. Becoming a wife is generally viewed as a more significant achievement than becoming a husband; and our culture glorifies motherhood more than it does fatherhood.

Both role status and role prestige refer to levels of public esteem, but, in the present terminology, whereas *status* differentiates *between* role occupants and nonoccupants, *prestige* distinguishes *among* occupants of a particular role. Not all workers, for example, enjoy the same level of public esteem. *Prestige* thus refers to the public esteem associated with a person's particular enactment of a role. Prestige has been analyzed quite differently for the three roles. In the case of the work role, it has traditionally been associated with one characteristic of jobs—namely, occupation. It is important to mention that other dimensions of jobs (e.g., industry, organization, hierarchical level within the organization) could and should also be scaled for prestige but, with a few exceptions (Stewart, Lykes, & LaFrance, 1982), have not been. Gender has important implications for the prestige of occupations. Witness the findings from research that have compared the prestige of the three classes of occupations: typically male, typically female, and mixed. These results may surprise some people. Highest on occupational prestige are the mixed occupations. Next come the typically male occupations and, just slightly below them, the typically female occupations (McLaughlin, 1978).

Prestige has not been studied separately for the marital and parental roles. Instead, what has been investigated primarily is the socioeconomic standing of the family. Traditionally, this has been measured in terms of the prestige of the husband's occupation. Research has indicated, however, that in families in which both husband and wife work, some weight should be given to the wife's as well as the husband's occupation in arriving at a family's social standing (Berk & Kingston, 1982). In short, whatever the particular formulation, family social standing derives from occupational prestige, a measure associated with the work role. Future research would do well to investigate the prestige associated with the marital role taken on its own, that is, separate from the parental role. Certain marital choices are considered substantially more prestigious than others (e.g., the colloquial notion of "a good catch"). A variety of the spouse's characteristics contribute to judgments about prestige. Spouse's occupation (or spouse's father's occupation) is important but so are such characteristics as spouse's physical attractiveness, personality, intelligence, education, income, et cetera. Parallel arguments about prestige associated with the parental role make somewhat less sense.

Role Power

The issue of power has been widely discussed in connection with both the work role and the marital role; it has received less attention in relation to the parental role. Power in the occupational context has many meanings: hierarchical position in the organization, control over valued work-related resources and rewards, degree of autonomy, and so on (Wolf & Fligstein, 1979). Power in the marital role frequently refers to the relative influence of husband and wife in family decision-making, a notion that has been investigated by both survey and observational means (Gray-Little & Burks, 1983). Power in the parental role makes most sense as influence over decisions regarding children. In intact families, parental power largely represents an extension of marital power.

The main challenge posed by the concept of role power—a challenge that remains entirely unmet—is to formulate an approach to measuring power that applies to all three major social roles. This chapter proposes that influence over decision making offers the necessary common thread. Incumbents in each role should be asked to rate the degree of influence they have over role-related decisions, especially when such decisions are contested by other relevant parties. Investigators should frame the question in absolute rather than in relative terms, thereby maximizing the capacity to make comparisons across roles and between the sexes.

Some information already exists on the question of sex differences in role power. By almost every criterion, men enjoy more power in the world of work than do women (Kanter, 1977; Wolf & Fligstein, 1979). Men's access to a power advantage appears to extend into most of the components of the marital role (Scanzoni, 1978) and the parental role, although in at least one instance (the housekeeper function) the power differential favors women (Nye, 1976). According to available data, then, power represents one role characteristic on which men outscore women in all three major social roles and often by large margins.

SUBJECTIVE ROLE CHARACTERISTICS

Role Satisfaction

The term *satisfaction* may be used to refer to a variety of types of measures, including direct ratings of satisfaction and happiness, as well as indirect questions about overall positive versus negative reactions to a role. Common to most measures of satisfaction is a weighing by the role incumbent of positive and negative factors associated with the role. Based on questions that measure some form of role satisfaction, we conclude that role incumbents report higher levels of satisfaction with marriage and with parenthood than with work, although we are unsure how much these reports of satisfaction are inflated by social desirability. We further conclude that the evidence does not allow us to determine relative levels of satisfaction with the marital and parental roles.

Actually, the evidence on relative levels of satisfaction with the three roles falls well short of robust. Veroff et al.'s (1981) interview schedule for their 1976 national survey does not contain parallel questions about how satisfied incumbents are with each of the roles. Instead, it includes an open-ended question about job satisfaction, a closed-ended rating of marital happiness, and no direct question about parental satisfaction. A further set of questions in the same study asked respondents how much satisfaction they derived from each role. This type of question emphasizes role gratifications but neglects role frustrations, and hence does not offer a particularly balanced assessment of satisfaction. Nonetheless, among role incumbents the items generated higher scores for marriage (80% reported a great deal of satisfaction) and parenthood (85%) than for work (53%) (Depner, 1978). Beyond the Veroff et al. study, Campbell et al. (1976) included standard questions about satisfaction with marriage and with one's job in their 1971 national survey, and obtained higher ratings of satisfaction with marriage (58% completely satisfied) than with one's job (36%). Obviously, a pressing need exists for a study that provides direct ratings of satisfaction with the three roles in comparable terms.

Next are the findings on sex differences in role satisfaction. For none of the three roles do large sex differences emerge. Based on a number of studies, we conclude that no consistent sex differences exist for satisfaction with work or parenthood but that men register higher marital satisfaction than women. In Veroff et al.'s (1981) survey, men and women did not differ on level of job satisfaction. Campbell et al. (1976) detected no sex differences in job satisfaction in their survey; and a review of several national survey findings on overall job satisfaction found no consistent difference by sex (Quinn, Staines, & McCullough, 1974). Husbands tend to give a more favorable impression of their marriages than do wives. Veroff et al. (1981) found that husbands registered slightly higher levels of marital happiness than did wives. Campbell et al. (1976) noted higher marital satisfaction among men than women and observed further that women were more likely to admit that the thought of getting a divorce had crossed their minds. Substantial sex differences favoring men are sometimes found on items that tap more-specific aspects of marital satisfaction (Veroff et al., 1981). Fathers and mothers do not display any consistent pattern of difference in their level of satisfaction with the parental role. In Veroff et al.'s (1981) study, fathers offered a slightly more positive account than mothers of how one's life is changed by becoming a parent (i.e., indirect measure of satisfaction). Campbell et al. (1976), however, found no appreciable sex differences on questions about enjoyment derived from the parental role and wishing to be free from the responsibilities of the role.

Role Gratification

The three major life roles presumably offer different types of gratifications or, more accurately, a different mix of gratifications. Veroff et al. (1981) asked spouses to specify the nicest things about their own marriages, parents to specify the nicest things about having children, and workers to specify the things they particularly liked about their jobs. The question wordings and associated open-ended codes are not exactly parallel for the three roles but the items permit some approximate comparisons. The present reporting of the data concentrates on a trio of gratifications (interpersonal, achievement, and power) that are for the most part relevant to each of the three major roles, and it omits gratifications that apply primarily to only one of the roles (e.g., sex). Based on Veroff et al.'s data, incumbents in all three roles place greatest emphasis on interpersonal gratifications (e.g., doing things together; love and affection) but these prove most important to spouses, followed by parents, and then workers. Achievement gratifications (e.g., sense of accomplishment, challenge, recognition) come most from the work role, followed by the parental role, and least from the marital role. Power satisfaction (e.g., leadership, independence) derives more from the work role than from the marital and parental roles.

Sex differences in types of role gratifications follow traditional lines. More women than men mention interpersonal gratifications for all three roles. For the work role, men are more likely than women to mention achievement gratifications. And for both the work and parental roles, men cite power gratifications more often than do women.

Role Involvement

Numerous measures of role involvement exist and raise questions about what is the most appropriate type of measure. One important issue concerns the distinction between role involvement and role satisfaction. The current discussion assumes that the two concepts are distinct and that higher scores on a measure of role involvement need not imply high satisfaction. The overall conclusions on levels of involvement with the different roles, however, resemble those for role satisfaction. Involvement is higher for the marital and parental roles than for the work role but the data do not allow one to pick between the two family roles. The available evidence is again less than definitive. Veroff et al. (1981) asked their respondents whether they would rather overhear someone saying that they were an excellent worker, a good spouse, or a fine parent. Actually, Veroff et al. required respondents to compare two roles at a time and to do so for three possible pairings (worker versus spouse, worker versus parent, and spouse versus parent). Veroff et al.'s data indicate substantially higher involvement with marriage and with parenthood than with work. Both marriage and parenthood outscore work by large ratios, and marriage prevails somewhat over parenthood. There remains a need for a study, however, that phrases separate and parallel questions on involvement for the three roles.

Data on sex differences in role involvement also prove inadequate. The overall trend of existing data is for men to score higher than women on work involvement and for women to score higher than men on involvement in marriage and parenthood. On an item about nonfinancial motivation to work, men show a greater readiness than women to continue working in the absence of financial necessity, according to data from several studies (Campbell et al., 1976; Veroff et al., 1981). Pleck's (1983) review of an array of studies likewise accumulates evidence that men are more involved than women in work and that women are more involved than men in family roles.

The foregoing comparisons among the three roles and between the two sexes take place at a high level of aggregation (or generality). Results for the comparisons actually vary according to a variety of additional factors, such as historical period, stage of the role, and demographic subgroup, but rarely have the comparisons taken these other factors seriously into account.

PRESCRIPTIVE EXPECTATIONS

In comparing the three major life roles (and the two sexes) one needs to recall the earlier distinction between prescriptive expectations and behavior. The discussion thus far has concentrated on various aspects of role enactment (i.e., behaviors and experiences in the role); and, in fact, most empirical studies do give much greater weight to behavioral data than to data on prescriptions. Some studies, however, have provided information on role-related prescriptions and permit us to consider the degree of normative pressure to perform certain role behaviors and allow us to detect discrepancies between normative requirements and actual enactment of the various roles.

A first prescriptive issue concerns whether individuals are obligated to enter the major life roles. What, in short, are the norms regarding role occupancy? Veroff et al. (1981) posed the issue for the two family roles. How much normative pressure is there for a single person to marry and for a childless couple to have children? Specifically, the investigators asked respondents what they would think about a person who did not want to get married and about a couple who decided to have no children. Normative pressure to enter the role is not particularly great for either family role but is somewhat stronger for parenthood than for marriage.

A second prescriptive question concerns whether individuals who have entered a role are obligated to enact the role—that is, to carry out its responsibilities. Available data suggest that normative pressure is much stronger to enact a role already entered than to enter it in the first place. Nye (1976) asked a sample of married couples in Yakima county, Washington, whether they would socially ostracize people who refused to perform various work and family roles. Nye's analysis makes it somewhat difficult to compare the three major roles because he disaggregates them into eight smaller roles. To be specific, his research refers to one work role (provider), five marital roles (housekeeper, therapeutic, sexual, kinship, recreational), and two parental roles (child care, child socialization). Nye found high levels of anticipated ostracism (over 80%) in the case of one role for men (provider) and two roles for women (child care, child socialization), and lower levels (about 50%) in the case of another role for women (housekeeper).

The third prescriptive question concerns the extent of role participation.

How much time and energy should people invest in the major social roles? How much responsibility and how many activities should they undertake in the role? As noted earlier, role participation may be measured in temporal-absolute terms (e.g., number of hours per week) or in activity–proportional terms (e.g., proportion of role activities performed by one spouse). Systematic normative data have, unfortunately, been collected mainly in activity–proportional terms—that is, mainly on the issue of what proportion of a particular role's activities should be undertaken by the husband as opposed to the wife. In other words, respondents have rarely been asked to specify in absolute terms how much time each sex should spend in the various life roles. As noted earlier, certain specific limitations follow from the decision to measure extent of role participation in activity–proportional terms. Respondents may believe, for example, that both sexes should spend a great deal of time with their children, but data collected in activity–proportional terms would never reveal this. Similarly, respondents may believe that people should spend twice as much time in one social role (e.g., parenthood) as in another (e.g., marriage), yet the activity–proportional approach allows us to compare roles only in the very restricted sense of comparing appropriate proportions for men and women.

Nye (1976) has collected the most systematic prescriptive data on extent of participation in work and family roles, albeit in activity–proportional terms. Of the roles on which he collected normative data on extent of participation, the provider role falls most clearly into the husband's domain of responsibility, with about half of all respondents assigning it to the husband solely and half to the husband mainly. Conversely, the housekeeper role is assigned either to the wife mainly (two-thirds of respondents) or solely (one third). Prescriptions for the parental roles prove more equally balanced. Among the other marital roles, kinship responsibilities are allocated more to wives than husbands, and recreational responsibilities tend to be allocated to both sexes equally.

Interestingly, Nye arrays his data so that role prescriptions and role behavior can be compared directly. Norms match behavior for some roles but not for others. In particular, role prescriptions and enactment are generally in line for the provider, kinship, and recreational roles. In the case of the two parental roles (child care and child socialization) and, to a lesser extent, the housekeeper role, wives do proportionately more and husbands proportionately less than norms prescribe.

A fourth and final prescriptive question involves the type (or nature) of role activities. At issue here is which types of role activities people believe that men and women ought to participate in. Of particular interest is whether contemporary norms favor men and women limiting themselves to the traditional sex-linked activities associated with each role. Once again, there arises the problem that most prescriptive data have been collected in activity–proportional terms (i.e., proportion of responsibility assigned to women versus men) rather than in temporal–absolute terms. As a consequence, existing data do not compare societal norms regarding the amount of time that should be spent in two activities within the same role (e.g., teaching children and playing with children), or two activities in different roles (e.g., housework and physical care of children).

Gecas's (1976) prescriptive data on types of role activities parallel Nye's prescriptive data on extent of role participation. His most detailed analysis of activities comes in the case of the parental role. Overall, wives are assigned more responsibility than husbands for the activities of child care, especially for keeping children clean, fed, and warm, but responsibility is about equal for keeping children from fright and protecting them from danger. Norms for the activities of child socialization prove more egalitarian. For all activities of child care and child socialization, moreover, role enactment is weighted more heavily in the wife's favor than role norms.

The foregoing prescriptive data from parallel research leave much to be desired. They come from just a few studies and cover only some of the relevant issues, thereby reflecting the present imbalance that favors research on role-related behavior over research on role-related prescriptions. Future research would be well-advised to (1) organize its collection of prescriptive data around the three major social roles; (2) cast its measures in temporal–absolute terms in order to allow comparisons across roles and among the components of roles as well as between the sexes; and (3) to assemble prescriptive data on role power as well as on the extent and type of role participation.

Interactions among Roles

The previous section's systematic comparisons among the three major social roles may suggest to some that the roles operate independently and exert little influence on each other. Nothing could be further from the truth. Accordingly, this section provides an analysis of how roles interact. It does so by examining the various pairings of roles and asking how each role in the pair affects the other. Of course, such effects within role pairings may vary appreciably by sex and the analysis will take particular note of any sex differences that emerge.

Available literature on the interactions within role pairs has pursued two different strategies. Each is considered here in turn. The first strategy focuses on statistically determined relationships. It requires the investigator to measure characteristics of each role and then search statistically for relationships between a characteristic of one role and a characteristic of another role. Sometimes the relationship between the two characteristics is purely bivariate; on other occasions, statistical controls are imposed on possibly confounding variables; and some analyses even formally test alternative causal hypotheses regarding the role characteristics. The characteristics for which most information is available on role interactions represent a subset of those characteristics reviewed in the previous section: role participation, role activities, role satisfaction, and role involvement. In the case of role participation, we select two indicators: *role occupancy* (currently participates in role versus does not) and *role time* (amount of time spent in role on a daily or weekly basis).

The second strategy for assessing how roles affect each other calls for respondents to report on the relationships they perceive among roles. Some studies have investigated interrole integration by asking individuals whether their experience in one role contributes positively to their experience in a second role. However, because of the widespread attention devoted to social problems, by far the more common use of the second strategy has been to explore interrole conflict.

STATISTICAL RELATIONSHIPS

Occupancy of Different Roles

Although each of the selected role characteristics has been involved in some of the statistical relationships reported, role occupancy (or incumbency) has received by far the most attention. This review of the statistical strategy for exploring how roles affect each other begins, therefore, by examining the effects of occupancy of one role on occupancy of a second role. It considers men and women separately because the data generate appreciably different patterns for the two sexes.

The limited available evidence is consistent with the view that, among men, being employed facilitates getting married and having children. Hogan (1978) demonstrates, using demographic data, that taking one's first full-time job typically precedes getting married and that only a small proportion of the male population reverses the order of these two events. In addition to being an empirical prerequisite to marriage in most cases, employment also appears to facilitate staying married. Studies have shown that families in which husbands experience unemployment are relatively unstable (Sawhill, Peabody, Jones, & Caldwell, 1975), although the issue of causal direction (if any) needs to be addressed here. Conversely, being married and having children increase the pressure on men to undertake or maintain employment. Normative data presented in the preceding section of the chapter indicate that occupancy of family roles activates breadwinning responsibilities among men. Furthermore, men's rate of labor-force participation increases when they acquire the marital role (Johnson & Waldman, 1981) and is at a maximum when they occupy the roles of both spouse and parent (Aneshensel, Frerichs, & Clark, 1981). As a final observation about men, it seems highly plausible that being married facilitates the decision to have children.

Among women, on the other hand, the effect of employment on marriage is more complicated. According to Hofferth and Moore's (1979a) conceptual analysis, employment renders a woman less economically in need of marriage (an independence effect). Yet, women who are working may be more likely to marry because a young couple can more easily afford to marry when both partners are working (an income effect), because working women's earning ability makes them more attractive (a dowry effect), or because working women have more opportunities to meet eligible men (an access effect). These authors have thus identified the positive and negative effects of working on marriage, but note that the relative importance of the different factors has not been documented. Hofferth and Moore further observe that the empirical literature on associations between working and marriage among women lacks consistency. They view existing data as most in line with the interpretation that employment leads to postponement, but not necessarily rejection, of marriage.

Likewise complicated is the effect of employment on remaining married. As with the decision to get married, the impact of women's employment on divorce can be either positive or negative (Hofferth & Moore, 1979a). On the one hand, a wife's working can raise the couple's joint standard of living, thereby increasing the benefits of remaining in the marriage. On the other hand, a woman with a job has an alternative means of support should her marriage prove unsatisfactory. According to Hofferth and Moore's review of studies, although the employment of women is linked in certain ways to divorce, there is no clear-cut body of evidence indicating that, in individual couples, employment of the wife leads to divorce or separation. Regrettably, research has not yet given sufficient attention to female unemployment to determine whether it poses a threat to marital stability, as appears to be true for male unemployment.

The effect of employment on parenthood among women also needs careful clarification. Working women tend to delay having their children (Wilkie, 1981), but there is little evidence that employment reduces the probability of a woman's ever having a child. The percentage of women who expect to be childless remains low (Moore & Hofferth, 1979).

Being married and being a parent continue to represent obstacles to the employment of women, but their historical role has changed. Whereas marriage was once the primary point at which women left the labor force and parenthood a secondary barrier to employment, marriage now reduces the probability of employment by only a small amount, and the advent of parenthood represents the critical stage at which a substantial portion of women leave the labor force (Taeuber & Sweet, 1976). Relative to marriage, that is, parenthood has over time become a stronger predictor of female employment, but in absolute terms, both marriage and parenthood have lost some of their power to deter women from working (Perun & Bielby, 1981). There is an additional reason why parenthood acts as less of a brake on the employment of women than it once did. The number of mothers who do not live with husbands (i.e., primarily the formerly married) has increased substantially, and available evidence (Taeuber & Sweet, 1976) indicates that the inhibiting effect of parenthood on employment is much lower for this group. Furthermore, the still-negative, if reduced, impact of marriage on employment can also be seen by focusing on those women whose marriages terminate in separation and divorce. Among childless women, those without a spouse (i.e., separated, divorced, or otherwise living apart from their spouse) record somewhat higher rates of labor force participation than those married with a spouse present (Taeuber & Sweet, 1976).

As was true of men, marriage would seem to facilitate parenthood among women (Waite & Spitze, 1978), but there is the additional observation in the case of women that parenthood in the absence of marriage makes marriage a more complicated proposition. Actually, one needs to distinguish here between two groups of mothers, the never married and the formerly married. According to Waite and Spitze (1978), never-married women who have borne a child may be less desirable as potential wives to all men but the child's father. Their chances of marrying the father of the child may be increased by the child's birth, but their chances of marrying anyone else may be reduced. Among formerly married women, those with children have lower rates of remarriage than those without children (Sweet, 1977).

It is worth emphasizing the important sex difference implicit in the foregoing relationships between occupancy of various roles. Among men, occupancy of the work role tends to be positively related to occupancy of the two family roles; among women, occupancy of work and family roles tend to be negatively related, especially in the case of work and parenthood. The point is underscored by Aneshensel et al.'s (1981) statistics showing that men's rate of labor force participation is at a maximum, and women's at a minimum, when they occupy the roles of both spouse and parent.

Role Occupancy and Role Time

Occupancy of one role can also affect the amount of time spent in a second role. Among men, one would expect being married and being a parent to increase the amount of time allocated to the work role. Specifically, husbands should work longer hours each week than men who have never married and, among husbands, fathers should work longer hours than nonfathers. Robinson (1977b) reported that, for time-budget data collected from employed persons in 1975, married men spent several more hours per week than single men in work-related activities. Published comparisons of the work time of fathers and nonfathers prove difficult to locate, however. In addition, it is obvious that, among fathers, being married increases the amount of time spent with one's children because nonmarried fathers tend not to live with their children. Interestingly, among husbands, being a father is associated with spending somewhat less time in the housework component of the marital role (Pleck, 1983).

Among women, being employed reduces time spent on the housework component of the marital role and also time devoted to the parental role (Pleck, 1983). Conversely, being married and being a parent appear to reduce the amount of time employed women spend at work each week, exactly the opposite of what was expected (and, to some degree, established) for employed men (Robinson, 1977a, 1977b). We may inquire further about the effect of marriage on the amount of time mothers spend with their children. Robinson (1977a) reported that married mothers have more total contact time with their children than do unmarried mothers but that the two groups do not differ on time spent in primary-activity child care. Parenthood, on the other hand, has a positive effect on women's time devoted to the housework component of marriage (Pleck, 1983).

Role Occupancy and Role Activities

Occupancy of one role may in addition, influence the type of activities performed in another role. According to one provocative hypothesis discussed by Aldous (1978), among married persons, the advent of parenthood means that the housework component of the marital role becomes more sex-differentiated. Husbands and wives, that is, come to share fewer chores around the house and instead tend to perform those activities traditionally associated with their sex. Few studies put the hypothesis to a direct empirical test. Berk (1979), for example, compared the weekday household activities of husbands with small children and of childless husbands but found only limited differences. Perhaps what should be emphasized is that the onset of parenthood has an appreciable impact on the total amount of housework and also the type of housework to be performed, and rather less effect on the degree of sex differentiation in household chores.

Role Occupancy and Role Satisfaction

Incumbency in one role also has important implications for satisfaction with other roles. Among men, being employed has a positive effect on satisfaction with marriage and parenthood. Research on unemployment during the Great Depression indicates that unemployment for men was associated with decrements in many indicators of satisfaction with family roles (Komarovsky, 1940). In a survey by Veroff et al. (1981), similarly, unemployed men were more likely than working men to describe their marriages as unhappy and to take a more restrictive (i.e., pessimistic) view of parenthood. These differences persisted even after a statistical control was imposed on age. Conversely, there is also evidence that, among men, being married (Bisconti, 1978; Crosby, 1982) and being a parent (Crosby, 1982) are both associated with increased satisfaction with the work role, but the issue of causal direction (if any) needs to be resolved.

Marriage would seem likely to improve men's satisfaction with the parental role because, in the absence of marriage, men are typically deprived of daily access to their children. The relevant evidence, however, is indirect and mixed (Campbell et al., 1976; Veroff et al., 1981). On the other hand, according to a number of studies (Campbell et al., 1976; Glenn & McLanahan, 1982), parenthood does have a clear-cut adverse impact among men on marital satisfaction.

In the case of women, the impact of employment on marital satisfaction raises new issues. For example, it becomes important to distinguish between unemployed women and housewives. Research (Veroff et al., 1981) establishes the same negative relationship between unemployment and marital happiness for wives as for husbands. In the comparison between working wives and housewives, employment has traditionally been thought to have a negative impact on marital satisfaction. Earlier in this century, when the employment of wives was much less common, it probably did (Nye, 1974), but more-recent research (Staines, Pleck, Shepard, & O'Connor, 1978) has suggested that the effect of employment on the marital satisfaction of wives in general (or heterogeneous) samples has become marginal, if present at all. Unfortunately, somewhat less is known about the effect of the employment of mothers on their satisfaction with the parental role. Veroff et al. (1981) did not search for differences between employed and unemployed mothers on measures of parental satisfaction, although, based on an analysis not confined to mothers, they observed that unemployed women adopted a more restrictive view of parenthood than did employed women.

According to two studies (Bisconti, 1978; Crosby, 1982), but not to a third (Andrisani & Shapiro, 1978), women, like men, tend to report higher levels of work satisfaction when they are married. Not entirely clear from available data is the effect of parenthood on work satisfaction among women (Andrisani & Shapiro, 1978; Crosby, 1982).

For women as well as for men, being married may enhance satisfaction with the parental role, but being a parent definitely reduces marital adjustment. Veroff et al. (1981) compared married mothers and those who were separated or divorced. With a statistical control imposed on age, the data show that the wives felt noticeably more adequate as parents. On the other hand, although not explicitly indicated, Campbell et al.'s (1976) finding of no association between marriage and the desire to escape parenthood appears to apply to women as well as men. Veroff et al. also compared the marital happiness of married mothers and childless wives and found the mothers to score considerably lower, a result confirmed by several other studies (Glenn & McLanahan, 1982; Glenn & Weaver, 1978).

Role Occupancy and Role Involvement

It might be reasonable to expect that, as a general rule, occupancy of one role reduces the degree of psychological involvement in another role. There may, however, be important exceptions. For example, a man who acquires the roles of husband and father may register greater involvement in his work because of his new breadwinner responsibilities. Few relevant data on men are available, however.

Despite occasional exceptions (White, 1967), virtually all studies of women find occupancy of the marital role to be associated with lower levels of work involvement (Perrucci, 1970; Spitze & Waite, 1981). One might likewise expect motherhood to have a negative effect on work involvement, but it does not. There are only two exceptions (Geerken & Gove, 1983; Parnes et al., 1970) to the general finding of a positive association between motherhood and work commitment (Perrucci, 1970; Spitze & Waite, 1981). Various factors may contribute to the positive effect of occupancy of the parental role on women's work commitment. Women who become mothers may find the activities of child care less congenial than those of employment. Alternatively, entry into the parental role may elicit certain breadwinning responsibilities among women, as it seems to among men.

Other Role Characteristics

Role characteristics aside from role occupancy also have effects across various role pairings, but because less is known about them we comment on them more briefly. Because of the normal constraints of time, amount of time spent in one role will tend to be negatively related to amount of time spent in another role. Investigations based on time budgets have tended to report negative relationships between time spent on paid work and on housework for both sexes (Robinson, 1977a; Walker & Woods, 1976). The evidence for a corresponding negative relationship between hours employed and hours devoted to child care has been less convincing (Pleck, 1981b; Robinson, 1977a). Role satisfaction tends to be positively correlated across roles, no doubt in part because of shared-method variance (i.e., using a single type of measure to assess different concepts). Evidence of positive correlations among husbands is available for each role pairing: job satisfaction and marital satisfaction (Staines, 1980), satisfaction with work and with parenthood (Depner, 1978) and satisfaction with marriage and with parenthood (Depner, 1978). By comparison, data on satisfaction with work and marriage among women have suggested a more marginally positive relationship (Staines, 1980). In addition, Depner (1978) found for women, as she did for men, positive correlations between satisfaction with work and with parenthood and also between satisfaction with marriage and with parenthood. Little research, unfortunately, has explored the similarity between the types of activities a person performs in different roles, or the relationships between a person's level of involvement in different roles.

PERCEIVED RELATIONSHIPS: ROLE INTEGRATION

As noted earlier, respondents may be asked about the *positive relationships* they perceive among major social roles (i.e., role integration) or about the *negative relationships* (i.e., role conflict). The most common approach to measuring role integration is to ask people whether their role partners in one role contribute to their performance in another role. In the 1977 Quality of Employment Survey, for example, Quinn and Staines (1979) asked workers living with one or more family members aged 14 years or older: "How often do family members in your household help you with or do things that are part of your job?" According to the data from this national survey, three-quarters of the workers reported that family members never helped them with their work. Moreover, the answers given by husbands and wives did not differ very much (Staines, 1978).

Lopata, Barnewolt, and Norr (1980) reported on a more extensive study of how spouses contribute to each other's work roles. Their probability sample of 996 women aged 25–54 in the Chicago area consisted of a broad spectrum. The investigators asked the wives in their sample how they helped their husbands and also, in the case of employed women, how their husbands helped them. At an aggregate level, their respondents presented themselves as giving more job-related help to their husbands than they received from their husbands for virtually all task areas listed by the investigators except providing transportation. Interestingly, employed wives differed very little from nonemployed wives in the amounts of different types of help they offered their husbands. When compared with Staines's (1978) study, Lopata et al.'s (1980) data show that if work-related help is defined in terms of a variety of specific activities and is thus interpreted more inclusively, higher rates of work–family integration are recorded and the advantage that husbands have over wives in terms of amount of work-related help from family members becomes more noticeable.

PERCEIVED RELATIONSHIPS: CONFLICT AMONG ROLES

A great deal of research has explored the conflicts that role incumbents experience among various pairings of the major social roles (Greenhaus &
Beutell, 1982). Different studies have, of course, formulated different conceptualizations of interrole conflict. In the first place, studies vary in their
designation of major social roles. Many studies go beyond the trio of roles
considered here (viz, worker, spouse, parent) and include other factors such
as leisure. Moreover, researchers quite commonly combine the spouse and
parent roles and investigate conflict between work and family life. Without
denying the utility of other approaches, we urge that future research include
a systematic study of conflict based on all possible pairings of the three major
social roles.

The few relevant studies of conflicts among all three major social roles
suggest the highest incidence of conflict for the pairing of worker and parent
roles (Holahan and Gilbert, 1979). The 1977 Quality of Employment Survey
provides a detailed analysis of conflict between work and family life (Pleck,
Staines, & Lang, 1980). The investigators examined the extent of work–
family conflict by posing the following question to a national sample of 1084
adults in the survey who were both employed and living with a spouse
and/or children: "How much do your job and your family life interfere with
each other—a lot, somewhat, not too much, or not at all?" About 10% of all
workers living in families reported "a lot" of interference between work and
family life, and 24% reported that interference occurred "somewhat." Contrary to common preconceptions, men and women experienced conflict to
almost the same degree. The relationship between marital status and extent
of work–family conflict also defies general expectations. Among employed
mothers, those with a husband reported higher levels of conflict than those
without a husband. Less surprising are the data on the effects of parenthood.
Parents reported conflict more often than nonparents across all comparable
subgroups.

Some studies have investigated conflict between work and specific family
roles. Holahan and Gilbert's (1979) research included questions about
work–spouse and work–parent conflict. Herman and Gyllstrom (1977) included a question about conflict between work and maintenance of the
home, as well as a general question about work and family responsibilities.
Herman and Gyllstrom found that women perceived significantly more conflict than men between work and home maintenance but that the sexes did
not differ on conflict between work and family responsibilities. They further
found that both marital and parental roles contributed to certain work–
family conflicts. Although several studies (e.g., Holahan & Gilbert, 1979)
have included spouse–parent conflicts in their analyses, none have

systematically investigated the nature of such conflicts. The most detailed research study available (Olson, 1979) explores the conflict between the housework component of the marital role and the responsibilities of parenthood. According to Olson, the common assumption that housework and children fit together neatly deserves to be questioned.

Although a number of comparisons are possible between the statistical and perceptual approaches to role interactions, we focus on two issues: one point of agreement and one point of difference. In the first place, both approaches indicate greater conflict among women between work and parenthood than between work and marriage. Second, the statistical approach consistently shows greater incompatibility between work and family roles for women than for men, but the perceptual data do not evidence any clear sex difference. Part of the issue here involves social selection. Statistically determined work–family interference is largely based on samples that include nonworkers as well as workers, whereas perceptually based work–family conflict is assessed using samples of employed people only. Thus the greater work–family conflict of all women compared to all men may disappear when confined to the subset of people (women especially) who have elected to work and have succeeded in finding work.

Consequences of Roles

This section examines the impact of roles on the incumbents who enact them. To gauge the impact that roles have, one needs a conceptual language independent of particular roles that allows one to assess the effects of any or all roles and to do so in as inclusive a fashion as possible. Along with other researchers (Andrews & Withey, 1976), we have chosen the general concept of well-being to capture many of the consequences of roles for individual incumbents. The concept of *well-being* covers many different areas, including the major dimensions of physical and mental health. Though to some degree intercorrelated (Northcott, 1981), the various measures of well-being cannot always be expected to provide the same (or even similar) results and the patterns of consistency and divergence among types of measures become topics of substantive interest.

One may reasonably ask how effectively the relevant literature establishes the causal direction from roles to well-being. The answer is unevenly. Although some research uses longitudinal designs (e.g., panel studies), and thus suffers from less causal ambiguity, the majority of studies proceed within the constraints of cross-sectional data. Some research entertains the reverse causal interpretation that well-being affects roles via a process of social selection (e.g., individuals low on well-being avoid entering roles);

this research sometimes provides interesting though not definitive tests of the reverse interpretation. Other research discusses and tests a further causal hypothesis (viz, third variables render spurious the association between roles and well-being) by introducing appropriate statistical controls. Few studies, however, formally and systematically investigate alternative causal hypotheses, and some make no attempt at all to reduce the equivocality on the causal issue.

CHARACTERISTICS OF A SINGLE ROLE

The discussion begins by analyzing how various characteristics of a single role affect an incumbent's well-being. As in earlier sections, role occupancy (one of the indicators of role participation) has received the greatest attention in the relevant literature.

Role Occupancy

Mere occupancy of a major life role can have important implications for a person's well-being. Each role offers both rewards and demands (Goode, 1960; Sieber, 1974). *Rewards* include gratifications, stimulation, and challenges; *demands* refer to obligations, constraints, and the like. Presumably, rewards and demands have opposite implications for a person's well-being, with rewards enhancing and demands reducing levels of well-being. Given that a role may be at once gratifying yet demanding, is there a net effect on well-being? In other words, for any particular role, one may ask whether the difference between the sum of the role's rewards and the sum of its demands amounts to a profit or a loss (Condie & Doan, 1978).

The issue of a role's net profit versus loss applies directly to occupancy of each of the three major social roles reviewed in this chapter. Existing literature indicates that occupancy in the *work role* provides a role profit to men. However, the comparison between men who work for pay and those who do not is complicated because the nonworkers consist of several subgroups: the unemployed, the retired, the disabled, and students.

The analysis begins with comparisons between employed and unemployed men. Verbrugge (1982) concludes from relevant evidence that currently employed men enjoy better physical health than unemployed men. Campbell et al. (1976) compared the mental health of men working full-time and unemployed men, and recorded appreciably higher levels of mental health for working men on a variety of measures. Statistical controls on family income, age, race, et cetera did not markedly reduce the impact of unemployment on mental health. Other studies of unemployment and mental health among men (Aneshensel et al., 1981; Veroff et al., 1981) have generated essentially similar results.

Campbell et al. (1976) also compared the mental health of working men and retirees. Retired men tended to characterize their lives in more favorable terms than did employed men. Campbell et al. then added a variety of statistical controls (e.g., age, health, family income, education, race, marital status) to their analysis but did so for the two sexes combined. After these additional controls, the employed were slightly more satisfied with their lives than the retired. Other studies comparing the well-being of employed and retired men (Aneshensel et al., 1981; Veroff et al., 1981) have typically introduced fewer statistical controls and have failed to generate a consistent pattern of differences. Giving greatest weight to Campbell et al.'s data because of the extensive statistical controls introduced, one may conclude that employed men experience better mental health than one category of nonemployed men (the unemployed) and probably experience better mental health than a second category of the nonemployed (retirees).

The effect of incumbency in the work role is even more complicated in the case of women because the nonemployed include the unemployed, retirees, the disabled, students, plus a major additional category, housewives. Verbrugge (1982) presents data from the 1977–1978 Health Interview Survey, which show that, controlling for age, employed women experience better physical health than unemployed women, based on nearly all measures.

In the case of mental health, Campbell et al. (1976) found that unemployment had a negative effect for women, just as it did for men, but the effect was not as large as for men. Moreover, when the effects of family income were controlled, unemployed women had almost the same scores on mental health as women with full-time jobs. Thus, the disadvantage of unemployment appear to be smaller and more exclusively income-related for women as compared to men. In general, other research (Veroff et al., 1981) has also found a negative relationship between unemployment and mental health among women that is smaller than the corresponding relationship among men.

As noted, Campbell et al.'s report on the effects of retirement does not present all relevant comparisons for each sex separately. Once age and other demographics are controlled, retirement exerts a negative effect on mental health for both sexes combined, but its effect for women separately is not known. Aneshensel et al. (1981) found that retired women experience more depression than women employed full-time, both before and after the imposition of statistical controls on age, education, and family income.

A good deal of research has compared the well-being of two groups of married women: employed wives and housewives. The results have proven somewhat contradictory and confusing. Some of the discrepancies may arise from the definition of the category of housewives. It has traditionally been assumed that any married woman who does not work is a housewife. Some research (Campbell et al., 1976) has distinguished between two groups of nonworking wives, the unemployed and housewives. Thus, comparisons between working wives and housewives will depend in part upon whether the unemployed are included among housewives. We will concentrate here on research that defines housewives in the more restricted sense.

Verbrugge (1982) compared the physical health of employed women and homemakers. On virtually all of her indicators of physical health, Verbrugge noted that, controlling for age, working women experienced better health than homemakers in the 1977–1978 Health Interview Survey. In the case of mental health, several studies (Campbell et al., 1976; Veroff et al., 1981) have found only minimal differences between working wives and housewives. Kessler and McCrae (1982), however, used multiple regression to reanalyze Veroff et al.'s data for white married couples but obtained a different pattern of results. Controlling for a variety of demographic variables (e.g., husband's income, respondent's age, number and ages of children), the investigators found that working wives scored significantly lower than full-time homemakers on five indices of psychological distress (e.g., ill health, psychological anxiety, depression, low self-esteem). Before concluding that the employment of wives improves their mental health, Kessler and McRae tested (at least indirectly) and rejected the reverse hypothesis that psychologically healthy women are more likely than distressed ones to enter the labor force. For example, they detected little evidence that homemakers who were planning to go to work in the future were any less distressed than homemakers who planned to remain at home.

To summarize, occupancy of the work role does not offer women the same degree of role profit it offers men. The advantages of employment for women are clearest in the comparison with the unemployed and are still probable in the cases of retirees and housewives. Even when employment has the most to offer women, as in the comparison with the unemployed, research shows that it offers them less than it does men.

Research indicates that occupancy of the *marital role* has clearer implications for well-being in the case of men than women. Virtually all studies agree that marriage represents a boon to men. Verbrugge (1982, 1983) reports that the physical health of married men surpasses that of nonmarried men. The data on mental health from a variety of studies generally concur (Campbell et al., 1976; Veroff et al., 1981).

Glenn (1975) raised the question of whether the association he found between marital status and reported happiness is partly or wholly spurious. He noted that if marriage selects persons with superior capacity for psychological adjustment, then being married is not necessarily conducive to happiness. Glenn reported several persuasive though not conclusive pieces of evidence, however, against the selection hypothesis. To cite one example, he argued that if the selection hypothesis were correct, late marriers would probably resemble the nonmarriers. If so, movement of the late marriers from the never married to the married category as a birth cohort grows older should tend to reduce the aggregate level of reported happiness among the married people in the cohort. Thus, everything else being equal, aggregate reported happiness among married people should be greater below than above age 30. In fact, the data evidenced no such pattern for either sex.

The impact of marriage on the well-being of women has generated much dispute. On the one hand, the data using attitudinal measures of mental health (e.g., avowed happiness and satisfaction) indicate that married women report more favorably on their lives than do women who are not married (Campbell et al., 1976; Veroff et al., 1981). On the other hand, a number of writers have offered a contrary impression of the impact of marriage on women, based on measures of well-being that emphasize physical health and nonattitudinal dimensions of mental health. In fact, several social scientists (Bernard, 1973; Gove & Tudor, 1973) have argued from data on mental illness that among women, marriage is associated with poorer mental health. Yet a careful review of evidence, giving consideration to appropriate statistical controls, does not support the contrary position. Verbrugge (1982) summarizes the data from a number of studies, including her own, on differences in women's physical health by marital status. Married women, she concludes, have better health status than nonmarried women, and have particularly low rates of chronic limitations. In the case of nonattitudinal measures of mental health, a number of studies (Campbell et al., 1976; Veroff et al., 1981) have generally found that married women score higher than nonmarried women. Reviewing all their measures of well-being, Veroff et al. (1981) concluded, nonetheless, that there are many more indicators that marriage is good for men than that it is good for women.

In short, marriage appears to be associated with higher levels of physical and mental health for both sexes. Although the evidence is not entirely consistent, the positive association with mental health appears to be stronger for men than for women, and stronger for attitudinal than for nonattitudinal measures of mental health.

Unlike the other two major life roles, occupancy of the parental role appears to offer a net loss from the role rather than a role profit. Becoming a parent appears to be associated with reduced well-being for both sexes, but the negative effects of parenthood tend to be small and occasionally are reversed (e.g., Aneshensel et al., 1981). Ambiguity of findings is greatest in the case of measures of physical health. A review of evidence by Verbrugge

(1982) could find no literature on how parenthood affects men's physical health and only inconsistent research evidence on how parenthood affects women's physical health. Among women, having several children (rather than one or none) was sometimes related to good health status and little restricted activity; by contrast, having very young children seemed to boost symptoms and curative care. A more-recent study by the same investigator (Verbrugge, 1983) found small positive associations among both sexes between parenthood and measures of physical health.

Several studies have examined the relationship between parenthood and mental health. Glenn and Weaver (1979) imposed statistical controls on marital status, age, and family income, and found the effect of the presence of a child on reported happiness to be small but negative for both males and females. Other studies, employing fewer statistical controls, have produced less evidence of the negative effects of parenthood on mental health (Campbell et al., 1976; Veroff et al., 1981). Even if the presence of children in the household is associated with poorer mental health, it remains possible, as Glenn and McLanahan (1981) have pointed out, that "the primary rewards derived from having children typically come during and after late middle age" (p. 410). Nonetheless, the investigators found that, for both sexes, having had children had very little impact on the global happiness of older Americans in the mid-1970s.

Other Role Characteristics

A modest amount of research has explored whether degree of role time and well-being are related, but it has obtained few significant findings for any of the three roles (Pleck, 1981b). Such research has typically searched for linear relationships between amount of role time and levels of well-being. It may well be, however, that levels of well-being change only after the number of hours in a role reaches a certain threshold (i.e., a decline in well-being once hours become excessive) (see Shamir, 1982).

Limited research has explored the link between types of role activities and well-being. For the housework component of the marital role, several studies have investigated whether performing sex-typical, as opposed to sex-atypical, activities makes a difference to mental health, and have found that men tend to gain some advantage from performing masculine and avoiding feminine chores (Keith, Dobson, Goudy, & Powers, 1981; Keith & Schafer, 1980). To the extent that subsequent research confirms such patterns among men, resistance can be expected to any efforts to reduce the sex-based division of household labor.

A positive relationship would certainly be expected between role satisfaction and well-being, although doubts would arise concerning the correct causal interpretation of such a relationship. One might also anticipate that the relationship between satisfaction with work and well-being would be stronger for men than for women but that the relationship between role satisfaction and well-being for the roles of spouse and parent would be stronger for women than for men. Available evidence supports a positive relationship between job satisfaction and mental health, but it is equivocal regarding the proposed sex difference in the strength of the relationship (Campbell et al., 1976; Glenn & Weaver, 1981). All relevant studies have found a positive correlation between marital satisfaction and overall mental health (Campbell et al., 1976; Glenn & Weaver, 1981) and several studies have noted a sex difference that, as expected, favors women (Depner, 1978; Glenn & Weaver, 1981). Two studies (Cleary & Mechanic, 1983; Depner, 1978) have detected a positive association between parental satisfaction and mental health for both sexes but no consistent sex difference.

Paralleling the issue of whether role occupancy enhances well-being is the question of whether subjective involvement in a role contributes to or detracts from well-being. On the positive side, psychological investment in a role would appear to enhance gratifications from the role, yet it may also exacerbate demands. The limited available evidence on mental health suggests that, among employed people of both sexes, involvement in the work role represents a profit rather than a loss (Baruch & Barnett, 1979; Pleck & Lang, 1978).

COMBINATIONS OF ROLES

Whereas the preceding discussion has focused on the effects of characteristics of individual roles, the analysis turns now to a consideration of the effects of combining roles. Men have traditionally enacted multiple roles. That is, they have performed the roles of worker, spouse and parent simultaneously. Women have traditionally tended to perform their roles sequentially rather than simultaneously, but the rise in women's rate of labor-force participation means that women now enact multiple roles with a frequency that is coming to approach that of men.

Is it advantageous to combine roles? The conventional argument holds that multiple roles create problems for role incumbents. In particular, multiple roles are thought to generate role conflict (i.e., conflict among roles) and role overload (i.e., excessive demands on the time, energy, and resources of role incumbents). Furthermore, the conventional view holds that the disadvantages of multiple roles become more pronounced as the number of roles increases (Goode, 1960). A contrary position articulated by Sieber (1974) contends that the benefits of role accumulation tend to outweigh any stress to which they might give rise, thereby yielding net gratification. Sieber spells out four different types of benefits that derive from combining roles: privileges, buffers, resources, and personality enrichment.

Number of Roles Occupied

An obvious way to focus the debate about the advantages and disadvantages of multiple roles is to introduce the concept of the number of roles a person occupies. The concept is quite clearly an extension of the earlier notion of role occupancy that was applied to a single role. The concept allows us to ask two important questions: (1) Does level of well-being increase or decrease as the number of roles increases? and (2) Do such increases (or decreases) become larger or smaller as the number of roles increases? The present discussion places the concept in the context of a particular trio of roles (worker, spouse, parent). Number of roles is thus a variable with four possible values: zero, one, two, or three.

Existing studies point to a positive relationship between number of roles held and well-being. Based on the 1978 Health in Detroit Survey, Verbrugge (1982) set forth age-adjusted scores for white women on eight measures of physical health for all permutations of work, marriage, and parenthood. Her data, which thus allow us to compare the physical health of women in zero, one, two, and three roles, convey an unmistakable impression. The more roles a woman has, the better is her physical health. Verbrugge's data further show that each additional role brings a smaller increment in physical health.

Similar findings have emerged for measures of mental health. In a preliminary analysis, Depner and Staines (1980) combined data from the 1977 Quality of Employment Survey (Quinn & Staines, 1979) and the 1971 Quality of Life Survey (Campbell et al., 1976) for a single-item self-rating of life happiness. They established that for both sexes, average levels of happiness increased monotonically as number of roles rose from zero to three. The same investigators examined scores on an index of life satisfaction from the 1971 survey and likewise found for both sexes a positive monotonic relationship between number of roles and mental health. Depner and Staines's data, however, do not show a clear relationship between the size of the increment in mental health and each additional role.

Particular Role Combinations

The concept of number of roles provides only a partial perspective on the topic of role combinations. Quite clearly, the concept of the number of roles pays no attention to which particular roles are held. In the first place, one may state the argument about particular roles in terms of their main effects on well-being. Individual roles differ from each other and do not have the same main effects. Similarly, holding two roles can refer to a number of different combinations and each combination may have substantially different consequences. In the second place, particular role combinations deserve individual attention because of their possible interactive effects on well-being (Verbrugge, 1982).

Sequencing of Role Combinations

Yet another qualification may be added to the utility of the concept of the number of roles as an approach to studying role combinations. Basically, the concept ignores issues of time and timing. For any role combination, the time that each role was entered can be important for well-being (and, in some cases, the time that a certain role was exited can also be important). Timing of role entry has been studied in a number of ways. Much research on individual roles has been devoted to the implications of the age at which various roles are undertaken (e.g., age of first marriage or first birth), with special attention given to role entries at young ages.

One useful approach to studying the timing issue in connection with role combinations is to consider the temporal order in which the roles were acquired. Some orders of role acquisition are much more common than others. They constitute the statistical norm and may also be normative in the sense of societally prescribed. They likewise define what is considered a normal sequence, thus allowing us to designate both normal and nonnormal sequences of role acquisitions. The same role combination, that is, can derive from a normal or a nonnormal sequence of role entries. The general hypothesis here is that role combinations arrived at in the usual sequence are associated with higher levels of well-being.

Our interest lies, predictably, in the order of acquisition of the roles of worker, spouse, and parent, and the implications of various orders for the well-being of men and, separately, women. Most of the available literature on sequencing is not organized along the lines of this trio of roles, however. In the case of men, the research on sequences typically focuses on the roles of student, worker, and spouse. It omits any explicit treatment of the parental role, apparently making the highly questionable assumption that marriage and starting a family may be grouped together as a single event. Analyses have studied the consequences of departures from the normative order: completion of schooling (actually, a role exit rather than a role entry), starting the first full-time job, and entry into marriage. Studies show that, controlling for standard demographic factors, men having nonnormative patterns experience higher rates of marital instability and lower earning power (Hogan, 1978, 1980).

In the case of women, discussions usually focus on yet another trio of roles: student, spouse, and parent. The normative ordering is not always explicitly stated, although it may be inferred that women typically complete their education first, marry, and then bear children. Thus, unlike the situation for men, marriage and having children are considered as different events in the transition to adulthood for women. Also, unlike the analysis for men, the beginning of the first job is not normally included as a formal event in a woman's transition to adulthood. A good deal of research has focused on the negative effects of early childbearing on later economic well-being (Hofferth & Moore, 1979b). Our particular interest concerns reversals of the normative order of role acquisitions.

One body of research has focused on the reversal of the marriage-to-parenthood sequence. Strictly, it focuses on what happens when pregnancy, but not actual parenthood, precedes marriage. Premarital pregnancies represent an unusual sequence, although one not as severely nonnormative as when actual parenthood precedes marriage (i.e., illegitimate births). Research on premarital pregnancies has generally focused on couples rather than women specifically and has shown that premaritally pregnant couples are at a substantial economic disadvantage after marriage (Coombs & Freedman, 1970).

Various explanations have been offered of the negative consequences of nonnormative sequences. While one can speculate about social sanctions imposed for counternormative behavior, some writers have been highly critical of such an abstract approach (Marini, 1981). As an alternative, some theorists (Hogan, 1978) have proposed that nonnormative sequences reduce the harmony between the individual and his or her social (or institutional) context, and that, as a consequence, various specific mechanisms explain the disadvantages of nonnormative patterns. For example, Hogan (1980) has suggested that men who marry before beginning their first job may be less geographically mobile than single men, thus depressing their earnings.

Existing research on role sequences leaves unanswered many of the issues raised by the current chapter. In general, research has not considered work, marriage, and parenthood as separate and significant roles for either sex. We believe that future research should study normative and nonnormative sequences associated with entry into each of this trio of roles and should do so for each sex separately, so that sex differences can be assessed systematically. Completion of schooling could be added as a fourth factor. The one study that follows the approach advocated here (Steel, Abeles, & Card, 1982) investigates role sequences for both sexes in terms of the four factors cited and presents useful data on sex differences in the extent of various nonnormative patterns and on the consequences of such nonnormative sequences for subsequent earnings. In addition, research should include a wider range of measures of well-being than the predominantly economic ones used in previous studies.

Role Combinations and Other Role Characteristics

The discussion thus far has featured the concept of number of roles held as the primary approach to studying role combinations and well-being, with qualifications added regarding particular combinations and sequences of role accumulation. Number of roles held is, as previously noted, simply an extension of the concept of role occupancy. Yet role characteristics other than occupancy prove relevant to the relationship between role combinations and well-being. To study the significance of the other role characteristics, one does not compare various combinations; instead, one examines a particular role combination, such as the case in which an individual holds all three major social roles. By focusing on holders of a particular set of multiple roles, one can ask how their overall level of well-being is affected by the amount of time they spend in the various roles, or the types of activities engaged in during enactment of the roles, or the degree of satisfaction with the roles, or the extent of involvement in the roles. The discussion has already examined how such role characteristics as applied to a single role affect well-being. What is at issue here is the direction and relative size of the unique contributions to well-being of the role characteristics for each role, controlling on all other roles.

Existing research has explored the unique effects of each role on well-being for only one role characteristic—namely, role satisfaction. Research, that is, has explored the relative contributions to mental health of satisfaction with work and family roles. In particular, such research tells us something about whether satisfaction with each of the roles makes a unique contribution to mental health, whether satisfaction with some roles makes a greater impact on mental health than satisfaction with other roles, and whether any of these results vary by sex. According to the relevant data (Campbell et al., 1976; Cleary & Mechanic, 1983; Depner, 1978), the contribution of role satisfaction to overall mental health does vary as a function of the role. Satisfaction with marriage makes the greatest unique contribution to mental health, followed by satisfaction with work; satisfaction with parenthood makes the smallest unique contribution, if any contribution at all. No compelling evidence of sex differences has emerged.

Conclusions

This chapter has advocated a revised (or role-specific) approach to gender roles; it views gender as modifying the experience of major social roles, especially work, marriage, and parenthood. The chapter criticizes the traditional (or global) approach to gender roles according to which sex defines two major roles (male and female). In particular, the chapter charges the traditional approach with operating at too high a level of aggregation (or generality) and indeed the evidence assembled here and summarized in Table 1 indicates that many of the sex differences in role experiences apply to only one or two social roles and not to all life experiences.

In summarizing the major findings obtained from the role-specific approach to gender roles, this section concentrates on a single theme: Work and the two family roles tend to cooperate in the case of men but compete (or interfere) in the case of women. Several facts underscore this important sex difference. Occupancy of the work role is positively associated with occupancy of the marital and parental roles among men, but negatively associated among women. Occupancy of the marital role is associated with longer work hours among men, but shorter work hours among women; in other words, marriage is linked to greater participation in the work role among men, but to less work participation among women. Occupancy of the work role is positively associated with marital satisfaction among men, but negatively (albeit marginally) associated among women. Job satisfaction and marital satisfaction display a stronger positive association among men than among women. Men experience higher levels of work–family integration than do women (i.e., wives give more job-related help to their husbands than they receive from them). On the other hand, the sexes do not always divide along the lines of role cooperation versus competition. Occupancy of the maternal role, for example, is associated with high, as opposed to low, work involvement, and no sex difference emerges in levels of perceived work–family conflict. Nonetheless, the greater harmony between work and family roles among men as compared to women is too evident to be ignored.

The findings summarized in Table 1 represent only a small portion of the potential contribution to social science of the revised approach to sex roles. Various additional research steps appear promising. As the table reveals, a number of empty cells remain to be filled in. Of particular importance here is a commitment by researchers to a truly comparative approach to the study of the three major social roles. The summary table also omits certain role characteristics (e.g., status) and certain permutations of role characteristics (e.g., the relationship between involvement and satisfaction) that need to be investigated. Likewise deserving additional attention are the major refinements to the basic paradigm (historical periods, role stages, and subgroups) and the need for normative, as distinct from behavioral, data on all relevant issues. Possible expansions of the proposed paradigm include the addition of other role characteristics (e.g., role performance and sense of role competence) and even other research questions that go beyond the issues of role comparisons, interactions, and consequences (e.g., relation-

TABLE 1
Summary of Selected Findings[a]

Comparisons among roles
Objective role characteristics
Daily time spent

Major findings
Work > housework > parenthood

Gender differences
Work (M > F)
Housework, parenthood (F > M)

Types of activity

Physical demands of work (M > F)
Interpersonal demands of work (F > M)
Frequent, repetitive housework (F > M)
Basic child care (vs. playing with children) (F > M)

Power

Work, marriage, parenthood (M > F)

Subjective role characteristics
Satisfaction

Major findings
Marriage, parenthood > work

Gender differences
Work, parenthood (M = F)
Marriage (M > F)
Interpersonal (F > M)

Types of gratification

Interpersonal
(marriage > parenthood > work)
Achievement
(work > parenthood > marriage)
Power
(work > marriage, parenthood)

Work-related achievement (M > F)

Power (M > F)

Involvement

Marriage, parenthood > work

Work (M > F)
Marriage, parenthood (F > M).

Interactions among roles
Statistical relationships
Occupancy

Major findings for men
Work → marriage, parenthood
Marriage, parenthood → work
Marriage → parenthood

Major findings for women
Marriage, parenthood → low probability of work
Marriage → parenthood
Work → low housework, parental time

Occupancy and time

Marriage → work time, parental time
Parenthood → low housework time

Marriage, parenthood → low work time
Parenthood → increased housework time

(Continued)

TABLE 1 (Continued)

	Major findings	Gender differences
Occupancy and satisfaction	Work → marital, parental satisfaction; Marriage, parenthood → work satisfaction; Parenthood → low marital satisfaction	Marriage → work satisfaction; Parenthood → low marital satisfaction
Occupancy and involvement		Marriage → low work involvement; Parenthood → high work involvement
Daily time spent	Work time → low housework time	Work time → low housework time
Satisfaction	Positive associations for all role pairings	Positive associations for all role pairings
Perceived relationships	Major findings	Gender differences
Integration		
Conflict	Work–parenthood > work–marriage, marriage–parenthood	Work-related help received from spouse (M > F)
Consequences of roles		
Single roles		
Occupancy	Major findings	Gender differences
	Work, marriage → well-being	Stronger effects for men
	Parenthood → low well-being	
Satisfaction	Satisfaction with work, marriage, parenthood → well-being	Stronger effect for women than men in the case of marital satisfaction
Involvement	Work involvement → well-being	
Combinations of roles		
Occupancy	Major findings	Gender differences
	Number of roles → well-being	
	Normal sequencing of roles → well-being	
Satisfaction	Work and marital satisfaction → well-being	

ᵃInequality signs indicate mean differences; unidirectional arrows indicate evidence of association but not necessarily causal relationship.

ships between two characteristics of a single role, such as time spent per day and level of involvement).

A further set of revisions have strong methodological overtones: the use of nonsurvey methods of data collection (and the corresponding pursuit of interactionist themes of role negotiation and emergence) and systematic efforts to disentangle causal directions. In the latter instance, the questions of role interactions and role combinations routinely raise the causal issue but rarely has it been set to rest. We need to know, for example, to what extent the occupancy of roles contributes to well-being and to what extent well-being determines entry into roles.

This chapter concludes by considering the implications of the revised (or role-specific) approach to gender roles for social relationships between individual women and men, an important component of this volume's overall theme of female–male relations. In particular, the previously discussed sex differences in role experiences appear to have important implications for the ways in which women and men interact, although available evidence does not allow us to go much beyond informed speculation.

In the case of the work role, various types of employment-related sex differentiation may affect the relationships between women and men on the job.[2] Because of occupational sex segregation, women and men tend to work in different occupations and tend not to interact as members of the same occupation. Industrial sex segregation further reduces the probability that women and men will work side by side. Sex-based differentiation can also take a number of organizational forms. Certain organizations (e.g., sections of the military) tend to hire members of only one sex. Many organizations tend to place men at higher levels and women at lower levels in the organizational hierarchy; and women and men may be organized into different work groups within the organization.

These different forms of sex segregation at work (occupational, industrial, organizational) have several implications for relationships between women and men. They imply that when men and women interact at work they do so on different terms. The sexes meet as people who do different types of work, come from different organizational niches, and have different levels of power and prestige. Further, the sexes tend not to meet in equal numbers. One sex is frequently in a substantial numerical majority and the other a corresponding minority. Such arrangements make gender highly salient, make tokenism and the problems of statistical minorities a live issue (Kanter,

---

[2]The twin and interrelated issues of how men and women interact in face-to-face task groups and how formal organizations are structured according to gender (i.e., the relative positions of the sexes in organizations) are explored in the following chapter by Bartol and Martin.

1977), and may detract from the level of satisfaction with relations with co-workers (O'Farrell & Harlan, 1982).

In the case of marriage, one can ask whether sex differentiation in role experiences (especially amount and type of housework, and level of marital power) affects the quality of the relationship between husband and wife. On the one side are arguments in favor of a specialized division of labor: the classical economic argument about efficiency (Nickols & Metzen, 1982), and the classical argument from role theory about role clarity and the absence of conflict (Turner, 1968). On the other side are arguments against specialization in marital responsibilities: the reduction in empathy and communication between spouses (Turner, 1968) and the reduction in shared activities and interaction between marital partners (Lundgren, Jergens, & Gibson, 1982).

Current research generally suggests a positive relationship between a more equal division of housework and wife's marital satisfaction (Veroff et al., 1981) and possibly between a more equal division of housework and husband's marital satisfaction (Lundgren et al., 1982) though it has less to say about the effect of type of housework on the marital satisfaction of either spouse. Further, most research on marital power indicates highest marital satisfaction among egalitarian couples and lowest satisfaction among wife-dominant couples (Gray-Little & Burks, 1983). Thus, available evidence is at least consistent with the view that specialization in marital responsibilities detracts from the marital relationship.

How does the connection between role-related sex differentiation and male–female relationships arise in the case of parenthood? One interpretation is that sex differences in extent of parental participation, types of parental activities, and parental decision-making power affect the quality of the relationship between husband and wife. The arguments for and against a sex-based division of labor essentially duplicate those for the marital role. Very little relevant research has been collected thus far, but at least one study (Pleck, 1981b) found that husbands who do their share of child care report higher marital satisfaction.

It is possible that a sex-differentiated division of labor will have highly variable effects on female–male relationships—different consequences for different roles and, within a role, different consequences for women and men. Yet we should remain alert to the possibility suggested by existing data that the absence of sex differentiation in roles (i.e., equal amounts of participation, similar types of activities, and equal power) may contribute to better social relationships between women and men in all major social roles. It is a possibility worth investigating.

References

Aldous, J. (1978). *Family careers: Developmental change in families.* New York: Wiley.

Andrews, F., & Withey, S. (1976). *Social indicators of well-being: Americans' perceptions of life quality.* New York: Plenum.

Andrisani, P. J., & Shapiro, M. B. (1978). Women's attitudes toward their jobs: Some longitudinal data on a national sample. *Personnel Psychology, 31,* 15–34.

Aneshensel, C. S., Frerichs, R. R., & Clark, V. A. (1981). Family roles and sex differences in depression. *Journal of Health and Social Behavior, 22,* 379–393.

Angrist, S. S. (1969). The study of sex roles. *Journal of Social Issues, 25*(1), 215–232.

Arvey, R. D., & Begalla, M. E. (1975). Analyzing the homemaker job using the Position Analysis Questionnaire (PAQ). *Journal of Applied Psychology, 60,* 513–517.

Ashmore, R. D., & Del Boca, F. K. (1979). Sex stereotypes and implicit personality theory: Toward a cognitive–social psychological conceptualization. *Sex Roles, 5,* 219–248.

Baruch, G. K., & Barnett, R. C. (1979, August). *Involvement in multiple roles and the well-being of adult women.* Paper presented at the meeting of the American Sociological Association, Boston, MA.

Berk, M. L., & Kingston, P. W. (1982). Working couples and class identification. *Sociological Spectrum, 2,* 31–39.

Berk, S. F. (1979). Husbands at home: Organization of the husband's household day. In K. W. Feinstein (Ed.), *Working women and families.* Beverly Hills, CA: Sage.

Bernard, J. (1973). *The future of marriage.* New York: Bantam.

Bisconti, A. S. (1978). *Women: Marriage, career, and job satisfaction. Special Topic Series No. 1.* Bethlehem, PA: CPC Foundation.

Brown, R. (1965). *Social psychology.* New York: The Free Press.

Campbell, A., Converse, P. E., & Rodgers, W. L. (1976). *The quality of American life.* New York: Russell Sage Foundation.

Cleary, P. D., & Mechanic, D. (1983). Sex differences in psychological distress among married people. *Journal of Health and Social Behavior, 24,* 111–121.

Condie, S. J., & Doan, H. T. (1978). Role profit and marital satisfaction throughout the family life cycle. *Journal of Comparative Family Studies, 9,* 257–267.

Coombs, L. C., & Freedman, R. (1970). Pre-marital pregnancy, childspacing, and later economic achievement. *Population Studies, 24,* 389–412.

Crosby, F. J. (1982). *Relative deprivation and working women.* New York: Oxford University Press.

Depner, C. (1978). *Adult roles and subjective evaluations of life quality.* Unpublished doctoral dissertation, University of Michigan.

Depner, C. E., & Staines, G. L. (1980). *Multiple roles and well being.* Proposal to National Institute of Mental Health, Institute for Social Research, Ann Arbor, MI.

Gecas, V. (1976). The socialization and child care roles. In F. I. Nye (Ed.), *Role structure and analysis of the family.* Beverly Hills, CA: Sage.

Geerken, M., & Gove, W. (1983). *At home and at work: The family's allocation of labor.* Beverly Hills, CA: Sage.

Glenn, N. D. (1975). The contribution of marriage to the psychological well-being of males and females. *Journal of Marriage and the Family, 37,* 594–600.

Glenn, N. D., & McLanahan, S. (1981). The effects of offspring on the psychological well-being of older adults. *Journal of Marriage and the Family, 43,* 409–421.

Glenn, N., & McLanahan, S. (1982). Children and marital happiness: A further specification of the relationship. *Journal of Marriage and the Family, 44,* 63–72.

Glenn, N., & Weaver, C. (1978). A multivariate, multisurvey study of marital happiness. *Journal of Marriage and the Family, 40,* 269–282.

Glenn, N., & Weaver, C. (1979). A note on family situation and global happiness. *Social Forces, 57,* 960–967.

Glenn, N. D., & Weaver, C. N. (1981). The contribution of marital happiness to global happiness. *Journal of Marriage and the Family, 43,* 161–168.

Glick, P. C. (1977). Updating the life cycle of the family. *Journal of Marriage and the Family, 39,* 3–15.

Goode, W. J. (1960). A theory of role strain. *American Sociological Review, 25,* 483–496.

Gove, W. R., & Tudor, J. F. (1973). Adult sex roles and mental illness. *American Journal of Sociology, 78,* 812–835.

Gray-Little, B., & Burks, N. (1983). Power and satisfaction in marriage: A review and critique. *Psychological Bulletin, 93,* 513–538.

Greenhaus, J. H., & Beutell, N. J. (1982). *Sources of conflict between work and nonwork roles: A review of the empirical research.* Faculty Working Paper Series. College of Business and Administration, Drexel University, Philadelphia, PA.

Herman, J. B., & Gyllstrom, K. K. (1977). Working men and women: Inter- and intra-role conflict. *Psychology of Women Quarterly, 1,* 319–333.

Hofferth, S. L., & Moore, K. A. (1979a). Women's employment and marriage. In R. E. Smith (Ed.), *The subtle revolution.* Washington, DC: The Urban Institute.

Hofferth, S. L., & Moore, K. A. (1979b). Early childbearing and later economic well-being. *American Sociological Review, 44,* 784–815.

Hogan, D. P. (1978). The variable order of events in the life course. *American Sociological Review, 43,* 573–586.

Hogan, D. P. (1980). The transition to adulthood as a career contingency. *American Sociological Review, 45,* 261–276.

Holahan, C. K., & Gilbert, L. A. (1979). Conflict between major life roles: Women and men in dual career couples. *Human Relations, 32,* 451–467.

Johnson, B. L., & Waldman, E. (1981). Marital and family patterns of the labor force. *Monthly Labor Review, 104*(10), 36–38.

Kanter, R. M. (1977). *Men and women of the corporation.* New York: Basic.

Keith, P. M., Dobson, C. D., Goudy, W., & Powers, E. A. (1981). Older men: Occupation, employment status, household involvement, and well-being. *Journal of Family Issues, 2,* 336–349.

Keith, P., & Schafer, R. (1980). Role strain and depression in two-job families. *Family Relations, 29,* 483–488.

Kessler, R. C., & McCrae, J. A., Jr. (1982). The effect of wives' employment on the mental health of married men and women. *American Sociological Review, 47,* 216–227.

Komarovsky, M. (1940). *The unemployed man and his family.* New York: Dryden.

Lopata, H. Z., Barnewolt, D., & Norr, K. (1980). Spouses' contributions to each other's roles. In F. Pepitone-Rockwell (Ed.), *Dual-career couples.* Beverly Hills, CA: Sage.

Lopata, H. Z., & Thorne, B. (1978). On the term "sex roles." *Signs, 3,* 718–721.

Lundgren, D. J., Jergens, V. H., & Gibson, J. L. (1982). Marital power, roles, and solidarity and husbands' and wives' appraisals of self and other. *Sociological Inquiry, 52,* 33–52.

Marini, M. M. (1981). *Age and sequencing norms in the transition to adulthood.* Unpublished manuscript, Battelle Human Affairs Research Center, Seattle.

McLaughlin, S. D. (1978). Sex differences in the determinants of occupational status. *Sociology of Work and Occupations, 5,* 5–30.

Miller, J., & Garrison, H. H. (1982). Sex roles: The division of labor at home and in the workplace. *Annual Review of Sociology, 8,* 237–262.

Moore, K. A., & Hofferth, S. L. (1979). Women and their children. In R. E. Smith (Ed.), *The subtle revolution.* Washington, DC: The Urban Institute.

Nickols, S. Y., & Metzen, E. J. (1982). Impact of wife's employment upon husband's housework. *Journal of Family Issues, 3,* 199–216.

Northcott, H. C. (1981). Women, work, health and happiness. *International Journal of Women's Studies, 4,* 268–276.

Nye, F. I. (1974). Husband–wife relationship. In L. W. Hoffman & F. I. Nye, (Eds.), *Working mothers.* San Francisco: Jossey-Bass.

Nye, F. I. (1976). Family roles in comparative perspective. In F. I. Nye (Ed.), *Role structure and analysis of the family.* Beverly Hills, CA: Sage.

Nye, F. I., & Gecas, V. (1976). The role concept: Review and delineation. In F. I. Nye (Ed.), *Role structure and analysis of the family.* Beverly Hills, CA: Sage.

O'Farrell, B., & Harlan, S. L. (1982). Craftworkers and clerks: The effect of male co-worker hostility on women's satisfaction with non-traditional jobs. *Social Problems, 29,* 252–265.

Olson, J. T. (1979). Role conflict between housework and child care. *Sociology of Work and Occupation, 6,* 430–456.

Parnes, H. S., Shea, J. R., Spitz, R. S., Zeller, F. A., & associates. (1970). *Dual careers: A longitudinal study of labor market experience of women: Vol. 1. Manpower Research Monograph 21.* Washington, DC: Government Printing Office.

Perrucci, C. C. (1970). Minority status and the pursuit of professional careers: Women in science and engineering. *Social Forces, 49,* 245–259.

Perun, P. J., & Bielby, D. D. V. (1981). Towards a model of female occupational behavior: A human development approach. *Psychology of Women Quarterly, 6,* 234–252.

Pfohl, S. J. (1975). Social role analysis: The ethnomethodological critique. *Sociology and Social Research, 59,* 243–265.

Pleck, J. H. (1981a). *The myth of masculinity.* Cambridge, MA: MIT.

Pleck, J. H. (1981b). *Wives' employment, role demands, and adjustment: Final report to NIMH and NSF.* Wellesley, MA: Wellesley College Center for Research on Women.

Pleck, J. H. (1983). Husbands' paid work and family roles: Current research issues. In H. Z. Lopata & J. H. Pleck (Eds.), *Research in the interweave of social roles: Vol. 3. Families and jobs.* Greenwich, CT: JAI Press.

Pleck, J. H., & Lang, L. (1978). *Men's family role: Its nature and consequences.* Working paper, Wellesley College Center for Research on Women, Wellesley, MA.

Pleck, J. H., Staines, G. L., & Lang, L. (1980). Conflicts between work and family life. *Monthly Labor Review, 103*(3), 29–32.

Quinn, R. P., & Staines, G. L. (1979). *The 1977 Quality of Employment Survey.* Ann Arbor, MI: Survey Research Center.

Quinn, R. P., Staines, G. L., & McCullough, M. R. (1974). *Job satisfaction: Is there a trend?* Washington, DC: U.S. Government Printing Office.

Robinson, J. P. (1977a). *How Americans use time: A social-psychological analysis of everyday behavior.* New York: Praeger.

Robinson, J. P. (1977b). *Changes in Americans' use of time: 1965–1975. A progress report.* Cleveland, OH: Communications Research Center.

Sawhill, I. V., Peabody, G. E., Jones, C. A., & Caldwell, S. B. (1975). *Income transfers and family structure.* Washington, DC: The Urban Institute Working Paper, 979–1003.

Scanzoni, J. (1978). *Sex roles, women's work, and marital conflict.* Lexington, MA: Heath.

Shamir, B. (1982). *Work schedules and the perceived conflict between work and nonwork.* Working Paper No. 3, The Hebrew University Bertelsmann Program, Jerusalem.

Sieber, S. D. (1974). Toward a theory of role accumulation. *American Sociological Review, 39,* 567–578.

Spitze, G. D., & Waite, L. J. (1981). Young women's preferences for market work: Responses to marital events. *Research in Population Economics, 3,* 147–166.

Stafford, F. P. (1980). Women's use of time converging with men's. *Monthly Labor Review, 103*(12), 57–59.

Staines, G. L. (1978, May). *Americans report on work and family life: A new national survey.* Paper presented to the Michigan Council on Family Relations' conference on "Family and work: A delicate balance." Dearborn, MI.

Staines, G. L. (1980). Spillover versus compensation: A review of the literature on the relationship between work and nonwork. *Human Relations, 33,* 111–129.

Staines, G. L., Pleck, J. H., Shepard, L., & O'Connor, P. (1978). Wives' employment status and marital adjustment: Yet another look. *Psychology of Women Quarterly, 3,* 90–120.

Steel, L., Abeles, R. P., & Card, J. J. (1982). Sex differences in the patterning of adult roles as a determinant of sex differences in occupational achievement. *Sex Roles, 8,* 1009–1024.

Stewart, A. J., Lykes, M. B., & LaFrance, M. (1982). Educated women's career patterns: Separating social and developmental changes. *Journal of Social Issues, 38*(1), 97–117.

Sweet, J. A. (1977). Demography and the family. *Annual Review of Sociology, 3,* 363–405.

Taeuber, K. E., & Sweet, J. A. (1976). Family and work: The social life cycle of women. In J. M. Kreps (Ed.), *Women and the American economy.* Englewood Cliffs, NJ: Prentice-Hall.

Turner, R. H. (1968). Role: Sociological aspects. In D. L. Sills (Ed.), *International encyclopedia of the social sciences* (Vol. 13). New York: Macmillan.

U.S. Bureau of the Census. (1980). *Statistical abstract of the U.S.: 1980* (101st ed.). Washington, DC: Government Printing Office.

Verbrugge, L. M. (1982). Women's social roles and health. In P. Berman & E. Ramey (Eds.), *Women: A developmental perspective.* Bethesda, MD: National Institute of Child Health and Human Development.

Verbrugge, L. M. (1983). Multiple roles and physical health of women and men. *Journal of Health and Social Behavior, 24,* 16–30.

Veroff, J., Douvan, E., & Kulka, R. A. (1981). *The inner American: A self-portrait from 1957 to 1976.* New York: Basic.

Waite, L. J., & Spitze, G. D. (1978, September). *Female work orientation and marital events: The transition to marriage and motherhood.* Paper presented at the annual meeting of the American Sociological Association, San Francisco.

Walker, K. E., & Woods, M. E. (1976). *Time use: A measure of household production of family goods and services.* Washington, DC: American Home Economics Association.

White, K. (1967). Social background variables related to career commitment of women teachers. *The Personnel and Guidance Journal, 45,* 648–652.

Wilkie, J. R. (1981). The trend toward delayed parenthood. *Journal of Marriage and the Family, 43,* 583–591.

Wolf, W. C., & Fligstein, N. D. (1979). Sexual stratification: Differences in power in the work setting. *Social Forces, 58,* 94–107.

Seven

Women and Men
in Task Groups*

KATHRYN M. BARTOL

DAVID C. MARTIN

Introduction

In the previous chapter, *worker* was one of the major sex-related roles considered. In the present chapter, a somewhat different—yet complementary—perspective is taken regarding men and women as workers. We look at women and men as participants in task groups. Our overall goal has two interlocking components: to explore the dynamics of women and men in small face-to-face groups and to relate this to the sex structuring of formal organizations and especially to the fact that women are underrepresented in upper-level management positions.

The underrepresentation of women in management is particularly significant given the phenomenal rise in the proportion of women who have become paid workers since the late 1940s. As of 1980, 51% of women worked outside of the home compared with 32% in 1947 (U.S. Department of Commerce, 1980). Yet women have not penetrated the managerial ranks in numbers proportionate to their presence in the work force. Women account for only 28% of the managers and administrators in the United States

*The authors are grateful to R. D. Ashmore and F. K. Del Boca for their encouragement and helpful comments during the preparation of this chapter.

and earn only about 60% of the salaries paid to their male counterparts (U.S. Department of Labor, 1982). One study of the 1300 largest U.S. companies showed only 10 women among the 6400 corporate officers (Robertson, 1978). Women are found in increasing numbers in nonmanagerial functions, even in organizations in which large percentages of the workers are women and in which the occupations, per se, do not appear to be gender stereotyped (Bartol, 1977; Mennerick, 1975). Acker and Van Houten (1974) have referred to these disproportionate conditions as the sex structuring of organizations.

Because of the paucity of females in leadership positions, this chapter is presented in a series of four sections, which are related in some degree to leading groups and organizations, with the ultimate goal of answering the obvious question: Why are women so underrepresented in managerial positions in organizations? This question is addressed from several perspectives. The first section reviews the literature pertaining to groups in which there are no designated leaders. The issues discussed relate to how males and females interact in these types of situations and to the factors that influence their perceived leadership potential and their actual effectiveness. The second section of this chapter consists of a review of the research concerning task-group situations in which there is a designated leader. A major issue is the extent to which males and females differ in leadership behavior and effectiveness. This latter issue is particularly important because leaders who are more effective usually get promoted to higher positions in the organization. Leader selection, a particularly germane issue to the preceding primary question, is reviewed in the third section of this chapter. Numerous factors appear to influence the selection of female versus male leaders. In the final section of the chapter, we present a set of conclusions based on our literature review. Several alternative explanations of our conclusions are discussed and an information-processing framework is proposed as a guide for future research.

To fully appreciate the role of gender in these discussions, one must understand the concept of leadership. *Leadership* here is defined as the behavior of an individual while he/she is involved in directing group activities (Hemphill, 1949). As is discussed later, task- and person-oriented behaviors are important in leading task groups. For purposes of this chapter, we use Shaw's minimal definition of a group as "two or more persons who are interacting with one another in such a manner that each influences and is influenced by each other person" (1981, p. 8). It should be pointed out that Shaw uses influence very broadly in this definition, noting that "interaction requires *mutual* influence" (p. 8). However, this chapter involves the additional requirement that the interaction take place for the purpose of completing one or more specified work tasks. Thus, familial groups and groups whose main function is social are excluded.

Before reviewing literature relevant to the issues raised, two caveats are in order. First, more license is taken than is typically the case in traditional literature reviews. The main focus is on areas where there is sufficient information to provide some guidance regarding male and female relationships in task groups. This means that selectivity is exercised in both the areas and studies reviewed. The concern is with relevance rather than with copiousness. Second, although the body of literature relating to groups is sizable, a large proportion of group studies have involved same-sex groups or have used mixed-sex groups without addressing gender issues. Hence many studies of task groups are not useful to this particular endeavor. Fortunately, the rising interest in gender-related issues during the late 1970s and the 1980s has brought an increase in group studies that are helpful in assessing female and male relationships in task groups.

Research on Groups without Designated Leaders

One advantage of reviewing research on leaderless groups is that it is possible to gain insights into how males and females relate in task situations where they work with peers. Such situations are common in most organizations where individuals frequently work together on tasks or parts of tasks, attend meetings of peers, and interact with one or more others informally on task-related issues.

Although such groups frequently do not have designated leaders, literature on groups suggests that one or more individuals tend to emerge as informal leaders. Following usual practice in group research, groups without designated leaders are sometimes referred to as leaderless groups, even though informal leaders frequently emerge. Groups that have formally designated leaders are discussed in a later section of this chapter. In the present section, a central issue is the extent to which males versus females emerge as leaders in leaderless groups and the types of behaviors that males and females tend to exhibit in such groups. Research on several related behaviors that have been the focus of controversy regarding the possible existence of gender differences and that could have an impact on long-term relationships between males and females in task situations is then reviewed. Finally, overall conclusions are highlighted and critical comments regarding the current state of the research are made. However, much of the commentary on the implications of the research on leaderless groups is reserved until literature on situations in which there are designated leaders has also been reviewed.

EMERGENT LEADERSHIP

An issue central to understanding relations between males and females in groups is the extent to which females versus males emerge as leaders. A task-group member tends to emerge or become viewed as a leader by demonstrating task and interpersonal competence while concurrently earning the respect and support of the other members of the group (Bass, 1981; Yukl, 1981). On an observable level, the fact that there are relatively few female managers when compared to the number of male managers in most organizations suggests that males emerge or are perceived as leaders more frequently than females. Along these lines, Mennerick (1975) provides evidence that females are less likely to be found in nonmanagerial positions, even in occupations that are heavily populated by women.

Several studies which indicate that females are not widely viewed as possessing managerial ability (Bass, Krusell, & Alexander, 1971; Schein, 1973) indirectly support the notion that females will tend to be underidentified as emergent leaders. Other reasons to expect a smaller proportion of female versus male emergent leaders are data indicating that females often are reluctant to accede to positions of leadership (Megargee, 1969) and that females need to have their positions legitimized in some way before engaging in high levels of leadership behaviors (Eskilson & Wiley, 1976).

Several empirical studies focusing on actual leaderless situations also support the notion that males are more likely than females to emerge or to be identified as leaders by members of task groups (e.g., Frank & Katcher, 1977; Tindall, Boyler, Cline, Emberger, Powell, & Wions, 1978). However, there also is evidence of no difference in the likelihood of males or females emerging as leaders (Schneier & Bartol, 1980).

It appears that the relationship between gender and emergent leadership is more complex than is frequently recognized. For example, Kimble, Yoshikawa, and Zehr (1981) found that males were more likely to be chosen as leaders in task groups, but not in groups without task assignments (i.e., groups that were told to talk about "absolutely anything you want to"). The researchers suggested that part of the reason for the difference in task versus nontask groups may stem from the different types of leader behaviors that are necessary in these groups.

Parsons and Bales (1955) have argued that males have instrumental orientations and females have expressive or interpersonal orientations in groups. Hence, it is possible that males emerge as leaders in task groups, where instrumental orientations are needed in order to complete the task, while instrumental and expressive orientations can be more balanced in unstructured groups (Kimble, Yoshikawa, & Zehr, 1981; Spence & Helmreich, 1979). Under this argument, in task groups, males may have the advantage of having the appropriate behavioral orientation for emergent leadership. In a related study, Maier (1970) investigated the effects of male versus female leaders using a role-playing situation where the foreman tries to induce three workers to alter their work procedures. When the solution to the work procedures problem was supplied to the leader, males and females performed similarly in getting the group to go along with a solution that was favorable to management. In contrast, when the solution was not supplied, female leaders became more permissive and the group was less likely than a male-led group to settle on a solution that resolved the conflict between the leader and the workers. These results suggest that females may be less able to deal with unstructured task situations. The females in the study may have been under a disadvantage, however, because the role play designated a male name for the leader role.

The assumption that females are necessarily expressive in orientation in groups is subject to considerable debate. On the one hand, several studies support this notion. For example, Strodtbeck and Mann (1956) used Bales's Interaction Process Analysis to study mock jury deliberations. They found that males tended actively to pursue a solution to a task, whereas females were more inclined to react and perform social–emotional acts. Heilbrun (1968) found that in short-term discussion groups, females were rated as more expressive than instrumental by both their male and female peers. However, no such differentiation was made for males by raters of either sex. Research by Bartol (1973) in leaderless task groups showed that females were not ranked significantly higher than males on expressive behaviors, but males were perceived by group members as ranking significantly higher on instrumental behaviors.

Other studies suggest that females may value expressive behaviors more than males do. Buss (1981) had female and male students rate dominant acts on their social desirability. Males judged self-enhancing and self-asserting acts as relatively more desirable than group-oriented, communal acts, which were rated as more desirable by females. Dominant females reported themselves as engaging in more group-oriented, communal acts; while dominant males reported engaging in both communal and self-enhancing/asserting acts.

The counter evidence to the notion that females tend to engage in expressive and males in instrumental behaviors in group situations suggests that the interpersonal orientations of males and females may depend on the situation (Deaux, 1976). It appears that females are more active in engaging in leadership behaviors when they are in same-sex groups (Aries, 1976) or in the majority in mixed-sex groups (Tindall, Boyler, Cline, Emberger, Powell, & Wions, 1978; Webber, 1976). When females are in the minority in mixed-sex groups, they are likely to exercise fewer leadership behaviors, either because they allow males to dominate (Aries, 1976; Kaess, Witryol, & Nolan, 1961; Webber, 1976) or because their efforts at leadership are rejected by the majority males (Bormann, Pratt, & Putnam, 1978; Wolman & Frank, 1975).

Although the evidence is limited, females appear to fare the least well as potential emergent leaders when they are the solo female in the group. Frank and Katcher (1977) found that when there was only one woman in groups of medical students, she was ranked low on both dominance and task orientation. In situations where there was more than one female, females continued to be ranked low on dominance; but there was less of a tendency to stereotype the females as low in task orientation and they were ranked relatively high on friendliness.

Data also suggest that males may behave differently depending on the sex composition of the group. For example, data provided by Aries (1976) indicate that males may engage in more competitive instrumental behavior when in all-male groups, but take on a more expressive personal orientation when in mixed-sex groups. Furthermore, Schneier and Bartol (1980) found that socioemotional or expressive behaviors were as characteristic of male as of female emergent leaders in the mixed-sex groups in their study.

Having members of the other sex in task groups may alter behaviors in ways that are seemingly inconsistent with group members' personalities. In one study, which measured actual dominant behaviors through observation (Aries, Gold, & Weigel, 1983), results showed that in all-female and all-male groups, a personality measure of dominance was a strong predictor of overall patterns of dominance-related behaviors. However, in mixed-sex groups, the ability of the dominance personality measure to predict either individual or overall patterns of dominance-related behaviors was negligible. These results support the notion that the gender composition of groups may influence members to act at variance with their personalities or at least to alter behavioral manifestations of personality.

There is evidence that females and males in group situations may demonstrate their personality characteristics in different, but sex-role-related, ways.[1] For example, Megargee, Bogart, and Anderson (1966) found that when leadership in a simulated industrial task was emphasized, the member of selected male pairs who had a high need for dominance assumed

[1]The term, sex role, is used here as it has been employed by the researchers whose work is being reviewed. Staines and Libby (Chapter 6, this volume) provide a broad critique of the notion of sex roles as generalized prescriptions for how men and women should behave.

leadership 90% of the time. In a follow-up study, Megargee (1969) formed four types of pairs based on sex and need for dominance: (1) a high-dominance male, low-dominance male, (2) high-dominance male, low-dominance female, (3) high-dominance female, low-dominance male, and (4) high-dominance female, low-dominance female. The pairs were given a mechanical task in one study and a dictating task in a second study. Both tasks called for one member of the pair to assume a leadership position, and the decision as to who should be leader was left to each pair. Megargee hypothesized that high-need-for-dominance women would not assume the leadership position when paired with low-need-for-dominance males, even though the high-need-for-dominance member of the pair would assume the leadership position under the other three conditions. Megargee's hypothesis was confirmed. He attributed the phenomenon to social-role prescriptions of women, noting that while it is acceptable for men to dominate women, the reverse is not true. An analysis of tape recordings of verbal interchanges between the pairs revealed that the high-need-for-dominance females tended to make the decisions that the males should be the leaders. Thus, the females appeared to have exerted their needs for dominance, but in a subtle, less visible manner.

Physical attractiveness may also be a factor in how males and females interact in group situations. Nadler, Shapira, and Ben-Itzhak (1982) found that subjects tended to seek less help from physically attractive than from unattractive helpers who were the same sex. When the potential helpers were the other sex, males were less likely to seek help from a physically attractive female than from an unattractive female, while females sought more help from a physically attractive than from an unattractive male. The researchers suggested that the results may be due to concern for positive self-presentation. In this view, males are likely to be more concerned with positive self-presentation when the female is attractive and thus may be reluctant to seek help (i.e., display inferiority and dependence). On the other hand, because it is more compatible with the female role, help seeking is consonant with positive self-presentation and, therefore, females are more motivated to seek help when the male is attractive.

Although the data are mixed, the nature of the relationship between females and males in groups also may depend on the duration of the interaction. Research by Frank and Katcher (1977) indicates that the nature of the relationships among the groups of male and female medical students became clear very early during the academic term in which their study was conducted and persisted until the end of the term. However, Spillman, Spillman, and Reinking (1981) found that both biological sex and psychological androgyny were predictive of leadership emergence on task and expressive dimensions during the first two group meetings but not for the final two sessions. The sessions took place over the first half of an academic quarter. The duration factor may partially explain why Schneier and Bartol (1980) found no difference in the proportion of males and females to emerge as leaders toward the end of a 15-week course.

In summary, the research on emergent leadership suggests that females frequently have a difficult time exerting leadership in groups containing males and that females tend to accept male leadership in groups. These effects depend on the nature of the group (e.g., the group's goals), the sex composition of the group, and characteristics of the participants, such as physical attractiveness.

RELATED BEHAVIORS

In addition to emergent leadership, there are three other task-group issues that have been the subject of considerable research and debate regarding gender effects and that are particularly germane to our interests here. The first involves the extent to which females in groups are more likely than males to engage in cooperative rather than competitive behaviors in task settings, a factor that may allow females to be bypassed in the competitive atmosphere of many organizations (Kanter, 1977). The second concerns the notion that females may engage in communication styles that are more deferent than males in group settings and that may cause task-group members to discount female input. The third issue addresses the possibility that females are more easily influenced than males in group settings. We review each of these issues in turn as they relate to male versus female effectiveness in task groups.

Cooperation versus Competition

A significant body of research has suggested that females in groups tend to be more cooperative and altruistic than males (Amidjaja & Vinacke, 1965; Brenner & Vinacke, 1979; Wall, 1976). Cooperative effects are particularly evident in situations involving reward allocations, and much of the research has centered on this area. There is evidence that females tend to pay themselves less than do males in similar situations and to pay themselves less than either males or females pay other females (Callahan-Levy & Messe, 1979). The females in the study appeared to be relatively unconcerned about the equity of their own pay. Mednick and Tangri (1972) have argued that one factor accounting for the differential pay of females and males in the work world is the relatively low emphasis of females on equitable pay for themselves. It may be that desire for pay is viewed as inconsistent with the female stereotype of concern for others. Alagna (1982) found that females

performed better in a competitive situation when they were given information suggesting that their peers held a positive view of competitive behavior.
Further support for the notion that females tend to be less competitive than
males is provided by Bartol, Anderson, and Schneier (1981), who found that
a significant difference between male and female business students on
motivation to manage was attributable to lower ratings by females on a
subscale measuring desire to engage in competitive games. A lesser number
of studies have found either no differences or evidence of greater competitive
behavior on the part of females (Bedell & Sistrunk, 1973; Caldwell, 1976;
Stake, 1983). As a result, research since then has focused on attempts to
understand the conditions under which females are likely to engage in more
cooperative or altruistic behaviors.

Some research suggests that females may tend toward cooperative rather
than competitive behavior because they place different values on various
rewards that frequently are available in task and organizational settings
(e.g., Bartol, 1976; Manhardt, 1972). For example, Bartol and Manhardt
(1979) found that female college graduates newly hired into entry-level
business jobs gave significantly less emphasis to career objectives and
significantly more emphasis to work environment and interpersonal job
aspects than did males. However, the research also provided some evidence
that the personal orientations of females may be changing. Analysis of
trends over a 9-year period showed a convergence of female preferences
toward those of males on the two job-orientation dimensions in which sex
differences were found.

Kahn, Nelson, and Gaeddert (1980) further argue that females have an
orientation that predisposes them to approach interaction situations with interpersonal agendas such as learning about other persons and establishing
rapport with them. Males, on the other hand, approach interaction situations more from the viewpoint of what they can gain or how they will perform relative to others. As a result, the authors argue, females tend to
allocate rewards equally, while males tend to allocate equitably. At the same
time, they point out that the preponderance of situations that tend to require
equity decisions and the overuse of same-sex groups may overstate the
strength of sex differences.

Reis and Jackson (1981) have offered an alternative explanation for the
tendency for males to allocate rewards equitably and females to allocate
equally. They argue that the sex differences may be due to the masculine
types of tasks used in much of the previous research. On a masculine task,
the males allocated equitably and the females equally; however, on sex-
appropriate tasks, the respective sexes allocated equitably. Questionnaire
data suggested that males and females evaluated performance differently
depending on the sex appropriateness of the task and that reward behaviors

were affected accordingly. Interestingly, both sexes gave more generous rewards to an other-sex partner than a same-sex partner regardless of the type of task. As more-recent research includes mixed-sex groups in study designs, the differential effects attributable to mixed-sex groups are becoming more apparent, although these effects are not fully understood.

Much of the research on cooperation versus competition in task groups has addressed reward allocation behaviors. Because competitive behaviors frequently involve competition for rewards, the emphasis on reward allocation has particular utility for task settings. However, most of the studies involved distribution of extrinsic rewards and have not considered very explicitly the availability and the importance of other more intrinsic rewards, such as accomplishing tasks, receiving recognition, and achieving status. Greater emphasis on intrinsic rewards would be helpful in more adequately assessing reward allocations. Further emphasis also needs to be placed on cooperative and competitive behaviors in pursuit of rewards.

In general, there appears to be a tendency in leaderless situations for females to make more equal distributions of rewards than for males to do so. While such cooperative behavior can be an asset under some circumstances, these tendencies also could allow more-competitive males to take advantage of female cooperativeness in task settings. At the same time, the female tendency toward more cooperative behavior is not pervasive and appears to be affected by the nature of the task as well as the gender makeup of the group.

Communication Style

Another area of current controversy is the extent to which female speech differs from male speech in ways that impact interactions in groups. In reviewing the relevant literature, Haas (1979) suggested that although the common stereotype is that women talk more than men, the limited empirical data indicate that males talk more than females in mixed-sex groups. Because there is some evidence that amount of verbal interaction is related to leader emergence in leaderless group situations, verbal predominance by males may work to their advantage in upward mobility (Bass, 1981).

Research also suggests that females tend to use more words that imply "feelings, auxiliary words, negations, evaluative adjectives, interpretations, psychological state verbs, and purposive cases" and that "males use more terms referring to time, space, quantity, destructive action, and perceptual attributes and more objective cases" (Haas, 1979; p. 622). Limited data indicate that males are more assertive and tend to give directions, while females are more tentative, supportive, and are more likely to make requests. There is, however, some disagreement over the extent to which male and female speech patterns differ. For example, Lakoff (1975) has argued that female speech patterns are characterized by deference, while Philips (1980) has proposed that there are few consistent differences in the linguistic forms used by females and males. A number of criticisms of gender related communications research have been raised on both methodological and conceptual grounds (see Putnam, 1982). One difficulty is that researchers sometimes attempt to generalize about communication differences between males and females from studies in a variety of contexts where male and female roles may differ, causing conclusions regarding gender to be confounded by role effects. Unfortunately, only a small proportion of gender-related communications research specifically addresses task situations.

In support of the notion that gender affects at least perceptions of communication patterns, Hall and Braunwald (1981) have found evidence of a stereotype that women tend to speak in a deferential manner to men, while men speak in a dominant manner to men. Yet judges asked to identify the gender of the individual being addressed on audiotaped short clips were accurate in judging that males who sounded dominant were addressing another male, but were inaccurate when they judged that females who sounded dominant were addressing another female. Citing evidence that visual cues often are weighted more heavily than auditory cues, the authors suggested the possibility that deference by females may be conveyed by visual cues rather than by the auditory cues made available to judges in the study.

In a particularly important study for the purposes here, Bradley (1981) attempted to determine the extent to which different speech strategies could alter the impact of female versus male speech. Her results showed that both males and females were more influential and viewed more positively when their opinions were accompanied by strong supporting arguments. However, the use of qualifying phrases lead to negative effects only when used by females. Females who used tag questions (e.g., "Don't you think?") or disclaimers (e.g., "I'm no expert, but") had lower influence and were perceived as having low intelligence and little knowledge. Thus, the use of stereotypic female speech strategies had adverse effects for females but not for males. On the other hand, females who used the strong supporting argument strategy, which is counter to the female stereotype, received the highest intelligence and knowledgeability ratings, although these were not statistically different from those received by males. The study also found that males received higher ratings of likability than females, regardless of the speech strategy used. One way to view these results is that there did not appear to be any particular penalty in terms of likability imposed on the females who used a speech strategy counter to the female stereotype, but influence was greater.

Characteristics of the situation may have important implications for the nature of verbal (what is said) and vocal (how it is said) communication patterns. Kimble, Yoshikawa, and Zehr (1981) found that in mixed-sex groups composed of two males and two females, the female who spoke last was less verbally assertive than the female who spoke first. The last female speaker also was less vocally assertive than the others in the group. These effects were more prevalent in task than in unstructured groups and did not occur in all-female groups. This research reinforces the notion that communication patterns are affected by the gender makeup of the group.

In the area of nonverbal communications, an extensive review by Hall (1978) indicates that females may be more adept at recognizing the meanings of nonverbal cues of emotion than males. The effect of the gender difference in decoding nonverbal cues was significantly larger for visual-plus-auditory studies than for studies that considered either just visual or just auditory cues. It is not clear just why this gender difference occurs. One possibility is that it fits with the female sex role in which females are supposed to be more concerned with interpersonal interactions. Presumably such sensitivity to nonverbal cues could be an asset in many situations involving interacting with others. However, there is little evidence of a female advantage in interacting in task groups.

There is a possibility that greater sensitivity to nonverbal cues could work to the advantage of females in situations where they are attempting to move into nontraditional roles. Their sensitivity to nonverbal cues may make them aware of areas where they are encountering resistance to their efforts. Awareness of resistance, however, could be a disadvantage if it served to undermine their confidence. There is evidence that females may respond more readily than males to the biases of interviewers, in the sense that their behaviors tended to confirm the interviewers' preinterview biases (Christensen & Rosenthal, 1982).

For the purposes here, the research on communication style suggests that females may tend to speak in a more deferent manner than males in task situations or may be perceived as doing so because of gender stereotypes (Foss & Foss, 1983). Kramarae (1981) has suggested that females may engage in different verbal strategies partially because unequal access to valued resources causes them to work in different ways to achieve their goals. At the same time, there is evidence that more-assertive communication styles on the part of females can lead to greater influence in leaderless groups. Although it appears that females may be more accurate than males at interpreting nonverbal communications, the causes of and operational implications of this greater nonverbal sensitivity are far from clear.

Influenceability

A number of studies have suggested that females are more easily influenced than males (Nord, 1969). If this trend were confirmed, gender differences in influenceability would have important implications for female and male relations in task groups. For one thing, leaders generally are expected to be able to influence others and not be easily influenced themselves.

Several reviews of the literature bear on the question of gender differences in influenceability (Cooper, 1979; Eagly, 1978; Eagly & Carli, 1981). In the most extensive review, Eagly and Carli (1981) conducted a metanalysis of a large number of studies, which indicated that women were more persuasible than men. Their analysis also showed that females were more conforming than men in group-pressure situations that involve surveillance by the influencing agent. These are situations where members of the group are the influencers and where the subject must express an opinion in their presence. In situations where there was no surveillance, women also showed more influenceability than males; but these results were more tenuous.

Because it has been argued that gender differences in influenceability may be due to masculine content in many of the influenceability studies (e.g., Sistrunk & McDavid, 1971), Eagly and Carli tested this possible explanation, but found little support. They also investigated possible gender-of-researcher effects, finding a significant relationship between sex of researcher and outcome of the experiment. Female influenceability findings were more likely to be found in studies by male authors than by female authors. To test for this trend in other related research, Eagly and Carli evaluated gender of author effects in the aforementioned nonverbal-cues literature review by Hall (1978). Although the strength of the relationship was smaller, they did find that male researchers tended to find that males are not as inaccurate in decoding nonverbal cues as female researchers find them to be. The reasons behind the gender-of-researcher findings are not clear. Perhaps the results are due to subjects behaving differently depending on the sex of the experimenter, although Eagly and Carli point out that the authors may not have actually run the experiments and in most studies of these types the experimenters are relatively unobtrusive. Among the other plausible explanations is the possibility that female and male authors differ in the importance that they attribute to sex differences data and their propensity to report such data.

Another possible explanation that has been advanced for the tendency for females to be more influenceable is a female interpersonal orientation related to sex roles. The interpersonal orientation argument has been discussed earlier in conjunction with the emergent leader, cooperation versus competition, and communication issues. A further study by Eagly, Wood, and Fishbaugh (1981), however, found no support for the notion that females tend to conform because they are concerned about positive interpersonal relationships.

More recently, Eagly and Wood (1982) have offered a status explanation for differences in social influence. Their data suggest that subjects make inferences that women hold lower status positions than men and that persons in lower status positions are likely to yield to the influence of higher status persons. When job titles were introduced in one of the experiments, subjects made inferences based on job titles rather than on gender. Thus, perceived status in the group may affect influenceability expectations on the part of both female and male participants. In fact, sex-role expectations and status considerations may induce males to feel that they must maintain high social influence. Eagly, Wood, and Fishbaugh (1981) found that males conformed less than females only under the surveillance condition in groups containing two males and two females.

Overall, the research has frequently found that women are more easily influenced in groups than are males. Further research into causal explanations, however, is beginning to suggest that influenceability is not an inherent gender characteristic. Rather, it appears that influenceability is affected by the gender makeup of the group and the status cues incorporated within the study setting.

SUMMARY AND CRITIQUE

In viewing representative research on female and male relationships in task groups without designated leaders, several major trends are evident. First, females tend to accept male leadership and to encounter male resistance if they attempt to exercise leadership in mixed-gender groups. Second, females are more cooperative in task groups, particularly with respect to reward allocations. Females also are more likely to be perceived by others as engaging in communication styles that are characterized as deferent. Finally, females appear to be more influenceable than males in task groups.

One common explanation given for the differential behavior of females is that they tend to be more interpersonally oriented than males. Indeed, there is evidence that females hold more interpersonally oriented values than males (e.g., Bartol & Manhardt, 1979) and may engage in more interpersonally oriented behaviors. However, counter evidence also exists to the notion that differential female and male behaviors in task groups are caused by inherent differences associated with gender characteristics. For example, several studies suggest that factors such as task setting and gender ratios in the group influence female and male behaviors (e.g., Kimble, Yoshikawa, & Zehr, 1981; Reis & Jackson, 1981). Eagly and Wood (1982) offer a broader explanation, suggesting that gender differences in status may explain male and female differences in social influenceability and other behaviors in task groups. We return to the status issue in our concluding section.

In fully assessing the trends in female and male relationships in groups without designated leaders, several limitations of the current research should be considered. One difficulty is that much of the research is based on college students engaged in simulated tasks over short time-frames. Several studies involving students did take place in settings where it was necessary for them to interact in the normal course of completing their programs of study (e.g., Frank & Katcher, 1977; Schneier & Bartol, 1980). However, more field research is needed, which can assess emergent leadership issues over a longer time frame and in contexts that more adequately reflect the complexities and realities of organizations. Longitudinal studies that track the career progress of newly hired male and female college graduates in similar nonsupervisory positions would be particularly useful in assessing factors that lead to their differential upward mobility. Although research indicates that task and interpersonal behaviors are related to emergent leadership (e.g., Schneier & Bartol, 1980), many of the dynamics associated with emergent leadership are not well understood (Bass, 1981). Hence, future attempts to increase knowledge regarding gender differences in emergent leadership must also be oriented toward extending understanding of emergent leadership itself.

Another limitation of current research is that many studies involving task groups without designated leaders have concentrated on male subjects or have failed to consider the gender of subjects in assessing study results. As a result, the bulk of gender-related research on task groups has focused on a few major areas where controversies have arisen—for example, the aforementioned cooperation versus competition, communication styles, and influenceability issues. Although these areas are important in assessing male and female relationships in groups, further gender-related research is necessary on such aspects of group dynamics as factors that lead to the inclusion of females versus males in task groups, behaviors that hinder or facilitate acceptance in the group, strategies for countering challenges to female leadership efforts, and approaches to building cohesiveness in mixed-sex task groups. Essentially, the base of inquiry needs to be broadened beyond the areas that have received the major attention to date in order to adequately evaluate female and male task relationships.

A further difficulty with current gender-related studies is that they have involved task groups with different numbers of participants and varying proportions of females and males. Because of evidence that both size and gender ratios can affect behaviors in groups (e.g., Shaw, 1981), greater emphasis must be placed on controlling for these variables. In addition, more studies are required that compare behaviors in same- and mixed-gender groups. Such comparative studies are particularly useful in isolating effects that are due to the gender makeup of the group rather than to other factors in the situation.

Greater consideration also should be given to types of tasks, because results sometimes differ, depending on the congruence of the task with existing sex stereotypes. It would be helpful if more studies could vary tasks systematically in order to determine the extent to which type of task affects male and female group relationships.

Although a number of task group studies have attempted to measure actual behaviors through observation methods (e.g., Aries, Gold, & Weigel, 1983), such methods should be utilized to a greater degree. Particular attention should be focused on determining whether females and males differ in the extent to which they engage in interpersonally oriented leader behaviors in leaderless groups. Additional directions for future research are discussed in the concluding section of this paper.

Research on Groups with Designated Leaders

As we have seen, the literature relating to female and male relationships in leaderless task groups indicates that females frequently have difficulty emerging as leaders and exerting leadership in situations where there are no designated leaders. This situation is mirrored in the working world where females hold a disproportionately small number of managerial and administrative positions in organizations. Several surveys suggest the existence of a general pessimism regarding the ability of females to serve as effective leaders, largely because of expectations that females behave differently than males in leadership positions (Brown, 1981). However, the data on leaderless groups do not allow one to conclude that females necessarily engage in different behaviors and achieve lesser results when they are the designated leaders of task groups. In order to adequately assess the issue of male versus female behavior in designated leadership positions, it is important to review related research evidence.

The major purpose of this section is to evaluate the extent to which the differences in female and male behaviors in leaderless situations are paralleled when females and males hold designated positions of leadership in task groups. In this section, comparative research on the leadership styles of female versus male designated leaders is reviewed. We then investigate related behaviors that are germane to controversies regarding male and female behaviors in leaderless group research. Because of the concern for the relative effectiveness of male and female leaders, research related to leader effectiveness and evaluation issues involving male and female leaders also is reviewed.

LEADERSHIP STYLE

One way of assessing female versus male leaders is to compare their leadership styles. Much of the research since the mid-1960s, on leadership in general, has centered on two types of leader behaviors or styles: initiating structure and consideration. The initiating-structure leadership style is closely akin to the task-oriented leader behavior previously discussed in conjunction with leaderless groups and concerns the degree to which the leader organizes and defines tasks, makes work assignments, establishes communications networks, and evaluates the performance of the work group. The consideration leadership style is analogous to the interpersonal or expressive orientation previously discussed and concerns behaviors that are aimed at giving support, building trust, establishing mutual respect, encouraging friendship, and showing concern for the welfare of the employee (Szilagyi & Wallace, 1980). Because of their importance in the leadership literature, the research on gender differences in leadership has tended to focus largely on the initiating-structure and the consideration leadership styles.

Paralleling leaderless situations, evidence suggests that the popular stereotype is that females will be interpersonally oriented rather than task oriented in leadership positions and, therefore, will not be suited to many leadership positions (Bass, Krusell, & Alexander, 1971; O'Leary, 1974; Schein, 1973, 1975). However, several literature reviews (e.g., Bartol, 1977; Terborg, 1977) have questioned the stereotype of female leaders as mainly interpersonally oriented. In fact, most of the evidence suggests that there are either no differences or relatively minor differences between male and female leaders on leadership style across a variety of settings.

For example, Bartol (1973) had student groups, playing a simulated management game, rank members on several aspects of interpersonal versus task behavior. No significant differences in the rankings received by male and female leaders were found. In a study by Day and Stogdill (1972), civilian Air Force supervisors were matched according to civil service level, type of work, length of service, and time in position. Subordinate descriptions on 12 leadership dimensions, including initiating structure and consideration, showed no significant differences in leader behavior between the male and the female supervisors. Subsequent studies (e.g., Bartol & Wortman, 1975, 1979; Chapman, 1975; Osborn & Vicars, 1976) have generally obtained similar results, indicating few differences between males and females on the initiating structure and consideration leadership styles. Adams and Hicks (1980) did find that West Point cadets described female platoon leaders as being higher in consideration, but there were no differences in descriptions of male and female leaders on structuring behavior. Because fewer differences in expressive and task behaviors appear when comparing males and females in actual leadership positions rather than in leaderless situations, it is possible that females adjust their behaviors to the perceived demands of the situation, at least when they feel that they have achieved a leadership position. There is some limited evidence for this adjustment view. In a laboratory study that attempted to measure actual leader behaviors, Eskilson and Wiley (1976) found that the mode of selection significantly affected female, but not male, leader behaviors. Females engaged in significantly more performance output and contributed a significantly higher proportion of task behaviors in the group when they achieved their leadership positions, albeit through a bogus test, than when they drew lots to choose the leader. Perhaps the achievement of the position legitimized the leadership position for the females and encouraged them to engage in behaviors less congruent with their sex role. Related findings are reported by Chacko (1982), who found that women who perceived that they were hired to fulfill affirmative action requirements experienced lower organizational commitment, lower satisfaction with their work, with supervision, and with co-workers, and reported more role conflict and role ambiguity than women who viewed their gender as an unimportant factor in their selection.

Further evidence of adaptability by women managers is provided by Moore and Rickel (1980), who compared women in managerial roles in a nontraditional setting—business—with women in managerial positions in a more traditional setting—nursing. They found that, compared with their more traditional counterparts, the women in the nontraditional managerial roles were more achieving, more production-oriented, and viewed themselves as having characteristics more like managers and men. Along similar lines, Brenner and Greenhaus (1975) found that female managers were significantly more dominant, more achievement-oriented, and less nurturant than female nonmanagers; but there were no significant differences between male and female managers on these personality characteristics. Data obtained by Steinberg and Shapiro (1982) also showed few differences in personality traits between female and male Master of Business Administration students. Based on assessment center results for 4846 women, Moses and Boehm (1975) found that similar dimensions—organizing and planning, decision making, and leadership—were the strongest predictors of subsequent management level for both males and females. The research also showed that the distribution of assessment center ratings for women and men were comparable when assessed using the same techniques. Similar findings based on a 7-year longitudinal study have been reported by Ritchie and Moses (1983).

Socialization processes in work environments may facilitate adaptation by female managers. Gomez-Mejia (1983) found that differences in work attitudes between men and women managers tended to decline with length of experience as managers and that the declines were due largely to increases in the task-related and job involvement orientations of women. It appears that as women move up in organizations they begin to take on the attitudes of job incumbents in similar positions (i.e., males). Schein (1974) discusses the processes by which managers become socialized in organizations.

Gender-related factors such as the gender composition of the group also appear to affect leader behavior or perceptions of it. Eskilson and Wiley (1976) found that male leader performance output and proportion of group task behaviors were highest with two male followers and lowest with mixed-sex followers. Further analysis suggested that, although the males cooperated in the all-male situation, when one female was present, the two males vied for actual leadership of the group. The study also indicated a tendency for two male followers to ignore a leader who was female, even though she alone possessed certain task-related information. A similar trend was found by Wexley and Hunt (1974), whose data suggested that male subordinates seek to dominate the group when the leader is female.

Gender of subordinates also is related to subordinate perceptions of leader behavior. Based on a study of nonacademic university employees, Petty and Lee (1975) reported that male subordinates of female supervisors described their superiors as lower in consideration and higher in initiating structure than did male subordinates of male supervisors or female subordinates of leaders of either sex. Bartol and Wortman (1975) did not find similar significant interactions between sex of leader and sex of subordinates in relation to leader behavior. They did, however, find that perceptions of the leader differed according to the sex of the subordinate on five leader behavior dimensions. In all cases, female subordinates perceived their superiors, regardless of sex, as engaging in the particular leader behaviors to a greater extent than did male subordinates. Along similar lines, a study by Lee and Alvares (1977) indicated that female subordinates described the same supervisors as engaging in more consideration behavior than did male subordinates. Lord, Phillips, and Rush (1980) also found that the rater's gender affected perceptions of emergent leadership in leaderless task groups. Female subordinates in a study by Adams (1978) perceived more self-determination and initiating structure from their managers than did male subordinates. It was not possible to determine the extent to which the results of these studies were due strictly to perceptions of the subordinates or to actual behaviors on the part of the leaders vis-à-vis female subordinates; but the findings support the idea that the gender of subordinates may affect superior–subordinate relationships. One study of leader communication patterns by Moore, Shaffer, Goodsell, and Baringoldz (1983) suggests that leaders may engage in differential behavior towards female versus male subordinates. Their data indicated that leaders of both sexes made more disapproval and productivity statements to males, while offering more instructions when directing females.

In general, comparative research indicates that there are few differences in the leadership styles of female and male designated leaders. Females appear to be more willing to engage in leader behaviors when they hold official leadership positions. There also is research indicating that female designated leadership may be challenged by male subordinates. Finally, gender of subordinates is related to perceptions of both male and female leadership styles; but it cannot be determined from available studies the extent to which these effects are due to actual behavioral differences toward females and males on the part of leaders or to strictly perceptual factors.

RELATED BEHAVIORS

Earlier, in discussing studies related to leaderless group situations, it was noted that differences between females and males in cooperative behaviors, communication, and influenceability had been the subject of considerable research and debate. The work reviewed suggested a tendency for females to engage in more cooperative behaviors, particularly with reference to distributing rewards; to communicate in a more deferent manner; and to be more influenceable in group situations. Because these results were not consistent across all studies, the possibility was raised that the effects may not be due to gender differences per se, but may be related to other factors such as gender-related status differences.

In this section, we review studies in designated leadership situations that are germane to the cooperation, communication, and influenceability issues. Our purpose here is to determine the extent to which the tendencies found in leaderless situations also apply when females and males hold official leadership positions. In general, fewer studies of designated-leader than of leaderless situations have addressed these issues. In addition, some of the studies cited here are not strictly comparable with the issues raised in the research on groups without designated leaders. However, they constitute the best comparison data that are available.

Studies in designated leadership situations, for example, generally have not considered the issue of cooperation versus competition. In the one study directly related to gender differences in reward allocation, Szilagyi (1980) found no significant differences in the reward behaviors of female and male managers in a merchandise distribution center.

In the area of communications, Birdsall (1980) studied the communication styles of male and female managers in two organizations and concluded that the managers used similar communication styles in their staff meetings. Based on a content analysis of tape recordings of a simulated leadership situation, Moore, Shaffer, Goodsell, and Baringoldz (1983) also found few differences in the spoken language of male and female leaders. Similar results are reported by Camden and Witt (1983), based on subordinate perceptions of female and male managers in three organizations.

Several studies have investigated issues related to leader power and influence in organizations. None has compared male and female leaders on influenceability, the focus of the leaderless group research discussed earlier. Rather, they have been concerned with a related issue—the degree to which female leaders might differ from their male counterparts in both the degree and manner in which they attempt to influence others. Instone, Major, and Bunker (1983) found that, when compared with male leaders, female leaders in a simulated organizational setting tended to make fewer influence attempts and used a more limited range of influence strategies, fewer rewarding strategies, and more coercive strategies. A study using a simulated organizational setting by Ayers-Nachamkin, Cann, Reed, and Horne (1982) also indicated that females attempt to influence subordinates to a lesser degree than do males. In both of these studies, the authors suggested that the magnitude of the differences appeared to be small. Further analyses by Instone, Major, and Bunker indicated that the results of their study were due mainly to sex-related differences in self-confidence, rather than to basic differences in behavioral orientation.

In the related area of decision making, Muldrow and Bayton (1979) found no significant differences between male and female managers on procedural and outcome variables related to a decision task, but female managers were less oriented toward risk taking than their male counterparts. On the other hand, a study by Jago and Vroom (1982) indicated that both female students and female managers chose more participative decision styles than their male counterparts on a problem set related to the Vroom and Yetton decision-making model (1973). The data also showed that the female decision style choices were more effective in that they fit more closely the prescriptive norms of the decision-making model than did male choices. It may be that females find it easier to select appropriate participative behaviors due to female sex roles that sanction such behaviors. Another possibility is that females may be more oriented toward participation because they are less confident than males. This prospect seems less likely, however, because the female managers apparently did not choose participation in situations where it was considered inappropriate according to the norms of the decision-making model.

Although relatively few studies have addressed gender effects on cooperation, communication, and influenceability in designated leadership situations, the overall results of related research suggest that the differences between female and male leaders in these areas are few. Where differences do exist, their magnitudes appear to be small. These results are consistent with studies of leadership style reviewed in the previous section, which showed relatively few differences associated with gender of the leader.

LEADER EFFECTIVENESS AND EVALUATION ISSUES

An important aspect of evaluating relationships among women and men in task groups is the extent to which the gender of the leader actually affects or is perceived as affecting important outcomes. For example, opinion survey results have suggested that employees may be less satisfied with their work situation and may put forth less work effort when the manager is female (e.g., Bass et al., 1971). At the same time, there is research suggesting that the same behaviors and outcomes are evaluated differently when the leader is female. In this section, we first review literature related to the job satisfaction and performance issues. We then explore the research on evaluations of male and female leaders and assess its implications for the upward mobility of females versus males.

JOB SATISFACTION AND PERFORMANCE

Several studies have focused on the job satisfaction of female managers themselves. Despite the apparent difficulties that females experience in achieving and maintaining leadership positions, the available evidence indicates that female and male managers experience equivalent job satisfaction (Bartol, 1973; Bartol & Wortman, 1976; Brief & Oliver, 1976; Herrick, 1973; Jacobson & Effertz, 1974; Reif, Newstrom, & St. Louis, 1976). A pending research issue is the reason for the equivalent job satisfaction given the inequitable treatment commonly afforded to female managers. For example, Veiga and Yanouzas (1976) found that salary levels did not predict managerial disillusionment among a group of female managers, even though an examination of their job descriptions indicated that at least some of the managers were clearly underpaid. Evidence in leaderless group situations also suggested that females place a relatively low emphasis on their own pay. Data provided by Varca, Shaffer, and McCauley (1983) indicate that the situation may be changing, at least for higher-level women, who were less satisfied with their pay than were their male counterparts. On the other hand, the study showed that women in lower-level jobs experienced relatively high satisfaction with their pay.

Given the negative evaluations that frequently are made regarding the capabilities of women to manage (Bass et al., 1971; Rosen & Jerdee, 1978), a major issue is the extent to which employees working for female managers experience lower job satisfaction than employees working for male managers. Generally, the studies that have investigated the job satisfaction of subordinates of female versus male leaders indicate few differences (Adams, 1978; Bartol, 1973; Bartol & Wortman, 1975; Maier, 1970; Osborn & Vicars, 1976; Reif, Newstrom, & St. Louis, 1976).

Some subordinate job satisfaction studies have shown interaction effects. For example, although Petty and Lee (1975) found that subordinates were more satisfied with work when supervisors were perceived as higher in consideration, the relationship was stronger for female supervisors. Their results also indicated a tendency for male subordinates to report lower job satisfaction when working for female supervisors perceived as higher on initiating structure. Similarly, Petty and Miles (1976) found that job satisfaction with the supervisor was more closely associated with consideration leader behavior when the leader was female. But the data further showed a close relationship between satisfaction with the supervisor and initiating structure when the leader was male.

A later study by Petty and Bruning (1980), which controlled for job level, failed to find interaction effects relating sex of leader and leader behavior to job satisfaction. Although there were minor differences, a study by Bartol and Wortman (1975) also found that perceived leader behavior and subordinate satisfaction with supervision were unrelated to sex of leader and sex of subordinates. Thus, the relationship between job satisfaction and leader gender appears to be minimal when managers at similar levels in the organization are compared.

Another important issue is the extent to which leader gender is predictive of managerial performance. Only a few studies in which performance was measured in some relatively objective manner have addressed the performance issue, and most of these studies have been laboratory studies. The available evidence does suggest that males and females perform similarly as leaders (Bartol, 1977; Eskilson & Wiley, 1976; Maier, 1970; Maier & Sashkin, 1971; Martin, 1972; Sashkin & Maier, 1971). The notion that male and female leaders perform equivalently also is supported by studies of assessment centers, which indicated that overall levels of performance of male and female assessees did not differ (Moses, 1973; Moses & Boehm, 1975; Ritchie and Moses, 1983).

Overall, there appear to be few differences in the job satisfaction levels of female and male managers or their subordinates when managers at similar levels are considered. Research findings also indicate that performance is equivalent in work groups with male versus female leaders.

Evaluations of Leaders

Because differences in job satisfaction and performance associated with male versus female managers appear to be minimal, other explanations are necessary for the sex structuring of organizations. One possible explanation is that the behaviors and outcomes associated with female leaders are evaluated differently than those associated with their male counterparts. Related studies have focused on evaluations of both leader behaviors and performance. (Some of these studies are discussed, from a slightly different perspective, by Del Boca, Ashmore, & McManus in Chapter Four, this volume.)

For example, Bartol and Butterfield (1976) attempted to study evaluative responses to male and female leader behaviors. Their results gave partial support to the notion that leader behaviors that conform more closely to stereotypes about male and female leaders are evaluated more highly. Female managers received more positive ratings than male managers on consideration style, while initiating structure behavior was valued more highly when engaged in by male managers. Along similar lines, Haccoun, Haccoun, and Sallay (1978) found that the directive style was rated least favorably when it was displayed by female supervisors. A study by Jago and Vroom (1982) showed that male and female managers perceived to be participative received equally favorable ratings. On the other hand, male managers perceived to be autocratic received modestly positive ratings, while female managers perceived to be autocratic received negative evaluations.

Somewhat contrary results were obtained by Butterfield and Bartol (1978), in a study that included managers as subjects. There were no significant differences in the evaluations of male and female leaders on initiating structure. Males using consideration were evaluated higher than females using that style, a finding opposite that in the Bartol and Butterfield (1976) study. Further discrepant results were obtained by Arnett, Higgins, and Priem (1980). In their study, male and female managers who were classified as distinctly accommodative received similar liking ratings from subordinates; but, among managers who were classified as distinctly directive, females were better liked than males. In a related study by Anderson, Finn, and Leider (1981), subjects gave greater subordination (willingness to work for) and strong friendship attraction ratings to democratic rather than authoritarian leaders depicted in cases. However, under the authoritarian condition, subjects gave higher subordination ratings to female leaders using the title, "Ms."

Interaction effects also have been found in studies that focus on evaluative responses to leader behaviors. A study by Jacobson, Antonelli, Winning, & Opeil (1977) indicated that females tended to be evaluated more negatively than their male counterparts when they were firm with a transgressing male subordinate and when they were lenient with a transgressing female subordinate. Rosen and Jerdee (1973) reported that a friendly, dependent style was rated more effective when exhibited by supervisors of other-sex subordinates.

In brief, there appears to be a slight trend toward more negative evaluations of initiating-structure leader behaviors when they are engaged in by female rather than male leaders. Again, however, this tendency is weak and is not found in all studies. Further studies will be necessary to isolate the conditions under which the same behaviors by female and male leaders are evaluated differently.

Gender of rater also has been found to influence evaluations of leadership styles, but there is no clear pattern (Bartol & Butterfield, 1976; Butterfield & Bartol, 1978; Haccoun, Haccoun, & Sallay, 1978; Lee & Alvares, 1977). Several studies suggest that females and males hold similar views regarding appropriate behavior for female and male leaders (Jacobson & Effertz, 1974; Jago & Vroom, 1982; Rosen & Jerdee, 1973; Szilagyi, 1980). Based on the inconsistencies here, and other research indicating that males and females hold similar stereotypes regarding female managers (e.g., Schein, 1973, 1975), it appears likely that gender of rater is not a major predictor of evaluations of the leadership styles of male versus female managers (Nieva & Gutek, 1980).

When one considers evaluations of actual performance, the situation is particularly complex. While females frequently are the targets of lower evaluations for the same behaviors, qualifications, and performance levels as males (Mohr & Downey, 1977; Rosen & Jerdee, 1974b; Terborg and Ilgen, 1975), differential ratings do not always occur (Morrow & Lowenberg, 1983; Nieva & Gutek, 1980; Wexley & Pulakos, 1982).

Sex bias in performance evaluations seems to depend partially on situational factors. For example, a study by Jacobsen and Effertz (1974) involved a task that made it difficult for the participants to gauge their success and that the researchers characterized as one of relative failure. Results indicated that followers rated the performance of female leaders higher than that of male leaders and perceived greater group success when the group was led by a female. The researchers attributed the results, in part, to the difficulty of determining actual performance. They speculated that the higher ratings for females were due to high expections for males, but not for females, in leadership roles. The research also supported the notion that, in situations of indeterminant performance, female followers may be judged more harshly than males because females are expected to be good followers. In a review of sex effects in evaluation, Nieva and Gutek (1980) concluded that competent males tend to be rated more highly than females of equal competence; however, relatively incompetent males are likely to be rated lower than females of equal incompetence.

The method of leader selection for task dyads also has been found to influence male performance ratings of female leaders. When female leader selection was equitable (based on performance or chance), as opposed to arbitrary (by virtue of her gender), in a study by Jacobson and Koch (1977), female leader performance was rated more highly and she was given more credit when the dyad succeeded and less blame when the dyad failed.

Research by Pulakos and Wexley (1983) suggests still another factor. Their study indicates that the degree to which subordinates perceive themselves as being similar kinds of people to their superiors may be a better predictor than subordinate gender of the level-of-performance ratings received from managers. Perceived similarity is likely to be a function of the quality of the relationship between the subordinates and their superiors.

Other data indicate that evaluations of male and female managers tend to be less influenced by sex stereotypes in situations where the job is one that is not sex typed as either male or female (Brief & Wallace, 1976) and where actual performance data are available (Hall & Hall, 1976). Butterfield and Powell (1981) also found that when performance indicators are given, leader performance, rather than leader gender or leadership style, best predicted evaluations of leaders.

Although gender effects in evaluations of incumbent managers vary widely, research that has involved recommended personnel actions presents more consistent findings. Females are less likely to be recommended for promotions, development (Rosen & Jerdee, 1974a), and pay raises (Reif et al., 1976; Terborg & Ilgen, 1975). Part of the reason for the lesser rewards for females may be a tendency to attribute the accomplishments of females to luck and simpleness of the task, while attributing male accomplishments to ability and effort (Deaux & Emswiller, 1974). This tendency may be more pronounced when evaluators, especially males, hold relatively negative attitudes toward women in management (Garland & Price, 1977).

SUMMARY AND CRITIQUE

In viewing representative research on gender issues in groups with designated leaders, several major trends are evident. Studies indicate that females and males engage in similar leader behaviors when they hold official leadership positions. Also, male and female leaders achieve equivalent results on two common measures of leader effectiveness: job satisfaction of subordinates and performance. Thus, differences in leader behaviors and important outcomes, per se, do not appear to account for the disproportionately small number of females in managerial positions. In addition, there is evidence that the same leader behaviors may be evaluated differently depending on the gender of the leader. For example, female leaders may be more negatively evaluated than male leaders when they engage in initiating-structure leader behavior; but male leaders appear to be susceptible to more negative evaluations than female leaders under some conditions as well. Overall, the evaluative differences related to leadership styles and leader gender are weak and inconsistent.

The availability of performance data appears to reduce the effects of leader gender in evaluations. Individuals may use gender of leader as relevant information in making evaluations when other, more objective, data are not available. Given the difficulties of measuring many aspects of managerial jobs (Carroll & Schneier, 1982), any tendency to use leader gender in the absence of objective data could have serious implications for the upward mobility of women. There also appears to be a tendency to attribute female performance to luck and simpleness of the task, particularly when the evaluators hold relatively negative attitudes toward women.

Finally, when personnel actions are recommended, evaluators are less likely to award promotions and raises to females than males. More research in field settings is needed to fully evaluate this latter trend, although there are ample aggregate data indicating that females tend to be clustered at lower levels and paid less in the work world in general (Brown, 1981).

In order to adequately assess these trends in designated leader studies, several methodological issues related to this research should be considered. For example, most of the research comparing male and female leadership styles has relied on subordinate descriptions (perceptions) of leader behaviors. Given the consistency of the no-difference findings in subordinate descriptions of male and female leaders, the reliance on perceptual data may not constitute a serious problem. However, studies using observational methods would help confirm the finding of no significant differences in leader behaviors. Observational studies could also aid in determining the extent to which perceived differences in leader behaviors on the parts of male and female subordinates are due to actual leader behavioral differences or can be attributed to perceptual influences.

As mentioned previously, research on gender differences in leader behavior has focused largely on the initiating structure and consideration leadership styles, which have figured prominently in a number of leadership theories. Alternative theories, which focus on other behaviors (e.g., Mintzberg, 1971), may also be useful. However, state-of-the-art leadership research has yet to explain adequately the various leader behaviors that lead to effective outcomes. As a result, for the purposes here, additional attention should be given to direct comparisons of leader outcomes. This is particularly true in the area of leader performance. In the past, it was difficult to find females in sufficient numbers in equivalent positions with males in organizations to conduct serious comparative performance studies in field settings. However, this situation is changing rapidly. Subordinate satisfaction as an outcome has already been the subject of considerable research, but other outcomes such as subordinate absenteeism and turnover have been largely ignored. Research also is necessary on factors that may differentially inhibit male and female leader performance, such as unequal access to resources, variations in support from supervisors, differences in availability of strategic information, and other indirect influences.

The rising numbers of females in managerial positions also make it possible for future studies to more easily control for job level. Some research results showing differences between female and male leaders may be due to the confounding effects of job-level differences. That is, typically a disproportionately large number of female managers, compared to male managers, are found in the lower managerial echelons of organizations. Additional numbers of female leaders also will facilitate obtaining sufficient sample sizes of males reporting to female leaders, a factor that may affect interaction effect findings.

Many of the studies on evaluations of male and female leaders have used short descriptions of leadership situations, rather than circumstances where subjects interact with leaders. The description approach has been used in order to standardize leadership situations for evaluation and to allow easy variation of the gender of the leader depicted (e.g., by altering leader names). Additional studies on evaluation issues with actual leaders in both laboratory and field settings are a necessary next step in this line of research. Further suggestions regarding future research needs are given in a later section on conclusions and future directions.

Leader Selection

Research on designated leadership situations indicates that male and female leaders are quite similar in leader behaviors and effectiveness. Thus the low representation of females in positions of leadership in organizations does not appear to be explained by inherent differences in the ability of males and females to hold leadership positions. An important issue, therefore, is the extent to which one's gender might inhibit or facilitate one's selection as the designated leader.

There is ample evidence that females frequently are viewed as less-desirable candidates than males for some types of organizational membership. For example, when Cecil, Paul, and Olins (1973) asked business students to evaluate 50 variables in terms of what an interviewer would consider important in interviewing a particular candidate "for a job as a white collar worker," candidates with male names were seen as potential administrative management employees, whereas candidates with female names were viewed as potential clerical workers. Rosen and Jerdee (1974b) found that business students accepted male applicants for managerial positions more frequently than female applicants with the same credentials. The more the hypothetical position was described as demanding in the sense of requiring aggressive and decisive behaviors versus clerical accuracy and dependability, the less likely a female was accepted for the job. Females also received lower ratings than males on the other dependent variables in the study: overall assessment, potential for technical aspects of the job, potential for long service to the organization, and potential for fitting in well in the operation. Similar findings were obtained by Dipboye, Fromkin, and Wiback (1975), using both college students and professional interviewers as evaluators and by Zikmund, Hitt, and Pickens (1978), in a study involving personnel managers.

There is some counterevidence to the notion that females are viewed as less-desirable leaders than similarly qualified males. Renwick and Tosi (1978) found that graduate students gave equal evaluations to male and female resumés of highly qualified candidates for managerial jobs. A study by Fidell (1970) showed that psychology department chairpersons gave equivalent job prospect ratings to male and female candidates for faculty positions and a Terborg and Ilgen (1975) study using an in-basket exercise indicated that undergraduates gave similar ratings to male and female candidates. In these latter two studies, however, lower starting-salary recommendations were made for the female candidates.

There has been some limited data indicating favoritism toward females in task settings. Although some interaction effects were obtained, Muchinsky and Harris (1977) found that college students gave higher ratings to female than male applicants for such jobs as mechanical engineer, day-care person, and copy editor. Similarly, Kryger and Shikiar (1978) provided evidence of favoritism toward females for a management trainee position. Based on letters of recommendation, personnel managers were more likely to recommend proceeding with an interview when the applicant was a female. Because the decision that the subjects were asked to make involved only the step of interviewing the individuals, it is still possible that a promale bias might have become visible at the actual hiring-decision stage.

One partial explanation for the disparate results in the willingness to include females in work groups and organizations may be the perceived congruency between the sex of the applicant and the type of job (Arvey, 1979). Under the sex-congruency notion, males tend to be favored for jobs, such as managerial positions, that have been traditionally held by males; and females are favored for positions that have been traditionally held by females (Cohen & Bunker, 1975; McIntyre, Moberg, & Posner, 1980; Rose & Andiappan, 1978; Rosen & Jerdee, 1974b; Shaw, 1972). Research on employment patterns in a number of different types of organizations strongly support the notion that females are routinely channeled into lower-level positions (Acker & Van Houten, 1974; Mennerick, 1975; Smith, 1979; Taylor & Ilgen, 1981). In fact, a study by Stewart and Gudykunst (1982) indicated that even though females tended to have a greater total number of promotions than their male counterparts, they still remained at lower levels in the organization.

Evidence indicates that physical attractiveness interacts with gender to produce complex stereotyping of job applicants. In general, physically attractive candidates are at an advantage in obtaining employment and are rated as more likable by co-workers *unless* their work role is perceived as being incongruent with their sex (Cash, Gillen, & Burns, 1977; Kleck & Rubenstein, 1975). As a result, both unattractive and highly attractive females seemed to be at a disadvantage as candidates for managerial positions (Dipboye, Arvey, & Terpstra, 1977). Attractive women appeared more likely to be channeled into positions consistent with traditional sex roles—for example, receptionist (Heilman & Saruwatari, 1979).

Characteristics of the evaluators of candidates for positions also may affect the access of women to leadership positions. Simas and McCarrey (1979) researched the possible effects of authoritarianism on personnel officers' assessments of female and male candidates for a position as administrative trainee. Their results showed that both female and male personnel officers who were high in authoritarianism rated male job applicants more highly than female applicants and recommended more job offers to male than female applicants. There also is evidence that high authoritarian individuals tend to assign inferior tasks to females, while designating males for decision-making tasks (Slotnick & Bleiberg, 1974).

Another possible reason for the relatively low numbers of female managers is that sex stereotypes may impede their selection. For example, women often are believed to be more reticent and passive than their male counterparts, a factor that could reduce their perceived desirability for leadership (Rosen & Jerdee, 1978; Schein, 1973). On the other hand, because sex-role norms dictate that women should be passive (Rosenkrantz, Vogel, Bee, Broverman, & Broverman, 1968), it is plausible that a passively oriented female may well be perceived as a more desirable addition to the organization than a more aggressive female. In testing this latter possibility, Dipboye and Wiley (1977, 1978) found that both male and female candidates for a supervisory position who utilized a moderately aggressive style were evaluated more favorably than males or females who used a passive style more in keeping with the female role. Thus, passive behavior may decrease the odds of being selected for a supervisory position regardless of one's sex.

Where females are selected for entry-level managerial positions, they may have difficulty achieving social integration among their peers. Such difficulties may inhibit further upward mobility. Based on a study of five organizations, Miller, Labovitz, & Fry (1975), concluded that women in male-dominated occupations who attempt to fully participate by acquiring greater expertise, by moving up occupationally, or by acquiring positions of authority also risk losing friendships, influence, and access to information. Other research indicates that competent women, particularly those who attempt to compete for the rewards of the organization, are less likely to gain acceptance than incompetent women, are more apt to be isolated from work groups, are likely to perceive that they are being treated less favorably than their male counterparts, and may be forced into more radical sex-role stances than they might otherwise take (Graddick & Farr, 1983; Hagen & Kahn, 1975; Kanter, 1977; Shaffer & Wegley, 1974; Spangler, Gordon, & Pipkin, 1978). Yet, there also is evidence that acquiring friends in the organization is particularly crucial for women wishing to move up (Stewart & Gudykunst, 1982).

The proportion of males and females in the work group also appears to influence acceptance, mainly in a negative direction when females are few (Kanter, 1977; Schmitt and Hill, 1977; Yerby, 1975). A study by Heilman and Kram (1978) suggests further that women tend to derogate their own performance and that the tendency is more pronounced when working with male colleagues. These multiple forces operate to reduce the possibility of social integration or at least to make it more difficult. The extent to which these pressures cause women to abandon efforts at upward mobility or group inclusion is unknown, but would appear to be substantial (O'Leary, 1974).

Ironically, women may have the advantage in one inclusion circumstance. Rosen and Jerdee (1979) found that male and female managers were less likely to recommend retirement for females than for males, the more so if the female was in a relatively high position in the organization. The authors hypothesized that the reluctance related to high position was based partially on concern for the equal opportunity position of the organization.

SUMMARY AND CRITIQUE

Essentially, the research on the selection issue is mixed, suggesting that females may or may not experience more difficulty than a similarly qualified male in obtaining entry-level managerial positions. Equality appears more likely when candidates have good credentials and the job is perceived to be appropriate for females and males. Once they are selected, evidence indicates that females may have a more difficult time than males achieving acceptance in the organization. This is particularly true if females attempt to gain further upward mobility.

Research on selection issues has relied heavily on students as subjects. Although student reactions to selection materials are reported to be not appreciably different from those of managers (Bernstein, Hakel, & Harlan, 1975), more field studies, particularly involving professional interviewers, need to be used in future research efforts that address selection (Arvey, 1979).

Study designs and procedures also deserve additional attention. Many studies have made available to subjects only data or paper credentials concerning those individuals ("paper people") to be selected or rejected for a particular position. Research by Gorman, Clover, and Doherty (1978) indicates sizable differences between selection decisions involving paper people and those that include interviews with real people. At any rate, organizations rarely make selection decisions based on paper credentials alone. In fact, when asked to make selection decisions based on paper credentials only, the professional interviewers in the Gorman et al. study continually indicated that a valid decision could not be made without a face-to-face interview.

Research should also be conducted on the strategies females versus males use to secure a job, select a sponsor or mentor, learn about potential and actual job openings, develop career plans, and seek promotions. Longitudinal studies also are needed that review male and female career aspirations and subsequent realizations, with attention to such issues as types of assignments, rates of promotions, and relationships with superiors, subordinates, and peers.

Conclusions and Future Directions

To this point we have reviewed literature related to females and males working in two types of task situations, those in which there are official leaders and those that are leaderless. In addition, literature relating to the selection of males versus females for leadership positions was reviewed. In this section, overall conclusions are drawn. Several alternative explanations for these conclusions are then discussed. Finally, an information-processing framework is suggested as a useful mechanism for further research on female and male relationships in task groups.

MAJOR CONCLUSIONS

Before drawing major conclusions, it is useful to point out that we draw on a diverse body of research. Many of the studies on leaderless task groups have only tangentially considered gender influences. Exceptions are areas where considerable controversy has arisen, such as the research reviewed here related to gender effects on cooperation, communication, and influenceability. The relevant research in designated leadership situations, on the other hand, has been more focused on gender-related issues, concentrating largely on possible differences in managerial style, job satisfaction, selection, and performance evaluation. Designated-leader research has given less attention to performance and other areas where male and female leaders may potentially differ. While leaderless-group research has concentrated mainly on laboratory settings, designated-leader research has included both laboratory and field settings. However, we note that gender-related results in designated-leadership situations have been consistent across laboratory and field settings (Bartol, 1977). Because of the difficulties in systematically observing behaviors in field settings, a larger proportion of the research on designated-leadership situations has dealt with subject perceptual data than has been the case with leaderless-group research. In addition, the selection-related research has relied heavily on limited simulated situations. Other shortcomings in the available research have been mentioned previously. Because of these limitations in the research bodies being compared, and because some areas of interest include only a few studies, our conclusions are necessarily tentative.

Based on literature related to male and female relationships in leaderless groups and in designated leaders situations, as well as research on selection issues, several major conclusions are suggested:

1. In mixed-sex leaderless groups, females frequently take a more passive role towards leadership and may engage in more expressive behaviors at the expense of instrumental or task behaviors (e.g., Heilbrun, 1968).
2. Females are more active in engaging in leadership behaviors in same-sex than in mixed-sex leaderless groups (e.g., Aries, 1976).
3. Males tend to resist leadership by females in leaderless groups (e.g., Wolman & Frank, 1975) and to a lesser degree in designated-leader situations (e.g., Eskilson & Wiley, 1976).
4. Females have a more difficult time achieving social inclusion in mixed-

sex leaderless groups if they attempt to actively engage in leadership behaviors (e.g., Miller, Labovitz, & Fry, 1975).

5. The behaviors of both males and females are influenced by the gender ratios in task groups (e.g., Tindall et al., 1978).

6. Females and males behave similarly in designated-leadership situations (e.g., Bartol, 1977).

7. Females have a more difficult time achieving social inclusion in designated-leader situations if they demonstrate a desire for upward mobility (e.g, Kanter, 1977).

8. Although females are less likely than males to be selected for leadership positions, to be promoted to higher-level managerial positions, and to receive equal performance ratings for similar performance, these sex effects are highly dependent on situation factors, such as the amount of data that are available to raters (e.g., Hall & Hall, 1976).

Each of the preceding tentative conclusions has important potential implications for understanding female and male relationships in groups. However, their major significance stems from their collective implication. In their extensive review of sex differences literature, Maccoby and Jacklin (1974) suggested that there are relatively few reliably established behavioral differences between the sexes (see Block, 1976, for a critique of this work). The data here are consistent with that conclusion, in the sense that the phenomenon isolated cannot be explained simply in terms of innate biological differences. If there were sex differences in task behaviors, which could be explained by inherently different characteristics of males and females, then we should see these effects consistently across a variety of situations. Instead, the effects vary greatly across situations. For example, the research review indicates that females behave differently in leaderless groups than they do when they hold official leadership positions, suggesting that a gender explanation for these phenomena is not adequate and that alternative explanations are needed.

ALTERNATIVE EXPLANATIONS

In seeking to explain the preceding conclusions, there are several potential explanations that help to provide a framework for further analysis: gender roles, status, and tokenism. We discuss each of these in turn.

Gender Roles

The notion of gender roles recognizes the possibility that an individual may or may not view males and females as having similar behavioral abilities but may still view certain behaviors as more appropriate for females or males under a given set of circumstances. For example, it may be viewed as acceptable for a female to hold the position of elementary school principal but not the position of manager in a major corporation.

The research reviewed contains numerous examples of situations where both males and females are channeled into positions that are congruent with commonly held sex stereotypes (e.g., Rose & Andiappan, 1978). There also is evidence that males and females frequently attempt to behave in consonance with behaviors and orientations considered appropriate for their sex (O'Leary, 1974). However, the gender-roles approach does not account for findings where females and males behave in ways that are not congruent with gender roles. This is particularly true for the research indicating that females and males behave similarly in official leadership positions. (Staines & Libby, Chapter Six, this volume, critique the notion of overarching or generalized gender roles.)

Status

Another means of explaining female and male relationships in task groups is through the concept of status. For example, Meeker and Weitzel-O'Neill (1977) have argued that behaviors in task-oriented groups can largely be explained by initial differences in the status of group members. Further they argue that gender is a status characteristic, in that males have higher status than females. Thus females may engage in more expressive behavior, such as agreeing, because of their perceived lower status in groups. At the same time, females may engage in more task-oriented behaviors in situations where their status has been altered by such means as data indicating particular competence or by being appointed leader. Thus the status explanation provides some flexibility in attempting to assess situational factors influencing female and male relationships in task groups.

Lockheed and Hall (1976) and Eagly and Carli (1981) also have suggested a status-inequalities explanation for apparent sex differences in influenceability. They argue that females tend to be found in lower-status positions and males in higher-status positions in most natural settings. Because lower-status individuals are more likely to have less influence and are expected to be more easily influenced, people are more likely to experience situations where females generally have less influence and are more easily influenced. Eagly and Carli suggest that the sex variable is a by-product and formal status inequalities actually explain the apparent influenceability differences between males and females.

While formal status inequalities may well be one of the important variables that can be linked to the formation and operationalization of sex role stereotypes, further analysis is needed to determine how the process works. The tendency for newly formed groups to emulate the status differences in the larger society is not clearly understood (Eagly, 1983).

Tokenism

Another potential explanation for the research results reviewed here is the tokenism concept advanced by Kanter (1977). According to Kanter, group dynamics are heavily influenced by the relative numbers of socially and culturally different (e.g., sex, race) people in a group. Skewed groups exist when there is a large preponderance of one type (the dominants) and a relative few of another type (the tokens). Under such skewed circumstances, the tokens have a difficult time becoming successfully integrated into the group. Their token status increases their visibility and results in abnormal performance pressures being brought to bear on tokens. Their minority status also causes polarization, where differences between the characteristics of the dominants and the tokens tend to be exaggerated to the point where the tokens are isolated from the rest of the group. Finally, the skewed nature of the group leads to assimilation difficulties including token role entrapment. Role entrapment involves making assimilation dependent on the token adapting a stereotyped informal role that preserves the usual form of interaction between the token and the dominants. Kanter (1977) observed four different informal roles for token women:

1. One was the mother role, in which the token was expected to be a good, sympathetic listener and a person in whom to confide about one's problems. Her major role became one of emotional support for others, rather than task performance.
2. A second role was seductress, in which the token was cast as a sex object. In this case, she was frequently protected by a high-status male in the organization, causing resentment among her male peers. This role may be closely related to sexual-harassment issues (see special issue of *Journal of Social Issues*, Winter, 1982) in that it encourages perceptions of the token as a sex object.
3. A third role was pet, in which the token became a mascot or cheerleader who was supposed to cheer from the sidelines, but not compete.
4. A fourth role reserved for tokens who resisted the other three roles was iron maiden, in which women were stereotyped as tougher than they really were and were thus effectively isolated.

All of the roles preclude assimilation as an equal to the dominants.

Some of the research reviewed here supports the notion that the gender ratios in the group affect interactions (e.g., Schmitt & Hill, 1977). Kanter

(1977) argues that numerical shifts to increase the proportion of tokens and thereby reduce their token status are necessary in order to bring about a more favorable work climate for the tokens. Fairhurst and Snavely (1983) have challenged the view that numerical shifts are necessary, pointing instead to various sources of power and status that may be used by tokens to alter their work situation. For example, they note the possibility that increased visibility may give tokens greater access to upper levels of the hierarchy and thereby give them greater power and status. Thus the tokenism view, particularly as expanded by Fairhurst and Snavely, is potentially compatible with the aforementioned status explanation of female–male relationships in task groups.

INFORMATION PROCESSING

Although the several aforementioned approaches all seem to have some utility in attempting to explain female and male relationships in task groups, none is able to fully explain how and why these factors have varying effects across situations. One promising approach to understanding and explaining these effects is research on human information-processing (Hamilton, 1981). As Schneider, Hastorf, and Ellsworth (1979) have pointed out, investigating the manner in which individuals process information may be useful in analyzing how people are perceived and how others react to them.

A number of researchers have suggested that individuals use schemas as a basis for social information processing (e.g., Markus, 1977; Neisser, 1976; Taylor & Crocker, 1981). Taylor and Crocker (1981) in particular have outlined a schema theory that has high potential for explaining the phenomena summarized in our preceding major conclusions section. In order to function, individuals must continually scan their environments, give attention to some items, absorb information about those items, and either store the information in some way for future use or use it immediately, probably in conjunction with stored information, for action. Because of the vast amount of data in the environments of individuals, they cannot process all of the available information. Rather, they must exercise considerable selectivity in choosing items for attention and subsequent processing. Taylor and Crocker suggest that individuals use various schemas that encompass "hypotheses about how the world works" to select and process information. They define a schema as "a cognitive structure that consists in part of the representation of some defined stimulus domain. The schema contains general knowledge about that domain, including a specification of the relationships among attributes, as well as specific examples or instances of the stimulus domain." A major function of a schema is to "answer the question, 'what is it?' " (p. 91). Schemas operate as templates that guide attention to stimuli and that provide a plan for interpreting and using the schema-related information.

According to Taylor and Crocker, there are at least three general classes of social schemas that individuals use to process social information. One class is *person schemas*, which involve impressions or representations of specific individuals. A second class is *role schemas*, which include schemas for particular occupations like manager or secretary, and stereotypic conceptions of groups such as women or ethnic groups. A third class, termed *event schemas*, are associated with particular situations such as a cocktail party or department meeting. Thus individuals possess a variety of schemas related to individuals, roles, and situations, which they use when they encounter social stimuli. In general, the schemas help them to recognize quickly the stimuli before them, to fill in missing attributes of the stimuli, and to make predictions regarding the likely implications. Evidence suggests that gender frequently figures in the schema of individuals (Taylor, Fiske, Etcoff, & Ruderman, 1978). Ashmore and Del Boca (1979) define gender stereotypes as "structured sets of beliefs about the personal attributes of women and men" (p. 222). Thus, gender stereotypes can be conceptualized as types of schemas (see Chapter Three, this volume for a cognitive–social-psychological framework for gender stereotypes, which is conceptually related to the schema approach proposed here).

Taylor and Crocker argue that schemas fulfill a number of vital and specific functions. First, they enable individuals to structure their environments by comparing stimulus configurations that they encounter to various schemas they possess. The schema used and the matching process may or may not be accurate. For example, one's schema of an office situation might lead one to assume, perhaps erroneously, that the female standing by the secretarial desk is the secretary and the male standing nearby is the boss.

Schemas also control what information will be encoded or retrieved from memory. It appears that schema-consistent information is processed rather easily, while highly inconsistent information tends to be rejected or discounted as erroneous (see also Cooper, 1981). Moderately inconsistent information may trigger a relatively high amount of cognitive work as the individual attempts to fit the information into an existing schema. However, it is not clear whether such information will be more easily recalled because of the extra attention it receives or less easily recalled because it is more difficult to fit into an existing schema.

Individuals are able to fill in data missing from a stimulus configuration through the use of schemas. This can occur in two ways. First, a schema may guide the search for data. For example, one might walk into a suite of offices and see an empty desk where, based on one's schema of office setting, one might expect to find a receptionist. Thus, one may begin to look around for the receptionist. Another way in which schemas help to fill in missing data is by providing best guesses about information when it is missing. For example, if one is told only that there is a new receptionist in the office, one may surmise (best guess) that the receptionist is a female.

Schemas also provide bases for solving problems. They can be utilized as heuristics or shortcuts to solutions. For example, in the case of the suite of offices with the empty receptionist desk, the perceiver may scan the various offices in the suite, surmise (perhaps erroneously) that the female in one of the offices is the receptionist and ask her for help.

Individuals can evaluate various experiences through templates provided by schemas. Schemas generate expectations and standards against which various social stimuli can be judged. For example, an individual may believe that females function best in traditional types of positions, such as secretaries and assistants. Therefore, when evaluating the credentials of applicants for various jobs, the individual may give low evaluations to female applicants for nontraditional jobs and/or attempt to channel female applications into more traditional jobs.

Finally, according to Taylor and Crocker, schemas provide a means for anticipating the future, devising plans, and developing behavioral routines for use in dealing with various social stimuli. For example, one may have a schema of a business meeting that suggests that when males and females are present, the males should do the leading. A male possessor of such a schema may be prompted to attempt to exert leadership, while a female possessor of such a schema may assume a relatively passive role toward leadership in the group.

Taylor and Crocker also point out various potential liabilities of schema use. Several of these are implied in the preceding discussion. For example, errors may occur due to the use of the wrong schema, as in the case of a perceiver applying the schema of receptionist to a female manager. There also is a tendency to accept data as compatible with a schema when the data actually are incompatible. This appears to occur for several reasons, including the tendency to match the schema to the situation based on only a few cues. Usage of schemas may lead one to fill in information based on one's schema, rather than seek sufficient information about the actual situation. This tendency may lead to an *illusory data base*, which Taylor and Crocker define as "a set of assumptions, inferences, or bits of information which are not actually present in the stimulus configuration encountered by the perceived, but that rather constitute the contribution the schema makes to the stimulus configuration" (p. 117). Thus much of a perceiver's knowledge of an individual may actually be based on very little information; yet the perceiver may feel in possession of considerable valid knowledge about the individual. Once a perceiver has categorized an individual, the perceiver is likely to pay most attention to the behaviors that are consistent with the categorization (Jones, 1982). One implication is that schemas are resistant to disconfirmation (Cooper, 1981; Hamilton & Rose, 1980).

There is evidence that maintenance of schemas or stereotypes becomes more difficult with continuous exposure to contrary information (Triandis, 1977). A variety of paradigms suggest that discrepancies between one's social beliefs and apparent reality create a tension to reconcile the discrepancy (Festinger, 1957; Triandis, 1977; Walster, Berscheid, & Walster, 1973). At the same time, individuals do not abandon their stereotypes easily (Schneider et al., 1979).

Bartol (1980) has hypothesized a series of measures that an individual observer might take to resolve apparent discrepancies between gender schemas held by the observer and the behavior of a person in a stereotyped category in a work setting:

1. **Attribute congruence**. If the perceived discrepancies are relatively minor, the observer may ignore the discrepancies altogether or easily make causal attributions that explain away the discrepancies. For example, the observer may attribute the presence of a stereotyped person in a nontraditional job to an effort to bring in a little extra money rather than serious interest in a career. Good performance may be attributed to luck rather than to ability (Garland & Price, 1977). Thus, an observer may be able to maintain stereotypes even while explaining discrepancies.

2. **Discount as exception**. If the discrepancies become too apparent to reconcile with gender stereotypes, the observer may be able to dismiss the discrepancies as exceptions to the rule. Evidence suggests that stereotyped persons may acquiesce and/or contribute to the exception designation, perhaps as a means of being less threatening to the system and increasing their own chances of survival (Laws, 1975).

3. **Control—role alignment**. If the attributions and discounting are insufficient to reduce perceived discrepancies, the observer will need to find more complex means to deal with the discrepancies. One possibility is to attempt to channel the stereotyped individual's behaviors into a role set that is more compatible with the observer's stereotypic expectations. For example, Kanter (1977) has noted attempts to channel females in nontraditional jobs by relating to them in roles such as mother, seductress, and pet. While each of these roles requires the female to behave in ways that are more compatible with sex stereotypes, such roles preclude high levels of job performance on the part of the role player.

4. **Control—deviant labelling**. If efforts at role alignment fail and the stereotyped individual persists in behaviors that are incompatible with existing stereotypes, the individual runs the risk of being labelled a deviant

(Epstein, 1970). Deviant labels, such as "women's libber," signal to the group that the individual has violated group norms and encourages suspicion and isolation of the individual (Davis, 1977; Wolman & Frank, 1975). Deviant labels constitute negative schemas, in the sense that they convey a negative evaluation and encourage others to use the negative schema to classify the individual. The use of the deviant labelling also allows the perceivers to maintain their gender stereotypes.

5. Control—expulsion. If the behavior of the stereotyped person cannot be controlled by role alignment or deviant labelling, the observer may attempt to expel the individual from the setting either through firing or pressuring the individual to leave through indirect means, such as poor assignments, short deadlines, inadequate resources, et cetera. Relatively little is known about the turnover and voluntary withdrawal patterns of individuals in nontraditional work roles. Home-related pressures from other persons in the stereotyped individual's role set may contribute to the success of the expulsion strategy (O'Leary, 1974).

If it is necessary to progress through the series and the series fails, the observer may begin to question his or her own gender schemas. It is possible that an observer may never need to use this entire series of measures because one of the earlier measures may resolve the discrepancy problem. Furthermore, an observer may not employ all measures because the individual does not perceive their potential availability. The order of usage of the measures also may vary, depending on the observer and the organization.

It is possible that the observer would not be able to use all of these measures because the stereotyped person has been able to acquire relative power in the organization. Fairhurst and Snavely (1983) have suggested a number of means that tokens may be able to use to acquire status and power in the organization, such as longevity in and knowledge about the organization, attractiveness and personality, visibility, and access to valued resources. Kanter's (1977) suggestion of a numerical shift toward more tokens also may have the effect of increasing the amount of discrepant information, while making some of the more drastic measures impractical. Thus, using an information-processing approach may help to explain why numerical shifts may aid the assimilation of tokens into the task environment. Another reason why increasing the number of tokens may help the assimilation process is that multiplying the numbers of tokens may reduce the degree to which they stand out as different. The accompanying reduction in visibility is likely to influence the schema selection of perceivers. Thus, if females are in the minority in a particular work setting, a perceiver may be inclined to use a gender-related schema rather than a job-related schema to evaluate the situation.

An information-processing approach also may be useful in attempting to understand why females and males frequently behave differently in mixed-sex than in same-sex task groups. Preliminary work suggests that individuals have self-schemas or knowledge structures that they develop to help them understand, integrate, or explain their own behaviors and social experiences. Furthermore, gender appears to be a salient aspect of many people's self-schemas (Markus, Crane, Bernstein, & Siladi, 1982). At the same time, we have argued, individuals hold various schemas, including stereotypes, regarding the behaviors of others. Although a discussion of origins of gender stereotypes is beyond the parameters of this chapter. Ruble and Ruble (1982) indicate that by the age of 5 years, children have acquired reasonably well-defined stereotypes about relatively concrete aspects of sex roles, such as toys and occupations. More-abstract concepts such as traits develop somewhat later. Thus individuals have notions regarding what should and does happen in terms of their own behavior and that of others across of variety of settings (see Chapter Three).

When a task group contains both males and females, individuals may use the gender of participants to select schemas that help them decide what are appropriate behaviors under the circumstances. The exact cues that individuals use to select schema have not been isolated and probably vary among individuals and across situations. We speculate that individuals use gender cues to select schemas when the sex ratios in the group are skewed or when specific roles are ambiguous, as is frequently the case in leaderless groups. Because female gender and low status tend to covary, gender schemas may incorporate low-status assumptions for females and suggest behavioral routines consonant with those assumptions both on the part of the perceivers and the focal individuals using self-schemas to select behaviors. In designated-leader situations, the roles are clearer; and it appears that perceivers are more likely to choose schemas related to roles rather than gender. For example, Eagly and Wood (1982) found that when job titles were introduced in a task experiment, subjects made inferences based on job title rather than on gender. Thus, we find fewer gender differences in behaviors in designated leadership situations. This interpretation is consistent with research indicating that when performance data or credentials provide clear information, perceivers are likely to use that information in making decisions (e.g., Hall & Hall, 1976). Perceivers seem more likely to use gender schemas in the absence of cues leading to more-appropriate schemas.

Because schemas (and self-schemas) provide guidelines for deciding what is appropriate action, the gender schemas of females may cause them to judge that males should be leaders when there are males in a leaderless group and that females should assume more passive roles. Conversely, even if a female adopts a schema that indicates that she should play a leadership role, the males in the group may possess schemas that indicate that leadership by a female in the situation is inappropriate and challenge her attempts at leadership. At the same time, it appears that appointing females to leadership positions may cause a shift in schemas from gender to role and thereby legitimize the female leadership role, at least to some degree, for both females and males. Thus usage of schemas does not exist in a vacuum, but is dynamically influenced by factors in the situation (Cummings, 1982).

Schemas allow individuals to order their worlds and to conduct means-end analyses that enable them to pursue the satisfaction of their various needs. Without some conceptualization of how the world does and should operate, individuals would be relegated to random actions with completely unpredictable consequences. The challenge to researchers of gender-related issues is to achieve a better understanding of the schemas or templates that individuals use to dynamically assess individuals, roles, and events where gender is a potentially relevant variable. As mentioned previously, research suggests that subject responses to gender-related situations are highly influenced by accompanying information cues, such as titles and objective performance data. As a result, special attention should be given to the cues that affect individual interpretations and concomitant actions. Such efforts, of course, will need to be closely tied to progress in general schema and information-processing research in order to ensure that "schemas" are adequately measured. A better understanding of the ways in which individuals dynamically interpret their environments offers rich prospects for intervention and change. An information-processing approach also may be useful in building knowledge regarding how gender-relevant schemas change over time.

The information-processing framework here proposed suggests that the twin objectives with which we began—how do the sexes relate in face-to-face groups and what are the causes of the sex structuring of formal organizations—require attention to both self- and other-schemata. This further suggests that gender identity (Chapter Two, this volume) and gender stereotypes (Chapter Three, this volume) play important roles in the social-psychological analysis of women and men in task groups.

References

Acker, J., & Van Houten, D. R. (1974). Differential recruitment and control: The sex structuring of organizations. *Administrative Science Quarterly, 19,* 152–163.

Adams, E. F. (1978). A multivariate study of subordinate perceptions of and attitudes toward minority and majority managers. *Journal of Applied Psychology, 63,* 277–288.

Adams, J., & Hicks, J. M. (1980). Leader sex, leader descriptions of own behavior, and subordinates description of leader behavior. *International Journal of Womens Studies, 3,* 321–326.

Alagna, S. W. (1982). Sex role identify, peer evaluation of competition and the responses of women and men in a competitive situation. *Journal of Personality and Social Psychology, 43,* 546–554.

Amidjaja, I. R., & Vinacke, W. E. (1965). Achievement, nurturance, and competition in male and female triads. *Journal of Personality and Social Psychology, 2,* 447–451.

Anderson, L. R., Finn, M., & Leider, S. (1981). Leadership style and leader title. *Psychology of Women Quarterly, 5,* 661–669.

Aries, E. (1976). Interaction patterns and themes of male, female and mixed groups. *Small Group Behavior, 7,* 7–18.

Aries, E. J., Gold, C., & Weigel, R. H. (1983). Dispositional and situational influences on dominance behavior in small groups. *Journal of Personality and Social Psychology, 44,* 779–786.

Arnett, M. D., Higgins, R. B., & Priem, A. P. (1980). Sex and least preferred co-worker score effects in leadership behavior. *Sex Roles, 6,* 139–152.

Arvey, D. (1979). Unfair discrimination in the employment interview: Legal and psychological aspects. *Psychological Bulletin, 86,* 736–765.

Ashmore, R. D., & Del Boca, F. K. (1979). Sex stereotypes and implicit personality theory: Toward a cognitive-social psychological conceptualization. *Sex Roles, 5,* 219–248.

Ayers-Nachamkin, B., Cann, C. H., Reed, R., & Horne, A. (1982). Sex and ethnic differences in the use of power. *Journal of Applied Psychology, 67,* 464–471.

Bartol, K. M. (1974). *Male and female leaders in small work groups.* Division of Research, Graduate School of Business Administration, Michigan State University, East Lansing, MI.

Bartol, K. M. (1976). Expectancy theory as a predictor of female occupational choice and attitude toward business. *Academy of Management Journal, 19,* 669–675.

Bartol, K. M. (1977). The sex structuring of organizations: A search for possible causes. *Academy of Management Review, 3,* 805–815.

Bartol, K. M. (1980). Female managers and quality of working life: The impact of sex-role stereotypes. *Journal of Occupational Behaviour, 1,* 205–221.

Bartol, K. M., Anderson, C. R., & Schneier, C. E. (1981). Sex and ethnic effects on motivation to manage among college business students. *Journal of Applied Psychology, 66,* 40–44.

Bartol, K. M., & Butterfield, D. A. (1976). Sex effects in evaluating leaders. *Journal of Applied Psychology, 61,* 446–454.

Bartol, K. M., & Manhardt, P. J. (1979). Sex differences in job outcome preferences: Trends among newly-hired college graduates. *Journal of Applied Psychology, 64,* 477–482.

Bartol, K. M., & Wortman, M. S. (1975). Male versus female leaders: Effects on perceived leader behavior and satisfaction in a hospital. *Personnel Psychology, 28,* 533–547.

Bartol, K. M., & Wortman, M. S. (1979). Sex effects in leader behavior self-descriptions and job satisfaction. *Sex Roles, 94,* 177–183.

Bass, B. M., Krusell, J., & Alexander, R. A. (1971). Male managers' attitudes toward working women. *American Behavioral Scientist, 15,* 221–236.

Bass, B. M. (1981). *Stogdill's Handbook of Leadership.* New York: Free Press.

Bedell, J., & Sistrunk, F. (1973). Power, opportunity costs, and sex in a mixed-motive game. *Journal of Personality and Social Psychology, 25,* 219–229.

Bernstein, V., Hakel, M. D., & Harlan, A. (1975). The college student as interviewer: A threat to generalizability? *Journal of Applied Psychology, 60,* 266–268.

Birdsall, P. (1980). A comparative analysis of male and female managerial communication style in two organizations. *Journal of Vocational Behavior, 16,* 183–196.

Block, J. H. (1976). Issues, problems, and pitfalls in assessing sex differences: A critical review of *The psychology of sex differences*. *Merrill-Palmer Quarterly, 22,* 283–308.

Bormann, E. G., Pratt, J., & Putnam, L. (1978). Power, authority, and sex: Male response to female leadership. *Communication Monographs, 45,* 119–155.

Bradley, P. H. (1981). The folk-linguistics of women's speech: An empirical examination. *Communication Monographs, 48,* 73–90.

Brenner, O. C., & Greenhaus, J. H. (1975). Managerial status, sex and selected personality characteristics. *Journal of Management, 5,* 107–113.

Brenner, O. C., & Vinacke, W. E. (1979). Accomodative and exploitative behavior of males versus females and managers versus nonmanagers as measured by the test of strategy. *Social Psychology Quarterly, 42,* 289–293.

Brief, A. P., & Oliver, R. L. (1976). Male–female differences in work attitudes among retail sales managers. *Journal of Applied Psychology, 61,* 526–528.

Brief, A. P., & Wallace, M. J. (1976). The impact of employee sex and performance on the allocation of organizational rewards. *Journal of Psychology, 92,* 25–34.

Brown, L. K. (1981). *The woman manager in the United States.* Washington, DC: Business and Professional Women's Foundation.

Buss, D. M. (1981). Sex differences in the evaluation and performance of dominant acts. *Journal of Personality and Social Psychology, 40,* 147–154.

Butterfield, D. A., & Bartol, K. M. (1978). Evaluators of leader behavior: A missing element in leadership theory. In J. G. Hunt & L. L. Larson (Eds.), *Leadership: The cutting edge.* Carbondale, IL: Southern Illinois University Press.

Butterfield, D. A., & Powell, G. N. (1981). Effect of group performance, leader sex, and rater sex on ratings of leader behavior. *Organizational Behavior and Human Performance, 28,* 129–141.

Caldwell, M. D. (1976). Communication and sex effects in a five-person prisoner's dilemma game. *Journal of Personality and Social Psychology, 33,* 273–280.

Callahan-Levy, C., & Messe, L. A. (1979). Sex differences in the allocation of pay. *Journal of Personality and Social Psychology, 37,* 433–447.

Camden, C., & Witt, J. (1983). Manager communicative style and productivity: A study of female and male managers. *International Journal of Women's Studies, 6,* 258–269.

Carroll, S. J., & Schneier, C. E. (1982). *Performance appraisal and review systems: The identification, measurement, and development of performance in organizations.* Glenview, IL: Scott, Foresman.

Cash, T. F., Gillen, B., & Burns, D. S. (1977). Sexism and "beautyism" in personnel consultant decision-making. *Journal of Applied Psychology, 62,* 301–310.

Cecil, E. A., Paul, R. J., & Olins, R. A. (1973). Perceived importance of selected variables used to evaluate male and female job applicants. *Personnel Psychology, 26,* 397–404.

Chacko, T. I. (1982). Women and equal employment opportunity: Some unintended effects. *Journal of Applied Psychology, 67,* 119–123.

Chapman, J. B. (1975). Comparison of male and female leadership styles. *Academy of Management Journal, 18,* 645–650.

Christensen, D., & Rosenthal, R. (1982). Gender and nonverbal decoding skill as determinants of interpersonal expectancy effects. *Journal of Personality and Social Psychology, 42,* 75–87.

Cohen, S. L., & Bunker, K. A. (1975). Subtle effects of sex role stereotypes on recruiters' hiring decisions. *Journal of Applied Psychology, 60,* 566–572.

Cooper, H. M. (1979). Statistically combining independent studies: A meta-analysis of sex differences in conformity research. *Journal of Personality and Social Psychology, 37,* 131–146.

Cooper, W. H. (1981). Ubiquitous halo. *Psychological Bulletin, 90,* 218–244.

Cummings, L. L. (1982). Organizational behavior. *Annual Review of Psychology, 33,* 541–580.

Davis, N. J. (1977). Feminism, deviance, and social change. In E. Sagarin (Ed.), *Deviance and social change.* Beverly Hills, CA: Sage.

Day, D. R., & Stogdill, R. M. (1972). Leader behavior of male and female supervisors: A comparative study. *Personnel Psychology, 25,* 353–360.

Deaux, K. (1976). *The behavior of women and men.* Monterey, CA: Brooks/Cole.

Deaux, K., & Emswiller, T. (1974). Explanations of successful performance on sex-linked tasks: What is skill for the male is luck for the female. *Journal of Personality and Social Psychology, 29,* 80–85.

Dipboye, R. L., Arvey, R. D., & Terpstra, D. E. (1977). Sex and physical attractiveness of raters and applicants as determinants of resume evaluation. *Journal of Applied Psychology, 62,* 288–294.

Dipboye, R. L., Fromkin, H. L., & Wiback, K. (1975). Relative importance of applicant sex, attractiveness, and scholastic standing in evaluation of job applicant resumes. *Journal of Applied Psychology, 60,* 39–43.

Dipboye, R. L., & Wiley, J. W. (1978). Reactions of male raters to interviewee self-presentation style and sex: Extensions of previous research. *Journal of Vocational Behavior, 13,* 192–203.

Dipboye, R., & Wiley, J. (1977). Reactions of college recruiters to interviewee sex and self-presentation style. *Journal of Vocational Behavior, 10,* 1–12.

Eagly, A. H. (1978). Sex differences in influenceability. *Psychological Bulletin, 85,* 86–116.

Eagly, A. H. (1983). Gender and social influence: A social psychological analysis. *American Psychologist, 38,* 971–981.

Eagly, A. H., & Carli, L. L. (1981). Sex of researchers and sex-typed communications as determinants of sex differences in influenceability: A meta-analysis of social influence studies. *Psychological Bulletin, 90,* 1–20.

Eagly, A. H., & Wood, W. (1982). Inferred sex differences in status as a determinant of gender stereotypes about social influence. *Journal of Personality and Social Psychology, 43,* 915–928.

Eagly, A. H., Wood, W., & Fishbaugh, L. (1981). Sex differences in conformity: Surveillance by the group as a determinant of male nonconformity. *Journal of Personality and Social Psychology, 40,* 384–394.

Epstein, C. F. (1970). Encountering the male establishment: Sex-status limits on women's careers in the professions. *American Journal of Sociology, 75,* 965–982.

Eskilson, A., & Wiley, M. G. (1976). Sex composition and leadership in small groups. *Sociometry, 39,* 183–194.

Fairhurst, G. T., & Snavely, B. K. (1983). Majority and token minority group relationships: Power acquisition and communication. *Academy of Management Review, 8,* 292–300.

Festinger, L. A. (1957). *A theory of cognitive dissonance.* Palo Alto, CA: Stanford University Press.

Fidell, L. S. (1970). Empirical verification of sex discrimination in hiring practices in psychology. *American Psychologist, 25,* 1094–1098.

Foss, K. A., & Foss, S. K. (1983). The status of research on women and communication. *Communication Quarterly, 31,* 195–204.

Frank, H. H., & Katcher, A. H. (1977). The qualities of leadership: How male medical students evaluate their female peers. *Human Relations, 30,* 403–416.

Garland, H., & Price, K. H. (1977). Attitudes toward women in management and attributions for their success and failure in a management position. *Journal of Applied Psychology, 62,* 29–33.

Gomez-Mejia, L. R. (1983). Sex differences during occupational socialization. *Academy of Management Journal, 26,* 492–499.

Gorman, C. D., Clover, W. H., & Doherty, M. E. (1978). Can we learn anything about interviewing real people from interviews of paper people? Two studies of the external validity of a paradigm. *Organizational Behavior and Human Performance, 22,* 165–192.

Graddick, M. M., & Farr, J. L. (1983). Professionals in scientific disciplines: Sex-related differences in working life commitments. *Journal of Applied Psychology, 68,* 641–645.

Haas, A. (1979). Male and female spoken language differences: Stereotypes and evidence. *Psychological Bulletin, 86,* 616–626.

Haccoun, D. R., Haccoun, R. R., & Sallay, G. (1978). Sex differences in the appropriateness of supervisory styles: A nonmanagement view. *Journal of Applied Psychology, 63,* 124–127.

Hagen, R. L., & Kahn, A. (1975). Discrimination against competent women. *Journal of Applied Psychology, 5,* 362–376.

Hall, F. S., & Hall, D. T. (1976). Effects of job incumbents' race and sex on evaluations of managerial performance. *Academy of Management Journal,* 476–481.

Hall, J. A. (1978). Gender effects in decoding nonverbal cues. *Psychological Bulletin, 85,* 845–857.

Hall, J. A., & Braunwald, K. G. (1981). Gender cues in conversation. *Journal of Personality and Social Psychology, 40,* 99–110.

Hamilton, D. L. (1981). Cognitive representations of persons. In E. T. Higgins, C. P. Herman, & M. P. Zanna (Eds.), *Social cognition: The Ontario Symposium* (Vol. 1). Hillsdale, NJ: Erlbaum.

Hamilton, D. L., & Rose, T. L. (1980). Illusory correlation and the maintenance of stereotypic beliefs. *Journal of Personality and Social Psychology, 39,* 832–845.

Heilbrun, A. B. (1968). Influence of observer and target sex in judgments of sex-typed attributes. *Perceptual and Motor Skills, 27,* 1194.

Heilman, M. E., & Kram, K. E. (1978). Self-derogating behavior in women—fixed or flexible: The effect of coworker's sex. *Organizational Behavior and Human Performance, 22,* 497–507.

Heilman, M. E., & Saruwatari, L. R. (1979). When beauty is beastly: The effect of appearance and sex on evaluations of job applicants for managerial and nonmanagerial jobs. *Organizational Behavior and Human Performance, 23,* 360–372.

Hemphill, J. K. (1949). The leader and the group. *Journal of Educational Research, 28,* 225–229.

Herrick, J. S. (1973). Work motives of female executives. *Public Personnel Management, 2,* 380–388.

Instone, D., Major, B., & Bunker, B. B. (1983). Gender, self confidence and social influence strategies: An organizational simulation. *Journal of Personality and Social Psychology, 44,* 322–333.

Jacobson, M. B., Antonelli, J., Winning, P. J., & Opeil, D. (1977). Women as authority figures: The use and nonuse of authority. *Sex Roles, 3,* 365–375.

Jacobson, M. B., & Effertz, J. (1974). Sex roles and leadership perceptions of the leaders and the led. *Organizational Behavior and Human Performance, 12,* 383–396.

Jacobson, M. B., & Koch, W. (1977). Women as leaders: Performance evaluation as a function of method of leader selection. *Organizational Behavior and Human Performance, 20,* 149–157.

Jago, A. G., & Vroom, V. H. (1982). Sex differences in the incidence and evaluation of participative leader behavior. *Journal of Applied Psychology, 67,* 776–783.

Jones, R. A. (1982). Perceiving other people: Stereotyping as a process of social cognition. In A. G. Miller (Ed.), *In the eye of the beholder.* New York: Praeger.

Kaess, W. A., Witryol, S. L., & Nolan, R. E. (1961). Reliability, sex differences, and validity in the leaderless group discussion technique. *Journal of Applied Psychology, 45,* 339–350.

Kahn, A., Nelson, R. E., & Gaeddert, W. P. (1980). Sex of subject and sex composition of the group as determinants of reward allocations. *Journal of Personality and Social Psychology, 38*, 737-750.

Kanter, R. M. (1977). Some effects of proportions on group life: Skewed sex ratios and responses to token women. *American Journal of Sociology, 82*, 965-990.

Kimble, C. E., Yoshikawa, J. C., & Zehr, H. D. (1981). Vocal and verbal assertiveness in same-sex and mixed-sex groups. *Journal of Personality and Social Psychology, 40*, 1047-1054.

Kleck, R. E., & Rubenstein, C. (1975). Physical attractiveness, perceived attitude similarity, and interpersonal attraction in an opposite-sex encounter. *Journal of Personality and Social Psychology, 31*, 107-114.

Kramarae, C. (1981). *Women and men speaking*. Rowley, MA: Newbury House.

Kryger, B. R., & Shikiar, R. (1978). Sexual discrimination in the use of letters of recommendation: A case of reverse discrimination. *Journal of Applied Psychology, 63*, 309-314.

Lakoff, R. (1975). *Language and woman's place*. New York: Colophon/Harper & Row.

Laws, J. L. (1975). The psychology of tokenism: An analysis. *Sex Roles, 1*, 51-67.

Lee, D. M., & Alvares, K. M. (1977). Effects of sex on descriptions and evaluations of supervisory behavior in a simulated industrial setting. *Journal of Applied Psychology, 62*, 405-410.

Lockheed, M. E., & Hall, K. P. (1976). Conceptualizing sex as a status characteristics: Applications to leadership training strategies. *Journal of Social Issues, 32*, 111-124.

Lord, R. G., Phillips, J. S., & Rush, M. C. (1980). Effects of sex and personality on perceptions of emergent leadership, influence, and social power. *Journal of Applied Psychology, 65*, 176-182.

Maccoby, E. E., & Jacklin, C. N. (1974). *The psychology of sex differences*. Stanford, CA: Stanford University Press.

McIntyre, S., Moberg, D. J., & Posner, B. Z. (1980). Preferential treatment in preselection decisions according to sex and race. *Academy of Management Journal, 23*, 738-749.

Maier, N. R. F. (1970). Male versus female discussion leaders. *Personnel Psychology, 24*, 221-238.

Maier, N. R. F., & Sashkin, M. (1971). The contributions of a union steward vs. a time-study man in introducing change: Role and sex effects. *Personnel Psychology, 24*, 221-238.

Manhardt, P. J. (1972). Job orientation of male and female college graduates in business. *Personnel Psychology, 25*, 361-368.

Markus, H. (1977). Self-schemata and processing information about the self. *Journal of Personality and Social Psychology, 35*, 63-78.

Markus, H., Crane, M., Bernstein, S., & Siladi, M. (1982). Self-schemas and gender. *Journal of Personality and Social Psychology, 42*, 38-50.

Martin, C. R. (1972). Support for women's lib: Management performance. *Southern Journal of Business, 7*, 17-28.

Mednick, M. S., & Tangri, S. S. (1972). New social psychological perspectives on women. *Journal of Social Issues, 28*, 1-16.

Meeker, B. F., & Weitzel-O'Neill, P. A. (1977). Sex roles and interpersonal behavior in task-oriented groups. *American Sociological Review, 42*, 91-105.

Megargee, E. I. (1969). Influence of sex roles on the manifestation of leadership. *Journal of Applied Psychology, 53*, 377-382.

Megargee, E. I., Bogart, P., & Anderson, B. J. (1966). Prediction of leadership in a simulated industrial task. *Journal of Applied Psychology, 50*, 292-295.

Mennerick, L. A. (1975). Organizational structuring of sex roles in a nonstereotyped industry. *Administrative Science Quarterly, 20*, 570-586.

Miller, J., Labovitz, S., & Fry, L. (1975). Inequities in the organizational experiences of women and men. *Social Forces, 54*, 365-381.

Mintzberg, H. (1971). Managerial work: Analysis from observations. *Management Science,* B97–B110.

Mohr, E. S., & Downey, R. G. (1977). Are women peers? *Journal of Occupational Psychology, 50,* 53–57.

Moore, L. M., & Rickel, A. U. (1980). Characteristics of women in traditional and non-traditional managerial roles. *Personnel Psychology, 33,* 317–333.

Moore, S. F., Shaffer, L., Goodsell, D. A., & Baringoldz, G. (1983). Gender or situationally determined spoken language differences? The case of the leadership situation. *International Journal of Women's Studies, 6,* 44–53.

Morrow, W. R., & Lowenberg, G. (1983). Evaluation of business memos: Effects of writer, sex and organizational position, memo quality, and rater sex. *Personnel Psychology, 36,* 73–86.

Moses, J. L. (1973). The development of an assessment center for the early identification of supervisory potential. *Personnel Psychology, 26,* 569–580.

Moses, J. L., & Boehm, V. R. (1975). Relationship of assessment-center performance to management progress of women. *Journal of Applied Psychology, 60,* 527–529.

Muchinsky, P. M., & Harris, S. L. (1977). The effect of applicant sex and scholastic standing on the evaluation of job applicant resumes in sex-typed occupations. *Journal of Vocational Behavior, 11,* 95–108.

Muldrow, T. W., & Bayton, J. A. (1979). Men and women executives and processes related to decision accuracy. *Journal of Applied Psychology, 64,* 99–106.

Nadler, A., Shapira, R., & Ben-Itzhak, S. (1982). Good looks may help: Effects of helper's physical attractiveness and sex of helper on male's and female's help-seeking behavior. *Journal of Personality and Social Psychology, 42,* 90–99.

Neisser, V. (1976). *Cognition and reality: Principles and implications of cognitive psychology.* San Francisco: Freeman.

Nieva, V. F., & Gutek, B. A. (1980). Sex effect on evaluation. *Academy of Management Review, 5,* 267–276.

Nord, W. R. (1969). Social exchange theory: An integrative approach to social conformity. *Psychological Bulletin, 71,* 174–208.

O'Leary, V. E. (1974). Some attitudinal barriers to occupational aspirations in women. *Psychological Bulletin, 81,* 809–826.

Osborn, R. N., & Vicars, W. M. (1976). Sex stereotypes: An artifact in leader behavior and subordinate satisfaction analysis? *Academy of Management Journal, 19,* 439–449.

Parsons, T., & Bales, R. F. (1955). *Family socialization and interaction process.* Glencoe, IL: Free Press.

Petty, M. M., & Bruning, N. S. (1980). A comparison of the relationships between subordinates' perceptions of supervisory behavior and measures of subordinates' job satisfaction for male and female leaders. *Academy of Management Journal, 23,* 717–725.

Petty, M. M., & Lee, K. (1975). Moderating effects of sex of supervisor and subordinate on relationships between supervisory behavior and subordinate satisfaction. *Journal of Applied Psychology, 60,* 624–628.

Petty, M. M., & Miles, R. H. (1976). Leader sex-role stereotyping in a female-dominated work culture. *Personnel Psychology, 29,* 393–404.

Phillips, S. V. (1980). Sex differences and language. *Annual Review of Anthropology, 9,* 523–544.

Pulakos, E. D., & Wexley, K. N. (1983). The relationship among perceptual similarity, sex, and performance ratings in manager–subordinate dyads. *Academy of Management Journal, 26,* 129–139.

Putnam, L. (1982). In search of gender: A critique of communication and sex-roles research. *Women's Studies in Communication, 5,* 1–9.

Reif, W. E., Newstrom, J. W., & St. Louis, R. D. (1976). Sex as a discriminating variable in organizational reward decisions. *Academy of Management Journal, 19,* 469–476.

Reis, H. T., & Jackson, L. A. (1981). Sex differences in reward allocation: Subjects, partners, and tasks. *Journal of Personality and Social Psychology, 40,* 465–478.

Renwick, P. A., & Tosi, H. (1978). The effects of sex, marital status, and educational background on selection decisions. *Academy of Management Journal, 21,* 93–103.

Ritchie, R. J., & Moses, J. L. (1983). Assessment center correlates of women's advancement into middle management: A 7-year longitudinal analysis. *Journal of Applied Psychology, 68,* 227–231.

Robertson, W. (1978, July 17). The top women in big business. *Fortune,* 58–63.

Rose, G. L., & Andiappan, P. (1978). Sex effects on managerial hiring decisions. *Academy of Management Journal, 21,* 104–112.

Rosen, B., & Jerdee, T. H. (1973). The influence of sex-role stereotypes on evaluations of male and female supervisory behavior. *Journal of Applied Psychology, 57,* 44–48.

Rosen, B., & Jerdee, T. H. (1974). Influence of sex-role stereotypes in personnel decisions. *Journal of Applied Psychology, 59,* 9–14.

Rosen, B., & Jerdee, T. H. (1974). Effects of applicant's sex and difficulty of job on evaluations of candidates for managerial positions. *Journal of Applied Psychology, 59,* 511–512.

Rosen, B., & Jerdee, T. H. (1978). Perceived sex differences in managerially relevant characteristics. *Sex Roles, 4,* 837–844.

Rosen, B., & Jerdee, T. H. (1979). Influence of employee age, sex and job status on managerial recommendations for retirement. *Academy of Management Journal, 22,* 169–173.

Rosenkrantz, P., Vogel, S., Bee, H., Broverman, I., & Broverman, D. M. (1968). Sex-role stereotypes and self-concepts in college students. *Journal of Counseling and Clinical Psychology, 32,* 287–295.

Ruble, D. N., & Ruble, T. L. (1982). Sex stereotypes. In A. G. Miller (Ed.), *In the eye of the beholder.* New York: Praeger.

Sashkin, M., & Maier, N. R. F. (1971). Sex effects in delegation. *Personnel Psychology, 24,* 471–476.

Schein, E. H. (1974). The individual, the organization, and the career: A conceptual scheme. In D. A. Kolb, I. M. Rubin, & J. M. McIntyre (Eds.), *Organizational Psychology,* Englewood Cliffs, NJ: Prentice-Hall.

Schein, V. E. (1973). The relationship between sex role stereotypes and requisite management characteristics. *Journal of Applied Psychology, 57,* 95–100.

Schein, V. E. (1975). Relationships between sex role stereotypes and requisite management characteristics among female managers. *Journal of Applied Psychology, 60,* 340–344.

Schmitt, N., & Hill, T. E. (1977). Sex and race composition of assessment center groups as a determinant of peer and assessor ratings. *Journal of Applied Psychology, 62,* 261–264.

Schneider, D. J., Hastorf, A. H., & Ellsworth, P. C. (1979). *Person perception.* Reading, MA: Addison-Wesley.

Schneier, C. E., & Bartol, K. M. (1980). Sex effects in emergent leadership. *Journal of Applied Psychology, 65,* 341–345.

Shaffer, D. R., & Wegley, C. (1974). Success orientation and sex-role congruence as determinants of the attractiveness of competent women. *Journal of Personality, 42,* 586–560.

Shaw, E. A. (1972). Differential impact of negative stereotypes in employee selection. *Personnel Psychology, 25,* 333–338.

Shaw, M. E. (1981). *Group dynamics.* New York: McGraw-Hill.

Simas, K., & McCarrey, M. (1979). Impact of recruiter authoritarianism and applicant sex on evaluation and selection decisions in a recruitment interview analogue study. *Journal of Applied Psychology, 64,* 483–491.

Sistrunk, F., & McDavid, J. W. (1971). Sex variable in conformity behavior. *Journal of Personality and Social Psychology, 17,* 200–207.

Slotnick, R. S., & Bleiberg, J. (1974). Authoritarianism, occupational sex typing and attitudes toward work. *Psychological Reports, 35,* 763–770.

Smith, C. B. (1979). Influence of internal opportunity structure and sex of worker on turnover patterns. *Administrative Science Quarterly, 24,* 362–381.

Spangler, E., Gordon, M. A., & Pipkin, R. M. (1978). Token women: An empirical test of Kanter's hypothesis. *American Journal of Sociology, 84,* 160–170.

Spence, J. T., & Helmreich, R. L. (1979). On assessing "androgyny". *Sex Roles, 5,* 721–738.

Spillman, B., Spillman, R., & Reinking, K. (1981). Leadership emergence: Dynamic analysis of the effects of sex and androgyny. *Small Group Behavior, 12,* 139–158.

Stake, J. E. (1983). Factors in reward distribution: Allocator motive, sender and Protestant ethic endorsement. *Journal of Personality and Social Psychology, 44,* 410–418.

Steinberg, R., & Shapiro, S. (1982). Sex differences in personality traits of female and male master of business administration students. *Journal of Applied Psychology, 67,* 306–310.

Stewart, L. P., & Gudykunst, W. B. (1982). Differential factors influencing the hierarchial level and number of promotions of males and females within an organization. *Academy of Management Journal, 25,* 586–597.

Strodtbeck, F. L., & Mann, R. D. (1956). Sex role differentiation in jury deliberation. *Sociometry, 19,* 3–11.

Szilagyi, A. D. (1980). Reward behavior by male and female leaders: A causal inference analysis. *Journal of Vocational Behavior, 16,* 59–72.

Szilagyi, A. D., & Wallace, M. J. (1980). *Organizational behavior and performance.* Santa Monica, CA: Goodyear.

Taylor, M. S., & Ilgen, D. R. (1981). Sex discrimination against women in initial placement decisions: A laboratory investigation. *Academy of Management Journal, 24,* 859–865.

Taylor, S. E., & Crocker, J. (1981). Schematic bases of social information processing. In E. T. Higgins, C. P. Herman, & M. P. Zanna (Eds.), *Social cognition: The Ontario Symposium* (Vol. 1). Hillsdale, NJ: Erlbaum.

Taylor, S. E., Fiske, S. T., Etcoff, N., & Ruderman, A. (1978). The categorical and contextual bases of person memory and stereotyping. *Journal of Personality and Social Psychology, 36,* 778–793.

Terborg, J. R. (1977). Women in management: A research review. *Journal of Applied Psychology, 62,* 647–664.

Terborg, J. R., & Ilgen, D. R. (1975). A theoretical approach to sex discrimination in traditionally masculine occupations. *Organizational Behavior and Human Performance, 13,* 352–376.

Tindall, J. H., Boyler, L., Cline, P., Emberger, P., Powell, S., & Wions, J. (1978). Perceived leadership rankings of males and females in small task groups. *Journal of Psychology, 100,* 13–20.

Triandis, H. C. (1977). *Interpersonal behavior.* Monterey, CA: Brooks/Cole.

U.S. Department of Commerce, Bureau of the Census. (1980, June). *Money income of families and persons in the United States: 1978.* Series P-60. no. 123.

U.S. Department of Labor, Bureau of Labor Statistics, (1982, March 7). *1981 weekly earnings of men and women compared in 100 occupations,* New Release.

Varca, P. E., Shaffer, G. S., & McCauley, C. D. (1983). Sex differences in job satisfaction revisited. *Academy of Management Journal, 26,* 348–353.

Veiga, J. G., & Yanouzas, J. N. (1976). What women in management want: The ideal vs. the real. *Academy of Management Journal, 19,* 137–143.

Vroom, V. H., & Yetton, P. W. (1973). *Leadership and decision making.* Pittsburgh, PA: University of Pittsburgh Press.

Wall, J. A. (1976). Effects of sex and opposing representative's bargaining orientation on intergroup bargaining. *Journal of Personality and Social Psychology, 33,* 55–61.

Walster, D., Berscheid, E., & Walster, W. (1973). New directions in equity theory. *Journal of Personality and Social Psychology, 25,* 151–176.

Webber, R. A. (1976). Perceptions and behavior—mixed sex work teams. *Industrial Relations, 15,* 121–129.

Wexley, K., & Hunt, P. J. (1974). Male and female leaders: Comparison of performance and behavior patterns. *Psychological Reports, 35,* 867–872.

Wexley, K. N., & Pulakos, E. D. (1982). Sex effects on performance ratings in manager–subordinate dyads: A field study. *Journal of Applied Psychology, 67,* 433–439.

Wolman, C., & Frank, H. (1975). The solo woman in a professional peer group. *American Journal of Orthopsychiatry, 45,* 164–171.

Yerby, J. (1975). Attitude, task, and sex composition as variables affecting female leadership in small problem-solving groups. *Speech Monographs, 42,* 160–168.

Yukl, G. A. (1981). *Leadership in organizations.* Englewood Cliffs, NJ: Prentice-Hall.

Zikmund, W. G., Hitt, M. A., & Pickens, B. A. (1978). Influence of sex and scholastic performance on reactions to job applicant resumes. *Journal of Applied Psychology, 63,* 252–254.

Eight

Male–Female Relations: A Summing Up and Notes toward a Social–Psychological Theory

FRANCES K. DEL BOCA

RICHARD D. ASHMORE

Introduction

We began in Chapter One by introducing "the social psychology of female–male relations" as a possible new field of study. Because social psychology focuses on the individual in a social context, it was argued that both the individual and the social context must be considered. In subsequent chapters of the volume, accumulated research and theory regarding three individual-level constructs—gender identity, gender stereotypes, and gender-related attitudes—were critically evaluated, and men and women were examined in three related, but distinguishable, social contexts: in close personal relationships, in role relationships, and in task groups. In this concluding chapter, we first summarize the six preceding chapters and identify unifying themes and new directions for research and theory. In the second major section, a preliminary general model for the social psychological analysis of intergroup relations is described, and male–female relations is discussed as a specific instance.

THE SOCIAL PSYCHOLOGY OF FEMALE-MALE RELATIONS

From Here to There:
Emerging Themes and Directions

The review of the six preceding chapters is divided into two sections. The first is devoted to the three chapters that deal with individual-level constructs (Chapters Two, Three and Four); the second focuses on those chapters that examine women and men in social relationships (Chapters Five, Six, and Seven).

GENDER AND THE INDIVIDUAL

Of the three individual-level concepts covered in this volume, gender identity has involved the most variation in conceptualization and operationalization. Katz began her chapter on this topic by directly confronting this problem. Various definitions of constructs that relate gender to self-definition were reviewed, and a working framework for gender identity was presented. Katz explicitly stated that gender identity is a multifaceted *psychological construct* that includes awareness of gender, internalization of norms, expectations and stereotypes, and affective evaluation. Further, she argued that the structure and the degree of differentiation of gender identity varies both across individuals and over the life course. In addition to specifying the nature of the construct, Katz brought some order to the terminological confusion that surrounds the concept by presenting a scheme for conceptualizing the relations between gender identity and other gender-related variables. Her Figure 1 identifies six major developmental antecedents (e.g., gender-role norms) and three classes of behavioral consequents (e.g., behavioral enactment including activity preferences, dress, sexual behavior and the like) of gender identity.

Katz dealt with a domain of inquiry where there are two separate (and very active) research traditions: one that is concerned with the early development of gender concepts and sex-typed behavior in the growing child, and a second focusing on masculinity–femininity and, more recently, androgyny as components of adult personality. Katz took a critical look at research and theory in both traditions. Her working conceptualization and review of the literature concerning the acquisition and change of gender identity over the life course set the stage for theory and research that will bridge the gap between the presently isolated two lines of work.

Chapters Three and Four adopted similar formats in examining the related concepts, gender stereotypes and gender-related attitudes. Each chapter began with a critical review of the major programs of research. In both chapters, it was concluded that research is largely method driven. Further, the major methods are self-report, and there is more inconsistency in findings than most secondary sources indicate. Because it is not possible to resolve conflicting results in the absence of guiding theory, a cognitive-social psychological framework for the study of sex stereotypes was proposed in Chapter Three. This same framework was elaborated in Chapter Four. More specifically, sex stereotypes and gender-related attitudes were located within the individual's long-term social memory and were embedded in a larger system of beliefs and evaluations pertinent to gender. For both concepts, two types of issues were raised: questions regarding structure (e.g., How are gender stereotypes and attitudes organized?) and those concerned with process (e.g., How do such constructs develop and change?). In addressing these issues, both chapters argued that work on gender-related topics should be informed by research and theory in "basic" social psychology. Accordingly, Chapter Three drew upon relevant work in the fields of person perception and social cognition; similarly, Chapter Four made use of concepts and methods from the general area of attitudes and the more specific area of intergroup prejudice.

Although they dealt with different concepts and relatively separate research literatures, the three chapters focusing on individual-level constructs converged in a number of respects. The common themes concern both conceptual–theoretical analysis and methodological issues. Regarding the latter, gender identity, sex stereotypes, and gender-related attitudes are assessed almost exclusively with self-report procedures. These are obtrusive (and, hence, susceptible to both conscious and nonconscious distortion), and, with few exceptions, there has been a remarkable lack of concern with the basic psychometric principles of reliability and validity (Beere, 1979).

Perhaps because so much of the work on individual-level gender-related constructs has been instrument driven, there has been a failure to be explicit and consistent with regard to the meaning of key concepts and with respect to their presumed causes and consequences. This lack of conceptual analysis is manifested in somewhat different ways in the gender identity literature, on the one hand, and in the work on gender stereotypes and gender-related attitudes, on the other. As Katz indicated, a wide variety of terms have been used to describe the place of gender in the individual's sense of self, personality and behavior. Further, these have been used inconsistently. The same term is used to describe different phenomena and different terms are used to describe the same thing. There are fewer labels to contend with in the areas of sex stereotypes and gender-related attitudes. However, these concepts are seldom explicitly defined and important areas of disagreement remain hidden.

With regard to the causes and consequences of individual-level, gender-related variables, there has been considerable effort directed at applying general psychological theories (e.g., social-learning theory) to understanding the acquisition of sex-typed traits and behavior. There has not been, however, a parallel concern with gender identity in adulthood or with gender stereotypes and gender-related attitudes. There has been implicit theorizing involving all three concepts. With regard to gender identity in the adult, the most popular measures currently in use—the Bem Sex-Role Inventory (Bem, 1974) and the Personal Attributes Questionnaire (Spence, Helmreich, & Stapp, 1974)—define masculinity, femininity, and androgyny in terms of attributes that are *believed to be* socially desirable in or characteristic of females and males—that is, in terms of gender stereotypes. This approach implies that an individual's sense of identity as a male or a female involves comparisons of self with culturally shared notions of what women and men are like or should be like. This perspective on gender identity replaces an older paradigm, in which gender differences (in self-reports of traits, activities, and the like) were used as the criteria for assessing individual differences in masculinity and femininity. The more contemporary view tacitly assumes that cultural stereotypes are important bases of self-definition, that the sources of gender identity are external rather than internal.

This connection between cultural stereotypes and self-concept has also been made by investigators interested in gender stereotypes. As noted in Chapter Three, all three prototypic programs of research in this area have documented an empirical association between descriptions of the sexes and descriptions of self, at least at the aggregate level. This association is regarded as evidence that cultural stereotypes are a major input into the individual's sense of self as a male or as a female. Because these same researchers have also sought to document the differential desirability of gender stereotypes, it is fair to conclude that cultural stereotypes are regarded not only as a primary basis for the individual's gender identity but also for his or her attitudes toward men and women.

This implicit, or only partially articulated, model predicts relatively high intercorrelations between gender identity, sex stereotypes, and gender-related attitudes. There is, however, accumulating evidence that these variables are only loosely interconnected (cf. Spence, Deaux, & Helmreich, 1985; Vaughter, 1983). There are a number of explanations that might account for this. First, because little attention has been paid to the reliability and validity of assessment procedures, the low correlations across constructs may be due to poor measurement. Second, different measuring devices may assess different aspects of the same construct (Ruble & Ruble, 1982, p. 195). Thus, low correlations between different concepts may reflect a failure to match subcomponents appropriately. For example, a measure of gender identity emphasizing work and play preferences may not relate to a gender stereotype instrument involving personality traits. Third, the implicit model, especially the central causal role assigned to cultural stereotypes, may be invalid.

Each of the three chapters covering individual-level gender-related constructs presented a conceptualization that is consistent with the model of human nature outlined in Chapter One. In all three chapters, (wo)man was depicted as a cognitive creature and as a social being. As a cognitive creature, (wo)man represents reality internally. The authors of Chapters Two, Three, and Four made it clear that gender identity, sex stereotypes, and gender-related attitudes are individual-level, cognitively represented phenomena. Beyond this general point of agreement, there are three additional features common to the conceptualization of these constructs.

First, although the cognitive aspects tend to be stressed, all authors argued that other kinds of elements should also be considered in conceptualizing the nature of belief systems and evaluative orientations pertinent to gender. Both Katz, with regard to gender identity, and Ashmore et al., concerning gender stereotypes, made a strong appeal for the inclusion of feelings. These latter authors also suggested that pictorial images (e.g., the picture in the head of Tom Selleck) are an important component of stereotypes.

Second, the individual's representation of self and others in terms of gender is multidimensional. Although the bipolar view of masculinity–femininity is currently out of vogue, researchers continue to describe the attributes thought to be associated with each sex as two coherent (if separate) clusters of characteristics. Probably the most popular summary terms for these trait clusters are instrumentality and expressiveness. The authors of Chapters Two, Three, and Four adopted a different view. Katz suggested that a sense of masculinity or femininity can be achieved in a number of different ways. Similarly, Ashmore et al. and Del Boca and her co-authors argued that perceivers partition the broad social groups, female and male, into gender subtypes and that different sets of attributes may be associated with these more narrowly defined categories. If stereotypes are indeed a basis of self-definition, a variety of options would seem to be available. For example, one male may derive a sense of masculinity from the demonstration of "rational competence," while another might accomplish the same thing with a view of self as "rugged and adventurous." In her frequently cited critique of traditional measures of M–F, Constantinople (1973) suggested that a profile of scores across separate dimensions of masculinity and femininity would be a more informative and more appropriate means of representing gender identity than a single summary score. The use of such profile scores is certainly one logical approach to representing the multidimensional nature of gender at the level of the individual.

Third, gender-identity and sex-relevant stereotypes and attitudes are embedded in a larger configuration of beliefs and affective orientations that may be directly or indirectly related to gender. This larger system includes representations of the individual's short-term and long-term goals, along with other knowledge about the social and physical environment. The form and the specific content of this system are constrained by cognitive maturation and influenced by actual physiological states and their social interpretations. There are two important implications of viewing gender-related constructs in this way: (1) This perspective highlights the fact that the individual has goals and purposes that influence how gender-relevant information is processed and represented. Thus, contrary to the implicit assumption of many investigators, the individual is not simply a passive recipient of culturally determined beliefs regarding the sexes that shape his or her perceptions of self and others. (2) The way in which the individual thinks and feels about self and others in terms of gender will vary as a function of developmental stage. Cognitive-developmental theorists have recognized that cognitive capabilities constrain the development of gender concepts in the growing child. Less often acknowledged is the impact of biological change and the set of physical processes (e.g., menstruation) and life events (e.g., childbirth) related to sexuality. As the authors of Chapters Two, Three, and Four emphasized, sexual content must be a part of gender identity and of sex stereotypes, and sexual conduct and related issues (e.g., abortion) are significant attitude targets relevant to gender.

The authors of the chapters focusing on gender-related constructs depicted (wo)man as not only cognitive but also social. This is clear in the attention devoted to process issues in all three chapters. Acquisition and change were used by Katz as a vehicle for organizing her discussion of gender identity in Chapter Two. Similarly, although they have been little researched to date, the processes of development and change of sex stereotypes and gender-related attitudes are discussed in Chapters Three and Four. These processes involve people—that is, they are social processes.

Gender and Interpersonal Relations

Although not neglected in the first part of the volume, which deals with individual-level constructs, the implications of the social nature of (wo)man were explored more fully in the second group of chapters, which examined women and men in three related but separate social contexts or types of relationships. In Chapter Five, Huston and Ashmore examined individuals in close, voluntary personal relationships (e.g., lovers). In the subsequent chapter, Staines and Libby focused on women and men in role relationships (e.g., wife and husband). Finally, Bartol and Martin considered face-to-face groups where participants are confronted with agreed-upon tasks.

In analyzing personal and role relationships, similar formats were adopted by Huston and Ashmore and Staines and Libby. Chapters Five and Six each began by proposing an innovative approach for investigating an aspect of male–female relationships. The remaining portions of both chapters were devoted to applying the new proposed frameworks to understanding the behavior and experiences of women and men in personal and in role relationships.

The conceptual apparatus suggested by Huston and Ashmore has two primary components. First, they argued that interpersonal relationships are best understood in terms of a descriptive–analytic model articulated by Kelley and others (Kelley, Berscheid, Christensen, Harvey, Huston, Levinger, McClintock, Peplau, & Peterson, 1983). The heart of this model is the notion of "interdependence." Quite simply, two individuals are interdependent if their thoughts, feelings, and behaviors are mutually influencing. A close or personal relationship for Kelley and his colleagues is one in which mutual influence is great—in terms of magnitude as well as frequency and duration. Second, Huston and Ashmore contended that gender-related patterns in personal relationships must be accounted for not only in terms of the dispositions of the individuals involved but also, and often more importantly, in terms of the qualities of their relationship and the immediate and the broader societal contexts within which their relationship is situated. The bulk of Huston and Ashmore's chapter was devoted to demonstrating the utility of this alternative framework for understanding one particular type of personal relationship: that between adult men and women.

Staines and Libby began their consideration of role relationships by arguing for a new approach to sex roles—what they term "role-specific," as opposed to the currently dominant "global" approach. According to the latter perspective, there are two sex roles (one male, one female) that apply to all domains of life. Suggesting that the global approach involves too high a level of aggregation with a resulting loss of information, Staines and Libby proposed analyzing male–female role relationships in terms of the differential experience and performance of three major pairs of social roles: spouse (husband–wife), parent (father–mother), and worker. The heuristic value of this alternative approach was demonstrated by a systematic comparison of male and female incumbents of these role categories.

Rather than first proposing a framework and then demonstrating its utility, Bartol and Martin took a more inductive approach in their chapter. They began with a review of the accumulated research evidence and concluded by considering various explanations for the behavior of men and women in task groups. The focus of the literature review was leadership, including work on both designated and emergent leaders. This review served as a backdrop for considering several explanations for the differential recruitment to and advancement in managerial positions by women and men. Bartol and Martin concluded by proposing an information-processing approach.

Just as the three individual-level gender-related constructs discussed in the first half of the volume are interconnected, the three types of social relationships considered in the second part are intertwined. Women and men involved in intimate relationships frequently enter into socially recognized roles that formalize their personal commitments (e.g., lovers often become husbands and wives). These individuals may enact another role—parent. And, spouses and parents of both sexes engage in paid labor outside the home. Although task groups can and do exist outside of the context of the workplace, it is in the worker role that individuals are most likely to interact in such groups.

Two pairwise comparisons of the previous three chapters are instructive. First, although similar in format, the chapters by Huston and Ashmore and by Staines and Libby are quite different in the nature of their analysis. Huston and Ashmore's approach to personal relationships involved a fine-grained examination of the way in which conduct is negotiated and coordinated in dyadic interaction between intimates. While recognizing the importance of face-to-face negotiation in role relationships, Staines and Libby took a more social-structural perspective. They regarded social roles as slots to be filled by individuals. Taking the three roles that are central to relations between the sexes, they systematically compared the way in which men and women differentially experience and perform them.

The social relationships here considered can be partitioned in yet another way: the dyad versus larger social units. Huston and Ashmore and Staines and Libby moved us from a consideration of the individual in Chapters Two, Three, and Four to an analysis of a pair of individuals. Bartol and Martin provide a first step toward a consideration of individual men and women in yet larger social contexts: face-to-face task groups. We say "first step" because the social psychology of female–male relations requires consideration of nontask, face-to-face groups and of individual men and women as members of larger and more inclusive human groups. It is to this topic (i.e., the social-psychological level of analysis in relation to the societal level) that we now turn.

Notes toward a Social-Psychological Theory of Male–Female Relations

We began this volume by suggesting the desirability of a field of inquiry, "the social psychology of female–male relations." In the ensuing chapters, the building blocks (central concepts) of this field were critically examined.

A high priority for future work is to tie these separate concepts together and to do so within an overarching theoretical framework. This framework, while focusing on social-psychological variables, would need to explicitly recognize different yet complementary levels of analysis. In this section, we offer notes toward the development of such a theory.

In introducing these notes we return to two points raised in our introductory chapter: male–female relations can be studied scientifically at various levels of analysis and are similar to, yet different from, other forms of intergroup relations. Concerning the first point, it is essential to explicitly recognize the necessity of different levels of analysis and to eschew reductionism. In short, human social behavior must be understood at a variety of levels and can not be reduced to biology (and ultimately chemistry) at one "end" or to social factors (and ultimately society) at the other. At the same time, it must be recognized that these levels, while different and nonreducible, are interconnected. Thus, analysis at any one level must take into account other levels. We have already at several points noted the societal and social-psychological levels. We now add a third—biological—in order to emphasize that (wo)man is not only a cognitive creature and a social being, but also a biological beast.

Not only must relations between the sexes be approached from a variety of complementary scientific perspectives, but also this topic should be construed as an instance of intergroup relations. *Male* and *female* are important social categories that are recognized by both individual perceivers and society at large. Women and men relate to one another not only as individuals, but also as major societal groups. Thus, relations between the sexes are similar to relations between racial, ethnic, religious, social class, and age groups.

A SOCIAL-PSYCHOLOGICAL FRAMEWORK
FOR INTERGROUP RELATIONS

Table 1 presents the components of a social-psychological theory of intergroup relations. Three levels of analysis are distinguished—*societal, social psychological,* and *biological.* The primary objective of the theory toward which we are aiming is to account for the thoughts, feelings, and behaviors of individuals in social contexts. Thus, the social-psychological portion of the table is larger and more detailed. However, because the individual is a biological organism, and because all social contexts occur within a society, the biological and societal levels are included.

As an aid to discussing these three levels, Table 1 distinguishes three types of factors that might be considered at each level: *units and unit relations, maintenance function, knowledge function.* The first refers to elements to be considered and how these are interconnected. At the societal level, social

TABLE 1

Elements of a Social Scientific Model of Intergroup Relations

Level of analysis	Units and unit relations	Maintenance function	Knowledge function
Societal	Social categories Size (numbers) Prestige Power Interdependence of social categories	Means of maintenance	Cultural belief systems

Social
Psychological
Interpersonal/
  social contexts
	Situations
	Groups
	Task
	Other
	Roles
	Relationships
		Local norms
		Formal and informal
		  structure
			Social representations

Individual in
  social contexts
	Thoughts
	Feelings
	Behavior
		Regulatory system	Individual belief systems
			Social
			Implicit theories of
			  personality
			Scripts
			Beliefs and feelings
			  about specific
			  individuals

Biological	Anatomical Physiological	Regulatory system	Brain

categories (e.g., women, Italian-Americans, white-collar workers) are the important elements for a model of intergroup relations, and the positive-negative nature of their interdependence is of primary concern. At the social-psychological level, the social context units of interest are relationships and roles (e.g., lovers, husband–wife), face-to-face groups (e.g., a hospital staff meeting, the same staff at the weekly softball game), and situations (e.g., intensive-care ward at a hospital, a bar). For the individual in a social context, the units are thoughts, feelings, and behaviors. Finally, at the biological level, the units are diverse but include anatomical and physiological factors.

The second column in Table 1, maintenance function, highlights the importance of regulating or maintaining animate systems at some satisfactory level. At the societal level, regulation is generally via laws, operating procedures of organizations, and formal political processes; informal and quasi-legal procedures may also be involved, however. The term, means of maintenance, is used to denote the variety of procedures that regulate relations between social categories. Similarly, with regard to social contexts at the social-psychological level, there are both formal (e.g., work rules in a factory) and informal means of regulating interpersonal relations. A regulatory system has been included for both the individual in social context and for the biological level. For the latter, this seems obvious—humans, as all living organisms, are "programmed" to survive (which requires intake of nourishment, maintenance of bodily functions, and protection from danger) and to reproduce; to do this requires biological structures to regulate the organism's functioning. We repeat the regulatory system at the level of the individual in a social context, because we wish to emphasize that the cognitive–social aspects of (wo)man are grounded in life maintaining functions (Norman, 1981).

The final column of the table, labeled knowledge function, refers to systems for organizing, manipulating, and generating knowledge. This is most clearly seen at the individual level where the term belief systems is used to denote this knowledge system. An individual's belief system is based on a biological structure, the brain, but cannot be reduced to the brain (Sperry, 1977). As is also indicated in the table, we posit shared cognitive systems. At the societal level, there are shared belief systems that are part of a society's nonmaterial culture. For the interpersonal level, we have borrowed Moscovici's term, "social representations."

Social-Psychological Level

Because this entire volume has been directed at this level, we address just two questions: How do the topics here discussed fit into the scheme depicted in Table 1? What fruitful new directions for research and theory are suggested by this framework? Concerning the first question, beliefs and feelings about self and others (including gender identity and sex stereotypes) and evaluative orientations (including gender-related attitudes) are located in belief systems at the individual level. Personal and role relations, as well as face-to-face task groups, are major components of the interpersonal/social-context aspect of the social-psychological level.

What potentially fruitful directions for research are suggested by Table 1? More attention to the interpersonal/social-contexts level would produce significant yields. In terms of units, we need to know more about "situations" independent of an individual's actions in these. Sherif (1981) has identified four classes of factors to be considered: (1) *location*, including natural versus man made and objects present (e.g., a university chemistry lecture hall or a 4-year-old boy's bedroom in a suburban American home); (2) *other individuals*, including gender and ethnic makeup, as well as degree of prior acquaintance (e.g., the Wednesday night bowling league or a wedding reception); (3) *activities*, including goals and communication (e.g., a production line in an automobile factory or a sensitivity training group); (4) *temporal organization*, including length and scheduled or not (e.g., a psychotherapy session or an impromptu jam session by a group of musicians).

Table 1 also suggests the need for research and theory on the maintenance and knowledge functions at the social-context level. The former involves consideration of social norms. Because most social scientists are acquainted with this concept, no more will be said. However, Moscovici's (1981) notion of "social representations" is not well known and, thus, requires comment. He begins with the assertion that individuals do not simply absorb dominant societal ideologies. As Moscovici explains, "We may assume that individuals and groups are anything but passive receptors, and that they think autonomously, constantly producing and communicating representations. People on the street, in cafes, at their places of work, in hospitals, laboratories, etc. are always making critical remarks, commenting and concocting spontaneous, non-official 'philosophies' " (p. 183). It is these nonofficial philosophies that result from face-to-face communication among individuals in the course of everyday life that Moscovici refers to as "social representations."

Biological Level

We noted the importance of the biological regulatory system for the individual. This is the only significant point regarding the biological level of analysis for a general model of intergroup relations. Although many societal ideologies concerning intergroup relations involve biological assumptions (e.g., members of group X have smaller brains than Y-group members), it is here assumed that intergroup conflict is best understood in terms of social-psychological and societal factors, not biological predispositions (e.g., an aggressive instinct). At the same time, however, it is suggested later that biological issues must be considered in analyzing female–male relations.

Societal Level

The following comments are intended as a first step toward linking the present social psychological analysis to societal-level factors. Societies are differentiated into social categories. We assume that social categories are ranked in terms of esteem or prestige. Although this proposed hierarchical arrangement may not be universal (the debate about male dominance is instructive on this point; cf. Rogers, 1978), it is certainly a feature of Western society, and hence this assumption is appropriate for the present analysis of female–male relations in the U.S. We further assume that those at the top actively attempt to maintain their advantage and that those at the bottom actively attempt to undermine or overthrow the system that puts them at a disadvantage.

In terms of actual material outcomes, any two social categories[1] can stand (in a Weberian ideal-type analysis) in one of three relations to each other: (1) positive interdependence (Deutsch's [1949] "promotive interdependence," Sherif's [1958] "superordinate goals"), in which the two groups' outcomes (i.e., material rewards and costs) are positively correlated; (2) negative interdependence (Deutsch's "contrient interdependence"), in which the two groups' outcomes are negatively correlated; (3) noninterdependence, in which the groups' outcomes are uncorrelated.

How negative intergroup interdependence gets "resolved" depends, in large part, on two interrelated factors: power and numbers. Often the larger of two groups is able to impose on the smaller group a solution that is to its advantage. Thus, the terms *majority group* and *minority group* have long been central to discussions of intergroup conflict. However, numbers of people is just one of the resources available to competing groups. As a consequence, the term *majority group* has come to denote not necessarily the numerical majority but the group with the preponderance of social power; "social power refers to control and use of resources, including human resources, and of access to society's core institutions, e.g., its economy, political and legal institutions" (Sherif, 1981, p. 19). To the degree that one group has greater power than the other, it can establish itself as the dominant group (gaining more rewards for its members) with the other as subordinate. Van den Berghe (1967) has identified two types of negative intergroup interdependence: paternalistic (in which the dominant group has so much more power that it can "enslave" the subordinate) and competition (in which the power differential is less and the groups openly compete for resources).

All societies have means of maintenance to regulate relations between conflicting groups.[2] Given the aforementioned assumption that a dominant group attempts to maintain or enhance its position, the societal-level regulatory system will favor the advantaged social categories. In a pater-

[1]For the sake of clarity, we oversimplify the fact that societies are partitioned into many groups and that these groups tend to be stratified in different ways by dealing with relations between groups taken two at a time (e.g., black–white, female–male). It is important to recognize, however, that in reality the situation is much more complex. Individuals can and do belong to different and cross-cutting groups at the same time (e.g., white male professor). Thus, there is considerable diversity within the social categories female and male and the factors that contribute to this within-group variability (especially race and social class) significantly impact the experience of individual women and men.

[2]Means of maintenance is similar to, but not coterminous with, van den Berghe's (1967) "social control mechanisms."

nalistic system, there is explicit legal and political maintenance of differential position buttressed by physical coercion. Again using an ideal-type analysis, two means of maintenance can be identified for the competitive form of intergroup conflict. In the first, competition is defused by legal and quasi-legal factors and via physical coercion. With respect to race relations in the U.S., the period from about 1890 to the late 1950s was one of "defused competition." Jim Crow laws and economic exploitation of sharecroppers combined with Ku Klux Klan intimidation to abridge black–white competition. Today the racial status quo is maintained not by explicit–coercive means but largely by impersonal, amorphous institutions. That is, racism has been institutionalized such that blacks and other ethnic minorities are discriminated against indirectly through the business-as-usual operation of political and economic institutions. For example, the benefits of seniority is a standard operating principal of many employment situations. If blacks were denied access to a particular job until recently, then they would have low seniority. Thus, when it is necessary to lay off workers, blacks are the first to go not because of present explicitly race-based discrimination, but because of an institutionalized non-race-based principle.

Thus far, it has been implicitly assumed that humans are simply concerned with material outcomes. We do not believe this is the case, and we have included cultural belief systems in Table 1 to highlight the importance of shared knowledge. We stress two interrelated points about cultural belief systems. First, economic interdependence exerts a strong directional influence on shared beliefs—positive interdependence fosters positive or flattering beliefs about the other group, whereas negative interdependence promotes negative cultural stereotypes about the out-group. That is, societal belief systems develop, in part, to explain the nature of intergroup interdependence. And, within a particular society, dominant groups can impose an "official" belief system (e.g., that taught in schools) that justifies their advantaged position. Thus, cultural belief systems can rationalize economic relations between groups within a society. This, of course, is the core of orthodox Marxist analyses of intergroup conflict where economic factors are seen to determine "ideology." It is not assumed, here, however, that economic relations singly and fully determine shared intergroup attitudes, beliefs, or actions. Extant or pre-existing belief systems are one other major input (cf. Chesler, 1976, p. 41). Thus, for example, currently emerging cultural beliefs regarding black–white relations in the U.S. are influenced by both past and present racial belief systems as well as the current economic interdependence of these social categories.

A second point to be emphasized about cultural belief systems is that groups can come into conflict not just over material outcomes but also over belief systems. In Chapter Four, we described symbolic racism and symbolic sexism where the core issue is not economic self-interest but a strong affective attachment to the American way of life (including not just "mom and apple pie" but also slow evolution of, rather than quick and major change in, the racial and sexual status quo). We add here Tajfel and Turner's (1979) notion of group social comparison and Blumer's (1961) interpretation of "race prejudice as a sense of group position." Although quite different in particulars, both formulations suggest that societal groups can be interdependent regarding status and esteem as well as regarding material outcomes.

To this point, we have treated material and symbolic relations between groups as static, but they are not. Many societal- (and individual-) level accounts of intergroup conflict seek to explain why and how a particular society (or individual) comes to be "racist" (or "prejudiced"), with this state implicitly treated as a stable equilibrium. We would argue that, in fact, racism and prejudice for societies and individuals is an unstable equilibrium and that much is to be learned about intergroup relations by, from the outset, viewing relations between groups as dynamic rather than static and by analyzing group conflicts through time.[3]

MALE–FEMALE AS AN INSTANCE OF INTERGROUP RELATIONS

From the outset, it has been asserted that relations between the sexes should be considered as an instance of intergroup relations. This assertion is supported by Babad, Birnbaum, and Benne (1983), who argue that sex, age, race, ethnicity, religion, and social class are "the most critical and certainly most pervasive (dimensions) in all modern societies" (p. 143). Conflicts between racial, ethnic, and religious groups, and between social classes, are widespread and can be a source of major social change (e.g., Northern Ireland and Lebanon in the early 1980s). "Sex and generational conflicts are evident and ubiquitous enough, both in societies at large, and in their constituent families . . . Generally, however, sex and generational conflicts do not in any fundamental way threaten the existing order" (van den Berghe, 1973, p. 99).[4] Gender, then, is a crucial intergroup dimension, yet, if van den Berghe is correct, somehow quite different from other fundamental social categories in modern nation states.

---

[3]There are, however, forces in the direction of stability/equilibrium. The dominant group in a society is able to fashion societal structures (e.g., laws and the legal system) and ideologies (e.g., official histories) that can perpetuate existing disparities. And, in many modern societies, mass communication systems and universal schooling are potent means of socializing new generations.

[4]Age- and gender-based conflicts can, of course, influence social change. The role of youth in the 1960s and the Women's Movement in the 1970s are prominent examples.

Social-Psychological Level

By returning to Table 1, it is possible to place the social-psychological analysis presented in the previous chapters within the general working model of intergroup relations and to note important directions for future work. The three individual-level concepts covered—gender identity, sex stereotypes, and gender-related attitudes—are part of individual belief systems. A potentially fruitful direction, to relate this knowledge system to the maintenance system, is discussed later. The three social-context chapters, covering women and men in personal and role relationships and in task groups, address major social-psychological interpersonal units and unit relations.

The chapter on task groups is a stepping stone to a broader analysis of men and women in a variety of groups: When, how, and why do men and women interact within and across sex? In American schools, children's play groups are more sex than race or ethnically segregated. And, boys' and girls' groups are quite different. Girls tend to play in smaller groups (often dyads) that are relatively equal in status, whereas boys generally play in larger groups with a relatively well-delineated status dimension (cf. Schofield, 1982, pp. 102–108). Sex segregation of play continues in adolescence, although individual boys and girls date and become couples. In adulthood, men and women interact as individuals within the family "group"; they also find themselves in other groups—the aforementioned task groups, but also, for example, for recreation. How do these experiences in mixed- and same-sex groups influence individual-level constructs (thinking about self and others) and interpersonal relationships?

It is such relationships that are crucial to understanding male–female relations as an instance of intergroup relations. In accounting for why sex conflicts seldom threaten social organization, van den Berghe (1973) suggested that "the main factor is probably the set of binary ties linking individual males and females to each other in a particularly intimate, all-encompassing, and long-lasting relationship" (p. 103).[5] That is, unlike all other forms of intergroup relations, individual men and women are drawn together, perhaps out of biological need, certainly for the species a necessity for survival. These relationships are recognized by the participants and others (e.g., "they are lovers") and can become legally recognized role relationships (e.g., husband–wife). As noted in Chapter Five, these close personal relationships do not develop in a social vacuum. We suggest here the need to consider the converse: How does one's experience in personal and role relationships in-

---

[5]Rising divorce rates, sex differences in mortality, and related phenomena suggest that the strength, scope, and duration of such binary attachments may have diminished in recent years in the U.S.

fluence the individual's beliefs and attitudes about self and the social categories male and female and ultimately have an impact on the societal-level relations between the sexes?

The foregoing logic leads to the suggestion of a systems approach to the social-psychological building blocks discussed in the previous chapters. As has been noted, the three individual-level concepts are interconnected, as are the three types of social relationships. It is now suggested that all six topics are involved in a reciprocal causal network. How might researchers begin to study this system? Two possibilities are offered. First, developments in causal modeling (cf. Reis, 1982) might be exploited. Any one of the present building blocks could be taken as the "dependent variable," with the others treated as predictors. For example, one could develop a causal model to account for marital satisfaction, which included measures of individual-level, gender-related concepts (gender identity, sex stereotypes, and gender-related attitudes), as well as variables concerning social relationships (e.g., nature and degree of interdependence with spouse, participation in other role relationships and social groups). Second, the life milestones pertinent to gender identified by Katz in Chapter Two could be treated as natural experiments in which the interconnected network of individual and social relationships variables is threatened. Intensive longitudinal study of individuals prior to, during, and following such events may provide insights into how the building blocks are organized. For example, having a baby could be studied in terms of its impact on the mother's and father's gender identities, beliefs about the sexes, and gender-related evaluative responses, as well as on their personal and role relationships and their participation in a variety of task and nontask groups.

Biological Level

The "binary ties linking individual males and females to each other" are rooted in the biological necessity to procreate and nurture the young. Thus, unlike other forms of intergroup relations (except age-based), the social-psychological analysis of male–female relations must be linked to the biological level of analysis. This means neither that "anatomy is destiny" nor that sociobiology is the answer. Rather, the thoughts, feelings, and behaviors of individual women and men in social contexts are not independent of biological factors.

There are just four ways in which the sexes differ with no overlap: gestation, lactation, and menstruation by females, and fertilization by males (cf. Money & Ehrhardt, 1972). These biological processes are sexual (in the sense of being related to reproduction), and, because they are dependent on hormones, these processes are linked to the biological regulatory system.

From a social-psychological perspective, how are these biological–sexual-regulatory processes important? A start toward answering this query can be made by relating these processes to each of the topics discussed in this volume. In terms of identity, it is not the case that genetic sex (XX and XY) fully determines the individual's sense of self as female or male or behavior as feminine or masculine (cf. Frieze, Parsons, Johnson, Ruble, & Zellman, 1978, Chapter 5). On the other hand, several major life events that serve as inputs to gender identity are rooted in biology: adolescence, parenting, menopause. (Although biologically based, these events have received a wide variety of cultural interpretations, and their shared meanings significantly influence the individual's response to biological change.) In Chapter Three, it was seen that many gender subtypes involve sexuality. Although not discussed there, it seems plausible that an important American gender stereotype is that men are more sexually driven. The possibility of this shared belief deserves serious research attention. If true (for at least some portion of the population—men?), it is likely to have an important influence on heterosexual interactions.[6] This leads directly to the issue of attitudes—sexual conduct is a significant component of traditional (and modern) sex roles. Attitudes toward sexuality (see Altemeyer, 1981, p. 154) are also important for relations between the sexes.

Biological–sexual factors figure in relationships as well. Close heterosexual relationships are often sexual relationships. Sex is also part of the spouse role, and the birth of a child to a couple has significant impact on their personal relationship and their husband–wife roles. Although sexuality was not discussed in the preceding analysis of task groups (Chapter Seven), it is a factor in organizational settings (e.g., sexual harassment). Further, women and men interact in a variety of nontask groups that may implicate sexuality.

Societal Level

Certainly female and male are fundamental and universal social categories, but are they "groups"? Because there is no universally accepted definition of "group", this question does not submit to an unambiguous answer. It is worth grappling with, however, because its consideration raises significant issues. Each of the following has been offered as a defining quality of "groupness": interdependence, interaction, structure, treatment by environment, definition (by group members and others) (cf. Cartwright & Zander, 1968; Shaw, 1981). Are all women (or men) in the U.S. interdependent? Do men (or women) interact more frequently with other men (or women) than with women (or men)? Are women (men) a structured social category with differentiated roles, a power-status dimension, and norms?

[6]We do not mean that men are, in fact, more sexually driven (i.e., that the stereotype is valid). Rather, we are pointing to the importance of the belief that they are.

Are all U.S. men (women) treated in the same fashion? Do women (men) define themselves as a group? A preliminary answer to each of these questions is, "Yes, but . . . "

To illustrate the potential yield of going beyond the "yes, but . . . " answer, we consider the implications of using a structure definition of groups. It is possible to argue that, according to this definition, men are (though implicitly and non-self-consciously) a group, but women are not. In childhood, boys play in groups with roles, power-status dimensions, and norms. Baseball, football, and basketball, whether organized or simply pickup games, are prime examples. Girls' play groups are generally smaller and often involve equal-status dyadic interactions. In adulthood, males predominate in public activities such as business and politics, which require interlocking roles, explicit power relations, and formal and informal norms. Until the 1970s, in the U.S., women's primary sphere was the home, where again ties were binary (to husband and children) and where there was little possibility of structuring the interrelations of all or even many women.

Beyond the issue of whether the sex social categories are groups, we note two other general considerations about societal-level units and unit relations—aspects of units themselves and interdependence of units. In terms of numbers, men and women are roughly equal,[7] but men have greater power and prestige in American society.

How are the sexes interdependent? The answer depends, in part, on the level of analysis. At the social-psychological level, individual men and women compete (for admission to graduate school, for jobs), but they also and quite commonly enter into relationships involving a high degree of promotive interdependence (e.g., marriage). At the societal level, many observers regard men and women as contriently interdependent, with males as the dominant group, which discriminates against the female subordinate group. However, large portions of the lay public, women included, do not agree. For them, men and women each have their own spheres and neither group is "on top" (cf. Frieze et al., 1978, pp. 296–298). Part of this difference of opinion about a "war between the sexes" at the societal level derives from the fact that as individuals and in face-to-face groups (i.e., at the social-psychological level), women and men are quite often positively interdependent. It is difficult to regard as an enemy soldier the man with whom one shares a home and a child, good times, and times of trouble.

Another factor militating against "seeing" the negative societal-level interdependence of the sexes is that the sexual status quo, including all the fac-

---

[7]The ratio of women to men can vary considerably from one society to the next and over time within the same society. According to Guttentag and Secord (1983), the "sex ratio" has important implications for male–female relations and society in general.

tors outlined in Table 1, is for humans analogous to water for fish. Male–female relations involves a large number of complex and interconnected units and systems, and individuals live their daily lives within these systems. It is, thus, quite difficult to have a detached or objective perspective. Because (wo)man is, in part, a scientist, (s)he develops theories to account for societal arrangements and these theories can become widely shared (hence, cultural belief systems). Again, in part because we are so close to the phenomenon, these theories (including the notion of natural spheres for the sexes) rationalize what exists rather than highlight what could or ought to be.

What Will Be (?)

The question of what ought to be raises the issue of social change and highlights the importance of time. Several nations (e.g., Sweden, U.S.S.R.) or subgroups within a nation (e.g., the kibbutzim in Israel) have attempted to implement planned, authority-supported changes in sex-role arrangements. The slowness and unevenness of such change is testimony to the complex set of systems maintaining traditional relations (cf. Weitz, 1977, pp. 206–231).

Bringing the topic closer to home, we began in Chapter One by placing this volume in context, both in space (the U.S.) and time (the early to mid-1980s). With respect to the latter, we noted that this is a period of much change (e.g., increasing numbers of women with young children are employed outside the home). We close by suggesting that analysis of change (especially regarding women and employment), nonchange (e.g., nonpassage of the ERA), and apparent but misleading "change" (e.g., a continuing high rate of occupational segregation in the face of increases in female labor force participation) will provide insight into where we will be in the future as individual men and women in society and as social scientists seeking to understand female–male relations.

References

Altemeyer, R. A. (1981). *Right-wing authoritarianism.* Winnipeg: University of Manitoba Press.
Babad, E. Y., Birnbaum, M., & Benne, K. D. (1983). *The social self: Group influences on personal identity.* Beverly Hills, CA: Sage.
Beere, C. A. (1979). *Women and women's issues: A handbook of tests and measures.* San Francisco: Jossey-Bass.
Bem, S. L. (1974). The measurement of psychological androgyny. *Journal of Consulting and Clinical Psychology, 42,* 155–162.

Blumer, H. (1961). Race prejudice as a sense of group position. In J. Masuoka & P. Valien (Eds.), *Race relations: Problems and theory*. Chapel Hill: University of North Carolina Press.

Cartwright, D., & Zander, A. (Eds.) (1968). *Group dynamics: Research and theory* (3rd ed.). New York: Harper & Row.

Chesler, M. A. (1976). Contemporary sociological theories of racism. In P. A. Katz (Ed.), *Towards the elimination of racism*. New York: Pergamon.

Constantinople, A. (1973). Masculinity–femininity: An exception to a famous dictum. *Psychological Bulletin, 80*, 389–407.

Deutsch, M. (1949). A theory of cooperation and competition. *Human Relations, 2*, 129–152.

Frieze, I. H., Parsons, J. E., Johnson, P. B., Ruble, D. N., & Zellman, G. L. (1978). *Women and sex roles: A social psychological perspective*. New York: W. W. Norton.

Guttentag, M., & Secord, P. F. (1983). *Too many women? The sex ratio question*. Beverly Hills, CA: Sage.

Kelley, H. H., Berscheid, E., Christensen, A., Harvey, J. H., Huston, T. L., Levinger, G., McClintock, E., Peplau, L. A., & Peterson, D. R. (1983). *Close relationships*. New York: W. H. Freeman.

Money, J., & Ehrhardt, A. A. (1972). *Man & woman, boy and girl: The differentiation and dimorphism of gender identity from conception to maturity*. Baltimore: Johns Hopkins University Press.

Moscovici, S. (1981). On social representation. In J. P. Forgas (Ed.), *Social cognition: Perspectives on everyday understanding*. London: Academic Press.

Norman, D. A. (1981). Twelve issues for cognitive science. In D. A. Norman (Ed.), *Perspectives on cognitive science*. Norwood, NJ: Ablex.

Reis, H. T. (1982). An introduction to the use of structural equations: Prospects and problems. In L. Wheeler (Ed.), *Review of personality and social psychology* (Vol. 3). Beverly Hills, CA: Sage.

Rogers, S. (1978). Women's place: A critical review of anthropological theory. *Comparative Studies in Society and History, 20*, 123–162.

Ruble, D. N., & Ruble, T. L. (1982). Sex stereotypes. In A. G. Miller (Ed.), *In the eye of the beholder: Contemporary issues in stereotyping*. New York: Praeger.

Schofield, J. W. (1982). *Black and white in school: Trust, tension, or tolerance*. New York: Praeger.

Shaw, M. E. (1981). *Group dynamics: The psychology of small group behavior*. New York: McGraw-Hill.

Sherif, C. W. (1981, August). *Social and psychological bases of social psychology*. G. Stanley Hall Lecture on Social Psychology at the annual convention of the American Psychological Association, Los Angeles, CA.

Sherif, M. (1958). Superordinate goals in the reduction of intergroup conflict. *American Journal of Sociology, 63*, 349–363.

Spence, J. T., Deaux, K., & Helmreich, R. L. (1985). Sex roles in contemporary American society. In G. Lindzey & E. Aronson, (Eds.), *Handbook of social psychology* (3rd ed.). New York: Random House.

Spence, J. T., Helmreich, R., & Stapp, J. (1974). The Personal Attributes Questionnaire: A measure of sex-role stereotypes and masculinity–femininity. *JSAS Catalog of Selected Documents in Psychology, 4*, 127.

Sperry, R. W. (1977). Bridging science and values—A unifying view of mind and brain. *American Psychologist, 32*, 237–245.

Tajfel, H., & Turner, J. (1979). An integrative theory of intergroup conflict. In W. G. Austin & S. Worchel (Eds.), *The social psychology of intergroup relations*. Monterey, CA: Brooks/Cole.

van den Berghe, P. L. (1967). *Race and racism: A comparative perspective.* New York: Wiley.

van den Berghe, P. L. (1973). *Age and sex in human societies: A biosocial perspective.* Belmont, CA: Wadsworth.

Vaughter, R. M. (1983). All things being equal, a behavior is superior to an attitude: Studies of sex typed and sex biased attitudes and behaviors. In B. L. Richardson & J. Wirtenberg (Eds.), *Sex-role research: Measuring social change.* New York: Praeger.

Weitz, S. (1977). *Sex roles: Biological, psychological, and social foundations.* New York: Oxford University Press.

Author Index

Subject Index